THE CENTER FOR CHINESE STUDIES
at the University of California, Berkeley, supported by the Ford Foundation, the Institute of International Studies (University of California, Berkeley), and the State of California, is the unifying organization for social science and interdisciplinary research on contemporary China.

RECENT PUBLICATIONS

Kataoka, Tetsuya. *Resistance and Revolution in China: The Communists and the Second United Front*

Kim, Ilpyong J. *The Politics of Chinese Communism: Kiangsi under the Soviets*

Larkin, Bruce D. *China and Africa, 1949–1970: The Foreign Policy of the People's Republic of China*

Moseley, George. *The Consolidation of the South China Frontier*

Rice, Edward E. *Mao's Way*

Schneider, Laurence A. *Ku Chieh-kang and China's New History: Nationalism and the Quest for Alternative Traditions*

Van Ness, Peter. *Revolution and Chinese Foreign Policy: Peking's Support for Wars of National Liberation*

Wakeman, Frederic, Jr. *History and Will: Philosophical Perspectives of Mao Tse-tung's Thought*

LIU SHAO-CH'I AND THE
CHINESE CULTURAL REVOLUTION

THE POLITICS OF MASS CRITICISM

This volume is sponsored by
THE CENTER FOR CHINESE STUDIES
University of California, Berkeley

LOWELL DITTMER

Liu Shao-ch'i and the Chinese Cultural Revolution

The Politics of Mass Criticism

UNIVERSITY OF CALIFORNIA PRESS

BERKELEY · LOS ANGELES · LONDON

University of California Press
Berkeley and Los Angeles, California
University of California Press, Ltd.
London, England
Copyright © 1974, by
The Regents of the University of California
ISBN 0-520-02574-1
Library of Congress Catalog Card Number: 73-85786
Printed in the United States of America

To
TANG TSOU

CONTENTS

vii

FIGURES

TABLES

ABBREVIATIONS

GENERAL

ACFL—All-China Federation of Labor

APC—Agricultural Producers' Co-operatives

CC—Central Committee

CCP—Chinese Communist Party

CCRG—Central Cultural Revolution Group

CPSU—Communist Party of the Soviet Union

CYL—Communist Youth League

GLF—Great Leap Forward

GPCR—Great Proletarian Cultural Revolution

MAC—Military Affairs Commission

MCC—Military Control Commission

NCNA—New China News Agency

PLA—People's Liberation Army

RC—Revolutionary Committee

SEM—Socialist Education Movement

URI—Union Research Institute

PUBLICATIONS

AS—*Asian Survey*

CL&G—*Chinese Law and Government*

CN—*China Notes*

CNA—*China News Analysis*

CQ—*The China Quarterly*

CS—*Current Scene*

CSN—*China Science News*

CW—*Collected Works of Liu Shao-ch'i*

DSJP—*Daily Summary of the Japanese Press*

ECMM—*Extracts from China Mainland Magazines*

FBIS—*Foreign Broadcast Information Service*

FEER—*Far Eastern Economic Review*

HCPP—*Hung-ch'i p'iao-p'iao* (The red flag waves)

IS—Issues and Studies
JPRS—Joint Publications Re-search Service
KMJP—Kuang-ming jih-pao [Il-lumination daily]
LAD—Liberation Army Daily [*Chieh-fang chün-pao*]
LD—Liberation Daily [*Chieh-fang jih-pao*]
LSWTC—Liu Shao-ch'i wen-t'i tzu-liao chuan-chi [A special col-lection of materials on Liu Shao-ch'i]
NYCHCS—Nung-yeh chi-hsieh chi-shu [Agricultural mechani-zation technique]

PD—People's Daily [*Jen-min jih-pao*]
PR—Peking Review
RF—Red Flag [*Hung-ch'i*]
SCMM—Selections from China Mainland Magazines
SCMP—Survey of the China Mainland Press
SRWM—Selected Readings from the Works of Mao Tse-tung
SW—Selected Works of Mao Tse-tung

NOTE: Each abbreviation in the text or notes is cited in full the first time it appears. If the abbreviation refers to an item in the Selected Bibliography, the full citation will not appear in subsequent notes, but titles not included in the Selected Bibliography are cited in full the first time they appear in each chapter.

ACKNOWLEDGMENTS

For his unstinting help at every stage in the preparation of this study, including a painstaking reading with extensive comments on every chapter in a long series of preliminary drafts, I am profoundly indebted to Tang Tsou of the University of Chicago, to whom this book is gratefully dedicated. Lloyd Rudolph, also of the University of Chicago, Parris Chang of Pennsylvania State University, Edward E. Rice of the Center for Chinese Studies at the University of California in Berkeley, and Ying-mao Kau of Brown University also read the entire work in manuscript form and made many helpful comments. Nathan Leites of the University of Chicago contributed useful comments on chapters 6 and 8, and the theoretical perspective that informs these chapters owes much to his teaching. For indispensable methodological aid on chapters 8 and 9, I am grateful to William Parish and Jim Call of the University of Chicago. I am grateful to my friend Hong Yung Lee of the same institution for permitting me to incorporate his illuminating analysis of the Red Guard movement into chapter 5. Gordon Bennett of the University of Texas at Austin wrote an incisive critique of chapters 4 and 5, containing suggestions for both stylistic and substantive improvements. Dennis Ray of California State College in Los Angeles made helpful suggestions on chapter 7. For stimulating comments on an earlier draft of the concluding chapter, which was presented to a regional seminar of the Center for Chinese Studies in the autumn of 1972, I am grateful to Chalmers Johnson, Alan P. L. Liu, Fred Wakeman, Harry Harding, Anderson Shih, et al. John Stewart Service, Robert A. Scalapino, Wen-shun Chi, John Jamieson, and David Milton gave me the benefit of their experiences on the mainland in informative conversations.

The Program for Contemporary China of the University of Chicago generously provided the financial support that made it possible for me to spend the 1972–73 academic year revising the final draft, and the Center for Chinese Studies of the University of California gave me full access to their research facilities and an excellent environment for work during this period. For permission to republish slightly revised versions of chapters 9 and 10 I wish to thank *Asian Survey* and *The China Quarterly,* respectively; some of the ideas presented in chapters 5 and 6 first appeared in abbreviated form in *Journal of Comparative Administration* and *Studies in Comparative Communism.* For their patient help with revisions and production, I am grateful to members of the University of California Press.

The ultimate *sine quibus nihil* was of course provided by my parents, whose love and faith sustained me during the entire gestation period.

Though all of the aforementioned helped me well beyond my ability to express my debt to them in footnotes, none should be held responsible for any errors of fact or interpretation that remain.

PART I
Liu's Fall

And it shall come to pass afterward, that I will pour out
my spirit upon all flesh; and your sons and daughters
shall prophesy, your old men shall dream dreams, your
young men shall see visions: And also upon the servants
and upon the handmaids in those days will I pour out my
spirit.   —JOEL 2: 28–29

It is good for them to argue. Let them rebel a little. What
good does it do to make them say "Yes, Papa" "Yes,
Mama" all the time? I don't approve of that. Yet I feel
to be strict to one's children is to love them.
                        —CHIANG CH'ING, April 12, 1967

Our actions are own own; their consequences belong to
Heaven.   —THOMAS FRANCIS

1

INTRODUCTION

To seek the meaning of Liu Shao-ch'i's life is to become embroiled in inevitable controversy, for, by an unexpected turn of events in 1966, Liu's life came to be subjected to the most far–reaching reinterpretation by a nationwide movement of militant young activists who claimed to speak on behalf of Mao Tse-tung and the Chinese people. Because of Liu's intimate involvement for more than four decades with the major events that have shaped contemporary China, this reinterpretation opened Chinese Communist history to reassessment as well. Study of the controversy is an experience at once frustrating and rewarding. It is frustrating because some of the questions that the reinterpretation have posed must remain open, while we can at best reduce others to a limited number of objective possibilities. It is rewarding because such study places us in the eye of the storm of "mass criticism" whereby meaning and history are publicly created in modern China.

Liu's life may be viewed as an attempt to combine order with revolution and equality with economic efficiency and technocratic values. Over a period of more than a quarter century, he served as a constructive and stabilizing force within the Party and the regime. Unlike most Chinese Communist leaders, who tended to distinguish themselves in some particular endeavor and then pursue their careers along related lines, Liu had experience in numerous aspects of the Chinese Communist movement—trade unions, mass movements, underground organizations, guerrilla bases—but in all of these fields he exhibited the same fundamental concerns. During the revolutionary period of the 1920s and 1930s, his role as a Party and trade union organizer led him to place particular emphasis on an attempt to synthesize order and revolution. "Criticism and self-criticism," as definitively set forth by Liu in his 1941 essay, "On Inner-Party Struggle,"

3

was the most successful and important attempt to institutionalize this combination. His more extensive experience in the "white areas," and later as the operational administrator of the "first line" in Liberated China, led him to try to combine equality and economic efficiency as well. Perhaps his greatest success in this endeavor was in pulling the nation back together after the debacle of the Great Leap Forward (GLF) of 1958–60 and achieving a sustained economic recovery.

In the end, however, Liu's vision of how this combination of order and revolution, equality and economic efficiency could be achieved was overwhelmed by the sweep and depth of the revolutionary drive in China, as symbolized by Mao Tse-tung. Liu was dismissed as heir apparent and then purged, bringing his civil existence to an end. But his greatest contribution to the Chinese revolution was his last, as its victim, a role he played according to the principles that had guided his previous career. From August 1966 to the spring of 1967, despite the rising tide of public criticism, he chose not to oppose Mao actively and thus plunge China into even greater chaos. In his dignified, "cultivated" bearing during two years of intense and relentless polemical attacks, Liu lived up to his own prescription for a good Communist:

Even if it is temporarily to his disadvantage and if, in upholding the truth, he suffers blows of all kinds, is opposed or censured by most other people and so finds himself in temporary (and honorable) isolation, even to the point where he may have to give up his life, he will still breast the waves to uphold the truth.[1]

This last phase of Liu's career began in the spring of 1966, when Mao Tse-tung launched a "Great Proletarian Cultural Revolution" (GPCR), which was designed to provoke mass criticism of a "small handful" of "Party persons in authority taking the capitalist road" and to bring China's "bourgeois" cultural superstructure into closer conformance with its socialist base. As the ranking vice-chairman of the Central Committee (CC) during Mao's absence from Peking, Liu dispatched work teams in June and July 1966 to various schools and government organs to supervise the burgeoning movement. Upon his return to Peking in late July, Mao sharply criticized the activities of the work teams and requested their withdrawal. At the Eleventh CC Plenum in August, Liu came under criticism for his dispatch of work teams and was demoted from second to eighth place in the Politburo and relieved of his office as vice-chairman of the CC.

Two months later Liu submitted a self-criticism, which was re-

[1] Li Shao-ch'i, "How to Be a Good Communist" (July 1939), in *Collected Works* (hereafter *CW*) (Hong Kong, 1969) 1: 184.

ported to have been accepted, but his status remained uncertain; then in the next six months he became the target of a nationwide polemical assault, which characterized him as "China's Khrushchev," the leader of a "bourgeois reactionary line" that had been leading China down the "capitalist road" and was continuing even yet to resist Mao's "proletarian revolutionary line." Despite Liu's apparently passive reaction to these allegations, the "great repudiation" campaign continued for nearly two years before it culminated in his formal dismissal from all leadership positions and banishment from the Communist Party at the Twelfth CC Plenum in October 1968.

It was in the course of the GPCR that Liu's life, which seemed to have achieved such logical and felicitous unity, was to distintegrate. By a sudden turn of events, Liu's control over the meaning of his life was wrenched from his hands and "took wings" in the critical communication process of the GPCR. Liu's person and his public meaning became completely estranged: the former was cut off from the instruments of policy and sequestered in his official residence at Chungnanhai, but the other "Liu" became the animating spirit of opposition against which the GPCR was waged, and indeed proved so dauntless and resourceful an opponent that he could be vanquished only after two years of fierce "struggle." Since his downfall, this "Liu" has allegedly inspired repeated counterattacks against the GPCR, led by his former opponents, Ch'en Po-ta and Lin Piao. Thus the meaning of Liu's life has passed from his hands to the Chinese people as a part of their heritage, and his name has become an integral part of the polemical vocabulary indicating the direction in which the continuing Chinese revolution should move.

We are, perforce, concerned with two Liu Shao-ch'is, and with the nature of the process that rent him in twain. Perhaps, like Humpty Dumpty, "Liu Shao-ch'i" can never be reassembled to form a fully convincing whole. Our objective is to understand the forces that unraveled his life and, in the process of putting him back together, to form a picture of Liu's China, as well as of China's Liu. The portrait that emerges will be in the cubist style, from several different perspectives, with rough edges.

This book consists of three parts. The first features a chronological reconstruction of Liu's attempt to impose form on the world, of the gradual, subtle deviation of Liu's order from Mao's vision of China's future in response to various exigencies of nation-building and modernization, and of the confrontation between that order and the revived forces of revolutionary change in China. Chapter 2 presents a brief biographical sketch of Liu's life before 1959, which relies almost entirely on pre–GPCR sources and skirts areas of controversy in the hope of establishing an acceptable factual framework in terms of which later reinterpretations may be understood. It seeks to show how Liu's vision of the political process emerged as a result of various formative experiences in his life. Chapter 3 reviews the decade between 1956 and 1966. By tracing the main criticism themes of the GPCR to their origins in a series of unresolved political disputes, it seeks to reconstruct the decision to launch the GPCR and to determine the relationship between that decision and the decision to subject Liu Shao-ch'i to mass criticism. In chapters 4 and 5, Liu is swept into the GPCR, which exposed him as the Chinese revolution's greatest and most consistent nemesis. In a recent article, Howard Boorman compared Liu Shao-ch'i "as a human being" to the submerged portion of an iceberg, noting that his real personality "scarcely emerges in the polemical pyrotechnics" of the GPCR.[2] Chapter 4 aims to correct this situation by describing the GPCR as Liu experienced it, as an interpersonal drama of crime and unsuccessful atonement involving Liu and those with whom he had contact and whom he may have influenced. Chapter 5, in contrast, describes Liu's fall "objectively," i.e., as a symbol caught up in the rhetoric of a mass criticism movement over which he exerted minimal influence. It views his fall as the outcome of the conflictual and cooperative interaction among political actors in a greatly expanded decision-making arena.

Part II consists of an analysis of the Chinese attempt to reconstruct the past of the Mao-Liu rupture, the so-called struggle between two lines. Both the "struggle" and the polemical distortion of its significance are of momentous importance for China's future—the latter because it is accepted as reality, the former because it is real. Chapter 6 compares the personalities and political styles of Liu Shao-ch'i and Mao Tse-tung; chapter 7 analyzes Liu's policies, and their political and economic ramifications, in the context of an evaluation of the Maoist criticisms of Liu. These two chapters attempt not only to explore the value implications and feasibility of two diverging roads to communism but to solve the puzzle of their origin: if Mao and Liu differed so profoundly, how were they able to cooperate for so long? And yet if they did not, why was Liu subjected to such comprehensive criticism?

Part III seeks to come to terms with Liu Shao-ch'i's impact on China's political future. Liu stood for a concept of socialist modernization that stressed the institutionalization of revolution within com-

[2] Howard L. Boorman, "Liu Shao-ch'i," in *Revolutionary Leaders of Modern China,* ed. Chün-tu Hsüeh (New York, 1971), pp. 535–561.

plex structures of elaborately qualified formal rules regulating nearly every aspect of life. "Criticism and self-criticism" may stand as a paradigm of this attempt, inasmuch as it sets forth the parameters for decision-making and discipline at every level in the Party organization, including the highest. Mao's GPCR involved a deliberate abrogation of the formal rules of criticism and self-criticism in the name of substantive justice. Liu, to the end, played the game according to rules that Mao, a more flexible man, altered to suit his ends. Part III analyzes "criticism and self-criticism," Liu's most significant legacy to Chinese politics, as it was transformed during the GPCR and as it seems likely to evolve henceforth. Chapter 8 first formalizes the process of "mass criticism" in a semiotic model of social roles and intended meanings, then analyzes the Liu Shao-ch'i case in terms of that model. Chapter 9 compares mass criticism to the "normal" functioning of the mass line: it attempts to assess the impact of such innovations as the displacement of a national organization of professional bureaucrats by an ad hoc network of amateur publicists, the partial eclipse of the orderly process of formally adopted central directives by the direct dissemination of polemics through the mass media, and, of course, the advent of unprecedented popular participation in the movement. The final chapter describes the structural evolution of the process of "criticism and self-criticism" in China from its origins in 1942–44 in the Cheng-feng (rectification) Movement as a system of mediated and regulated collegial conflict to its climactic emergence in 1966 as a national mobilization and rectification technique.

I have been deliberately eclectic in assembling sources on the assumption that, if an "objective" analysis of the meaning of Liu's life and fall is probably impossible, a consideration of the widest possible array of subjective judgments will at least facilitate a balanced perspective. The sources include original and translated materials from the Chinese and Japanese press, as well as a wide assortment of secondary monographs in English, German, and French.

With regard to methodology, I have taken to heart Lewis Edinger's proposal that "for the analysis of individual political leaders we employ conceptual models and quantitative analysis in conjunction with a frank but disciplined use of empathy and other forms of imaginative speculation." [3] Quantitative indices are of course much scarcer and of more doubtful validity in China than in West Germany, but chapters 8 and 9 do make use of content analysis in an attempt to attain somewhat more precision in the characterization of meanings. Much of the

[3] Lewis J. Edinger, *Kurt Schumacher: A Study in Personality and Political Behavior* (Stanford, Calif., 1965), p. 4.

book, however, is based on evidence that is neither quantitative nor of assured validity. Whereas I continually try to move beyond available evidence to propose theories that plausibly link discrete events, some-times going so far as to suggest alternative hypotheses to explain the same sequence, these explanations should conform to the Weberian methodological criteria of "objective possibility" and "subjective meaningfulness." [4]

Despite occasional forays into neighboring disciplines, this is a political biography and should be evaluated in terms of its ability to shed new light on Chinese politics at a critical transition point. In placing Liu's biography within the broad social and political milieu that lent meaning to his life, and in using various social science techniques to analyze the structure of that milieu, this study hopes to contribute to innovation in the uniting of political biography and political history.

[4] Cf. Max Weber, "Objective Possibility and Adequate Causation in Historical Explanation," in *The Methodology of the Social Sciences,* trans. and ed. Edward A. Shils and Henry A. Finch (Glencoe, Ill., 1949), pp. 164–187.

2

THE LIFE AND TIMES
OF LIU SHAO-CH'I

Liu Shao-ch'i [1] was born at Huakungtang, Nantang, in Ninghsiang
Hsien, Hunan, in about 1898 (the exact date is in dispute), of mod-
erately well–off peasant stock, the youngest in a family of four boys
and two girls. His father was a primary-school teacher. Only a mountain range separated his home town from Shaoshan Ts'un, Hsiangtan,
where Mao Tse-tung was born. Very little is known of his family of
origin or boyhood. In contrast to Mao, he seems to have maintained
an amicable, if necessarily distant, relationship with his family.

STUDENT RADICAL

Following graduation from junior middle school, Liu attended Hunan First Normal School in Ch'angsha, where Mao and Ts'ai Ho-sen
had established the "New People's Study Society" (Hsin-min hsüeh-
hui). In 1917 Liu joined the society, which sponsored a "work-study"
program to enable students to continue their education in France; the
following year Liu became a work-study student in the Yüte Middle
School in Paoting, Hopei.[2] The training was vocational with an
orientation toward factory work. Possibly at this time Liu first acquired his penchant for mechanical efficiency and a functional division
of labor; in any event, he made repeated proud references to his

---

[1] Unless otherwise noted, this narrative is based on Howard L. Boorman, "Liu
Shao-ch'i," in *Revolutionary Leaders of Modern China,* ed. Chün-tu Hsüeh (New
York, 1971), pp. 535–561; and on Donald W. Klein and Anne B. Clark, "Liu
Shao-ch'i," in *Biographical Dictionary of Chinese Communism* (Cambridge, Mass.,
1971), 1: 616–626.
[2] "Down with Liu Shao-ch'i—Life of Counterrevolutionary Liu Shao-ch'i," *Chingkangshan* (Peking, May 1967), in *Current Background* (hereafter *CB*) (Hong Kong),
no. 834 (August 17, 1967): 1.

proletarian beginnings throughout his life. "When I was a work-study student preparing to go to France, I learned to operate many kinds of equipment," he told workers on a factory tour during the Great Leap Forward. "Carriage, pliars, wood plane, drill press—I know how to use them all." [3] In 1964 he again touched upon this experience while promoting the part-work, part-study system:

I had led the life of a work-study student for one year. Originally I had no thought of going to the Soviet Union. . . . That preparatory class provided a four-hour session in the morning. I learned French and engineering. . . . I learned both of them for one year! That year was quite a successful one.[4]

Unable to go abroad, Liu in the summer of 1920 joined the Socialist Youth League, which had been organized in October of that year by Grigory Voitinsky of the Comintern, and studied Russian under Mrs. Voitinsky at the League headquarters in the French settlement of Shanghai. "At that time," he recalled four decades later, he "only knew that socialism was good"; he had "heard about" Marx, Lenin, the October Revolution, and so forth, but was "not clear" about the nature of socialism, or the means of implementing it.[5] Toward the end of 1920, he was one of eight students selected by the Socialist Youth League to study in the Soviet Union. He described his feelings upon his first departure from the homeland in a poem titled "On the Tientsin Bridge," which he scrawled on the back of a photo and mailed to a close friend:

An unusual man seven feet tall,
Why are you so sad and angry, and sighing all the time?
Your life is short and your fortune is also bad,
Wealth and high office you can hardly expect in life.
Why not then enjoy life while you can,
Why drift a thousand miles, undergoing numerous hardships?
Talents are going westward,
Which frontier are you gazing at by raising your head?
Do you want to follow the footsteps of Marquis Pan to conquer distant land?
Your eyes are wistful with thoughts of the autumn.

[3] Hsi Yüan, "Liu Shao-ch'i t'ung-chih tsai T'aiyüan chung-hsing chi-ch'i chan" [Comrade Liu Shao-ch'i in a T'aiyüan heavy equipment factory], in Liu Shao-ch'i, Chou En-lai, Chu Te t'ung-chih tsai ch'ün-chung chung [Comrades Liu Shao-ch'i, Chou En-lai, Chu Te among the masses] (Peking, 1958), p. 3.

[4] "Selected Edition on Liu Shao-ch'i's Counterrevolutionary Revisionist Crimes" (August 18 Red Rebel Regiment of Nank'ai University, Tientsin) (April 1967), in Selections from China Mainland Magazines (hereafter SCMM) (Hong Kong), no. 653 (May 5, 1969): 27.

[5] "Chairman Liu Shao-ch'i's speech at the Moscow Meeting" (December 7, 1960) in SCMP, no. 2398 (December 15, 1960): 29.

Your aspirations are foolish, and your sentiments silly.
Nobody knows me standing here on the Tientsin bridge.
I can only mail it far away to my intimate friend who knows me.[6]

Liu reached Moscow in the spring of 1921, by way of Vladivostok and Chita, and studied for about seven months at the Communist University of the Toilers of the East, founded for the specific purpose of training cadres from minority peoples in the eastern Soviet Union and from Asian countries. Chang Kuo-t'ao, a senior classmate at Toilers of the East, recalls his first impression of Liu Shao-ch'i:

As I take up my pen, I recall the face of a serious young man whom I first saw forty-six years ago in Soviet Russia. At the time, a famine had engulfed the Soviet Union, and even the Communists who publicly presented a bold front were mumbling in private. But this tall, skinny, pale young man endured the hunger and cold without observable murmur or depression. In 1922, the Communists were passionate and full of verve; but he seldom displayed any excitement. He was somewhat bookish, thoughtful, rather taciturn, but clearly presevering. His friends soon recognized these characteristics as genuine, cultivated from childhood. Some people, however, found him a bit too glum and devoid of youthfulness.[7]

In the winter of 1921–22, Liu joined the Communist Party in the Soviet Union. "The reason that I joined the Party was that I knew I could not solve my personal problems, and by solving the problems of national interest and of the country and society, my personal problems could also be solved," he reminisced to his children. "With the interests of the public raised, the interests of the individual would also be raised." [8] Although "Toilers of the East" offered no systematic course of study and no interpreters, he apparently did learn some Russian, for he later drew Chinese students' attention to "some nouns which, in my opinion, have not been translated correctly." [9]

TRADE UNION ORGANIZER

Apparently disappointed with the study program in Moscow, Liu asked to be transferred home for "practical" work. In the spring of 1922 he returned to China and was appointed to the Secretariat of the

6 *Red Flag* (Peking Aeronautical Institute Red Flag Combat Corps), nos. 10–11 (February 10, 1967): 8, in *CW* 1: 2.

7 Chang Kuo-t'ao, "Introduction," Liu, *CW*, p. i.

8 Liu T'ao and Liu Yün-chen, "Look at Liu Shao-ch'i's Ugly Soul," quoted in "Selected Edition," *SCMM*, no. 653, p. 5.

9 "Speech at the Ceremonial Meeting for the School-Opening of Chinese People's University" (October 3, 1950), *CW* 2: 239.

Chinese Labor Unions (*Chung-Kuo lao-tung tsu-ho shu-chi-pu*), which Nym Wales later called China's first "systematic program for unionizing labor along modern lines." According to Liu, the organization consisted "mostly of students" recently returned from Moscow or France, or from Peking colleges.[10] The First Secretary was Chang Kuo-t'ao, who described his working relationship with his former assistant in the Shanghai headquarters:

My work often required me to travel, and, even when I was in Shanghai, there were other duties to attend at the CCP Central Committee, so I left all the daily work of the Secretariat for Labor Organization to Liu Shao-ch'i, and he assisted me wholeheartedly. Sitting face to face in the small office, we worked for six months in perfect cooperation.[11]

Liu's first major assignment was under Mao Tse-tung, then Secretary of the CCP District Committee in Hunan. In September 1922, Liu was sent to work among the coal miners of Anyüan at P'inghsiang Hsien (Hunan) as Deputy Director to Li Li-san, then Director of the Anyüan Miners' Labor Union. "At Anyüan, Li Li-san was the one in the limelight, but it was I who hammered away at work," Liu later boasted.[12] His working relationship with Li was analogous to his earlier relationship with Chang Kuo-t'ao and his later relationship with Mao Tse-tung. Chang describes this Sancho Panza role as follows:

Li Li-san and Liu Shao-ch'i were a good combination in the labor movement. Liu Shao-ch'i once remarked that Li Li-san had a strong impetus and was an expert in agitation, capable of launching offensives and capturing new beachheads, but the programs he set up were always chaotic, requiring Liu Shao-ch'i to put in a lot of hard work to sort them out, to get the masses organized and the programs functioning. I was often called upon to help them solve their difficulties and found this a recurrent pattern.[13]

One of the workers at Anyüan, to whom Liu taught the meaning of such simple Marxist concepts as "exploitation" in the extramural school for P'inghsiang and Anyüan miners (founded by Li Li-san in January 1922), recalls that Liu was careless about his clothing and personal appearance, self-effacing, and "extremely patient." [14] In mid-

10 Nym Wales [Helen Foster Snow], *The Chinese Labor Movement* (New York, 1945), pp. 32–34.
11 Chang Kuo-t'ao, "Introduction," Liu, *CW*, p. iii.
12 "Down with Liu Shao-ch'i," *CB*, no. 834, p. 1.
13 Chang Kuo-t'ao, "Introduction," Liu, *CW*, p. iv.
14 Chung P'in-kao, "Tsai Liu Shao-ch'i t'ung-chih shen-pien" [By the side of comrade Liu Shao-ch'i], in *Hung-ch'i p'iao-p'iao* [The red flag waves] (Peking) 12: 161–16; Jean Chesneaux, *The Chinese Labor Movement, 1919–1927*, trans. H. M. Wright (Stanford, Calif., 1968), p. 179.

September Liu assisted Li in organizing "the most notorious strike in the annals of the Chinese labor movement" at the Anyüan Coal Mine and Peking-Hankow Railroad, involving "an overwhelming body of 20,000 miners and 1,500 railway workers." [15] In the general suppression of labor unions in Hunan following this strike, the Anyüan union collapsed, but the 100,000 militant unionists who lost their jobs became the hard core of the armed workers in Ch'angsha, Hankow and other cities in Central China during the Northern Expedition, many of them later joining the Red Army.[16] In an article published more than a decade later, Liu recalled his experience in the Anyüan strike and the lesson he derived from it, which he was to make one of the central tenets of his conception of "democratic centralism":

The workers' enthusiasm to struggle was surging high. The great majority of workers and Party members under the branch advocated the call of a strike. However, on the basis of an analysis of the objective conditions, a strike called at that time would be doomed to failure. Therefore I did not agree to it. The comrades of the branch and workers disagreed with me and went ahead to get up a strike committee of which I was elected chairman. . . . What should I do? The strike, if called in compliance with the wish of the great majority, was to fail for certain. . . . What would have happened had I acted according to my personal opinion? I would have violated democratic centralism and the organizational principles and created a situation whereby I would have isolated myself from the branch and the mass of workers. Hence, I decided to call the strike according to the wish of everyone and actively and energetically to lead it. Before the strike was called, I declared that it was going to fail and that since the majority wanted to call it, I could only comply with their wish. The strike ended in a disaster as I predicted. Fortunately, as it was under my command, I took precaution, and the losses were not great. Afterwards . . . most comrades had greater confidence in me.[17]

By early 1923, Liu had assumed direction of the Anyüan Labor Organization, which he continued to run until early 1925, when the mines closed down; he also joined the Kuomintang (KMT) around 1923 and established a joint KMT-CCP Headquarters to organize underground work in Ch'angsha. His first writings also date from this period, describing the activities of the Hanyehp'ing Iron and Steel Company. "I carry out the revolution outside and must succeed," he

[15] T. Y. Chang, "Five Years of Significant Strikes," *Chinese Students' Monthly* 21, no. 8 (June 1926): 19, in Wales, *Labor*, p. 34; later reports provide rather more conservative estimates of the number involved.

[16] John E. Rue, *Mao Tse-tung in Opposition, 1927–1935* (Stanford, Calif., 1966), p. 35.

[17] "Training in Organization and Discipline" (n.d.), *CW* 1: 400.

explained to relatives during a visit home in 1923. "If I do not succeed, China will fail. By that time, I shall go abroad, and you don't have to look for me." [18]

In the spring of 1925 Liu traveled to Canton to take part in preparatory work for the convocation of the Second National Labor Congress; when the Congress was held in May, Liu was elected one of the vice-chairmen of the newly established All-China General Union (ACGU), which replaced the Labor Secretariat. He then returned to Shanghai, where he worked with Li Li-san once again to organize anti-British agitation following the May 30 incident (in which police opened fire on unarmed demonstrators), which blossomed into a nationwide protest and strike movement directed against foreign interests. But when the ACGU (chaired by Li Li-san) was suppressed in September, the leadership fled to Wuhan. Liu was arrested and detained for a brief period in Ch'angsha, then returned to Canton, where he helped organize the 16-month Canton–Hong Kong strike of 1925–26. Liu took part in the 1926 Northern Expedition and was put in charge of the Hupei Federation of Trade Unions when the Expeditionary Forces reached Wuhan. Liu reached Wuhan ahead of Li Li-san, and, as a representative of the ACGU, plunged into labor agitation that resulted in thirty-odd strikes within a month, causing serious trouble in Wuhan's industry, commerce, and transportation. In December he and Li-Li-san organized anti-British demonstrations that led to a clash with marines guarding the concession; these demonstrations forced the British to abandon their Hankow concessions in April 1927.[19]

UNDERGROUND ORGANIZER IN "WHITE AREAS"

Following the collapse of the 1925–27 revolution with Chiang Kai-shek's suppression of the Communists, Liu went underground, where he continued to organize and lead labor movements. He worked for a few months in the Party underground in and around Wuhan, then returned to Shanghai, and, in early 1928, was assigned to the Hopei Party Committee, where he became a leader in the "workers' movement in North China." This brought him into contact with many

18 Ting Hsüeh-lui, "Class Struggle Essential to Communist Party—Exposure of the Reactionary Nature of the Book on 'Self-cultivation' with Its Departure from Actual Class Struggle," *Jen-min jih-pao* [People's daily] (hereafter *PD*), May 6, 1967, in *Survey of the China Mainland Press* (hereafter *SCMP*) (Hong Kong), no. 3944 (May 23, 1967): 23.

19 "Appendix 2: A Biographical Sketch of Liu Shao-ch'i," in *Quotations from President Liu Shao-ch'i*, ed. C. P. FitzGerald (New York and Tokyo, 1968), p. 147.

North China intellectuals, and he also made the acquaintance of P'eng Chen.[20] In the summer of that year he was in Moscow for the CCP's Sixth Congress, where he was reelected to the Central Committee (his first election to the CC was at the Fifth Congress in 1927 in Hankow) and appointed head of the CC Labor Department.[21] In 1929, he worked in the Party headquarters in Shanghai; in the summer, he became secretary of the Manchurian Party committee in Fengtien, where he was again arrested in August of that year by Chang Hsüeh-liang, according to Red Guard allegations.[22] In 1930 and again in 1931, he left his post to attend the Third and Fourth Plenums of the Sixth CC; in the latter meeting he was elected to the Central Executive Committee of the Chinese Soviet Republic and possibly to the CC Politburo also (other sources say he was first elected to the Politburo in 1932). In the period after the Japanese seizure of Manchuria in September 1931, Liu took part in anti-Japanese activities among workers and students. In the following February, he was recalled from Manchuria to become labor commissioner in the Communist areas along the Kiangsi-Fukien border, where he spent two years at the Central Soviet base organizing labor for work on the primitive arsenals that supplied the Red Army.

Although there is conflicting evidence on this point, most reports indicate that Liu accompanied the Long March at least as far as Tsunyi, initially as the CC's representative to the Eighth and then to the Fifth Army Corps, still later as political commissar in P'eng Te-huai's Third Army Corps.[23] From Tsunyi, he moved northeast to take charge of the Manchurian Party committee; his assignment was to contact the anti-Japanese volunteer units scattered over the northeast "white areas" and to strengthen Communist influence over them.

20 *Chung-kung jen-min lu* [Who's who of the CCP], pp. 607–609, cited in T. K. Tong, "Liu Shao-ch'i, the Liu Shao-ch'i Faction and Liu Shao-ch'i-ism," *Collected Documents on the First Sino-American Conference on Mainland China*, ed. Wu Chen-tsai (Taipei, 1971), pp. 235–259.

21 Jerome Ch'en, *Mao and the Chinese Revolution* (London, 1965), p. 148.

22 James Pinckney Harrison, *The Long March to Power: A History of the Chinese Communist Party, 1921–72* (New York, 1972), p. 193.

23 According to Hans Heinrich Wetzel, the former German Communist, Liu left for Shanghai on the eve of the Long March to do underground work under a false passport identifying him as Chao Kang-ming, a professor of history from Yünnan. Wetzel, *Liu Shao-ch'i, Le Moine Rouge* (Paris, 1961), p. 166. However, according to Chen Jan (alias Kuo Chien), a participant on the March, Liu attended the Tsunyi Conference, where he extended Mao's criticisms of the CCP response to the fifth encirclement campaign to "white" area policies, which had been so "leftist" as to make urban work impossible, and demanded a general policy review. Cited in Dick Wilson, *The Long March, 1935: The Epic of Chinese Communism's Survival* (New York, 1971), p. 97.

Liu next surfaces as an undercover organizer of the December Ninth Movement in 1935–36 in Peking, whose success "proved the correctness of these [Liu's] tactical principles for work in the white areas," according to Mao Tse-tung. Liu arrived in Peking as Secretary of the Party's North China Bureau in 1936, shortly after the movement began; with the assistance of P'eng Chen and An Tzu-wen, he made contact with the protesting students and was able to recruit many of them to the Youth League or the CCP. It was at this time that Liu became implicated in granting a number of Party cadres authorization to sign public "confessions" in exchange for release from KMT prisons, as he admitted in a July 1967 self-criticism:

The Head of the Organization Department of the Northern Bureau at that time, comrade K'o Ch'ing-shih . . . said that there were a number of comrades in Peking prisons and that most of them had already served their sentences but that without going through certain formalities they could not be released; he asked me whether or not I could go through the formalities. . . . I immediately wrote a letter about this reporting it to the Party CC of Shen-Pei and asking the CC for a decision. But it wasn't long before I received the CC's answer, namely that the affair should be handled by comrade K'o Ch'ing-shih.[24]

Some of these men, such as Po I-po, Liu Lan-t'ao, Yao I-lin, and others, later rose to prominent Party positions, allegedly remaining closely associated with Liu throughout their careers. Throughout 1936, in Shansi, Hopei, Peking, and Tientsin, Liu promoted the "Resist Japan National United Front" strategy, expanding the North China Student Federation into the Peip'ing Student National Salvation Association, which called for an end to the civil war and unified national resistance against Japan. One eyewitness account of the movement notes only rumors of his presence, indicating how furtive his modus operandi was at the time.[25]

For most of the next decade, Liu remained in "enemy-occupied areas" with only occasional intermissions to attend conferences: from 1936 to 1942, he was successively Secretary of the Party's North China Bureau (1936), its Central Plains Bureau (1939), and its Central China Bureau (1941). According to the recollections of a former cadre, Liu was a model "secretary" during this period, one who "had a quiet nature, did not talk much, and who, if he wasn't sitting all day read-

24 "Tzu-wo chien-ch'a" [Self-examination] (August 2, 1967), in *Liu Shao-ch'i wen-t'i tzu-liao chuan-chi* (hereafter *LSWTC*) [Special collection of materials on Liu Shao-ch'i] (Taipei, 1970), p. 628.

25 Helen Foster Snow, *Notes on the Chinese Student Movement, 1935–1936* (Stanford, Calif., 1959), p. 37 *et passim*.

ing a book, would be writing something." [26] His strategy in the "white areas" was to "act chiefly on the defensive" and to rely on "utmost possible exploitation of overt, legitimate means" (e.g., "grey" organizations), and to coordinate underground activities in urban areas with armed struggle in rural areas. He stressed mobilization of the masses at the grass roots level, and at the elite level promoted a policy of uniting with anyone who could be united with, utilizing internal contradictions among the enemy to play lesser foes off against the major one.[27]

Following a CC conference in Yenan in April 1937, Liu addressed students at a meeting dealing with work in KMT-controlled areas, warning them that the moment had come to "legalize our hitherto illegal activities and make the mass movement widespread." Moreover, he added, because war against Japan was "imminent, the comrades in North China should get ready to take off their robes and bear weapons and join guerrilla bands." [28] On July 7, 1937, war with Japan began; Japanese intelligence reports suggested that Liu's men had touched off the Marco Polo Bridge incident that precipitated hostilities.[29] When war broke out, Liu transferred the North China Bureau to T'aiyüan, then headquarters for Yen Hsi-shan, governor of Shansi and KMT-appointed Commander-in-Chief of the Second War Zone, comprising all of north Shansi. There Liu played a central role in this phase of united front diplomacy, formally subordinating his organization to Yen's overall command while at the same time seeking to manipulate Yen's actions.[30]

For much of 1938–39, Liu stayed in Yenan (in a cave next to Mao's, which has since been closed to the public) as Director of the Cadre Training Department, which shared a good deal of organizational power with the central Organization Department, while concurrently serving as Central Plains Bureau Secretary. He also taught CCP history at the Yenan Party School during this period, delivering (*inter alia*) a

26 Sun Yün-p'eng, "Anniversary of the All-China General Labor Union Congress," *Chinese Worker*, no. 2 (1957), in Hsü Kuan-san, "Liu Shao-ch'i and Mao Tse-tung, 1922–1947," *Chinese Law and Government* (hereafter *CL&G*) 3, nos. 2–3 (summer–fall 1970): 206–251.

27 Cf. "Some Basic Principles of Organizing the Masses" (May 1, 1939), "On Open and Secret Work" (September 1939), "What We Are Doing Behind Enemy Lines" (June 3, 1949), *CW* 1: 99–115, 283–303, 411–437, *et al.*

28 Cited in Klein and Clark, "Liu Shao-ch'i," pp. 616–626.

29 Tetsuya Kataoka, *Resistance and Revolution in China: The Communists and the Second United Front* (Berkeley and Los Angeles, 1974), pp. 44, 72 (prepublication text).

30 Henry G. Schwarz, *Liu Shao-ch'i and "People's War": A Report on the Creation of Base Areas in 1938* (Lawrence, Kans., 1939), p. 21.

series of lectures that were compiled and first printed in pamphlet form in 1939 as *How to Be a Good Communist*. The publication later became one of the most influential and controversial tracts in the history of the Communist movement.[31] In this essay, cited by a Western sinologist in 1956 as an exemplary synthesis of "Communist Ethics and Chinese Tradition," [32] Liu blends quotations from Marxist and Confucian classics to preach the virtues of "steeling and cultivation" through "practical struggle," the "unconditional subordination of personal interests . . . to the interests of the Party," and an appropriate equilibrium between compromise and "principle." [33]

As Central Plains Bureau Secretary, Liu spent the latter part of 1939 and most of 1940 with various New Fourth Army units in Hunan, Anhui, and Kiangsu, concentrating on ways to develop bases behind Japanese lines.[34] In January 1941, Commander Yeh T'ing was captured and Political Commissar Hsiang Ying killed in the New Fourth Army Incident, which Mao characteristically attributed to their faulty leadership; he subsequently appointed Liu as the Army's

[31] "Self-cultivation" was originally delivered by Liu as a series of lectures in two parts: the first part, dealing with ideological self-cultivation, was presented on July 8, 1939, at the Institute of Marxism-Leninism in Yenan; the second part, focusing on organizational and disciplinary self-cultivation, was probably delivered soon afterward at the Central China Party School. The official English version, *How to Be a Good Communist*, was merely a translation of the first part of the lectures, although the second part was more frequently criticized in connection with Liu's theories of organization. Ying-mao Kau, "Editor's Introduction," *CL&G* 5, no. 1 (spring 1972): 10–11.

[32] David S. Nivison, "Communist Ethics and Chinese Tradition," *Journal of Asian Studies* 16, no. 1 (November 1956): 51–75.

[33] *CW* 1: 151–219.

[34] Liu pursued this goal with vigorous aggressiveness. Teng Tzu-hui, then deputy chief of the New Fourth Army's Political Department, wrote: "After analyzing the situation, comrade Liu Shao-ch'i deemed it important to seize northern Kiangsu and then build up northern Kiangsu and northern Anhui as anti-Japanese base areas in Central China. . . . Therefore, comrade Liu Shao-ch'i . . . submitted the following proposal to the central leadership: 'In our attempt to thrust eastward to seize northern Kiangsu, the die-hard troops of Han Te-ch'in pose a major stumbling block. Han holds concurrent posts as a member of the KMT CC, Kiangsu Provincial Governor and Commander of the 24th Group Army. . . . To get rid of this stumbling block and seize all northern Kiangsu, the strength of our troops presently stationed north of the Yangtze is insufficient. It is suggested that the central leadership move one division of the 8th Route Army to the south and order a northward push by troops under Ch'en Yi and Su Yu south of the Yangtze. All these units should be placed under the unified command of the CCP Central Plains Bureau.' " The Center approved his proposal; in the battle of Huangchiao of October 1940, the troops of Ch'en Yi and Su Yu annihilated the main force of Han Te-ch'in, while the 5th Column moved into Yencheng in northern Kiangsu. Teng Tzu-hui, "The Growth of the New Fourth Army in the Struggle Between Two Lines," in *A Spark to Set the Prairie Fire*, 6: 394; quoted in Warren Kuo, *Analytical History of the Chinese Communist Party* (Taipei, 1971), Bk. 4, p. 268.

Political Commissar (with Ch'en I as Acting Commander) and assigned him to rectify the erroneous policies. Liu vigorously pursued two complementary objectives: to protect and develop CCP troop strength, which he did through a reorganization of Yeh T'ing's "bandit remnant" into a more professional military unit; [35] and to use those troops to capture territory and establish political authority. Thus "friction" between the guerrilla forces of the New Fourth Army and their KMT allies became impossible to avoid. As concurrent Secretary of the Party's Central China Bureau, Liu also promoted formation of X "regional governments" and Party cells in various guerrilla bases. In his memoires, Tan Hsi-lin, once a division commander of the New Fourth Army, recalls a conversation with Liu during the battle of Tingyüan in March 1940:

I asked comrade Liu Shao-ch'i, "When we drive out Wu Tzu-chang, will the Nationalists appoint a good magistrate in his stead?" "We shall appoint our man," said comrade Liu, "and we have the right to appoint even a provincial governor. We shall appoint a magistrate for any county we occupy; when several counties are under our occupation, a specal district commissioner will be appointed. We need approval from nobody so long as approval is given by our Party and by the people.[36]

To those who, like Chang Kuo-t'ao, opposed such tactics on ethical grounds, Liu wrote an essay in 1941 justifying their adoption in terms of Marxist orthodoxy as well as political expedience:

But in the Party there are many comrades, even among the leaders, . . . [who] see the Party's united front policy and the policy of class conflict as being in contradiction. They take the Party's united front policy to be something that transcends classes and parties. . . . Because of this, they will necessarily impair their own independence, and become the tools of other classes. . . . In the united front, one aspect is unity, the other aspect is struggle.[37]

In late 1942, Liu was recalled to Yenan to serve as Secretary-General of the Party's Central Secretariat and Vice-Chairman of the CCP Military Affairs Commission, in which capacity he helped make arrangements for the Cheng-feng rectification movement, whose purpose was the consolidation of Mao's ideological authority within the Party. His 1941 lecture, "On Inner-Party Struggle," was published in pam-

35 For a detailed account of Liu's work with the New Fourth Army in northern Kiangsu, see Chalmers Johnson, *Peasant Nationalism and Communist Power: The Emergence of Revolutionary China, 1937–1945* (Stanford, Calif., 1962), pp. 140–155.

36 Cited in Warren Kuo, *Analytical History*, Bk. 4, pp. 231–232.

37 "Fan-tui tang-nei ke-chung pu-liang ch'ü-hsiang" [Opposing various evil trends existing in the Party] (1941), *LSWTC*, pp. 116–117.

phlet form as one of the major texts of the movement, replacing Wang Ming's 1931–32 pamphlet on the same subject. Although this essay did not achieve the wide popular impact of *How to Be a Good Communist*, it was of formative influence in the intra-Party evolution of "criticism and self-criticism," which has since Liberation become one of the primary categories of political participation in Chinese society. In an apparently successful bid to institutionalize the revolutionary impulse within a rational organizational context, Liu encouraged "principled" (i.e., impersonal, "reasonable," issue-oriented) struggle but called for compromise on "unprincipled" disputes.[38]

For the remainder of the war years, except for a brief inspection trip to Shantung and Hopei in late 1942, Liu remained in Yenan. While there, he continued to occupy himself with the consolidation of base areas, which even included promotion of industry at the Shensi-Kansu-Ninghsia border region. As he notes in 1944:

Although the scale of our industry is still very small, its development made over the past few years is surprising. In 1935, there was only a repair shop with several tens of workers there, but now the number of workers has increased to more than ten thousand.[39]

Liu's experience as the highest Party leader in enemy-occupied areas during the war enabled him, more than any other senior leader, to gain a first-hand acquaintance with many of the top and second-echelon leaders who emerged during the war years in Communist base areas in North and East China. During a period when Party membership increased from 40,000 in 1937 to 5.8 million by 1950, he built up the Party machine in a vast territory stretching from the Yangtze River to Manchuria and from the China Sea to the Yellow River. In October 1943, Liu was elected a member of the five-man Secretariat of the CC (with Mao, Chu Teh, Chou En-lai, and Jen Pi-shih) and a vice-chairman of the governmental Revolutionary Military Council (also chaired by Mao); following these appointments he began taking charge of the daily work of the CC.[40]

FIRST "MAOIST"

Liu apparently first became acquainted with Mao while working at Anyüan, which Mao would occasionally visit in his capacity as secretary of the CCP district committee in Hunan. Liu reportedly had

---

[38] *CW* 1: 327–369.

[39] "Speech at the Meeting of Factory Representatives" (May 20, 1944), *CW* 1: 449.

[40] Edgar Snow, *Red China Today: The Other Side of the River* (New York, 1970), pp. 333–336.

many meetings with Mao at Chingshuitang, which marked the beginning of their friendship; Liu was undoubtedly the first of the Russian returned students to give Mao his impressions of life in the Soviet Union.[41] When he was working in the Communist areas along the Kiangsi-Fukien border in 1932–34, Liu at one time went into hiding with Mao at Shachoupa village, 5 *li* west of Juichin, when Mao fell into disfavor with the Party Center.[42]

Liu and Mao evidently entered their mutually beneficial alliance due to their common opposition to the "returned student group," which dominated the leadership of the Party at the time. In the Fifth Plenum of the Sixth CC and the Second National Congress of the Chinese Soviet Republic, both held in Juichin in January 1934, the "returned students" attacked not only Mao, but Liu's work in the "white" areas with urban labor, categorizing both Mao and Liu under a "rightist" label.[43] Thus Liu sided with Mao against the "returned students" at the Tsunyi Conference in 1935, facilitating Mao Tse-tung's takeover of the Military Affairs Commission, as Mao remembered in October 1966:

At the Tsunyi Conference he played a good role. In those days they were quite useful. Lo Fu [Chang Wen-t'ien] was stubborn. Comrade Shao-ch'i opposed them, and so did Nieh Jung-chen.[44]

According to Chang Kuo-t'ao, who left the Party in 1938 in a dispute over the relative priorities of "unity" and "struggle" in the second united front, the Mao-Liu coalition was a *mariage de convenance* lacking any basis in principle. According to Chang's retrospective account, Liu wrote a 10,000-character petition to the CC in 1937 (never published) in which he opposed the seizure of big cities and advocated conservation of strength by carrying on undercover activities. Chang contended that this petition (which criticized Ch'en Tu-hsiu as "left adventurist" rather than "right opportunist") demonstrated that Liu was "more rightist than Chang Kuo-t'ao," but Mao suppressed Liu's letter and (again according to Chang) "exploited Liu for the purpose of suppressing Chang Wen-t'ien." [45] In one of Chou En-lai's attacks on Liu during the GPCR, Chou also alluded to the allegedly unprincipled character of the alliance: because both Liu and Teng Hsiao-p'ing had been attacked by the "third left line," he said,

41 Rue, *Mao Tse-tung,* p. 33; "Liu Shao-ch'i," in Union Research Institute (hereafter URI), *Who's Who in Communist China* (Hong Kong, 1969), 1: 457–459.
42 "A Biographical Sketch," in *Quotations,* ed. FitzGerald, p. 145.
43 Harrison, *The Long March,* pp. 234–235.
44 "Speech at a Report Meeting" (October 24, 1966), "Long Live Mao Tsetung Thought," in *CB,* no. 891 (October 8, 1969): 72.
45 Chang Kuo-t'ao, "Introduction," Liu, *CW,* pp. vii–viii.

"after the Seventh Party Congress, these two had to be trusted." [46] This would seem to imply that Mao temporarily moved to the right because his opponents were on his "left," whereas Liu was a more "sincere" rightist. While such a "revisionist" interpretation is obviously more consonant with the ultimate fate of the Mao-Liu alliance, few indeed were those able to discern the spurious character of the coalition before then. At the time, we find only indications of mutual accord and esteem. In his concluding speech to the Sixth Plenum in 1938, Mao availed himself of Liu's support in an attack on Ch'en Shao-yü's advocacy of "everything through" the united front:

Comrade Liu Shao-ch'i has rightly said that if "everything through" were to mean "through" Chiang Kai-shek and Yen Hsi-shan, then that will only mean unilateral submission, and not "through the united front" at all. Behind the enemy lines, the idea of "everything through" is impossible, for there we have to act independently and with the initiative in our own hands while keeping to the agreements which the KMT has approved.[47]

Henceforth, Liu's position as urban spokesman and chief of the North China organization in the occupied areas steadily improved. According to Chang, "Mao Tse-tung went out of his way to win Liu Shao-ch'i, sympathizing with his frustrations, accepting many of his opinions, making concessions and awarding him with Politburo membership [sic]." [48] Liu, in turn, began "working to build up Chairman Mao's personality cult." In 1940, he was telling underground workers in the area north of the Huai River:

Only the Thought of Mao Tse-tung is able to inspire us to go from victory to victory. . . . If we want the revolution to succeed this is impossible without the right leadership. Mao Tse-tung is the great revolutionary leader of all the people of China, and we should learn from him.[49]

[46] "Premier Chou Bitterly Refutes Liu Shao-ch'i—Excerpts from His August 16 Speech," *Ko-ti t'ung-hsün* [Revolutionary bulletin from various places] (Dairen) 4 (September 13, 1967), in *SCMP*, no. 4081 (December 15, 1967): 2.

[47] "The Question of Independence and Initiative Within the United Front" (November 5, 1938), *Selected Works* (hereafter *SW*) (Peking, 1965) 2: 213–217.

[48] Chang Kuo-t'ao, "Introduction," Liu, *CW*, viii. Other sources indicate that Liu had achieved Politburo membership independently by 1931 or 1932; in fact, Mao was apparently removed from the Politburo in 1927 and remained in limbo until the Tsunyi Conference in 1935, when he seized control of the Politburo by packing the meeting (it was an "expanded" conference) with Red Army leaders sympathetic to his critique of the previous military strategy. Cf. Henry G. Schwarz, "The Nature of Leadership: The Chinese Communists, 1930–1945," *World Politics* 22, no. 4 (July 1970): 496–518.

[49] Shao-ch'i t'ung-chih tsai Huai-pei k'ang-jih ti hou" [Comrade Shao-ch'i in the war behind the enemy lines north of the Huai], in *HCPP*, p. 79.

The immediate political intent of "On Inner-Party Struggle" was to evolve a non-Stalinist procedure for purging Mao's "leftist" rivals. Liu's 1943 essay, "Liquidate Menshevist Ideology in the Party," was likewise aimed at the "international faction" led by the "returned students," accusing the latter of being doctrinaire; it included the first published tribute to Mao's Thought:

Our comrade Mao Tse-tung is a resolute and great revolutionary who has undergone long tempering in the many strenuous and complicated revolutionary struggles of these twenty-two years, who has completely mastered the strategy and tactics of Marxism-Leninism and who possesses infinite loyalty to the cause of the liberation of the Chinese working class and the Chinese people.[50]

As the war drew to a close, Mao and Liu both grew more prolix in their expressions of mutual esteem. In April 1945, immediately before convocation of the Seventh Party Congress, the CCP adopted a "Resolution on Certain Questions in the History of Our Party," which is included in Mao's *Selected Works*. The Appendix contains the following encomium:

Comrade Liu Shao-ch'i's ideas on tactics for work in the White areas are likewise a model. Correctly taking into account the glaring disparity between the enemy's strength and our own in the White areas, and particularly in the cities, after the defeat of the revolution in 1927, Comrade Liu Shao-ch'i advocated systematic organization of our retreat and defense and "the avoidance of decisive engagements with the enemy for the time being, while the situation and conditions are unfavorable to us," in order to "prepare for revolutionary attacks and decisive engagements in the future." He also advocated that the Party's open organization in the period of the 1924–27 revolution be transferred systematically and strictly into underground organizations, while "utilizing open legal means as far as possible" in mass work to enable the Party's organizations to conceal their strength for a long time in such mass work, to go deep among the masses and "accumulate and strengthen the forces of the masses and heighten their political consciousness." With respect to leadership in mass struggles, Comrade Liu Shao-ch'i held that it was necessary, "in accordance with the situation and the specific conditions at a given time and place and the degree of political consciousness of the masses, to advance limited slogans, demands, and forms of struggle acceptable to the masses in order to set the mass struggle to a higher stage or, 'knowing how far to go,' temporarily to conclude the battle so as to prepare for the next battle at a higher stage and on a larger scale." On the question of utilizing the enemy's internal contradictions and winning temporary alliance, he held that it was necessary "to push these contradictions to the breaking point and form a temporary alliance against the chief enemy

[50] *CW* 1: 438.

with those elements in the enemy camp who may cooperate with us, induce them to join with us and participate in common action and then influence them and win over their mass following.[51]

Three weeks later, Liu presented his "Report to the Seventh Party Congress," in which he referred to Mao Tse-tung or his Thought no less than 105 times. In the revised Party Constitution, which Liu also drafted, Mao's Thought was put on the same footing with Marxism as a "guiding principle for all the works of the Party," and every member was required to study it.[52] "Mao Tse-tung had no prestige until the seventh general meeting of the Party," Liu's wife later remarked privately to his daughter. "Your father and other leaders established the prestige for him." [53]

One of the likely purposes of this "mutual admiration society" was to integrate the Party, which for nearly a decade had been split into two halves, meeting only for infrequent conferences: the "red area" (hung-ch'ü) forces, which consisted of peasant guerrilla armies under the leadership of Mao Tse-tung, and the "white area" (pai-ch'ü) forces, which consisted of urban intellectuals, workers, and some peasants, operating under Liu Shao-ch'i.[54] In 1945, Liu grafted his "white area" machine to the center, in an institutional merger that combined the Party's leading military strategist and symbol of revolution (Mao) with its leading organizational genius (Liu). Many of Liu's followers felt that the objective preconditions were not yet ripe for reforms as sweeping as those Mao proposed and were more amenable to Ch'en Shao-yü's line of separate workers' movements, women's movements, and youth movements. "The policy has been decided by the Center, you cannot discount it (ta che-k'ou) in the slightest," Liu informed leading cadres in Shantung. "There is nothing left to consider" except tactics of implementation.[55]

---

[51] "Appendix: Resolution on Certain Questions in the History of Our Party" (April 20, 1945), SW 3: 202–203. The 1966 edition of Quotations of Chairman Mao Tse-tung (Peking: Foreign Languages Press) included a statement on p. 242 in which Mao spoke favorably of Liu. The statement was not deleted until the 2d revised edition in May, 1967—along with the title of Chapter 24, "Ideological Self-Cultivation" (which became "Correcting Mistaken Ideas").

[52] "On the Party" (May 1945), CW 2: 9–119.

[53] Minoru Omori, "Mao's Worst Crisis," New Republic, January 28, 1967, pp. 17–19.

[54] Schwarz, "The Nature of Leadership," pp. 496–518. A second purpose was to use Mao as a symbol to capture the allegiance of the masses, for which it was considered necessary to create a charismatic hero cult rivaling that of Chiang Kai-Shek.

[55] Hsü Kuan-san, "Yenan shih-tai ti Liu Shao-ch'i" [Liu Shao-ch'i in the Yenan period], Jen-wu yü ssu-hsiang [Men and ideas] (hereafter Jen-wu), no. 38 (May 15, 1970): 9–16.

In remarks made in February 1967, Ch'en I claimed that Mao's Thought had been '"developed" in Liu's writings.[56] Indeed, it seems that Lin Piao's projection of the validity of Mao's theory of people's war to the rest of the world was prefigured in Liu's statements as early as 1945. In his "Report to the Seventh Party Congress," Liu "for the first time . . . put forward the idea . . . that China was not merely the pioneer but the leader and ideological mentor of anti-imperialist revolutions throughout Asia and Africa." [57] In an interview with Anna Louise Strong in 1946, Liu attributed theoretical originality and international relevance to Mao's Thought. "The basic principles of Marxism are undoubtedly adaptable to all countries, but to apply their general truth to concrete revolutionary practice in China is a difficult task," he noted. "Mao Tse-tung is Chinese; he analyzes Chinese problems and guides the Chinese people in their struggle for victory. He uses Marxist-Leninist principles to explain Chinese history and the practical problems of China. He is the first that has succeeded in doing so." He went on:

China is a semi-feudal, semi-colonial country in which vast numbers of people live at the edge of starvation, tilling small bits of soil. Its economy is agricultural, backward and dispersed. In attempting the transition to a more industrialized economy, China faces the competition and pressures—economic, political, and military—of advanced industrial lands. This is the basic situation that affects both the relations of social classes and the methods of struggle toward any such goal of national independence and a better, freer life for the Chinese. There are similar conditions in other lands of Southeast Asia. The course chosen by China will influence them all.[58]

In November 1949, at the Asian and Australasian Trade Union Conference, Liu called for "national liberation movements" in which "armed struggle can and should become the main form" of "people's liberation." These movements would take place under a "people's liberation army" led by the Communist Party; conditions in Vietnam, Burma, Indonesia, Malaya, the Philippines, Korea, Thailand, even Australia, he suggested, might foster such movements.[59]

56 Ch'en I, "K'an wen-hua ta ko-ming" [The GPCR observed], Red Flag (Peking Aeronautical Institute) (April 4, 1967), in Chung-kung wen-hua ko-ming tzu-liao hui-pien [Compendium of materials on the Chinese Communist Cultural Revolution], ed. Ting Wang (Hong Kong, 1967) 1: 640–649.

57 Stuart Schram, Mao Tse-tung (New York, 1966), p. 217.

58 Anna Louise Strong, "The Thought of Mao Tse-tung," Amerasia 11, no. 6 (June 1947): 161–174.

59 CW 2: 183–189.

HEIR APPARENT

Ch'en I said that Liu was recognized as Mao's successor as early as the Seventh Congress in 1945. Formally speaking, this is incorrect; when members of the CC were elected, Liu received the third highest total of votes and hence became third-ranking CC and Politburo member after Mao and Chu Teh. Yet it is likely that Liu was already second to Mao in actual authority. When Mao flew to Chungking in August 1945 for peace negotiations with Chiang Kai-shek, Liu acted in his place in Yenan for several months and took the concurrent job of head of the Organization Department. In March 1947, when a KMT drive forced the CCP to evacuate Yenan, the Politburo split up; Mao, Chou, and Jen Pi-shih remained in the Shensi-Kansu-Ninghsia Border Region to carry on the fight against the KMT, while Liu, Chu Teh, and an alternate central committee moved to the Communist-controlled Shansi-Chahar-Hopei Border Region. Mao had given the entire CC to understand that if his group were wiped out, Liu's committee was empowered to act as the CC. This alternate committee remained in the Shihchiachuang area of southern Hopei until Mao and the central organs of the Party arrived in May 1948. Again in 1950, when Mao visited the Soviet Union, Liu presided in his absence over the Fifth Meeting of the central People's Government. When Mao fell ill in March 1951, he again handed the reins of government over to Liu.[60]

From 1945 through 1955, when Teng Hsiao-p'ing succeeded him, Liu was General Secretary of the CC Secretariat and in this capacity seemed to act as de facto supervisor of the routine administration of domestic affairs. He also delivered reports introducing important legislative initiatives and began to fill certain ceremonial functions. In June 1950, he reported on the new Agrarian Reform Law, which introduced class demarcation to the countryside. In September 1952, he led a delegation to Moscow to attend the Nineteenth Soviet Party Congress, remaining there for more than three months. He headed the Electoral Law Drafting Committee and delivered its report to the First National People's Congress in 1954. In September 1956, he delivered the keynote political report to the Eighth Party Congress, in which he first proposed visits by responsible personnel to subordinate levels (hsia-fang) as one means of curtailing "intra-Party bureaucracy." In late 1957, "a radical group headed by Mao . . . and Liu . . . finally succeeded in imposing [its] policy of social mobilization on the Politburo, in opposition to the more cautious advocates of gradual eco-

[60] Robert Payne, *Portrait of a Revolutionary: Mao Tse-tung* (New York, 1961), p. 299.

nomic development." [61] At the Fortieth Anniversary of the Russian Revolution, and again in his keynote speech to the Second Session of the Eighth Party Congress in May 1958, Liu issued strong endorsements of the Great Leap Forward. To get a first-hand view of the situation, he and other top leaders went on extensive tours throughout the country.

Following an announcement at the end of December 1958 that Mao intended to relinquish his governmental responsibilities, Liu was officially elected Chairman of the People's Republic at the Second National People's Congress on April 20, 1959. At around the same time, he began to be described in official publications as Mao's "closest comrade-in-arms." Although many province chiefs, important mayors, ministers, and a large proportion of the CC could already be termed "Liu's men," Liu's new position further strengthened his authority, particularly after the reorganization of the Party's regional structure into six bureaus in January 1961. In an interview with Lord Montgomery in 1961, Mao replied to a query concerning his succession that this was clear and had been laid down—Liu Shao-ch'i was the choice.[62]

CONCLUSION

Liu's attempt to realize his particular vision of socialism achieved its pervasive impact on the Chinese political system through his personal example, through the educational impact of his extensive writings, through his origination or (more often) successful mediation of policies, and through his organizational influence. In all of these realms of endeavor, Liu sought to combine elements of revolution and order, equality and efficiency. Given the relatively late appearance and limited compass of the "cult of Liu Shao-ch'i," the power of Liu's personal example remained confined to those who worked with him; but among this select but influential group of Party and government officials Liu's stature was impressive. "When directing work, he would always try to exhaust the possibilities . . . of raising the theoretical consciousness of the cadres . . . to get at the theoretical principle of the thing before taking action to solve the problem in practice," a former subordinate wrote.[63] As Chang Kuo-t'ao noted in regard to Liu's early career:

61 Franz Schurmann, *Ideology and Organization in Communist China,* 2d ed. (Berkeley, Calif., 1968), p. 360.

62 Field Marshal Viscount Montgomery, "China on the Move," *The Sunday Times* (London), October 15, 1961.

63 "Shao-ch'i t'ung-chih tsai Huai-pei," *HCPP,* p. 79.

In practical work, Liu Shao-ch'i not only obeyed the decisions of superiors and carried them out, but also proposed his own ideas in proper ways. At that time there were over a dozen young leaders in the Shanghai labor movement working under Liu Shao-ch'i; they all got along with him very well, and their programs were orderly arranged.[64]

Liu's are the only doctrinal works besides Mao's to have attained catechismic status in the Party: In his writings on "self-cultivation" and on inner-Party struggle, he indoctrinated Party members with an inner feeling of disciplined responsibility and "Communist morality," which "combined an anti-traditional spirit and will to change with a neo-Confucian ethic wherein everyone stood in a definite relationship to everyone else—an authoritarian pattern, but permeated with the concept of reciprocal responsibility and tempered with an appreciation of the value of balance." [65] His writings also contributed to the transformation of class categories from ascriptive to achievement criteria, opening the way to recruitment of both intellectuals and broad masses of peasants to the Party and to the extensive promotion of "thought reform" as a functional substitute for a secret police system.[66]

In addition to the moral impact exerted through his personal example and writings, Liu had a significant effect on the formulation of certain policies. He promoted the idea of a second united front as early as 1936 and originated the "united yet independent" (chi t'ung-yi yu tu-li) compromise formulation that the Party successfully adopted in 1937.[67] In a pioneering 1938 talk Liu outlined concrete steps to be taken in the organization of base areas, and in a series of leadership positions in North and Central China he supervised the development of these steps, organizing the peasantry to support Communist troops and building up industry and primitive arsenals.[68] His administration of the Cheng-feng Movement in Yenan, together with the model of "inner-Party struggle" he articulated in direct connection with it, set a pattern for later rectification movements and purges that was followed with remarkable consistency up to the time of the GPCR. The pattern consisted of treating high-ranking deviators with lenience (usually reinstating them to lesser leadership positions) while sub-

[64] Chang Kuo-t'ao, "Introduction," CW, p. iii.

[65] Rhoda Sussman Weidenbaum, "The Career and Writings of Liu Shao-ch'i," Researches in the Social Sciences in China, ed. John E. Lane (New York, 1957), pp. 76–78.

[66] Cf. Susan Han, "The Concept of the Proletariat in Chinese Communism" (Ph.D. diss., University of Chicago, 1955).

[67] Hsü, "Yenan shih-tai ti Liu Shao-ch'i," Jen-wu, pp. 9–16.

[68] Cf. Schwarz, Liu Shao-ch'i and "People's War," pp. 24–27.

mitting their followers to intensive "study" and "reeducation" sessions. In 1956 Liu introduced the idea of "transfers down" (*hsia-fang*) to combat bureaucratic ossification, an idea Mao welcomed enthusiastically; in 1961 Liu himself spent forty-four days in three communes in three different *hsien* in Hunan; and in 1964 his wife spent nearly a year on a commune at T'aoyüan.[69]

Of even more importance than Liu's contribution to specific policy decisions was his pervasive influence over the processes of organization and institution building. Upon Mao's defeat of the "internationalist faction," Liu and his colleagues moved in to assert organizational control over the northern base areas in which the returned students held sway. When Chang Wen-t'ien and Ch'in Pang-hsien were removed, the Party administration fell under the complete domination of the Mao-Liu team, with Mao holding the policy-making offices at the top and Liu controlling the organizational apparatus.[70] Throughout the war with Japan and the civil war, Liu was the "Politburo chief (or first commissar) among all the Communist forces in eastern and northeastern China." [71] Liu thus assumed command over the urban-based, intellectual segment of the Party in those areas that had previously looked to the "returned students" for leadership, bringing them under the banner of Mao Tse-tung while also winning their personal allegiance. When Liu was first elected to the CC Secretariat in late 1942, significantly enough, he took the vacated position of Ch'en Shao-yü. Through his unstinting praise of Mao over the next two years, and by maintaining strict organizational discipline, Liu engineered, at the Seventh Congress in 1945, the merger of the Party's organizational apparatus with Mao's peasant armies. As leader of the "first line," Liu continued to whip this apparatus into line over the next two decades— as in 1954, when he acted as Mao's principal spokesman in a campaign to check regionalism, or 1958, when he publicly supported and helped to implement the "three red flags" program of building socialism, the Great Leap Forward, and the people's communes. The coherence of

69 "Uncover Liu Shao-ch'i's Counterrevolutionary Words and Deeds—Comments on Liu Shao-ch'i's 1961 Hunan Visit," *Tung-fang-hung* [East is red] (Education Department, Peking Institute of Geology) (March 9, 1967), in Chang, "Power and Policy," pp. 235–236. In a comment that the Red Guards took to be aimed at Mao, Liu expressed his contempt for those who "do not go to the grassroots level themselves, but expect other people to go there and carry out their instructions. As a result, they know nothing and when they are criticized by other people, they turn a deaf ear to them. They are high officials drawing a fat pay . . . arrogant, complacent, and conservative." Criticize Liu, Teng, T'ao Liaison Station and Tientsin Investigation Group, in *Pa-i-san hung-wei-ping* [August 13 Red Guard] (Tientsin) 68 (May 13, 1967), in *SCMM*, no. 588 (August 14, 1967): 23.

70 T. K. Tong, "Liu Shao-ch'i," pp. 607–609.

71 Edgar Snow, *Red China Today*, pp. 333–336.

this machine over time,[72] and its (suspected) continued first loyalty to Liu Shao-ch'i, is attested by the pattern of GPCR purge casualties: December Ninth cadres, "prison cadres," and "white area" cadres were purged in disproportionate numbers.[73]

[72] According to Derek J. Waller, the CCP between 1945 and 1965 has a "continuity and homogeneity of membership unmatched by any other ruling Communist Party." In 1945, at the Seventh Party Cogress, seventy-seven men were elected to the CC (forty-four full and thirty-three alternate members); eleven years later, seventy-one of these men were still alive, of whom sixty-seven (94 percent) were reelected to the Eighth CC in 1956. However, membership was expanded to 170 (ninety-seven full and seventy-three alternate members). "Elite Composition and Revolutionary Change in Communist China, 1965–1969" (paper presented at the Twenty-fourth Annual Meeting of the Association for Asian Studies, New York, March 27–29, 1972), p. 1.

[73] Parris H. Chang, "Mao's Great Purge: A Political Balance Sheet," *Problems of Communism* 28, no. 2 (March–April 1969): 1–11.

3

PROLOGUE: THE STORM GATHERS

This chapter attempts to trace the origins of the GPCR and of Liu's fall, two events so intimately linked (in that Liu stood for what the GPCR was intended to renounce) that to disentangle their respective causes is an exercise in informed speculation. The inquiry will proceed by way of testing two "ideal types," each of which proposes a different sequence of action and motive preceding the GPCR, each of which contains a different implicit conception of the nature of top-level politics in China in the early 1960s.

The first, and by far the most widely accepted type of explanation, we call the "conspiracy" theory.[1] The Maoist version ascribes conspiracy to the Liuists, the Western version to the Maoists, but both see the GPCR as an extension of factionalism: for a long time, the argument goes, a fierce inner-Party struggle over a host of issues raged between Mao Tse-tung and Liu Shao-ch'i and their followers behind the pacific facade of Party unity. In the GPCR, Mao boldly exposed this deadlocked struggle to the public and, following a "Great Strategic Plan" (ta chan-lüeh pu-shu), aroused a mass constituency to decide the outcome in his favor. The rudiments of this "Plan," according to Chou En-lai, were conceived in January 1965; Lin Piao dated its inception as early as 1962.[2] The Maoists have never divulged the details of this "Plan," but Western adherents of a somewhat more complex version of this Machiavellian perspective have inferred them. According to

1 Among those who have supported this theory are Philip Bridgham, "Factionalism in the Chinese Communist Party," *Party Leadership and Revolutionary Power in China*, ed. John W. Lewis (New York and London, 1970), pp. 203–239; Harry Gelman, "Mao and the Permanent Purge," *Problems of Communism* 15, no. 6 (November–December 1966): 2–14; Chu-yüan Cheng, "Power Struggle in Red China," *Asian Survey* (hereafter *AS*) 6, no. 9 (September 1966): 469–484.

2 Lin Piao said in 1969 that in 1962 Mao was "first to perceive the danger of a counterrevolutionary plot by Liu Shao-ch'i and his gang." "Report to the Ninth National Congress of the CCP" (April 1, 1969), in *CB*, no. 880 (May 9, 1969): 22.

Philip Bridgham, "The strategy was to incite 'revolutionary teachers and students' . . . in June and July 1966 to rise up against the work teams, and then to attack Liu for attempting to suppress the 'revolutionary Left.' " [3] According to Jerome Ch'en and William Whitson, the PLA secretly initiated these risings: "No other political force in China was so well organized and disciplined as to be able to carry out a nationwide operation in such well-guarded secrecy." [4]

The second type of explanation we call the "spontaneity" theory, which considers Mao a "great experimenter" who conceived of the GPCR as a mass mobilizational and educational experience and had formed no prior verdict on Liu Shao-ch'i or anyone else. When asked whether the GPCR was being directed from the top, Anna Louise Strong replied: "To some extent, but not in the sense that a person gives out a definite plan and gives out orders. It means arousing the people and then noticing trends you want to give publicity to." [5] James Hsiung concurs:

Contrary to early impressions, the Cultural Revolution does not seem to have followed any master plan. There was little logic to its series of spontaneous eruptions, and its erratic course of development suggests that even Mao did not foresee certain specific events. . . . Prior to the spring of 1966, Mao probably had no definite plan to remove such Party leaders as P'eng Chen and Liu Shao-ch'i. Nor did he seem to have any clear plan for the use of the Red Guards.[6]

These two possible interpretations are not exhaustive, but rather logical extremes on the continuum of prior intention and preparation between which the truth may be expected to reside. The first would imply that Liu was a marked man whom Mao, on the basis of a long series of policy disagreements, had determined to purge at the first opportunity. Moreover, he had laid plans to create such an opportunity: the GPCR was a trap, laid in secret, to spring shut on those assigned to implement it. This theory's implicit conception of the nature of high-level politics is one of ceaseless clandestine maneuvers between power-maximizing factions, from which the GPCR diverged

[3] Bridgham, in Lewis, ed., Party, pp. 223 ff.

[4] Jerome Ch'en, ed., Mao (Englewood Cliffs, N.J., 1969), p. 40; also William W. Whitson, The Chinese High Command: A History of Communist Military Politics, 1927–1971 (New York, 1973), pp. 373, 375.

[5] Bob Reece, "An Octogenarian Red Guard," Far Eastern Economic Review (hereafter FEER). 59, no. 11 (March 14, 1968): 456–459.

[6] James C. Hsiung, Ideology and Practice: The Evolution of Chinese Communism New York, 1970), pp. 218–219. See also Lily Abegg, Ostasien Denkt Anders: Eine Analyse West-Östlichen Gegensatzes, rev. ed. (Munich, 1970), pp. 368 ff.; and Wenshun Chi, "The GPCR in Ideological Perspective," AS 9, no. 8 (August 1969): 563–579.

only tactically, owing to Mao's loss of control over the institutionally legitimate purge mechanism.[7] According to the second interpretation, Mao's intentions for the GPCR were concerned with the rectification of the "bourgeois cultural superstructure," with providing a suitable *rite de passage* for China's "revolutionary successor" generation, and with a general revival of socialist ideals in China. Liu fell because of his unanticipated blunders in achieving these objectives and was later made the central target of criticism in order to give polemical focus to a movement that threatened to get out of hand. This interpretation implicitly allots a greater role to mass initiative in the unpredictable, dynamic interplay between elites and masses in the movement.

The method we have adopted to research these questions is essentially a "sociology of knowledge" approach: it consists of tracing the main polemical themes of the GPCR back to their apparent origins, at the same time watching for specific prior indications of a Mao-Liu rift. The criticisms themes are not original, and so by tracing them to their origins and reconstructing the political context in which they first appeared we may draw certain inferences about the decisions behind the themes. The themes originated in a series of unresolved disputes that arose between 1956 and 1966, the most important of which revolved about the following incidents: (1) the abortive attempt at liberalization in the "Hundred Flowers" Campaign, (2) the failure of the "Great Leap Forward," (3) the increasingly bitter ideological dispute with the Communist Party of the Soviet Union (CPSU), (4) the political decline of Mao Tse-tung and the corresponding rise of Liu Shao-ch'i, (5) Mao's theoretical conceptualization of the emergence of an inner-Party opposition, and (6) the frustration of Maoist attempts to revolutionize the cultural superstructure through institutional means.

THE "HUNDRED FLOWERS"

When Mao delivered his famous speech, "On the Correct Resolution of Contradictions Among the People," in February 1957, several things seemed to be on his mind. First was the 1956 Hungarian uprising, and the prospect of similar eruptions in China unless a way could be found to give vent to repressed grievances: "If one persists in using the methods of terror in solving internal antagonisms, it may lead to transformation of these nonantagonistic contradictions into

[7] Andrew J. Nathan has advanced the most sophisticated presentation of this model in his article, "A Factional Model for CCP Politics," *China Quarterly* (hereafter *CQ*), no. 53 (January–March 1973): 34–67.

antagonistic ones, as happened in Hungary." Mao claimed that "certain people" even hoped this would happen, that "thousands of people would demonstrate in the streets against the People's Government." Second, Khrushchev's denunciations of Stalin at the Twentieth CPSU Congress seemed already to be bothering him, raising the spectre of a rude disinterment of his own reputation after he died, which he hoped to anticipate. "To those who do not follow that teaching of Marx, I would address an old saying: 'He who does not allow himself to be criticized during his life will be criticized after his death.'" [8] Third, under the optimistic impression that thought reform had legitimated the new regime among all sectors of the populace, he felt that this movement would stimulate the flow of ideas which would assist socialist construction and give intellectuals a greater sense of participation.

The sharpness of the criticism that eventually "bloomed" and the Party's almost immediate punitive response to that criticism cause one to wonder to what extent such criticism was sanctioned or expected. As for its sanction, Mao seems indeed to have issued a sweeping carte blanche to all critics:

People may ask: Since Marxism is accepted by the majority of the people in our country as the guiding ideology, can it be criticized? Certainly it can. Marxism, being a scientific truth, fears no criticism. . . . Quite the contrary, Marxists need to steel and improve themselves and win new positions in the storm and stress of struggle. Fighting against wrong ideas is like being vaccinated—a man develops greater immunity from disease after the vaccine takes effect. Plants raised in hothouses are not likely to be robust.[9]

And in a speech to the Party's National Conference on Propaganda Work the following month, Mao said:

To "open wide" means to let all people express their opinions freely, so that they dare to speak, dare to criticize and dare to debate; it means not being afraid of wrong views and anything poisonous; it means to encourage argument and criticism among people holding different views, allowing freedom both for criticism and countercriticism. . . . It is the policy which will help us to consolidate our country and develop our culture.[10]

If the criticisms were sanctioned, why were they so quickly quashed? First, although he gave blanket sanction to all criticisms, Mao's ap-

[8] See Sidney Gruson's unexpurgated version of the speech (via Warsaw) in *New York Times* (hereafter *NYT*), June 13, 1957, pp. 1, 8.

[9] From the official (edited) version in *Selected Readings from the Works of Mao Tsetung* (hereafter *SRWM*) (Peking, 1971), p. 465.

[10] "Speech at the CCP's National Conference on Propaganda Work" (March 12, 1957), *SRWM*, p. 493.

parent magnanimity must be seen in the context of the reluctance of the intellectuals and former independent businessmen to respond to earlier, more hedged appeals. Mao first set forth the idea of a "Hundred Flowers" in a secret speech before the Supreme State Conference as early as May 2, 1956, but, despite subsequent invitations by Chou En-lai and Lu Ting-yi, no one ventured a serious criticism until more open-ended appeals were made the following spring.[11] Second, Mao clearly expected any antisocialist criticisms spontaneously to provoke vigorous mass countercriticism; that no such countercriticism appeared, he was later to conclude, was due to the survival of traditional respect for scholars and to domination of the nation's cultural and educational establishment by bourgeois intellectuals. Finally, even at their most magnanimous, Mao's appeals suggest that he expected criticism to be directed against isolated sectors of the Party-government bureaucracy, not at such fundamentals of socialism as the vanguard Party or the dictatorship of the proletariat. This was implicit in his prior classification of the expected criticisms as "contradictions among the people." Mao's a priori conviction that any friction between elites and masses could be attributed to "bureaucracy" is evident in his analysis of incidents of grass-roots protest that occurred the previous year, in which he dismisses the protesters' stated grievances and advances his own theory:

In 1956, small numbers of workers or students in certain places went on strike. The immediate cause of these disturbances was the failure to satisfy certain of their demands for material benefits, of which some should and could have been met, while others were out of place. . . . But a more important cause was bureaucracy on the part of the leadership. In some cases, the responsibility for such bureaucratic mistakes falls on the higher authorities, and those at lower levels are not entirely to blame.[12]

In power-political terms, Mao apparently intended the movement to provide popular legitimation for a purge of the bureaucracy:

But what to do if this ["Hundred Flowers"] is hampered by bureaucracy, which in turn leads to demonstrations and strikes? Such incidents should be considered as warning signals to sectors of the administration where bureaucracy has made its nest.[13]

[11] On May 2, 1956, Mao made a bold pronouncement on the subject of intellectuals in a secret speech before the Supreme State Conference, in which he set forth the idea of a hundred flowers. The speech was not published, but its main features were made known on May 26 in a speech by Lu Ting-yi.

[12] "On the Correct Resolution of Contradictions Among the People," SRWM, p. 470.

[13] Gruson, in NYT, June 13, 1967, pp. 1, 8.

Given Mao's manifest intention to use the bourgeois democratic parties and the intellectual community as an extraparliamentary lobby to rectify the bureaucracy, it is not surprising that the bureaucrats opposed the idea. From the bureaucracy's point of view, to be made a target of criticism destroyed an official's authority and made it impossible for him to do his job: "If the masses criticize the cadres, the cadres can no longer successfully lead the masses," contended a cadre during a later movement. "It is in order for higher officials to criticize the cadres. But when the masses do so, everything becomes chaotic." [14] At the highest level, Mao was apparently supported by liberal elements in the Party and by officials responsible for economic affairs who were pushing for a greater role for experts, including Chou En-lai, P'eng Te-huai, Lin Piao, and Ch'en I; he was opposed by Liu Shao-ch'i, P'eng Chen, and most members of the middle and lower Party bureaucracy.[15] In a meeting of Communist cadres in Shanghai in April 1957, Liu agreed that the nature of contradictions between proletariat and bourgeoisie had become "nonantagonistic" but held that the appropriate way of handling them was through unity, inasmuch as exposure and struggle would only make them "unnecessarily tense and delicate." [16] There was such strong resistance in the bureaucracy against criticism "from the outside" that Mao had to invoke the authority of his Party leadership to get his way; he is said to have told friends "he would prefer not to be Chairman in order to get involved in 'a hundred flowers blooming.' " [17]

Many of the ensuing criticisms prefigured GPCR themes, such as the attack on the privileges of the bureaucratic "new class." "Gross inequality exists in the political treatment of Party members and the masses. . . . Party members enjoy many privileges that make them a race apart," said a professor at Wuhan University.[18] A New China News Agency (NCNA) correspondent alleged in a letter to the CC and Chairman Mao that "with the exception of rice, more goods are con-

14 Hu-pei jih-pao [Hupei Daily], December 20, 1964, cited in Adrian Hsia, The Chinese Cultural Revolution (New York, 1972), p. 123.
15 Hsü Liang-ying, Tsu-kuo [China Monthly], no. 241 (August 12, 1957): 3; also Ch'ien Wei-ch'ang, "Firmly Support the Leading Power of the Party in Scientific Work," PD, July 17, 1957, p. 2.
16 Kuang-ming jih-pao (hereafter KMJP) [Illumination Daily], August 12, 1957, in Ch'in Ssu-k'ai, "The Mao-Liu Struggle from Another Angle," CL&G 3, nos. 2–3 (summer–fall 1970), p. 191.
17 Ma Che-min, "I Want to Renew Myself," PD, July 18, 1957, p. 10, cited in Richard Solomon, "One Party and 'One Hundred Schools': Leadership, Lethargy, or Luan?" Current Scene (hereafter CS) 7, nos. 19–20 (October 1, 1969): 25–26.
18 Quoted in Roderick MacFarquhar, The Hundred Flowers (New York and London, 1960), p. 92.

sumed by the revolutionaries who make up 5 percent of the population than the peasants who make up 80 percent of the population. . . .
A new ruling class has arisen." This new class had grown corrupt:
"Our Party is not as bad as the KMT, but since it took over the cities
seven or eight years ago, some signs of resemblance have now
emerged." [19] Lin Hsi-ling, a leading student activist, argued:

All the people should be allowed to air their views to their hearts' content.
The present "blooming and contending" is confined to the upper strata
only. This won't do. . . . Let the broad masses discuss and air their
opinions.[20]

But some of the criticisms went too far in a "bourgeois liberal"
direction, denouncing the proletarian dictatorship and demanding
competitive elections (in which the bourgeois parties would be entitled to bid for votes among all classes), academic freedom, greater
political power for the People's Consultative Conferences (in an arrangement resembling a bicameral legislature, with the CC as the
other "house"), and the like. A teacher at Peking Third Middle
School complained that criticism had become a one-way medium
through which the authorities intimidated the people and stifled
democracy:

A wide gap existed between the Party faction and the masses, and people
generally dared not say anything. There was one teacher who often accused
the school of being undemocratic and unconcerned with the masses; he was
made a target during the movement against counterrevolutionaries and subjected to repeated struggles. Finally it was found that there was nothing
wrong. Although the district Party committee and the Party fraction did
apologize to him, yet it was explained that the whole thing was not started
without reasons. Has this man still the courage to bloom now? [21]

Well in advance of any public indication of Sino-Soviet discord,
Lin Hsi-ling attributed the suppression of liberty to "wild copying of
the Soviet Union." Others, however, likened the proletarian dictatorship to the Nazi regime. Some teachers and students demanded that
Party committees either be withdrawn from educational institutions
or limited in power in order to "let the professors run the universities." The Chairman himself came under attack. A "rightist" Party
member and journalist was reported to have said he "early had had

[19] "Report of a People's Publishing House Forum," New China News Agency
(hereafter NCNA) (Peking), July 12, 1957, quoted in Solomon, "One Party."
[20] Quoted in Dennis Doolin, Communist China: The Politics of Student Opposition (Stanford, Calif., 1964), pp. 23–27.
[21] Quoted in MacFarquhar, The Hundred Flowers, pp. 120–121.

his doubts" about Mao, and that after the CPSU's Twentieth Congress (at which Khrushchev denounced Stalin) he had "begun to suspect that Chairman Mao had committed errors." [22] Ch'en Ming-shu, a member of the KMT Revolutionary Committee, said Mao was "hot-tempered," "impetuous," and "reckless," and that "these characteristics . . . have often affected his decisions in matters of policy, causing unnecessary deviations in the implementation of governmental policy." [23]

After hardly three weeks of "blooming," pressures began to build within the Party leadership to cut off open criticism. One "rightist" Party member was reported to have said: "Chairman Mao was under very great pressure, and in this domestic crisis the telegrams [from opponents] flew like snowflakes, all demanding restriction [of rectification]." [24] Mao reversed himself and joined with the organization men in the anti-rightist campaign; this change was signaled by a denunciation of the press in his unsigned article, "Things Are Undergoing a Change," which appeared in late May 1957.[25] Whether or not Liu Shao-ch'i supported the anti-rightist campaign at the time, he later expressed regret at its severity. At a 1963 forum on cultural and artistic work, he said, "It is necessary to criticize . . . those who oppose the Party, but criticism and repudiation should not be carried out so fiercely as during the anti-rightist campaign." [26]

The impact of the "Hundred Flowers" Campaign on the GPCR lies both in what it did and in what it failed to do. What it did was to expose the depth of political discontent with certain basic elements of the Chinese political system among even the more privileged elements of the populace at a time of economic prosperity and political success: many of the educated youth activists who had been prized as "successors" to the Chinese revolution attacked their government for

22 "NCNA Besieges Tai Huang on Successive Days," PD, August 8, 1957, p. 2, in Solomon, "One Party," p. 35.

23 "KMT Revolutionary Committee Holds Symposium Exposing Ch'en Ming-shu and the Rightists on July 14th," NCNA (Peking), July 14, 1957, in CB, no. 475 (August 28, 1957): 45.

24 "The Treachery of Yüan Yung-hsi Being a Rightist and Promoting Attacks on the Party," PD, July 22, 1957, p. 2. According to Lin Hsi-ling, "The 'Blooming and Contending' suggested by the Party CC has encountered much resistance. The Chairman said that more than 90 percent of the high-ranking cadres were opposed to the idea." Quoted in Doolin, Communist China, p. 33.

25 Hung-ch'i [Red Flag] (hereafter RF) (Peking), no. 2 (1968), pp. 12–13, in CB, no. 891 (October 8, 1969): 24.

26 "Liu Shao-ch'i's Counterrevolutionary Revisionist Utterances on Culture and Art," Hung-se hsüan-ch'uan ping [Red propaganda soldier] (Peking), no. 4 (May 10, 1967).

its elitism and insensitivity to the people, its failure to realize the ideals of socialism in practice.

What the "Hundred Flowers" failed to do was to evolve any institutional means for the articulation and peaceful resolution of "contradictions between the government and the people." The expression of popular grievances was ruthlessly suppressed in the anti-rightist campaign that followed the "Hundred Flowers." Although a moderate stage set in in 1959, after the Sixth Plenum at Wuch'ang, with the *hsiao ming-fang* (small blooming), it limited the expression of criticism to the academic establishment—a highly unsatisfactory *denouement* from Mao's point of view, since these "bourgeois liberals" focused their subtle attacks on the "cult of personality" rather than on the bureaucracy. The covert "revisionist" inclinations of China's "revolutionary successor" generation were of particular concern to Mao, as he revealed in later conversations with Malraux and Snow. In January 1962, he again proposed that popular criticism of the bureaucracy should be encouraged, even calling for his own self-criticism (for errors committed during the Leap) to be circulated to set an example, but there was no apparent response to this proposal. Eight months later, at the Tenth Plenum of the Eighth CC, the "small blooming" was terminated because of its "revisionist" propensities; there was to be no further "blooming and contending" until the GPCR.

THE GREAT LEAP FORWARD

At the end of the "Hundred Flowers," there were differences of opinion concerning China's economic policy, which found Mao Tse-tung, Liu Shao-ch'i, Teng Hsiao-p'ing, and P'eng Chen ranged against Chou En-lai, Ch'en Yün, and other "moderates." Liu announced the Great Leap program on behalf of Mao in his address to the Second Session of the CCP Eighth National Congress in May 1958, abruptly reversing the moderate objectives of the 1958–62 Five-Year Plan which he had outlined before the First Session in September 1956; his subsequent statements in support of the "three red flags" were so positive that one scholar (incorrectly) surmised it was "Liu rather than Mao who must be regarded as the main sponsor of the Great Leap Forward." [27] The commune program was started in the spring of 1958, and, by the end of August, 30 percent of all farming households were already communized. Although adjustments were made in the subsequent fifteen

[27] Harold C. Hinton, "Intra-Party Politics and Economic Policy in Communist China," *World Politics* 12, no. 4 (July 1960): 515.

months, Liu portrayed the commune as a model for the entire Communist world as late as October 1959, seven months after Khrushchev's stinging, if implicit, criticism of the idea at the Twenty-First Congress of the CPSU.[28]

Although difficulties began to emerge in unmistakable form by October and November 1958, there is no public record of opposition to the "three red flags" prior to the Lushan Plenum, which met from August 2 to 16, 1959. The initial reaction was to attribute responsibility for these difficulties to middle and lower level cadres: on November 14, the Shantung Province chief, Chao Chien-min, was purged, and with him a considerable number of local and provincial officials in Shantung and Honan. At the Wuch'ang Sixth Plenum (November 28–December 10, 1958), a moderating trend began; the construction of barracks was terminated; and the peasants were guaranteed private ownership of dwellings, gardens, and small pets. The proposal to supplement time-rates with task-specific work points was made at a Politburo conference in February 1959 and approved at the Shanghai Seventh Plenum (April 2–5, 1959).[29]

Thus when P'eng Te-huai wrote his initial memorandum on July 14, 1959, detailing his criticisms, the Leap's vulnerability had already been sensed, if not acknowledged. At issue were basic questions about relative sectoral priority, power distribution at different levels of society, and the nature of the Chinese army. P'eng's memorandum tactfully avoided imputation of blame, but it nonetheless constituted a serious challenge to the moral basis of Mao's authority, suggesting that his policies had contributed to the immiserization of the peasantry, and P'eng's criticisms initially drew strong (perhaps majority) support from other Politburo members. For the next twenty days, P'eng continued his criticisms of "petty-bourgeois fanaticism" in a series of caucuses. "Let us stiffen our scalps to stand it and listen to them for a couple of weeks," Mao instructed his followers, "and then counterattack." Toward the end of July, he sent for other CC members not present at Lushan whose support he needed.[30]

28 Liu, "The Victory of Marxism-Leninism in China," *Peking Review* (hereafter *PR*) (October 1959), p. 14.

29 Jürgen Domes, *Von der Volkskommune zur Krise in China* (Duisdorf b. Bonn, 1964), p. 55.

30 "Speech at the Eighth CC Plenum," *CL&G* 1, no. 4 (winter 1968–69): 61. Li Hsien-nien confessed in the spring of 1967 that he first voted for P'eng Te-huai but at the second ballot voted against him. *China News Analysis*, no. 761 (June 20, 1969), pp. 1 ff. This indicates that there were two ballots concerning the same issue, implying that Mao was defeated on the first one and finally prevailed only by convening a full plenum of the CC.

On August 2, Mao turned the enlarged Politburo conference into a formal CC plenum; confident of support from his "reinforcements," he launched a counterattack:

P'eng Te'huai's letter of opinion constitutes on anti-Party outline of rightist opportunism. . . . It is by no means an accidental or individual error, but it is planned, organized, prepared, and purposeful.

Mao's bitter words suggest that he had taken P'eng's criticisms personally. "The fact is that you have all refuted me, though not by name perhaps," he said and threatened to organize guerrilla bands "if the PLA chooses to follow P'eng Te-huai." [31] In the showdown, only one of the seven Standing Committee members (Chu Teh) supported P'eng; four opposed him, and two (Ch'en Yün and Teng Hsiao-p'ing) were absent. Liu Shao-ch'i played a conciliatory role, supporting Mao, but counseling for "unity" and leniency in dealing with P'eng and his followers. In accord with this counsel, a resolution was passed that was ideologically strict but surprisingly lenient in its imposition of organizational sanctions: P'eng, Chang Wen-t'ien, Huang K'o-ch'eng, and Chou Hsiao-chou were officially named members of an "anti-Party clique" and dismissed from their executive posts, but they retained membership in the Politburo and the CC.[32] According to an unconfirmed report, Lin Piao expressed misgivings about P'eng's dismissal, whereupon Liu held a three-day meeting with Lin in order to explain P'eng's errors to him in detail.[33]

The Leap did not immediately succumb to P'eng's attack. Following the Lushan Plenum, a nationwide rectification campaign was launched against "rightist opportunists" in the Party, accompanied by ardent reaffirmation of Leap policies. For instance, the system of "production responsibility"—output quotas based on individual households (pao-ch'an tao-hu), which had been acclaimed in the spring—was now denounced as "reactionary." [34] Yet the thought preparation for revival of the Leap in 1959–60 had a defensive quality rare in Chinese Communist writings; there was a spate of articles on rightism, pessimism, methods of work, and lower-level leadership which indicated a sense

[31] "Speech at the Eighth Plenum," pp. 34, 67.
[32] David Charles, "The Dismissal of Marshal P'eng Te-huai," China Under Mao: Politics Takes Command, ed. Roderick MacFarquhar (Cambridge, Mass., 1966), pp. 20–34.
[33] Fernand Gigon, Vie et Mort de la Révolution Culturelle (Paris, 1969), p. 42. This book contains a good deal of interesting information, with a bibliographical note (pp. 287–288) attributing some of it to a confidential Hong Kong newsletter.
[34] Chang, "Power and Policy," pp. 206–209.

of insecurity. The surge on the industrial front lasted into 1960, but the withdrawal of Soviet technicians and a second bad harvest brought the Leap to a close at the end of the year.[35]

In the next few years an economic depression struck China that was comparable in severity to the depression of the 1930s in the West; [36] at the low point of 1960–62, gross national output dropped by 20 to 30 percent from the high point reached during the Leap, per capita income by roughly 32 percent, industrial production by 40 to 45 percent.[37] These staggering figures signified that Mao had won the battle at Lushan but lost the war. Although the "three red flags" were at no time publicly criticized, the next three years witnessed a gradual but sweeping rollback of most of its programs. In November 1960, the Party dispatched a secret "Urgent Directive on Rural Work" ("Twelve Articles") to cadres at all levels, which restricted the powers of the commune and made the brigade the operational unit of planning, production, and accounting. Similar in spirit to the "Twelve Articles" but with more detailed and workable provisions were the "Draft Regulations Concerning the Rural People's Communes" (or "Sixty Articles on Agriculture") drafted by Teng Hsiao-p'ing and P'eng Chen and approved by a central work conference in Canton in March 1961. After Liu called a meeting in October 1961 to discuss the prevention of commodities from flowing onto the black market, provincial authorities began to extend free markets to villages and made 5 to 10 percent of the land available for private plots, thus nominally halting illegal activities by granting them legitimacy. On January 1, 1962, the production team became the basic accounting unit; in effect, this meant a retreat to the level of collective organization under the lower Agricultural Producers' Cooperatives (APCs), since both units had about twenty households.[38]

Following the Tenth Plenum in September 1962, the Party reemphasized class struggle and increased its ideological control by attacking "revisionist" trends in all fields.[39] The Party prohibited the prac-

35 J. D. Simmonds, *China: Evolution of a Revolution, 1959–1966* (Canberra, Australian National University, Department of International Relations Working Paper No. 9, 1968), pp. 6–15.

36 Nai-ruenn Chen and Walter Galenson, *The Chinese Economy Under Communism* (Chicago, 1969), p. 86.

37 Barry Richman, *Industrial Society in Communist China* (New York, 1969), p. 613.

38 Byung-joon Ahn, "Adjustments in the Great Leap Forward and Their Ideological Legacy, 1959–1962," in *Ideology and Politics in Contemporary China*, ed. Chalmers Johnson (Seattle, Wash., 1973), pp. 270–282.

39 Charles Neuhauser, "The Chinese Communist Party in the 1960's: Prelude to the Cultural Revolution," *CQ*, no. 32 (October–December 1969): 3–37.

tice of allotting output quotas to individual households, cut back excessive private cultivation, again stressed collective undertakings, and tightened control over rural trade fairs. But inasmuch as Mao presented no alternative to the objectionable policies, the plenum also guaranteed the right of peasants to private plots and domestic industries and formalized the revisions introduced since 1961, including production team accountability, smaller communes, and allotting output quotas to small groups.[40] It seems in retrospect that in order to procure support for his ideological initiative, Mao had to make policy concessions that had the effect of neutralizing the initiative.

The debacle of the GLF and the wholesale rescission of its programs had two implications for the fall of Liu Shao-ch'i in the GPCR. First, for various reasons, Mao found the use of the conventional rectification and purge technique, which had been evolved at the time of the Cheng-feng Campaign and followed quite closely ever since, highly unsatisfactory in dealing with the deviations of P'eng Te-huai. Less important than P'eng's own partially successful attempt to reverse verdicts in 1962 (P'eng was not rehabilitated, but most of his followers were) was the fact that the usual combination of ideological censure and organizational lenience had failed to discredit the policy line he represented, with the result that while P'eng fell, his line triumphed, making P'eng something of an unsung martyr (a "Hai Jui") in some quarters. Future purges, Mao may have concluded, must include an intensive mass education campaign to impress the people with the import of the purge.

Second, Liu Shao-ch'i, under the apparent illusion that Mao agreed that the Leap approach had been thoroughly discredited, presided over the reversal of its essential programs and even criticized it in closed meetings. In a written report to a conference for 7,000 cadres in January 1962, he said:

In the past several years many shortcomings and mistakes have occurred in our work. The cadres and members of the whole Party and even the great majority of the people all have had personal painful experience of this. They have starved for two years.[41]

Mao, on the other hand, continued to identify himself with the Leap's objectives; he seems to have felt that the Leap's failure did not reflect its intrinsic demerits but only the incorrigible contumacy of the reactionary forces. He said in 1963:

40 Ahn, "Adjustments in the GLF," pp. 270–282.
41 "Selected Edition," *SCMM*, no. 652 (April 28, 1969): 24.

In social struggle, the forces representing the advanced class sometimes suffer defeat not because their ideas are incorrect but because, in the balance of forces engaged in struggle, they are not as powerful for the time being as the forces of reaction; they are therefore temporarily defeated, but they are bound to triumph sooner or later.[42]

Mao had become so closely identified with the GLF that its failure discredited the charismatic vision that legitimated his leadership; in the ensuing years it became increasingly clear that any Maoist attempt to recoup the initiative must be preceded by an ideological vindication of the Great Leap Forward, whether the Leap's programs were revived in practice or not. Thus it is not coincidental that P'eng Te-huai was sought out by Red Guards during the GPCR and forced to submit a public self-criticism. The criticisms of Liu's economic adjustment policies are based in large part on their deviations from the policies of the GLF, implicitly assuming the Leap's essential correctness.

THE SINO-SOVIET DISPUTE

The Sino-Soviet dispute originated with Khrushchev's secret speech denouncing Stalin, was aggravated by rebuffed Chinese solicitations for nuclear armament (and for Soviet nuclear backing in the 1958 Taiwan Strait crisis), by Soviet dislike for the theoretically presumptuous GLF and their consequent withdrawal of advisers and termination of economic assistance, and became public in October 1962. In that month, two further provocations occurred: Khrushchev "capitulated" to Kennedy in the Cuban missile crisis, evoking open scorn from the Chinese, and the Chinese PLA suddenly struck across the Indian border. Having supplied the Indians with MiG-21s they had denied the Chinese, as well as other military assistance, the Russians maintained conspicuous neutrality during the border dispute—it was too similar to their own incipient border dispute with China for them to welcome a settlement favorable to the Chinese. More important, the Soviets seemed well on their way to weaning India from the U.S. to use as a balance against China, a policy that came to full fruition in 1971.

Unlike the one-sided GPCR disputes in which the Maoists could only accuse their opponents of "waving a red flag to oppose the red flag" because of the absence of any articulate opposition, the Sino-Soviet dispute resulted in a clear-cut cleavage on a number of issues. The Soviets said publicly many of the things domestic revisionists were later accused of having said privately. In 1959, Khrushchev said that

[42] "Where Do Correct Ideas Come From?" (May 1963), in *SRWM*, p. 503.

the development of nuclear weaponry had made large-scale war un-
feasible; the prevention of war had become "the question of questions." In 1961, he advocated the "parliamentary road" as a legitimate
alternative to violent revolution: "The transition to socialism in
countries with developed parliamentary traditions may be effected by
utilizing parliament, and in other countries by utilizing institutions
conforming to their national traditions." Soviet relations with the
Third World accordingly emphasized "revolution from above" by support for "national bourgeois" leaders (even without proletarian hegemony) and also through technical assistance to newly emerging nations. Chinese criticisms of these Soviet policies later found their
echoes in GPCR allegations that Liu Shao-ch'i advocated a "parliamentary road," "peaceful coexistence" with capitalist imperialism and
reaction, reduction of aid to wars of national liberation, and so on.[43]

Thus the Sino-Soviet dispute gave birth to a model of "social imperialism" that was later turned on Chinese foreign-policy makers;
even more important, however, the dispute served as a sounding
board for articulation of a critique of domestic revisionism. The Russians argued that the class struggle had been completed victoriously
and that the dictatorship of the proletariat had been transformed into
a "state of the whole people," permitting a relaxation of the repressive
policies necessary during the preceding historical stage. The Soviet
version of utopia was formulated in the program of the Twenty-
Second Congress in October 1961, where Khrushchev pictured a state
of collectivized affluence (mocked by the Chinese as "goulash Communism") that contrasted with the Chinese stress on social equality in
a condition of material deprivation. The domestic aspect of the dispute climaxed in the Chinese accusation, spelled out most fully in
1965, that the Soviet Union was actively engaged in the restoration of
capitalism. Mao Tse-tung made a substantial personal contribution to
these polemics in the form of nine lengthy commentaries, which he is
reliably reported to have written in collaboration with K'ang Sheng
and Ch'en Po-ta between 1963 and 1964.[44] It is in these polemics that
most of the themes of the GPCR first appeared in fully articulate form.

In "The Origin and Development of the Differences Between the
Leadership of the CPSU and Ourselves" (September 6, 1963) and "On

---

[43] Quoted in Robert C. North, "Two Revolutionary Models: Russian and Chinese," Communist Strategies in Asia: A Comparative Analysis of Governments and
Parties, ed. A. Doak Barnett (New York, 1963), pp. 44–48; also Zbigniew K. Brzezin-
ski, The Soviet Bloc: Unity and Conflict, rev. and enl. ed. (Cambridge, Mass., 1967),
p. 398.

[44] Chalmers Johnson, "The Two Chinese Revolutions," CQ, no. 39 (July–September 1969): 24.

the Question of Stalin" (September 13, 1963), Khrushchev is accused of posthumously attacking Stalin's "personality cult" in order to negate the "dictatorship of the proletariat." The implication was that it is a "characteristic common to all revisionists" that they oppose "absolute personal power." The rationale for such power, most clearly articulated in "Is Yugoslavia a Socialist Country?" (September 26, 1963) and in the final commentary, "On Khrushchev's Phony Communism and the Historical Lessons for the World" (July 14, 1964), is that "capitalism will always try to make a comeback"; i.e., with the result that economic or professional expertise in service of personal interest will displace selfless dedication to the collective interest as the motivating dynamism of the economy, and society will become restratified according to control over property.

This lesson [Yugoslavia] . . . shows that not only is it possible for a working class party to fall under the control of a labor aristocracy, degenerate into a bourgeois party and become a flunky of imperialism before it seizes power, but even after it seizes power it is possible for a working-class party to fall under the control of new bourgeois elements. . . . It shows that a restoration of capitalism in a socialist country can be achieved not necessarily through a counterrevolutionary coup d'état or armed imperialist invasion and that it can also be achieved through the degradation of the leading group in that country.

In the final essay, Mao began to apply the revisionist critique to his own country: "Is our society today thoroughly clean?" he asked. "No, it is not. Classes and class struggle still remain, the activities of the overthrown reactionary classes plotting a comeback still continue." [45] In his conversation with André Malraux a year later, he returned to the same theme, acknowledging that the analogy of revisionism with capitalism broke down but now basing his use of class categories on the estrangement between leaders and led, which he equated with the exploitative economic relationship between "bourgeoisie" and "proletariat":

Humanity left to its own devices does not necessarily reestablish capitalism (which is why you are perhaps right in saying they will not revert to private ownership of the means of production), but it does reestablish inequality. . . . You remember Kosygin at the Twenty-Third Congress: "Communism means the raising of living standards." Of course! And swimming is a way of putting on a pair of trunks! . . . I know his theory; you begin by no longer tolerating criticism, then you abandon self-criticism, then you cut

45 These tracts, nominally written by the editorial departments of RF and PD, were published in Peking on the dates indicated.

yourself off from the masses, and since the Party can draw its revolutionary strength only from them, you tolerate the formation of a new class.[46]

Based on this analogy between bureaucratic estrangement and economic exploitation, which implicitly held elites responsible not only for the hiatus between elites and mass but for increasing income stratification among the masses, Mao began in 1965 to refer to Chinese Communist bureaucrats as "bourgeois":

The bureaucratic class is a class sharply opposed to the working class and the poor and lower-middle peasants. These people have become or are in the process of becoming bourgeois elements sucking the blood of the workers. How can they have proper understanding? [47]

In tune with Mao's concerns, Liu Shao-ch'i made occasional references to "revisionism" in his speeches in the 1960s, but he invariably used the term in an international context. That he may have been unprepared for its extrapolation in a critique of Chinese domestic policies is suggested by a comment he made to members of a work team as late as August 4, 1966:

At present, we have proletarian dictatorship. The CCP is Marxist. It is not justified to rebel against the Communist Party. If the Party becomes a revisionist Party, then we should rebel against it! [48]

POWER STRUGGLE

It may seem contradictory for Mao, who was after all Chairman of the CCP and supreme leader of the state, to begin referring to his government as "bourgeois elements sucking the blood of the workers" and to call on the masses to criticize it. As the GPCR was to make obvious, Mao precluded himself when he referred to the "bureaucratic class," and some political analysts have seized upon this fact to infer that Mao had been excluded from the decision-making arena by power-hungry colleagues, and that his dominant motive in launching the GPCR and purging his heir apparent was to seize back power that had been "usurped." This "power struggle" interpretation in its pure form views Mao's arousal of the masses as a cynical manipulation of discontents to create a constituency powerful enough to assail a

[46] André Malraux, *Anti-Memoirs*, trans. Terence Kilmartin (New York, 1968), pp. 369–370.

[47] "Comment on Comrade Ch'en Cheng-jen's Report on Stay in Selected Spot" (January 29, 1965), in "Long Live the Thought of Mao Tse-tung," *CB*, no. 891 (October 8, 1969): 49.

[48] "Talk to the Work Team of the Peking College of Construction Engineering" (August 4, 1966), *CW* 3: 351.

network of bureaucratic vested interests that had coalesced to deny him power. This interpretation implicitly dismisses Mao's ideological charges on behalf of the masses as self-serving cant, viewing Mao's relationship to the masses as essentially manipulative.

This interpretation, in its pure form, does an injustice to Mao's identification with the masses, which seems to be long-standing and genuine. In Snow's autobiography, Mao relates to Snow that his father had treated him like the servants, which led Mao to identify with them; rather than submit, he formed a "united front" with the servants and his mother and brothers in opposition to paternal authority. When he went to school this identification with the oppressed and exploited was reinforced: because his father refused to spend money to clothe him adequately, Mao was always poorly clad, and his classmates referred to him as a "dirty little peasant from Shaoshan." On one occasion, while collecting debts for his father, he met some poverty-stricken peasants and gave them all the money he had just collected. Mao spent most of his adult life as a rebel against authority and a champion of the oppressed, and there seems no reason to doubt the authenticity of his identification with the underprivileged.[49]

If the power struggle hypothesis is thus inadequate in accounting for Mao's motives, neither can it be dismissed outright. In the words of C. K. Yang, "Though deeply intertwined with ideological issues, Mao's implacable insistence on complete personal dominance has a separate significance for the authoritarian . . . leadership structure of the Communist organizational system."[50] Identification operates in two directions, and it seems safe to assume that Mao interprets from his own perspective the degree of oppression the masses are suffering, i.e., that he would be more sensitive to reports that the masses were being oppressed or exploited if he felt that his own authority were being demeaned, and if he were in a position to detach himself from the putative source of oppression. On this assumption, it seems quite relevant to ascertain Mao's position in the configuration of power during the period prior to the GPCR—without assuming, however, that this information suffices to explain his motives.

Mao's retrospective comment that he was being treated like a parent at his own funeral illustrates his flair for poetic hyperbole but has a grain of truth. There is little doubt that Mao lost power after his resignation as Chief of State in December 1958, and some have ques-

49 E. Snow, Red Star over China (New York, 1961), pp. 130–138; see also the chapter on Mao in Wilfried Daim, Die Kastenlose Gesellschaft (Munich, 1960).
50 C. K. Yang, "Cultural Revolution and Revisionism," China in Crisis, ed. Ping-ti Ho and Tang Tsou (Chicago, 1968), 1, bk. 2, 501–525.

tioned whether that loss was altogether voluntary, speculating that Mao may have been obliged to step down in the light of the Leap's debacle. But Mao maintained from first to last that his retirement was voluntary, and there is no plausible reason for him to lie. When in October 1966 T'ao Chu observed that power had "slipped" from Mao's grasp, Mao said he had "deliberately let it slip that way," but that his would-be successors had then formed "independent kingdoms." [51] His wish to retire was first mentioned in his "Sixty Articles on Work Methods," written in February 1958, at the *outset* of the Leap. In the final article he wrote:

My retirement from the Chairmanship of the Republic and concentration on [the duties] of the Chairman of the Party Centre will enable me to save a great deal of time in order to meet the demands of the Party. This is also the way most suitable to my condition. If during discussions the masses are opposed to this proposal, it must be explained to them. Whenever the nation is urgently in need [of my services] and if the Party decides [to recall me], I will shoulder this leadership task once again.[52]

In a conversation with a visiting Asian diplomat that same month, Mao mentioned other reasons for wishing to retire, which reflect his mood and the more relaxed ambience of his decision. Winters in Peking were too cold, and he disliked the snow and dust storms that whistled in out of Mongolia. He was tired of the ceremonial performances of a chief of state, especially attendance at the interminable formal dinners for visiting dignitaries; they left him little time to think. He wanted to compose poetry.[53]

During the period of economic retrenchment, Mao began to spend much of his time away from the capital, disengaging himself from routine decision making to allow time for reflection and writing, as he had done several times earlier in his career. At Hangchow he used a specially constructed villa in the hills skirting the west side of the lake, and in Shanghai he took over the former French Club, chiefly because of its excellent swimming pool.[54] His circle of diurnal associates shifted from fellow Politburo members to an ad hoc circle of intimates who shared his broad theoretical and polemical concerns, including his former secretary, Ch'en Po-ta, his wife, Chiang Ch'ing, and her old friend, K'ang Sheng.

[51] "Speech at a Report Meeting" (October 1966), in "Selections from Chairman Mao" (Part I), *Joint Publications Research Service* (hereafter *JPRS*), no. 49826 (February 12, 1970): 10.

[52] *Mao Papers,* ed. Jerome Ch'en (London, 1970), p. 75.

[53] Albert Ravenholt, "The Red Guards," *American Universities Field Staff,* East Asia Series, 14, no. 3 (April 1967): 2.

[54] *Ibid.*

In accord with his more leisurely and reflective life style, Mao's role in the policy-making process changed from a definitive one to an episodic, provocative one.[55] He retained his position as Chairman of the Party, and Mao's colleagues are known to have sought him out for final approval on major policy decisions. As leader of the "second line," he began to issue a series of broad, programmatic statements: in May 1963, he issued a policy paper on the need to correct certain deficiencies in rural work; in September and October 1963, he discussed shortcomings in the propaganda field; in 1964, he focused on weaknesses in the educational system; in June 1965, he delivered strong criticism of the management of public health. In a matter of days after Mao had issued one of his edicts, newspaper editorials, Party pronouncements, and the speeches of high officials echoed his thoughts, work conferences were held, and the ponderous bureaucratic apparatus was set in motion.[56] Mao was unhappy with the bureaucracy's performance, however, and periodically returned to Peking to lobby for his programs. He seems to have prevailed in the policy-making process in 1962, 1963, 1964, and 1965, although by 1966 his automatic majority had grown dubious. He convened the Tenth Plenum of the Eighth CC in September 1962 and dominated the proceedings, putting the authority of the CC behind the program of waging class struggle and consolidating the collective economy, thus reversing the trend of economic retrenchment that had prevailed since 1960. He also "personally supervised" the drafting of the "First Ten Points" in 1963, which initiated the Socialist Education Movement; when he felt that the movement was not being implemented properly, he again interceded in January 1965 with his "Twenty-Three Articles," which assailed Liu's "Revised Later Ten Points" of September 1964,[57] a revision of P'eng Chen's September 1963 "Later Ten Points."

But although Mao could intercede at will and be certain to carry the day, as soon as he withdrew again the leadership under Liu Shao-ch'i would adopt policies based on its own criteria of economic efficiency and administrative rationality. For instance, when Mao convened a central work conference in Canton in March 1961 to consider reorganization of communes, he discovered to his irritation that, without his prior knowledge, several key provisions of the plan had already

[55] Michel C. Oksenberg, "Policy Making Under Mao, 1949–1968: An Overview," in *China: Management of a Revolutionary Society*, ed. John M. H. Lindbeck (Seattle, Wash., 1971), pp. 79–115.

[56] Michel C. Oksenberg, *China: The Convulsive Society* (New York, December 1970), p. 37.

[57] Ahn, "Adjustments in the GLF," *passim*.

been drafted under the supervision of Teng Hsiao-p'ing.[58] And even the policies he proposed had to go through regular channels, where Party functionaries would construe his usually vague directives in the light of their own biases.

Since the failure of the Leap, there seems to have been a silent loss of faith in the Maoist vision in many sectors of Chinese society. Visitors to the mainland on the eve of the GPCR were struck by an atmosphere of relaxation that contrasted sharply with the ideological intensity of the Leap.[59] Charles Taylor observed in early 1966:

The ever adaptable Chinese has learned to live with the campaigns. Bewildered at first, he has come to understand the mechanics and the methodology, since these hardly vary from campaign to campaign. Anticipating the required response, he can often beat the cadre at his own game. . . . All the evidence indicates that the reservoir of enthusiasm has been badly depleted. While it is impossible to deny that great numbers still show revolutionary fervor and genuine idealism, there is a growing apathy to the demands of the regime that borders on cynicism.[60]

Such a political atmosphere was anathema to all Mao cherished as vital to the creation of a revolutionary society. Cadres became entangled with their local constituency in webs of reciprocal obligation that made it difficult to pursue national goals, and corruption at lower levels became quite widespread, both among rich peasants and low-level cadres.[61] Among CC members, there was apparent covert opposition, or at least resistance, to Mao's policy views and leadership, mingled with the hope that he would genuinely retire from active participation in policy. Although Mao retained the deference granted to a "Buddha" (as he once sarcastically put it) [62] and was usually able

[58] In criticizing Teng and P'eng Chen at the subsequent Canton conference, Mao reportedly asked, "Which emperor decided this?" Ting Wang, ed., *Chung-kung*, pp. 486, 491.

[59] "A country like this changes rapidly. Someone who visited China in 1960 could report quite truthfully that the people in the towns were at the mercy of the street committees, that private enterprise was prohibited, that cooking-pots had been turned into steel . . . that research and education were completely controlled by the cadres. But someone who visited China in 1962 would dismiss this description as sheer nonsense. . . . People were eating at home. . . . In most schools and institutions administrative power was divided between cadres and specialists. Private enterprise is now allowed in professions ranging from doctors to barbers, actors to shoemakers, and black market prices for important commodities such as meat and cereals have been legalized in the free market." Sven Lindqvist, *China in Crisis*, trans. S. Clayton (New York, 1963), p. 100.

[60] Charles Taylor, *Reporter in Red China* (New York, 1966), pp. 160–161.

[61] Cf. C. S. Chen, ed., *Rural People's Communes in Lien-chiang*, trans. C. P. Ridley (Stanford, Calif., 1969), pp. 99–102 *et passim*.

[62] *NYT*, October 26, 1970, 6: 4.

to get his way, this deference now seemed to be based on fear rather than faith, and he was no longer so frequently sought out for advice.

The star of Liu Shao-ch'i was in the ascent during this period. Liu's leadership of the "first line" gave him the authority to convene conferences, select speakers, and thus secure passage of the measures he supported. For example, in an expanded CC meeting of January 21–27, 1962 (the "meeting of the 7,000" cadres), Liu Shao-ch'i presided and gave a speech (on the 26th) in which he reported that Hunan peasants had told him that the failure of the Leap was only 30 percent due to natural catastrophes and 70 percent due to "human errors." At the same time, Liu called for the following reforms: (1) immediate cessation of work on projects from which no "economically relevant results" were expected; (2) shutting down enterprises that make no profit or operate on a loss; (3) reintroduction of free markets and higher prices for agricultural produce; and (4) use of the production team as the basic accounting unit. This conference was followed by the Hsilou conference of the Politburo Standing Committee, which was held from February 21 to 26, 1966 and again chaired by Liu. At the meeting, Ch'en Yün submitted a report pointing to a deficit of two billion *yüan*. The report, which was accepted and distributed to local levels, justified retrenchment and increased reliance on local initiative to solve economic problems. At the Peitaiho Politburo Conference in August 1962, Liu Shao-ch'i again raised the questions to be discussed and dominated the meetings.[63]

Liu's promotion to chief of state in 1959 considerably enhanced his public visibility. His essay, "How To Be a Good Communist," was revised and republished in pamphlet form in 1962, following its serialization in *People's Daily*. Beginning in 1959, the appellation "Chairman Liu" [Liu *chu-hsi*] began to be used in tandem with "Chairman Mao," and the two "Chairmen's" pictures started appearing side by side.[64] As Chief of State, he made frequent ceremonial appearances where he gave brief talks for public consumption, including several well-publicized junkets through South and Southeast Asia. Roughly one-third of the unofficial Union Research Institute (URI) edition of

---

63 From Liu's October 1966 self-criticism, excerpted below on pages 97–99.

64 NCNA (Peking), September 28, 1965. "But formerly pictures of Liu Shao-ch'i and Chairman Mao were published together. The NCNA had sought his [Liu's] advice on this. He did not object and so Chairman Mao was reluctant to show his attitude. Presumably, he did not realize the full significance the first time and the pictures were published in this way. He should have realized it the second time. . . . This began in 1959. Why were such pictures published in the same way the following year? He was basically not humble." "Premier Chou En-lai's Criticisms of Liu Shao-ch'i," *Wen-ko t'ung-hsün* [Cultural Revolution bulletin], October 9, 1967, in *SCMP*, no. 4060 (November 15, 1967): 10.

his *Collected Works* (the last of three volumes) consists of statements made between 1958 and 1962—most of them ceremonial in nature and of no theoretical importance but nonetheless featured quite prominently in the media. In contrast, Mao made almost no public statements after publication of "On the Correct Resolution of Contradictions Among the People" in 1957. In December 1966, a Japanese correspondent noted that:

Last spring, when I stayed in Peking, I noticed that the picture of Mao was gradually decreasing in the streets, and when I called at the Central Headquarters of the Communist Youth League [CYL] in October last year, its CC members did not go beyond touching on Mao's ideology. A tendency to shelve Mao was steadily permeating the CCP.[65]

To be sure, Mao's declining and Liu's increasing public salience should not be blown out of proportion: a check on 200 major articles published between 1959 and 1966 shows that only thirteen contained favorable references to Liu, while Mao's name cropped up too often to be worth a precise count.[66]

Probably of much more importance than Liu's improving public image was his hold on the loyalty of the Party bureaucracy. One of his biographers said of Liu:

As soon as problems which arise in Party locals are passed to him to be disposed of, they are easily solved. . . . In the next few years, when he becomes head of the Chinese Communist organization, this will be all the more so. . . . Although Mao Tse-tung is capable, he is not as capable as Liu Shao-ch'i.[67]

These feelings seem to have been shared widely in ruling circles. A Hong Kong reporter noticed that "When Chou [En-lai] had dinner with CC leaders at Restaurant Chuan Chu-te in Peking, they called Mao by the name of 'Chairman' and Chou by the name of 'Prime Minister' but called Liu 'Shao-ch'i' familiarly. They adored Mao religiously and showed high respect for Chou but regarded Liu as an existence closer to them." [68] Mao's retinue seems to have noticed this premature leakage of their patron's authority and resented it, per-

65 *Tokyo Shimbun*, December 21, 1966, in *Daily Summaries of the Japanese Press* (hereafter *DSJP*) (Tokyo), December 23, 1966.

66 Leo Goodstadt, *Mao Tse-tung: The Search for Plenty* (London, 1972), p. 167.

67 Chao Kuang-yi, "Liu Shao-ch'i," *Chung-kung jen-wu ssu-miao* [Sketches of prominent Chinese Communists] (Hong Kong, 1952), p. 6. Apart from its marked anti-Communist bias, this book seems to be based largely on hearsay evidence of uncertain validity.

68 Chou Yu-jui, *Wanderings and Choice*, quoted in *Tokyo Shimbun*, December 23, 1966, in *DSJP*, January 5, 1967, pp. 21-23. Chou is Secretary and President of *Ta-kung pao* in Hong Kong.

haps even more than did Mao himself. Chiang Ch'ing said in a 1967 speech to an enlarged session of the Party's Military Affairs Commission (MAC):

The Chairman is still in sound health and very much alive, but some persons think that what the Chairman says can be ignored. When I was in Shanghai [in 1965–66], the situation was rather delicate in the East China Bureau and the Shanghai Municipal Committee. They paid no heed to what the Chairman said, much less to [my words]. But they regarded the words of a certain person simply as sayings in the Bible.[69]

Mao was forcibly, perhaps decisively, alerted to the extent of his authority's erosion in late March 1966, when a Japanese Communist Party delegation headed by Secretary Miyamoto Kenji met with him at Tsunghua near Canton. Members of the Japanese delegation got the impression that Mao had been convalescing a long time, that he was out of touch with events, and that CCP leaders had been quietly bypassing him. When Miyamoto suggested that the Chinese needed to expedite their handling of Soviet goods, shipped through China to North Vietnam, Mao looked bewildered and turned to his aide (believed to be Teng Hsiao-p'ing) for clarification. The aide replied that the Soviet Union had been providing military equipment to North Vietnam via overland shipment through China, but that "we are sabotaging some of their equipment in an effort to discredit the Soviet assistance in the eyes of the North Vietnamese." Mao appeared perturbed that he had not been kept informed.[70]

PERCEPTIONS OF INNER-PARTY OPPOSITION

We have established the objective tendency of the ruling group prematurely to transfer its allegiance from Mao to a collective leadership of Liu Shao-ch'i and Teng Hsiao-p'ing, but until Mao's subjective reaction to this tendency can be ascertained, the possibility cannot be pre-

[69] "Do New Services for the People" (April 13, 1967 speech to enlarged session of Military Affairs Commission), *Tung-fang-hung* [East is red], (Peking Institute of Geology), June 3, 1967, in *Issues and Studies* (hereafter *IS*) 6, no. 10 (July 1970): 82–91. According to Ralph Powell, Mao attempted to increase his dwindling control over the bureaucracy by militarizing the administration of enterprises. "The Increasing Power of Lin Piao and the Party Soldiers, 1959–1966," *CQ*, no. 34 (April–June 1968): 38–66. However, Liu countered by sending the military commissars to deal with "foodgrain, cotton, oil, and trivial commercial commodities," Red Guards alleged. *China News Analysis* (hereafter *CNA*), no. 735 (November 29, 1968): 1 ff.

[70] For a report on the February 10–April 4 JCP visit, see Kikuyo Ito and Minoru Shibata, "The Dilemma of Mao Tse-tung," *CQ*, no. 35 (July–September 1968): 58–59.

cluded that this tendency was consistent with Mao's own desire for a less active role in the policy process. Mao's statements about his opponents were invariably made in the context of his theoretical conception of the Chinese revolutionary movement and the nature of the threats confronting it. The theory seemed to evolve first, on the basis of Mao's analysis of the socioeconomic system as a whole; his polemics against opponents were implicit within that theory and were applied to specific persons on the basis of sometimes idiosyncratic circumstances.

The principal threat confronting the realization of Communism, according to Mao's basically consistent theoretical analysis of the situation from 1957 to 1966, was "revisionism." In March 1957 he wrote:

For a long time now, people have been leveling a lot of criticism against dogmatism. That is as it should be. But they often neglect to criticize revisionism. . . . In present circumstances, revisionism is more pernicious than dogmatism. Revisionism is one form of bourgeois ideology.[71]

This statement, with its fleeting reference to "bourgeois ideology," is the first signal of Mao's reversion to class categories after a period in which he had attempted to deal with "contradictions" within a more inclusive "whole people's" conceptual framework. In 1956–57, without entirely abandoning the category of "class," Mao introduced a distinction between "people and enemies of the people" (corresponding to "nonantagonistic and antagonistic contradictions"), which crosscut class categories.[72] In his essay, "On the Correct Resolution of Contradictions Among the People," he made clear that his purpose in introducing this categorization was to make possible the inclusion of members of nonproletarian classes among the "people": "In our country, the contradiction between the working class and the national bourgeoisie belongs to the category of contradictions among the people." [73] In the same vein, the essays, "On the Historical Experience of the Dictatorship of the Proletariat," and "More on the Historical Experience of the Dictatorship of the Proletariat," written under Mao's supervision during the same period, chided Stalin for *exacerbating* "class struggle, with the result that the healthy development of socialist democracy is hampered."

[71] "Speech at the CCP's National Conference on Propaganda Work" (March 12, 1957), in *SRWM*, p. 496.
[72] John Bryan Starr, "Mao Tse-tung's Theory of Continuing the Revolution Under the Dictatorship of the Proletariat: Its Origins, Development, and Practical Implications" (Ph. D. diss., University of California at Berkeley, 1971), p. 149.
[73] "On the Correct Resolution of Contradictions Among the People," *SRWM*, p. 434.

With the appearance of unexpectedly trenchant criticisms during the "Hundred Flowers," followed by P'eng Te-huai's criticisms at Lushan, Mao reverted to class categories to characterize his opponents. In a brief note written on August 16, 1959, some two weeks after P'eng's initial attack, he wrote:

The struggle that has arisen at Lushan is a class struggle. It is the continuation of the life-or-death struggle between the two great antagonists of the bourgeoisie and the proletariat in the process of the socialist revolution during the past decade. In China and in our Party, it appears that such a struggle will continue for at least another twenty years, and possibly for half a century.[74]

And again on September 11, Mao said, apparently in reference to the P'eng Te-huai group, that there were "several comrades" who had "never been Marxist" but rather were "bourgeois elements" who had "infiltrated into our Party." [75]

With the purge of the P'eng clique, Mao seems to have temporarily satisfied himself that "bourgeois elements" had been eliminated from the Party, for he made no further references to them for several years. At the Tenth Plenum in 1962 he did announce, "It can now be affirmed that classes do exist in socialist countries" and warned his colleagues to "never forget class struggle," but his call for renewed "class struggle" was, later claims to the contrary notwithstanding, rather mild:

In regard to the problem of work, it is incumbent on our comrades to pay attention to the truism that our work must not be affected by class struggle. . . . All localities and sectors should place work first. Work and class struggle should be undertaken side by side. One should not place the class struggle conspicuously. . . . Our work must not be jeopardized just because of class struggle.

Much of his address was devoted to a discussion of foreign affairs ("the contradiction between us and the world is the primary one"), with an emphasis on the Sino-Soviet dispute, which had preoccupied him. Although he continued to refer to his inner-Party opposition with class categories, he was not prepared to infer that "class struggle" was an appropriate means of resolution and in fact gave assurances that dissidents would be treated leniently:

As to how the Party should deal with the problem of revisionism and the problem of a bourgeoisie within itself, I think we should adhere to our

74 "The Origin of Machine Guns and Mortars, etc." (August 16, 1959), in *CL&G* 1, no. 4 (winter 1968–1969): 73.

75 "Speech at the Enlarged Meeting of the MAC of the CC of the CCP and the Foreign Affairs Conference" (September 11, 1959), *ibid.*, pp. 79–80.

traditional policy. No matter what errors a comrade may commit, we should follow the line of the rectification movement of 1942–45, that is, if he should change himself earnestly, we should welcome him and rally with him. We must aim at solidarity . . . and adopt a process of unity-criticism-unity. . . . We permit the commission of errors. Since you have erred, we also allow you to rectify them. Don't try to proscribe errors or prevent the rectification of errors.[76]

It seems to have been the unsuccessful Socialist Education Movement (SEM), more than anything else, that brought class struggle to an acute stage and indicated the location of "bourgeoisie" within the CC. When Mao initiated the movement in May 1963, with the dissemination of the "First Ten Points," he conceived it to be a semi-permanent movement "requiring five or ten generations"; "bourgeois" tendencies were attributed to "the exploiting class, landlords, and rich peasants who have been overthrown" but were "trying to make a comeback," not to the Party bureaucracy. Beginning with his "Twenty-Three Articles," which were approved in January 1965, Mao located the bourgeoisie at various levels within the Party, and coined a more specific term to refer to them:

The key point of this movement is to rectify those people in positions of authority within the Party who take the capitalist road, and progressively to consolidate the socialist battlefront in the urban and rural areas. Of those Party persons in authority taking the capitalist road, some are out in the open and some are at the higher levels. . . . Among those at higher levels, there are some people in the commune districts, *hsien,* special districts, and even in the work of provincial and CC departments, who oppose socialism.[77]

Thus it was not until 1965 that Mao specified the possibility that "Party persons in authority taking the capitalist road" might be located in the CC, a possibility he alluded to again in the CC work conference of September and October 1965, when he proposed criticism of Wu Han. Yet this conclusion did not *eo ipso* entail any particular method of discipline. In his writings Mao has proposed two methods of resolving contradictions, one emphasizing long and patient persuasion, "curing the sickness to save the patient," [78] and the second giving "the patient a good shake-up by shouting at him, 'You are ill!' so as to administer a shock and make him break out in a sweat." [79]

---

[76] "Speech at the Tenth Plenary Session of the Eighth CC," *ibid.,* p. 91.

[77] "Appendix F: The Twenty-Three Articles," in Richard Baum and Frederick C. Teiwes, *Ssu-ch'ing: The Socialist Education Movement of 1962–1966* (Berkeley, Calif., 1968), p. 120.

[78] "Rectify the Party's Style of Work" (February 1, 1942), *SW* 3: 50; see also "Speech at the CCP's National Conference on Propaganda Work," *SRWM,* pp. 493–494.

[79] "Oppose Stereotyped Party Writing" (February 8, 1942), *SW* 3: 56.

These two "therapies," however, were coterminous neither with intra-class-class conflict nor with nonantagonistic-antagonistic contradictions. Antagonistic contradictions were to be resolved by the application of "dictatorship," not necessarily by "shock therapy"; their application seemed rather to depend on the subjective intransigence of the "patient." By 1965, Mao seems to have concluded that the appropriate technique for treating bureaucrats who had become alienated from the masses was "shock" therapy:

Let those who will make fierce attacks, demonstrate in the streets, and take up arms to provoke change. I definitely approve. . . . Right now one-third of the nation's power is controlled by the enemy or by enemy sympathizers. After fifteen years, we now control the other two-thirds.[80]

Liu Shao-ch'i also conceived the main threat to the achievement of socialism during this period to be the "restoration of capitalism," but he did not locate "revisionist" tendencies within the leadership. He continued to assume that the *embourgeoisement* of certain sectors of the peasantry and the corruption of local cadres was the main problem and proposed to press the struggle all the more determinedly along the same lines. In September 1964, he doubled his estimate of the time needed for completion of the SEM to five or six years, and "spot testing" (*shih-tien*) was to last six rather than three months. At the same time, new emphasis was placed on the need to have "staunch" work teams.[81] A Hunan cadre representative of the Liuist persuasion scorned the idea of a "superficial upsurge" and emphasized the need for painstaking mass-level work, which would carefully organize the struggle from the top down through work teams. On March 21, 1964, Liu told Ho Wei:

At present we have two ways to guard against the restoration of capitalism. One way is to arouse the masses to carry out the four clean-up movements, and the other way is to reform the educational system and the labor system.[82]

At the enlarged meeting of the Politburo later that year, Liu added the third way: sending cadres down to perform labor.

Mao's abstract terminology makes it difficult to say whether he had at this point positively identified Liu as one of the "Party persons in authority taking the capitalist road" to whom his threats were addressed. In his December 1964 government report to the Third Na-

80 "Conversation with K'ang Sheng and Ch'en Po-ta," *JPRS*, no. 49826 (February 12, 1970): 26–28.

81 Schurmann, *Ideology*, pp. 503–597.

82 "Down with Liu Shao-ch'i—Life of Counterrevolutionary Liu Shao-ch'i," *Chingkangshan* (May 1967), *CB*, no. 834 (August 17, 1967): 1.

tional People's Congress, Chou En-lai noted the reprehensible "three reconciliations and one reduction" (reconciliation with capitalist imperialism, social imperialism, and reaction, and reduction of aid to national liberation wars, later to be labeled a prime example of Liuist revisionism) had been raised in the 1959–62 period, but he added that this policy had been *checked* by Mao at the Tenth Plenum in 1962 —as Liu's later self-criticism confirmed.[83] *After* Liu became the main criticism target of the GPCR, Chou En-lai disclosed that Mao had decided upon Liu's purge at the time he presented his "Twenty-Three Articles" in January 1965.[84] Mao Tse-tung related to Snow in 1970 that "on January 25, 1965, at a decisive meeting, and not before," he had decided that Liu had to go, because Liu opposed the mass rectification of the Party that Mao was then contemplating.[85]

Should such post hoc explanations by the victors of the historic "struggle between two lines" be given credence over the accounts of the victims, who insisted they first learned of such a "struggle" after they had lost it? If Mao's decision was so obvious in January 1965, why did Chou, allegedly at Mao's behest, continue to shield Liu from Red Guard assaults until February 1967? Why did Mao, at an October 1966 work conference, direct that no big-character posters should be posted against Liu in the streets and include Liu among the top leaders to appear with him on the T'ienanmen Square rostrum at eight mass rallies in the fall of 1966? If Liu was the leader of an opposing "line," why did he abandon P'eng Chen to the Maoists? How could he be so naïve as to implicate himself so thoroughly in a Maoist "trap"? And why did he capitulate without sign of resistance when Mao called him to account? If Mao's verdict seems predictable in retrospect, it seems to have been much less clear to anyone at the time. The above questions can only be answered in the light of an understanding of the circumstances of the GPCR, but they do seem to becloud the possibility that Mao had formed a definite verdict on Liu before its launching.

CULTURAL REVOLUTION

Under his assumption that a bourgeois superstructure had survived the socialization of the means of production in China and continued to exert an influence over the people's thinking, Mao made the reform of

---

83 Chou's address is in *PR*, no. 1 (January 1, 1965): 12–13.

84 "Premier Chou En-lai Bitterly Refutes Liu Shao-ch'i," *Ko-ti t'ung-hsün* (Dairen), no. 4 (September 13, 1967), in *SCMP*, no. 4081 (December 15, 1967): 10.

85 E. Snow, *The Long Revolution* (New York, 1971), p. 17.

the cultural superstructure an integral part of his attack on "revision-ism." The Maoist attempts to reform the cultural superstructure were of consequence for at least three reasons. First, they originated the *utopian* as opposed to the polemical objectives of the GPCR: the in-tention to make sweeping changes in the curricula and clientele of education, science, and the arts, as opposed to the decision to rebuke certain "revisionist" officials. Second, a loose organizational infra-structure coalesced around Chiang Ch'ing in her attempts to push through cultural reforms and formed the nucleus in May 1966 of the Central Cultural Revolution Group (CCRG), the radical agitational center of the GPCR and a body of considerable independent impor-tance. Third, through Chiang Ch'ing, these attempts at cultural re-form directly involved the Chairman himself in the launching of the GPCR. In assembling her informal group of radical publicists, his wife had (perhaps coincidentally) formed an alternative "staff" to which Mao could turn when he became impatient with the formal bureaucracy.

Chiang Ch'ing's efforts to revolutionize the cultural superstructure, according to her own later testimony, were initially undertaken inde-pendently of her husband's wishes but with his tacit forebearance. Beginning around 1960, she would call together young assistants and outstanding students of Peking University at the Summer Palace and assign them to write radical literary criticism. Ch'i Pen-yü and Nieh Yüan-tzu, who were to become prominent radical publicists during the GPCR, were both very active in these sessions.[86] Because Chiang's activities were given no formal sanction, the administrative organs charged with this duty resented her unsolicited incursions into their spheres of competence.[87] For instance, when she asked Cho Lin for an audience with her husband Teng Hsiao-p'ing to seek support for her drama reforms at the 1964 Peking Opera festival (incidentally, Chiang's revolutionary repertoire did dominate the festival), Teng reportedly declined to see her, saying: "For her drama reform I would raise two hands to show my approval, but I would not care to watch the show." [88] Chiang's cavalier treatment at the hands of the official bureaucracy may well have suggested to her that she and other informal associates

---

[86] *Tokyo Shimbun*, December 21, in *DSJP*, December 23, 1966, pp. 17–19.

[87] When Chiang Ch'ing declared in 1965 that the four Peking operas she had staged were "model operas," P'eng Chen allegedly retorted: "What kind of models are these? As the head of the CC's Group of Five I have no knowledge of them at all!" "Use Mao Tse-tung's Thought to Create Heroes' Images," *PD*, May 14, 1967.

[88] "The Tempestuous Combat on the Literature and Art Front," *Shou-tu hung-wei-ping* [Red Guards of the capital], June 7, 1967, in *CB*, no. 842 (December 8, 1967): 17, 22.

of Chairman Mao stood to be frozen out of the successor regime as then known, and she began to organize outside the system.

Beginning in December 1963, Mao tried to stir the CC Propaganda and Cultural departments into action with a blistering critique of the field: "Problems abound in all forms of art such as the drama, ballad, music, the fine arts, the dance, the cinema, poetry, and literature." In July 1964, he repeated his warning in more qualified terms.[89] Within twenty days of Mao's first instruction, Liu Shao-ch'i personally presided over a forum on literature and art on behalf of the Politburo. Propaganda Deputy Director Chou Yang delivered a self-criticism but was on the whole optimistic about the state of the arts, and Liu generally endorsed this view. About the time Mao issued his second warning, P'eng Chen was named Chairman of a Group of Five with authority to review the entire field of art and literature, and the reform movement began to gather somewhat more momentum. Member associations of the Federation of Literature and Art Circles launched rectification campaigns against the playwright T'ien Han and the critic Shao Ch'üan-lin. Vigorous (academic) criticism was also launched against Party educator Yang Hsien-chen's theory of "two combined into one" and historian Chou Ku-ch'eng's *Zeitgeist* theory. A number of films were also criticized.

This intensification of the rectification campaign excited the anxieties of those elites who based their ambitions for China's economic development on the cooperation of its intelligentsia. On March 3, 1965, Teng and Liu convened a meeting of the CC Secretariat, at which they called the 1964 criticisms "excessive," hampering "prosperity in creation." "Right now, some people have not dared to write articles. The NCNA is in receipt of only two manuscripts today," complained Teng. "We are forbidden to stage this and that." Henceforth, criticisms of notables must have "approval of the CC" and should be carried out in conformance with Liu's "gentle breezes and mild rain" formula rather than Chiang Ch'ing's populist approach. Chou Yang set forth five rules:

(1) Don't use erroneous labels. (2) Treat everyone equally. (3) Don't trace old cases. (4) Make concrete analyses so that not everything is affirmed or negated. (5) Give attention to pecularities of people in the literary and art field so as to avoid the old habit of intellectuals despising each other.[90]

[89] Alan P. L. Liu, *Communications and National Integration in Communist China* (Berkeley, Calif., 1971), pp. 64–71.

[90] Quoted in Wang Chang-ling, "Overt and Covert Struggles Between Mao and Liu over Literature and Art, *IS* 4, no. 3 (December 1967): 1–12.

Meanwhile, rather than circuit her proposals through P'eng Chen's censorious Group of Five, Chiang Ch'ing began to take her projects underground; beginning in June or July 1965, her group started work on a political expose of Wu Han:

One day a comrade gave the Chairman a copy of Wu Han's *Biography of Chu Yüan-chang*. . . . I said, "Don't, the Chairman is very tired, the author only wants a fee for the manuscript or a name for himself. Let him publish it. We'll review and criticize it after publication. I want to criticize the same author's *Hai Jui's Dismissal* too!" [N.B.: The wife as "gatekeeper."] At that time the Chairman argued with me and said that he wished to read it and that he wanted protection for a number of historians. He said that I had seen the whole circle of historians in a dark light without any trace of merit. In fact, this was an injustice. I asked the Chairman if I could reserve my opinion. He said I could. . . . Because he promised me to reserve my opinion it gave me courage to proceed with writing that article and to keep it secret. The secret was kept for seven to eight months during which the article was revised countless times.

Although Yao Wen-yüan was credited with authorship of this famous critique, it was in fact the fruit of long collaboration between Yao, Chiang Ch'ing, and Shanghai Party leader Chang Ch'un-ch'iao. Chiang Ch'ing continues:

Whenever Chang Ch'un-ch'iao came to Peking, some counterrevolutionaries thought that his coming had something to do with the criticism . . . of Wu Han. Although this was true to some extent, yet he also came to deal with the play, hear tape recording, and revise the music. But he also made a secret of that article on *Hai Jui's Dismissal* which he brought with him. The reason was that once they learned of it, they would strangle it.[91]

Mao Tse-tung convened a CC work conference in late September 1965, at which he said, "I felt the need to criticize the revisionists within the CC." On October 10 at the same conference, he proposed specifically that Wu Han be criticized. It has been speculated that a majority opposed Mao's proposals.[92] While this cannot be certified, the response to Yao's article when it was published in November was hardly indicative of widespread enthusiasm for a criticism campaign. In late October, after waiting two weeks for P'eng Chen to act, Mao lost patience and moved to Shanghai. As he later explained:

At this time I suggested to XX [P'eng Chen] to criticize *Hai Jui's Dismissal*, but in that Red city, I could not do anything [*wu neng wei li*] and had to go to Shanghai to organize.

[91] Chiang Ch'ing, "Speech at the Enlarged Session of the MAC of the CCP CC" (April 12, 1967), in *IS* 6, no. 10 (July 1970): 82–91.
[92] Jürgen Domes, *Die Aera Mao Tsetungs* (Stuttgart, 1971), p. 137.

Upon his arrival in Shanghai on October 24, Mao went on to say, he read Yao's article and approved it for publication:

Finally the essay was written. I read it three times, and felt that it was basically good. I had comrade XX publish it. I suggested to have a few comrades in the CC also read it again, but comrade XX suggested that it could be published the way it was, not to let comrade En-lai or comrade K'ang Sheng read it.[93]

The article, "Comments on the Newly-Written Historical Opera, *Hai Jui's Dismissal*," first appeared in the Shanghai *Wen-hui pao* on November 10. With its appearance, the GPCR had begun.

CONCLUSION

To return to the question posed at the beginning of this chapter as to the relationship between the decision to purge Liu and the decision to launch a cultural revolution, the evidence presented thus far suggests that the former was *not* the central focus of the GPCR as it was originally conceived. We find no before-the-fact indication that a definite verdict had been reached on Liu prior to the actual launching of the GPCR. To infer an inverse time sequence in making these two decisions would be to dismiss the weight of public evidence and give full credence to the after-the-fact explanations of the Maoists, who had a vested interest in construing any antecedents to the Mao-Liu break to fit its subsequent reality.

What then *was* the objective of the GPCR? Its objectives seem to have been to remedy an accumulation of frustrations from which Mao had suffered during the previous decade. Mao alluded to the multiple, cumulative nature of GPCR objectives at the September–October 1965 work conference [94] and again in a February 1967 speech:

In the past we waged struggles in rural areas, in factories, in the cultural field, and we carried out the SEM. But all this failed to expose our dark aspect openly, in an all-round way and from below.[95]

The coalescence of various frustrated goals and cumulated grievances was what gave the GPCR its wide, explosive appeal when their expression was legitimated by the "Thought of Mao Tse-tung"; to have distinguished between different objectives would have fractionalized

93 "Speech to Foreign Visitors" (August 1967), in "Mao Tse-tung ti yen-chiang ch'üan-wen" [Mao Tse-tung's complete speeches], *Ming pao*, July 5, 1968, p. 1.
94 "Previously, the criticism of *Wu Hsün Chuan* and *Hung Lou Meng* were just [attempts to] kill a pain in the head or in the feet, and that method did not do the trick." Ch'en, *Mao Papers*, p. 43.
95 *JPRS*, no. 49826.

the movement into a congeries of competing special interest groups. We have sought to support this "pressure cooker" interpretation by tracing GPCR criticism themes to their origins in five seminal conflicts, each of which contributed a distinctive cluster of themes.

The "Hundred Flowers" Campaign witnessed the birth of Mao's desire to launch a rectification movement on a nationwide scale that would include the non-Party masses and be relatively free of organizational restrictions, a desire that was thwarted but never given up, as he indicated in a comment made in 1965:

It is therefore necessary to mobilize everybody to assume responsibility, speak out, give encouragement and make criticism. Everybody has a pair of eyes and mouth. They should be allowed to use their eyes and mouth.[96]

At the same time, the ensuing criticisms by bourgeois intellectuals of the "cult of personality" and "proletarian dictatorship" were one of the reasons for the movement's hasty abortion. These criticisms, and their suppression in the "anti-rightist campaign," created bad blood between Mao and the intellectual establishment, forming the basis for an enduring enmity, which was certainly aggravated by the intellectual satires of Mao that appeared in the early 1960s and reciprocated on Mao's part by tirades on the uselessness of book learning, the need to reform the "bourgeois cultural superstructure," and the like. Thus the GPCR was to begin with a critique of Wu Han and then spread to other intellectual notables, with the enthusiastic support of the natural enemies of academics, their students.

The Great Leap Forward revived and strengthened Mao's ideals of distributive justice, martial mass solidarity, and the participation of the masses in the economic and political decisions immediately affecting their lives. The reaction to its incipient debacle at Lushan suggested to Mao that doubts about the validity of his charismatic vision had spread from the bourgeois intelligentsia to include members of the leadership, and the drastic cutback of Great Leap programs during retrenchment suggested that disaffection had spread beyond the original purge victims, replacing an economic crisis with an ideological one. Mao defiantly clung to the ideals of the Leap in the face of its failure and consequent apparent elite defections from them and made those ideals the basis for later criticisms of the liberal retrenchment policies.

In the Soviet Union, Mao thought he could descry the eventual outcome of such policies, and the Sino-Soviet dispute gave him his first

[96] "Comment on Peking Normal College's Investigation Material Report" (July 3, 1965), CB, no. 891 (October 8, 1969): 50.

public forum to articulate his critique of "revisionism." The critique began with Soviet foreign policy, then focused on unequal division of property, and finally, when the critique was brought home and applied to domestic trends, it was broadened to include all forms of invidious distinctions among people, including in particular the domination-subjection patterns characteristic of a "tall" bureaucratic hierarchy. The first public airing of the critique of "revisionism" in the context of steadily worsening relations with the Soviet Union made its later use against domestic dissidents (e.g., "China's Khrushchev") doubly effective by automatically implying collusion with a hostile foreign power.

As for the "power struggle" thesis, the evidence presented heretofore suggests that to speak of an extended conflict among sharply divided and organized factions overstates the case. The position of the Liu-Teng group within the legitimate institutions of policy making and implementation was such that it simply did not require factional organization. The multitude of charges against Liu and his followers do not indicate a usurpation plot (which would of course be superfluous), but the misuse of powers legally exercised. Mao's loss of authority seems rather to be attributable to his voluntary retirement to the second line and to the subsequent failure of policies with which he had been publicly identified, placing that retirement in the meaning-context of defeat, rather than the crowning triumph he had intended, and throwing doubt on the validity of his vision as an enduring model for China's development. In this altered meaning-context, Mao grew dissatisfied with his retirement and periodically sought to intercede with policy initiatives that would vindicate his political vision. These initiatives failed to achieve their objectives, and Mao blamed their failure on the bureaucracy, complaining that his colleagues thought his ideas "out-of-date" and tended to exclude him from an active role in policy. The subsequent claim that leadership had been "usurped" was a polemical formulation of Mao's accumulated dissatisfaction with an arrangement he had approved under more auspicious circumstances. Mao's retirement from the operational aspects of government seemed also to limit his understanding of (and tolerance for) the problems of policy implementation, freeing him to pursue his theories to their logical conclusions without too much regard for these problems. Retirement moreover resulted in his physical detachment from his Politburo colleagues, as he assembled his own "kitchen cabinet" in Shanghai and Hangchow, consisting of personal favorites who held relatively low positions in the official hierarchy and stood to be excluded from the designated successor regime.

Mao's feelings of exclusion and irrelevance to the developing scheme of things, reinforced by conversations with an apparently sycophantic and ambitious personal staff, thus set the stage for a conception of the GPCR as a revolt by the "outs" against the "ins," a "movement to seize power."

Mao formulated his dissatisfaction with the developing scheme of things within a theoretical framework that underwent no basic change after 1959, when he first announced his discovery that classes and class struggle persisted even after socialization of the means of production, even within the Communist Party. The practical implications that could be drawn from this theoretical framework were that since his inner-Party opposition consisted of class enemies, the contradiction could be resolved through "revolution," but Mao did not draw these problematic implications until 1965, when the disappointing results of the SEM became apparent. Certain subtle signs of Mao's rising impatience seem detectable in retrospect though they were hardly unambiguous warnings: before 1965, he occasionally spoke of "bourgeois elements in the Party," for example, while in January 1965 he introduced the more menacing term, "Party persons in authority taking the capitalist road" and specified their possible location in the CC.

While we fail as yet to find convincing evidence of a definite verdict on Liu Shao-ch'i prior to the GPCR, it is possible that the immanent logic of the evolving and converging GPCR themes pointed to Liu as one of its victims. Liu was a patron of "bourgeois liberal" cultural and educational policies, but his sweeping purge of school administrations and CC Propaganda and Cultural departments in the spring of 1966 indicates that he was prepared to abjure that patronage and hence proof against the specifically cultural criticism themes with which the movement began. The most dangerous themes from Liu's standpoint were the criticism of "Party persons in authority taking the capitalist road" and the idea of mass rectification of the CCP leadership without organizational constraints; the combination might result in an unstructured witch-hunting atmosphere that would be anathema to a man whose theories placed such consistent emphasis on the unity, predictability, and integrity of the organization.

4

THE FALL OF LIU SHAO-CH'I

The GPCR brought Liu Shao-ch'i's attempt to balance revolution
with order, equality with economic efficiency, into direct confrontation with the revived forces of revolution in China, a confrontation
in which Liu's order was to fall asunder. In this study of how the
flames of revolution were reignited, and how Liu was trapped and
consumed in the conflagration, we shall for analytical purposes divide
the complex causal processes involved into two dimensions: in the
first Liu is a *subject* participating actively in the direction of affairs,
and in the second he is an *object* of revolution. This chapter analyzes
Liu's fall from the first perspective, viewing the GPCR as much as
possible through Liu's eyes and trying to delineate his personal responsibility; the following chapter will essay an analysis of Liu's "objective" role in the GPCR as a vehicle of communicative action. In
the conclusion, along with an evaluation of Liu's subjective reaction
to Red Guard criticisms, we shall offer more definitive answers to the
questions posed in the introduction to Chapter 3: why, and how, was
it decided to submit Liu to mass criticism? How was this decision related to the decision to launch the GPCR?

Liu's subjective actions vis-à-vis the movement showed an overall
trend of declining efficacy, which may be periodized in three phases.
In the first, from November 1965 to the end of May 1966, Liu's involvement in the unfolding GPCR was only indirect: Wu Han, and
through Wu his patron, P'eng Chen, were the initial targets of the
movement, and our attention during this phase will therefore be focused on Liu's relationship to these early targets. In the second phase,
from June 1, 1966, until late July, Liu assumed temporary command
of the CC in Mao's absence and dispatched "work teams" to "exercise
leadership" over the rising movement. It was at this time that Liu
committed the errors that defined his essential guilt, and we shall

67

therefore analyze these errors in considerable detail. During the third phase, beginning with Liu's criticism and demotion at the August 1966 Eleventh Plenum and ending with his formal purge from the Party at the October 1968 Twelfth Plenum, Liu underwent a gradual decline and fall as the nature of his error was progressively redefined by the mass movement from its initial "nonantagonistic" status to that of "antagonistic" contradiction. Due to this chapter's concern with the subjective dimension of Liu's fall, we shall focus during this phase on Liu's attempts to atone for his errors through self-criticism and analyze the reasons for his failure to achieve that modest goal.

THE FALL OF P'ENG CHEN

Liu was not the initial objective of the revolution, and to establish that he was the ultimate objective one must therefore demonstrate some clear connection between the initial objective and Liu Shao-ch'i. When such a connection is inferred (to support the "conspiracy" theory outlined in Chapter 3), it is usually conceived as follows: Wu Han, Peking's Vice-Mayor under P'eng Chen was attacked to implicate P'eng Chen; P'eng Chen, an old protégé of Liu Shao-ch'i, was then purged to implicate Liu, or to weaken his inner-Party power base. According to this line of reasoning, there was a chain of implication leading from Wu Han through P'eng Chen to Liu Shao-ch'i. The basis for this chain is the assumption that a leader is responsible for the errors of his subordinates and is thereby bound to defend them, for if they fall, his own position is jeopardized. However, several facets of this argument seem open to question. First, we shall investigate whether Mao had necessary and sufficient reason to attack Wu Han *independently* of a wish to attack P'eng Chen, for if he did, the assumption that his ultimate target was P'eng Chen is gratuitous. Second, we shall investigate whether P'eng Chen had a *viable choice* when Mao demanded the head of his protégé. Would Wu Han's loss destroy P'eng Chen, or would it merely tarnish his prestige and signal his submission to Mao? If P'eng's survival was not at stake, the chain of implication between Wu and P'eng was by no means a *necessary* one: P'eng *chose* to protect Wu, and because of his protection (and concomitant insubordination to Mao), he was implicated when Wu finally fell. Finally, we shall analyze the relationship between P'eng Chen and *his* presumptive patron, Liu Shao-ch'i.

First, it seems that Mao clearly had necessary and sufficient independent reason to attack Wu, making it causally unnecessary to construe that attack as an opening wedge for an attack on P'eng Chen.

For Mao to mount a criticism campaign against Wu for the reasons stated does not deviate from previous policy: since 1950, Mao had periodically mounted criticism campaigns against various cultural targets, beginning with the attack on *Story of Wu Hsün* in 1950, on Yü P'ing-po's critical study of *Dream of the Red Chamber* (and on Hu Shih *et al.*) in 1954, on Hu Feng in 1955, and so forth. It seems equally clear that Wu Han's 1961 play, *Hai Jui's Dismissal*, was an attack on Mao by historical analogy. Even if P'eng Chen's defensive plea, "Investigation shows that Wu Han and P'eng Te-huai have neither organization nor direct contact," [1] is correct, it is evident not only that the Peking satirists were familiar with the documents of the P'eng-Mao dispute,[2] but that their satirical objective was clear to political cognoscenti at the time.[3] P'eng Te-huai perceived the analogy between himself and the famous sixteenth-century minister of Wu's play who dared criticize the Chia-ching Emperor: "I cannot remain silent any longer. I want to be a Hai Jui," P'eng "cried" upon submitting an 80,000-character "memorial" in 1962 requesting a reversal of verdicts.[4]

It is ironic, to say the least, that it was precisely the mayor of Peking who was given responsibility for "rectifying" Wu Han, inasmuch as Wu and other anti-Maoist satirists had originally published their essays in Peking journals with P'eng's presumed knowledge and forebearance. For P'eng to subject his vice-mayor and other intellectuals

1 "P'eng Te-huai ti kung-tse" [P'eng Te-huai's Confession] (December 8, 1966–January 5, 1967), in *P'eng Te-huai*, ed. Chung-kuo wen-t'i yen-chiu so, (Hong Kong, 1969), p. 112.

2 For example, P'eng Te-huai, in his letter to Mao of July 14, 1959, said: "I am a simple man like Chang Fei, and really have his crudeness without possessing any of his sensitivity." In a satirical essay written on February 22, 1962, Teng T'o includes a parallel discussion of the "courage and artlessness" of Chang Fei, which he contrasts with the "great cleverness" of Chu-ko Liang. Teng T'o, "Can One Rely on Cleverness?" trans. in Joachim Glaubitz, *Opposition gegen Mao* (Olten, Switzerland, 1969), pp. 31, 75–79; for the original texts see *Tsu-kuo*, no. 48 (March 1968); Ma Nan-ts'un [Teng T'o], "Yen-shan yeh-hua" [Evening conversations at Yenshan], *Hsüan-chi* [Selected works] (Hong Kong, 1966); *Teng T'o shih-wen hsüan-chi* [Teng T'o's selected poems] (Taipei, 1966).

3 "To use novels to attack the Party is a great invention," Mao dryly observed in his address to the Tenth Plenum of the CC in September 1962. As James R. Pusey notes, "The fact that Wu Han's play was indeed suppressed . . . three years before he was criticized still proves that the political criticisms against Wu Han were not fabricated in 1965 but had been harbored, most likely by Mao Tse-tung, at least since 1961." *Wu Han: Attacking the Present Through the Past* (Cambridge, Mass., 1969), p. 61.

4 The record of his interrogation by Red Guards quotes P'eng as again saying: "He [Mao] dismissed me from office; I agreed, but had my reservations. I felt very much relieved without my official position. As I was no good and others were better, then I must be replaced. Since the Lushan meeting, I, as 'Hai Jui,' was finished [*wan-tan*]." "P'eng Te-huai ti kung-tse," in *P'eng Te-huai*, ed. Chung-kuo wen-t'i yen-chiu so, pp. 112, 114.

who had attained posts in his administration to full public exposure would mean an implicit acknowledgment and repudiation of his earlier responsibility for sanctioning those intellectuals and would entail disrupting his own "independent kingdom" and pledging undivided loyalty to Mao Tse-tung. It may have occurred to Mao that P'eng would be required to make a personal sacrifice; Mao's doubt that P'eng Chen would do so is suggested by the fact that when Mao asked P'eng to criticize Wu he did not disclose his contact with Chiang Ch'ing's group, which had already prepared a critique in secret. But as Edward Rice has pointed out, Mao frequently resorts to this sort of "test" to discipline subordinates whose loyalty is in question; P'eng's choice was difficult, but the record of others in the same dilemma who acquitted themselves satisfactorily shows that he did have a viable choice.[5] Again, in all fairness, it should be added that Mao had independently sufficient reason to assign Wu's purge to P'eng Chen: as the leader of the Group of Five with a special mandate for cultural reform and as one who had earned the public accolade "Chairman Mao's close comrade-in-arms" in September 1965 for his success in the 1964–65 reform of Peking Opera, P'eng was the most logical person to lead such a purge. Who would be a more plausible choice to clean up the Peking Party Committee than the mayor of Peking?

It is a measure of the erosion of Mao's authority that P'eng, forced to choose between protection of his own power base and obedience to Mao, opted for the former alternative. Mao waited only briefly for P'eng to take action before moving to Shanghai, where he read and approved for publication a trenchant critique Yao Wen-yüan had prepared with Chang Ch'un-Ch'iao and Chiang Ch'ing,[6] without discussing the decision with the rest of the Politburo. The article first appeared in the Shanghai *Wen-hui pao* on November 10 and was subsequently reprinted in several provincial and regional papers, all in the eastern China region. P'eng was immediately informed of the identity of Yao's "backstage backers" through his informal information network. According to a Red Guard report, "A few Shanghai Municipal Committee secretaries, led by East China Bureau Secretary Ch'en P'ei-

[5] According to Rice, at earlier times in his career Mao had placed Ch'en I and Ho Lung in analogous positions: Ch'en I in his suppression of the "Anti-Bolshevik Corps" at Fut'ien in 1930, Ho Lung in conducting a post-purge investigation of P'eng Te-huai in 1960. Ch'en acquitted himself satisfactorily, Ho did not. Edward E. Rice, *Mao's Way* (Berkeley, Calif., 1972), pp. 68–69, 185. It should be noted that Rice holds a "conspirational" view of the purge of P'eng Chen and Liu Shao-ch'i.

[6] A Shanghai Red Guard confided to Neale Hunter: "Yao Wen-yüan wrote his original article in Shanghai. . . . At that time, Chairman Mao's wife, Chiang Ch'ing, was also in Shanghai and she gave him concrete assistance." *FEER* 7, no. 5 (August 3, 1967): 245–248.

hsien and Shanghai Mayor Ts'ao Ti-ch'iu, were . . . afraid of P'eng Chen and even more afraid of Liu Shao-ch'i. So, as soon as the article was published, they warned P'eng Chen . . . of his danger." [7] P'eng called a special (enlarged) meeting of the Peking Party Committee and, on November 11, 1965, had Lu Ting-yi, Director of the CC Propaganda Department, call Shanghai to demand who gave them permission to attack Wu without consulting the Group of Five. Chang Ch'un-ch'iao reportedly answered that it was Mao himself, whereupon Lu hung up without a word. [8]

Yet P'eng was not easily intimidated; in fact, he seemed determined to keep the lid on. On November 28, P'eng called a second meeting at which he asked Teng T'o, "How is Wu Han now?" "Wu is nervous, for he is aware that this criticism originates from a source," Teng replied. "Source or not, we seek only the truth," P'eng assured him. "In truth, everyone is equal." [9] As Chiang Ch'ing recalled the sequence of events leading to the nationwide publication of Yao's article: "Nineteen days had passed without seeing its publication in Peking [then the axis of the national communications network]. Then, the Chairman got angry and said he would issue a pamphlet. The pamphlet was published but it was not released to the public in Peking." [10]

On November 29, Mao broke the deadlock by releasing the article over the nationwide radio network and having it published in the *Liberation Army Daily* (*LAD*), signaling to P'eng that the array of forces against him now included the PLA. The *Peking Daily* reprinted the article the same day in its column of academic criticism, and on the next day *People's Daily* (*PD*) followed suit, but whereas the *LAD* publication included a provocative editorial note condemning Wu Han's play as a "big poisonous weed," *PD* relegated the article to its column on academic research and, in an editorial note written by P'eng himself, called for wide discussions without condemning the work. [11] Due to P'eng's skillful editorial handling of the critique, it failed to arouse much attention: by December, 1965 it had been re-

[7] "Ch'en P'ei-hsien Is the Shanghai Vassal of the Liu Dynasty's Revisionist Headquarters," Speech by the representative of Red Revolutionaries at the January 6 rally in Shanghai, quoted in N. Hunter, *Shanghai Journal: An Eyewitness Account of the Cultural Revolution* (New York, 1969), p. 21.

[8] Gigon, *Vie et Mort*, pp. 37–38; also see Ch'i Pen-yü's article in *RF*, no. 7 (May 11, 1966).

[9] "Wu-ch'an chieh-chi wen-hua ta ko-ming ta chih-chi" [GPCR—A record of major events], (hereafter "Record"), *Chingkangshan* (February 1967), in *JPRS*, no. 42349 (August 25, 1967): 3.

[10] Chiang, "Speech to the MAC of the CC CCP" (April 12, 1967), *IS* 6, no. 10 (July 1970): 82–91.

[11] Chang Man, *The People's Daily and the Red Flag Magazine During the Cultural Revolution* (Hong Kong, 1969), pp. 9–10.

printed (without commentary) in only fourteen of the more than thirty-five regional papers; the other papers took no notice whatever.[12]

P'eng Chen sought for as long as possible to avoid choosing between outright defiance and a purge of his municipal committee by permitting public criticism of Wu Han to escalate within set limits. For three months the debate continued, hewing fairly closely to historiographical issues and confined to academic contributors, whose articles appeared on the *PD* page for academic research under the regular caption, "Let a hundred flowers bloom, let a hundred schools of thought contend." On December 14, P'eng called a work conference of the Peking Party Committee, at which he said to Wu Han, "You should examine your thinking where you are wrong and persist where you are right, upholding the truth and correcting mistakes." Wu published self-criticisms on December 28 and again on January 12 that were in tune with this mild reproof, relegating disagreement to a historicist methodology that gave its due to the values of earlier eras. Between December 21 and 23, Mao held a series of talks with central leaders, including P'eng Chen. According to Red Guard accounts, although Mao made clear his dissatisfaction with P'eng Chen's conduct of the campaign, which had thus far evaded the "key question" of the connection between *Hai Jui* and P'eng Te-huai, P'eng Chen deliberately misconstrued the import of his remarks: "The Chairman says that a conclusion will be reached on the Wu Han question in two months," he announced after a private audience with Mao. "Chairman Mao agrees with my viewpoint that Wu Han is not a political question." [13]

Beginning in the middle of January, P'eng, worried by the publication of articles by leftist gadflies Ch'i Pen-yü and Yao Wen-yüan, which injected political issues into the dispute,[14] moved to throttle debate. On January 17, Hsü Li-ch'ün called a conference of the newspapers *Liberation Daily* (*LD*), *Peking Daily*, and *PD* and the periodicals *Frontline, New Construction,* and *Red Flag* (*RF*) to announce: "In the future, articles of criticism to be carried by the three newspapers and periodicals must be reviewed in advance. *RF* will not engage in criticism." Following this decision, an article by Ch'i Pen-yü criticizing the "key questions" was rejected and there was a general diminution of criticisms dealing with Wu Han.[15]

12 *Viz.*, Shanghai, Chekiang, Fukien, Kiangsu, Shantung, Anhwei, Kiangsi, Hopei, Honan, and Kwangtung. Cf. Chao Ts'ung, "A Report on the Development of the Cultural Revolution," *Tsu-kuo*, no. 53 (October 1, 1968): 10 ff.

13 "Record," *JPRS*, no. 42349, p. 5.

14 Ch'i Pen-yü, "Study History for Revolution," *PD*, December 8, 1965.

15 "Record," *JPRS*, no. 42349, p. 6.

In preparing and disseminating the notorious "February Outline," P'eng Chen carried his insubordination one step further. P'eng invited eleven colleagues to an enlarged session of the Group of Five, which was held from February 2 to 5. There P'eng raised the possibility of launching a rectification campaign against the "leftists." The fruit of this meeting, an "Outline Report on the Current Academic Situation," was approved by the Politburo Standing Committee on February 5 and disseminated in the name of the CC between February 12 and 14. The "February Outline" drew the lines quite clearly between P'eng's and Mao's conceptions of the purpose of the rectification campaign. The "Outline's" import, most clearly stated in its second paragraph, was to limit debate to Wu's academic peers and avoid any "political conclusion." Although Mao repeated to P'eng on February 8 that "the key question concerns dismissal," asking him twice, "Is Wu Han opposed to the Party and socialism?" on February 13, P'eng sent Hu Sheng to warn Chang Ch'un-ch'iao: "The key points in the Wu Han question are not to be discussed. Nor can the question be related to the Lushan Conference. Wu Han is not opposed to the Party and to socialism. This is what the Chairman said." [16]

According to the "conspiracy" theory, the Wu Han–P'eng Chen relationship of mutual obligation and responsibility was the first link in a chain of implication leading to Liu Shao-ch'i. But examination of the events leading to P'eng Chen's implication indicates that Mao did not *necessarily* intend his attack on Wu Han to implicate P'eng, and that P'eng had a choice between his patron-client obligation to Wu and his official obligation to Mao, a choice that Mao gave him ample time and opportunity to make. From the outset P'eng chose to protect Wu, whose fall would have disrupted his municipal committee by exposing Teng T'o, Liao Mo-sha, and other coopted anti-Maoist intellectuals to like treatment. As pressure from the Maoists increased, P'eng began brazenly to misconstrue Mao's wishes to imply support for his own policies, spinning a web of self-protective lies that could not bear the stress of continuing Maoist pressures. By tenaciously clinging to Wu Han in the face of Maoist demands that he draw a "political conclusion," P'eng ultimately brought about the purge and reorganization of the entire Peking Party Committee.

If the link between Wu Han and P'eng Chen was not binding, but a matter of conscious choice, what is the case for a link between P'eng Chen and Liu Shao-ch'i? In the following account of the P'eng-Liu relationship we find: first, the evidence for assuming a relationship

[16] *Akahata*, August 15, in *DSJP*, August 16, 1967, p. 19; also "Record," *JPRS*, no. 42349, p. 8.

of obligation and responsibility between P'eng and Liu is tenuous; second, even if there was such a relationship, Liu did not honor it; and third, despite the absence of a functioning link, it is possible that Liu's relatively noncommittal behavior throughout the P'eng episode led some of the Maoists to suspect the presence of a link.

The putative historical basis for a P'eng-Liu link is their collaboration in the December Ninth Movement in Peking in 1935–36, but it seems doubtful that this early association would necessarily create sufficient basis for blind, enduring loyalty—after all, Ch'en Po-ta also collaborated with Liu in the December Ninth Movement. While it is true that P'eng tended to align with Liu in inner-Party debates, organizationally he was closer to Teng Hsiao-p'ing (Teng was General Secretary, P'eng Deputy General Secretary of the CC)—and yet Teng was one of the first to come out in criticism of P'eng.

The utter absence on Liu's part of any involvement on one side or the other during the entire period of P'eng's implication is so striking as to suggest that Liu was deliberately evading the issue. He attended the CC work conference in late September and early October 1965, at which Mao's plans for an escalated cultural reform movement were broached; then, on November 27, following an enlarged Politburo meeting, he dropped out of sight for seven weeks. When Mao convened a three-day meeting in Hangchow in December 1965, Teng Hsiao-p'ing, K'ang Sheng, and Ch'en Po-ta all attended and seconded Mao's criticisms of P'eng Chen's handling of the Wu Han affair. Liu did not attend, but, alerted by rumors in Peking, he reportedly telephoned; Lin Piao, in a long conversation with him, told him of the intensity of Mao's concern with revisionism and urged him to take swift action. Liu listened closely, intermittently posing a few questions, but made no commitments.[17]

As for the "February Outline," Liu must bear command responsibility, inasmuch as he chaired the February 5 Politburo Standing Committee meeting where the document was ratified, but this approval was apparently pro forma. At a later interrogation, Liu claimed he could not remember what he said at the meeting; Teng said he approved the "February Outline" because "P'eng Chen deceived me. I ratified it because I was told that Chairman Mao had agreed to it." [18] A Red Guard chronology (which can hardly be accused of pro-Liu bias) confirms Teng's version of the affair: P'eng spoke with Mao on February 8 and then two days later telephoned the Standing Committee to have the "February Outline" changed into

17 Gigon, *Vie et Mort*, pp. 38–39, 42.
18 *Sankei*, August 15, in *DSJP*, August 16, 1967, p. 19.

a formal document on the strength of Mao's alleged approval, and it was then released.[19] We have seen that Mao did not in fact approve P'eng's handling of the criticism campaigns, much less the "February Outline." P'eng's deceptions thus implicated Liu and Teng in the approval of a document that was shortly to come under sharp and authoritative attack. At the same time, the possibility cannot be ruled out that Liu heard of Mao's remarks but chose to accept P'eng's version of the event.

Mao launched his counterattack in the latter part of March, first attempting once more to set his plans in motion through a series of meetings with other elites. He held a meeting of the Standing Committee from March 17 to 20, at which Liu was present, and there gave vent to his mounting anger with the CC cultural and propaganda departments, which he said were "controlled by bourgeois intellectuals" who were "opposed to Communism"; Wu Han, he alleged, was a "Kuomintang element." On March 26, Liu Shao-ch'i and Ch'en I and their wives departed on a state visit to Pakistan and Afghanistan. From March 28 to 30, Mao held a CC work conference, which was the occasion for his first express denunciation of P'eng Chen (who was not, however, present): "If P'eng Chen, the Peking Municipal Committee, and the Central Propaganda Department continue to harbor bad people, then [they] . . . should be disbanded," he said. He went so far as to call the Propaganda Department the "headquarters of the king of Hell," which should be "overthrown" because it published anti-Mao satires but impeded publication of leftist critiques of the satirists: "I call on local provinces for a rebellion and an attack on the Center." [20] At this time, P'eng Chen disappeared. His last appearance was in connection with the visit of Kenji Miyamoto and the Japanese Communist Party delegation of March 28–29, and he was not seen again in public in an official capacity.

Frustrated by the dilatory tactics of the elites he had delegated to lead the movement, Mao now took his cause directly to the masses via a sweeping critical offensive in the media: whereas only ninety articles had appeared concerning Wu Han in the three-month period between January and March, in April, 4,000 articles appeared within three weeks criticizing Wu Han and other Peking intellectuals of his ilk: T'ien Han, the dramatist; Teng Kuang-ming, the historian; Chien Po-tsan, a philosopher, et al.[21] *LAD* led the offensive, but the Peking

[19] "Record," *JPRS*, no. 42349, pp. 7–8.

[20] *Akahata*, November 8, 1967, in *DSJP*, November 8, 1967, pp. 46–48.

[21] Marianne Bastid, "Origines et Développement de la Révolution Culturelle," *Politique Étrangère* 32, no. 1 (summer 1967): 68–87.

newspapers now followed suit, spurred by attacks by *LAD* and *LD* on *Peking Evening News, Peking Daily,* and *Frontline.* The papers also began publishing the opinions of peasants, workers, and soldiers. At the end of April, students were also participating in the criticism of Wu Han and the "three-family village" (comprising Wu, Liao Mo-sha, and Teng T'o, all members of the Peking Municipal Party Committee).[22]

The timing of the initial assault on P'eng Chen two days after Liu's departure suggests an alliance between P'eng and Liu. Liu's trip had in fact been arranged in March 1965 after Pakistan President Ayub Khan visited Peking, though this would not necessarily have dispelled suspicion among interested Chinese observers.[23] In any case, P'eng's fate was already in jeopardy by the time Liu returned from Burma on April 19. At a meeting of the CC Secretariat, held from April 9 to 12, Teng Hsiao-p'ing, Chou En-lai, Ch'en Po-ta, and K'ang Sheng criticized P'eng Chen for a series of grave errors, including opposition to Mao. "I have never, do not, and will not oppose Chairman Mao," P'eng insisted. "I merely persist in my opinion regarding 'blooming.' " The meeting adjourned by issuing a protocol recommending dissolution of the Group of Five, annulment of its reports and orders, and eventual appointment of a new Central Cultural Revolution Group. Mao, who had remained in Shanghai, convened a Standing Committee meeting in Hangchow on April 16 to consider the Secretariat's protocol. Mao sharply criticized P'eng in this meeting and objected in particular that he made no personnel changes after the April 10–15 meeting of the Peking Party Committee, merely approving the self-criticisms of his subordinates. Heated discussions between Politburo members arose.[24] Liu Shao-ch'i, who apparently went directly from K'unming to Hangchow upon his return from Burma on April 19, tried to resolve the differences by criticizing P'eng on certain points and absolving him on others:

P'eng Chen is actually the Deputy General Secretary of our Party. Since he is often asked to attend meetings of the Standing Committee, he is actually with the core of the leadership. This man is capable but has quite a number of shortcomings and has committed many mistakes. He does not understand the thought of Mao Tse-tung.[25]

22 Henry G. Schwarz, "The Great Proletarian Cultural Revolution," *Orbis* 10, no. 3 (fall 1966): 803–823.

23 Byung-joon Ahn, "The Making of the Cultural Revolution: November 1965–August 1966" (unpub. paper), p. 18.

24 "Record," *JPRS,* no. 42349, pp. 10–11.

25 "Selected Edition," *SCMM,* no. 653 (May 5, 1969): 15.

While the protocol was adopted on April 24, P'eng's purge was not considered final until P'eng was personally presented with evidence of his mistakes and induced to confess. "Concerning P'eng Chen," Chou En-lai recalled in a December 1966 speech, "the Party Central carried out debates for as long as twelve days in continuation, and upon P'eng Chen's personally recognizing his crimes, the Central decided, for the first time, that 'he is an anti-Party element.' " These debates were conducted in a Politburo meeting held from May 4 to 16; the results of the meeting were published in the "May 16 Circular," which was circulated within the Party as far down as the *hsien* level, announcing P'eng's dismissal, dissolution of the Group of Five, and formal annulment of all its decisions. A "Central Cultural Revolution Group" (CCRG) was also set up at this time, led by Ch'en Po-ta and Chiang Ch'ing.[26]

Certain inconclusive clues suggest that Liu's responsibility for approval of P'eng's "February Outline" made Liu an object of suspicion in the Maoist camp, if not at the highest echelons almost certainly at middle and lower levels, where the circumstances surrounding production of that notorious document were not fully known. Suspicion may have also been engendered by Liu's scrupulous neutrality throughout the Mao-P'eng contest and his seemingly tepid attitude toward the GPCR. For example, both Teng Hsiao-p'ing and Chou En-lai took advantage of the welcome ceremonies held for a visiting Albanian delegation in late April to praise the GPCR: Chou lauded Mao's Thought no less than eleven times in a speech on April 30 and praised the GPCR; Teng, who had rarely taken the spotlight previously, led a mass rally on May 6, where he also hailed Mao's Thought and the GPCR. Liu mentioned neither in his April 28 address to the Albanian delegation.[27] Maybe Liu was "sitting on the mountain to watch the tigers fight," coolly calculating the balance of forces before committing himself; maybe he simply did not wish to dirty his hands with the purge of an old colleague. In any case, the "May 16 Circular," reportedly drafted in large part by Mao himself, contained the following warning:

Those representatives of the bourgeoisie who have sneaked into the Party, the government, the army, and various cultural circles are a bunch of counterrevolutionary revisionists. Once conditions are ripe, they will seize political power and turn the dictatorship into a dictatorship of the bourgeoisie. Some

26 *Yomiuri*, December 14, in *DSJP*, Dec. 15, 1966, pp. 9–10; "Circular of the CC of CCP" (May 16, 1966), in Jerome Ch'en, *Mao Papers*, pp. 105–113.
27 Cheng, "Power struggle," pp. 379–480.

of them we have already seen through, others we have not. Some are still trusted by us and are being trained as our successors; persons like Khrushchev, for example, who are still nestling beside us.[28]

It was not known at the time to whom this statement might refer, but Kuan Feng, a CCRG radical, alleged on February 12, 1967, that it was aimed at Liu Shao-ch'i.

THE "FIFTY DAYS"

"No sooner was the signal sent out than our enemies began to act," Mao later remarked concerning the events that followed dissemination of the "May 16 Circular." "Of course, we should have acted too." [29] The "enemies" Mao referred to were Liu and his colleagues on the CC, who indeed had begun to act soon after the "signal" (the "May 16 Circular") was sent out. Was Liu's purpose in dispatching work teams to repress the revolutionary masses, as Mao seems to have inferred? What was the nature of the "error" that was to prove Liu's undoing, and how did he come to commit it? The following section will describe the creation of a radical student opposition and the organizational overreaction to it that later acquired national notoriety as the "bourgeois reactionary line."

The first development was the creation of a radical student opposition. Student participation in the GPCR began at the end of April within the framework of existing Party youth organizations and came in response to the stepped-up media critique of Wu Han and the "three-family village." Participation was extended by a number of incidents that unexpectedly revealed high-level elite support for a radical student minority opposed to the Party organization. The first of these was Nieh Yüan-tzu's posting of the first big-character poster on May 24.

Nieh, a philosophy teacher at Peking University, had conducted a running battle for several years with university President Lu P'ing over the relative importance of ideology among subjects in the curriculum. The issue culminated in early February in an interfaculty dispute over the political implications of Wu Han's play, which Lu resolved by sending several protesters to the countryside. As a member of the university Party committee, Nieh was privy to the "May 16 Circular," which repudiated P'eng Chen. Seeing in this document the basis for a counterattack on Lu, on May 24 Nieh met with six colleagues in the philosophy department to draft the first big-character poster, which

28 Jerome Ch'en, *Mao Papers*, pp. 112–113.
29 Mao, "Speech to Foreign Visitors," *Ming pao*, July 5, 1968, p. 1.

exposed Lu P'ing's relations with P'eng and implicated the three top men in Peking's political and academic power structure.[30] To the student majority, Nieh's act must have seemed one of quixotic bravado. The poster went up on May 25 at 2:00 P.M., and by 6:00, recollected Nieh, "Our poster was covered by many posters abusing us." Lu P'ing immediately reported the event to his superior in the Education Ministry, and by the evening of the same day a member of one of the CC departments brought him instructions. On May 26, Nieh's poster was reproduced and distributed to the students, who began to take their own positions and post big-character posters; by the time a Party task force consisting of Chou En-lai, K'ang Sheng, and Ch'en Po-ta arrived at the university later that day to assess the situation and meet with Lu P'ing, the campus was covered with posters. By May 27, things had begun to quiet down, and the Youth League even began to exert pressure on the Nieh group for written confessions, which the latter resisted.[31]

This incident was rescued from obscurity by the Chairman himself. On June 1, Nieh's poster came to Mao's attention, and he called K'ang Sheng to request that it "should be at once broadcast and published in the newspapers." The poster was broadcast over the national radio network the same day, and, on June 2, a PD editorial ("Sweep Away all Freaks and Monsters") appeared hailing the poster as having "unveiled a sinister gang." [32] On June 3, the CC announced reorganization of the Peking Party Committee with the appointment of Li Hsüeh-feng to replace P'eng Chen, dismissal of Lu P'ing and the dispatch of a work team to Peking University to supervise reorganization of the Party committee there. Inasmuch as no explanation was given for the sudden reorganization and dismissals, the masses could only speculate about the nature of the dispute dividing their leadership.

Nieh's vindication demonstrated to the students that an unpopular minority might win high elite backing and prevail against the supposedly monolithic Party organization on purely ideological criteria and thus established an important precedent for the "rebels." Its immediate effect was to unleash a widespread outburst of wall posters against local counterparts of Lu P'ing.[33]

---

[30] Bastid, "Origines," pp. 70–73.

[31] Anna Louise Strong, Letter from China, no. 49 (May 30, 1967): 1 ff.

[32] Yomiuri, January 7, in DSJP, January 7–9, 1967, pp. 28–30.

[33] "In all the excitement, is seemed as though the Red Guards were to sprout like bamboo," recalled Dai Hsiao-ai. Gordon Bennett and Ronald Montaperto, Red Guard: The Political Biography of Dai Hsiao-ai (Garden City, New York, 1971), p. 71.

Before trying to understand the nature of Liu's error in dealing with the student mobilization that followed publication of Nieh's poster, it may be helpful to submit to critical scrutiny several incomplete characterizations of that error. First, there is no reason to suspect that Liu's dispatch of work teams, which "had been recognized as the proper means of organization in every movement since the liberation in 1949," was anything more than a standard response to organizational disruption precipitated by extra-Party mass agitation.[34] "The sending of work groups is based upon the successful experience gained in past movements," Liu explained. "When the Party committee of a school rots, it is necessary to send a work group to seize power from it. If the school Party committee has fewer problems, the leaders of a work group must also be sent to help it to exercise leadership." When Lu P'ing's administration went the way of P'eng Chen's, the seven who had led the attack on it were of course unable to administer the university, so the CC sent the first work team under Chang Ch'eng-hsien to assume temporary leadership during reorganization of the school's Party committee.[35] The fall of Lu P'ing and of the "P'eng [Chen]-Lo [Jui-ch'ing]-Lu [Ting-yi]-Yang [Shang-k'un]" complex discredited other administrations likewise linked to that complex, and a new wave of revolutionary orthodoxy swept the school system as one administration after another came under rebel attacks, resulting in a deluge of calls to the CC to dispatch more work teams. In Liu's words:

At that time, requests came from many quarters for work teams. The requests became more urgent after newspapers published the report that a work team had been sent to Peking University. At that time, if we had not considered the requests for work teams or had not sent work teams to schools and government organs, in what other way could we have acted? There would have been people who thought we did not fully comprehend the Great Cultural Revolution.[36]

If the dispatch of work teams did not deviate from accepted organizational procedures for handling crises at lower levels, perhaps Mao had issued special instructions for organizing the movement that were

[34] *Ibid.* In an editorial note to his 1956 article, "Socialist Upsurge in China's Countryside," Mao approved the dispatch of work teams with reservations: "Work teams must be sent, but it must be stated very clearly that they are being sent to help local Party organizations, not replace them." Stuart Schram, ed., *The Political Thought of Mao Tse-tung* (New York, 1963), p. 321.

[35] Fan Shu-cheng, "Liu Shao-ch'i ti tzu-wo chien-ch'a pao-kao" [Report on Liu Shao-ch'i's self-examination], *Ming pao yüeh-k'an* [Ming Pao monthly], no. 14 (February 1967): 30 ff.

[36] "Tzu-wo chien-ch'a" [Self-examination] (October 23, 1966). in *LSWTC*, pp. 621–625.

more consistent with what he wished the GPCR to achieve? Chiang Ch'ing contended in a November 1966 speech that Mao had insisted "as early as June" (at the Hangchow conference on June 9, according to the Chingkanshan *Record*) that "work teams should not be sent out hastily" (*mang-mang chi-chi*). But she also admitted, in a passage deleted from the official version of her speech published a week later, that "our understanding of the work teams also underwent a process of change" (*kuo-ch'eng*).[37] While it is true that Mao was the first to decide that conventional mobilization techniques were inappropriate for achieving the degree of mass initiative he sought, there is no evidence that he issued any definite order against their dispatch or requested their withdrawal until late July, about fifty days after they were sent.[38]

Nor was Liu's fault a rigid commitment to the organizational status quo that precluded purges or major structural reform. The speed with which the Party organization purged unpopular school administrations and Party committees (June 2, 4, 5) belies any such impression. An incomplete tabulation showed that thirteen high officials in eleven universities were dismissed and publicly humiliated during the fifty days, including Li Ta (President of Wuhan University), Ho Lu-ting (Shanghai Municipal College), *et al.*[39] Liu also dissolved the Communist Youth League in early June because of its involvement with the cultural-academic establishment,[40] and it was this act (rather than an undercover network of People's Liberation Army (PLA) agents, an early speculation which has never been documented)[41] that most facili-

[37] I am indebted to Professor Tang Tsou for these quotations from the unexpurgated text of Chiang Ch'ing's November 28 address; the official version is in *SCMP*, no. 3908 (March 30, 1967): 9–16.

[38] Chou En-lai claimed Mao was not even aware that work teams had been sent: "The Chairman has not been in Peking for several weeks and is thus not responsible for the comrades who badly interpret his instructions, and in particular he does not know about the work teams sent to the universities and municipal governments." Quoted in Gigon, *Vie et Mort*, p. 99.

[39] Parris H. Chang, "Provincial Party Leaders' Strategies for Survival During the Cultural Revolution," in *Elites in the People's Republic of China*, ed. Robert A. Scalapino (Seattle, Wash., 1972), p. 510.

[40] "Self-Examination" (October 23, 1966), *LSWTC*, pp. 621–625.

[41] "This opposition had to be the army; no other political force in China was so well organized and disciplined as to be able to carry out a nation-wide operation in such well-guarded secrecy." Jerome Ch'en, *Mao*, p. 40. In endorsing the same suspicion, Whitson admits that "Unfortunately, there is little evidence of low-level commissar support for and participation in the Red Guard movement. We can, therefore, only speculate that commissars did in fact select and advise students at various universities and middle schools." *The Chinese High Command*, p. 373. Such a "speculation" is based on the estimate that open opposition to the Party would not have materialized without clandestine support from "backstage backers." However, opposition did materialize during the "Hundred Flowers" without such

tated the organization of extra-Party Red Guard groups. In response to student complaints of "discrimination against descendants of workers and peasants" in the schools, the Party moved swiftly to reform the school system, anticipating many of the "Maoist" reforms adopted after the GPCR. On June 13, the CC announced abolition of the existing admissions system of exams in institutions of higher learning on the grounds that the exam system shut out children of good class background. On June 17, Liu ordered the Propaganda Department to tackle the question of educational reform, teaching reform, and pedagogical methods. Beginning in the fall of 1966, students would be admitted by recommendation and selection and new teaching materials would be compiled under the guidance of Mao's Thought, "putting politics in command." [42]

If the dispatch of work teams cannot in itself be considered either a deviation from standard organizational procedures or a clear case of disobedience, and if Liu opposed neither a purge of the Party nor structural reforms of the cultural-educational establishment, was his "error" then merely a contrived pretext to purge him on the basis of accumulated but unstated grievances? The overstated and somewhat inconsistent nature of the Maoist criticisms of Liu's actions during the "fifty days" gives rise to this impression, but we must take into account the Maoists' need to simplify their criticisms in terms readily comprehensible to all. The strongest reason to assume that Liu indeed committed errors during the fifty days comes from Liu, who bore witness to them in eloquent detail in his self-criticisms. The magnitude of his error and what portion of blame may justly be ascribed to him for difficulties that continued to plague the GPCR even after he was rendered powerless are intrinsically more equivocal issues and will receive further consideration later, but neither Liu nor his supporters ever denied that he had committed errors.

The essence of Liu's error was to place a higher priority on order than on spontaneous mass self-expression, to put adherence to procedural rules of discussion and debate above Mao's desire to maximize the mobilization-participation aspects of the movement. "Shanghai is very orderly. There is no disruption," he complimented Ts'ao Ti-ch'iu on his way through the city in July. "This shows that your municipal

---

backing. There was a tendency throughout the GPCR to suspect that all political action was secretly choreographed, but one can no more infer the existence of secret organization from the fact of widespread opposition to the Party than one can impute secret organization to Liu from the continuing opposition of Party capitalist-roaders to Red Guard mobilization.

42 "Record," *JPRS*, no. 42349, pp. 22–23.

committee enjoys high prestige and commands the obedience of the masses." [43] Indeed, Liu's notion of authority seemed to equate "prestige" with "obedience" and give rather short shrift to participation, and he viewed the revolutionary activities inspired by the CCRG not as encouraging manifestations of revolutionary elan, but as signals of a crisis of authority demanding immediate countermeasures. "We considered it an extremely bad situation," confessed Teng Hsiao-p'ing. "Confounded by the so-called 'chaos' and putting fear above everything else, we were in a hurry to find medicine and hastily sent work teams to control the movement in the name of strengthening leadership. This actually had the effect of strangling the movement." [44] As Liu put it in the concluding passages of his October self-criticism:

I did not understand that the Great Cultural Revolution marked a new stage of more intensive and extensive development in the socialist revolution, nor did I understand how the Cultural Revolution could be carried out. . . . I distrusted the masses and could not make up my mind to mobilize the masses to conduct self-education and self-liberation. On the contrary, I believed completely in the functions of the work teams, wanting to monopolize the mass movement. I was gripped by the fear of confusion, great democracy, rebellion by the masses against us, and uprisings of counterrevolutionaries. [45]

Although the Maoist contention that Liu erred in sending work teams is not altogether logically satisfying, as we have seen, Liu's handling of the work-team difficulties symptomized and symbolized his misconceived approach to the GPCR. "My mistakes aggravated the teams' blunders," he later admitted. "Although it was no more than fifty days, the damage was enormous. Up to now the results of such damage have not been reckoned. It accounts for the acuteness of opposition among the masses in certain places." [46]

In organizational terms, the Liu-Teng error may be attributed to a problem familiar to organization theorists everywhere, that of *systematically blocked communication*. This blockage may in turn be subdivided into three aspects for closer scrutiny: (1) blocked lateral communication; (2) blocked vertical communication; and (3) the "mechanical" application of excessively severe sanctions by lower levels acting in quasi-autonomous self-defense.

[43] Speech by a representative of the Revolutionary Rebels in the Shanghai Municipal Committee's Urban Socialist Education Office in the Shanghai Municipal Committee's Cultural Revolution Group at the January rally in Shanghai, quoted in Hunter, *Shanghai Journal*, p. 42.

[44] "Teng Hsiao-p'ing's Self-Criticism at the Work Conference of the CCP CC" (October 23, 1966), *CL&G* 6, no. 12 (September 1970): 84–90.

[45] Liu, "Self-Examination" (October 23, 1966), in *LSWTC*, pp. 621–625

[46] *Ibid.*

(1) The most fundamental impediment to lateral communication was created by the organization's use of discriminatory ascriptive criteria for participation in the movement, which formed the basis for enduring factional cleavage. Upon Liu's dissolution of the CYL organization within which student mobilization had commenced in June, the CYL grouped its members into two categories: those with "five good" class backgrounds (worker, peasant, cadre, soldier, and revolutionary martyr) were released and urged to participate in the GPCR; children of the "free professions" (including doctors, shop clerks, teachers, technicians, middle peasants, and the like) received no definite assignment but were allowed to participate; children of the "five black'" classes (landlords, rich peasants, counterrevolutionaries, bad elements, and rightists) were categorically excluded from either CYL or GPCR.[47] This initial "class" segregation by the Party organization created the basis for two opposing factions. "The 'August 1st Regiment' supported you, and other corps put up big-character posters against it. Chia Chien asked you to stay at the college; other students raised objections!" Liu exclaimed in a talk with work-team representatives on August 4, "I can't blame you for your activities, the question is that a group of people supported you and another group of people did not support you." [48]

Just as participants were segregated from nonparticipants within the schools, making each school a honeycomb of different categories, they were also confined to the campuses and barred from contact with rebel groups at other schools or from recruiting expeditions among the populace; students were treated like the lower echelons of the bureaucracy and expected to conform to the discipline of inner-Party struggle.[49] In early June, Liu hurriedly convened a central work conference in Peking to formulate the "Eight Articles of the CC," which stipulated: (1) no big-character posters in the street; (2) no rallies in the street; (3) no parades in the street; (4) no encirclement of residences; (5) the drawing of a clear distinction between the inside and the outside; (6) watchfulness against sabotage by bad elements; (7) a ban on manhandling and insulting others; and (8) the prevention of the undesirable development of the movement. Each member of the work team in a given school was assigned to one class, and each class,

---

47 Giovanni Blumer, *Die Chinesische Kulturrevolution, 1965–1967* (Frankfurt / M., 1968), pp. 197–204. Blumer resided in Peking from 1965 to 1967.

48 *CW* 3: 350; see also Ken Ling, *Revenge of Heaven: Journal of a Young Chinese*, trans. Miriam London and Ta-ling Lee (New York, 1972), p. 22.

49 Jean Daubier, *Histoire de la Révolution Culturelle Prolétarienne en Chine* (Paris, 1971), 1: 81, 84–85. Daubier lived in Peking from 1966 to 1968 and bases his report solely on his personal observations.

department, and school was strictly isolated. The work teams conducted "anti-interference movements" to catch those "wandering fish" (i.e., outside agitators) who defied injunctions against communication between schools. Liu subsequently insisted that such actions were undertaken at work-team initiative, but a work-team representative pointed out that "it was not only tacitly accepted but also arranged for" by the Peking Party Committee.[50] Of course, all of these barriers on lateral communication impeded the sort of extensive mobilization Mao had in mind, and created friction between students and work teams.

(2) Liu and Teng acknowledged the Party as the only legitimate channel of vertical communication, deliberately isolating the center from information that did not go through this channel. When K'uai Ta-fu, an outspoken Tsinghua University rebel, tried to appeal his conviction as a "counterrevolutionary" to the CC, Liu refused to see him, and when K'ang Sheng complained that his refusal was "at least not in correspondence with state law and is in contravention to the Constitution," Liu told K'ang he "failed to understand the situation." By systematically limiting their sources of information to what was filtered through the bureaucratic apparatus, which became more slanted and self-vindicating as the struggle polarized, the Liuist center reinforced its commitment to its originally misguided policy. Liu did counsel flexibility and tolerance in dealing with dissident students, and when the work teams became embroiled in insuperable difficulties, he replaced them; but he did not, until Mao requested it, withdraw the work teams. Even when he counseled greater tolerance in dealing with the rebels, he did so as a tactic for achieving more effective control: "Let them dominate for a period of time and then put Communist Party members under rectification; they will betray themselves!"[51]

From Liu's point of view, the monopolization of vertical communication by the Party was necessary to preserve its structural legitimacy, which was based on a hierarchical relationship of "democratic centralism" between the center and the branches rather than on each individual branch's claim to ideological legitimacy. The Party was the organizational embodiment of Mao's Thought and sole legitimate mediator of the mass line and could not tolerate the organization of autonomous political groups. According to the Tsinghua "Record," Liu referred to the Red Guards as an "illegal organization": "Teachers and students are not permitted to hold meetings in secret. The Red

50 "Talks on Work Groups, June through July, 1966," SCMM, no. 653 (May 5, 1969): 17–19.
51 Ibid.

Guard is a secret organization and illegal." He called for prompt restoration of the leadership functions of the Party branches and foresaw
early termination of the movement. Early in July, Liu and Teng
ordered one-third of the middle schools to end the movement in mid-
August and the rest to do so by October 1, to be ready to reopen
school on September 1; "Further discussion of it will be tasteless." [52]
Liu thus identified himself from the outset as the chief foe of the
organization of autonomous Red Guard units and of the interpretation of Mao's Thought that legitimized such organization.

(3) The apparatus was taken aback by the strength and intensity
of student resistance to the work teams and registered its shock by invoking punitive sanctions of Draconian severity against all "trouble-
makers," whatever their ideological bent. Most of the work teams
had been formed during the SEM in 1964; certain of them remained in
the same place and resumed their activities in 1966; others were freshly
formed and sent into a situation utterly foreign to them under the
leadership of high-ranking cadres.[53] The teams were usually comprised
of uneducated basic-level cadres of peasant background who were not
accustomed to "trouble-shooting" in educational institutions. Both
students and work-team members were conscious of the status differences between them, which seemed to engender intellectual contempt
on the part of the students [54] and "commandism" on the part of the
work teams: "the work teams made mistakes and refused to answer the
questions raised by fellow students," K'uai Ta-fu complained. "The
work team had divorced itself from the masses." [55]

Due to the selective constraints on vertical communication, which re-
layed the work teams' version of the situation but precluded any
objective presentation of the case of their opponents, the center backed
the work teams to the hilt. On July 8, Liu told his daughter T'ao that
"he regarded all students opposed to the work group as bourgeois
elements and gave them no freedom and democracy," on the contrary proposing that K'uai Ta-fu should be "shot at as a living tar-

52 "Record," *JPRS*, no. 42349, p. 24.

53 Daubier, *Histoire* 1: 70–80.

54 As one former rebel later put it, "The working style of the work team members
was very bad: They had all come in from the Four Clean Movement in the
countryside. Maybe peasants listened to them when they talked so arrogantly, but
we weren't peasants. We were mature students who could not be treated like
clods." William Hinton, "Hundred Day War: The Cultural Revolution at
Tsinghua University," *Monthly Review* 24, no. 3 (July–August 1972): 46–47.

55 "K'uai Ta-fu's Speeches at the June 27 Debate: First Speech," in *Selected
Big-Character Posters of Tsinghua University*, compiled by Chingkangshan Red
Guard Propaganda Team of Tsinghua University (n.d.), p. 1.

get." [56] Organizational constraints on communication thus facilitated the application of blind, "mechanical" sanctions—sanctions defined routinely without much concern for extenuating circumstances or ideological considerations.

If Red Guard reports may be believed, the actions of the Tsinghua work team (which included Liu's wife Wang Kuang-mei, operating under the pseudonym "Hou P'u") set forth a disciplinary regimen that was particularly drastic. According to the criticisms, the work team promptly dismissed the university's president and replaced the Party committee; all lower-level cadres were challenged to present comprehensive self-criticisms to the students in a special meeting called for this purpose and thus "pass the test," with 70 percent of the 500 cadres being sent to be reformed in labor teams; higher-ranking cadres were spared self-criticism and referred to higher authorities for disciplinary action. Student resistance to the work teams was rewarded by dispensation of "counterrevolutionary" labels by the hundreds; one person was killed and several reportedly committed suicide.[57]

Such punishment contributed to the formation of a bitter personal vendetta against the Lius, particularly at Tsinghua. As Chingkangshan rebels noted in a statement attached to the copy of Liu's first self-criticism when they published it six months later, "When work teams oppressed the revolutionary masses, we were forced to write self-examinations 10,000 characters long. Liu Shao-ch'i writes only a short one; can this be considered adequate?" [58]

In its contumacy, Liu's error resembled that of P'eng Chen before him. Like P'eng, who committed himself to Wu Han from the outset and then found it impossible to abandon him when the conflict intensified, finally coming into direct confrontation with Mao, Liu initially backed the Party organization; his support was then fortified by the opposition the work teams precipitated, and ultimately he found his position polarized to that of a "bourgeois dictator." However, while P'eng knew as early as November 1965 that Mao was behind the criticisms of Wu Han and still chose to protect Wu, Mao took no clear stand on the work-team issue until he returned to Peking in late July, leaving the Liuist "center" to take the initiative, then condemning Liu's errors in retrospect. This makes the subsequent con-

56 Cf. Liu T'ao, "Rebel Against Liu Shao-ch'i, Follow Chairman Mao to Make Revolution for Life—My Preliminary Self-Examination," *Chingkangshan*, December 31, 1966, in *CB*, no. 821 (March 16, 1967): 1–25.

57 "Down with Liu Shao-ch'i," *Chingkangshan* (Peking) (May 1967), in *CB*, no. 834 (August 17, 1967): 27; also *RF*, no. 5 (1967).

58 Fan Shu-cheng, "Tzu-wo chien-ch'a pao-kao," *Ming pao yüeh-k'an*, pp. 30 ff.

demnation of Liu for deliberately perpetrating a "bourgeois reactionary line" *ethically* problematic; but in an analysis of organizational
dynamics it becomes an even more interesting error than P'eng Chen's,
for while P'eng deliberately violated an organizational norm (democratic centralism), Liu in good conscience followed norms that were
systematically misconceived. In Louis Althusser's terms, whereas P'eng's
error was one of "transitive causation," Liu's was one of "structural
causation," [59] revealing as it did certain propensities inherent in the
Party organization, particularly when that organization was confronted
by challenges "from below." This may be illustrated by an example
from Liu's earlier career when the organization was also so challenged
—the land reform campaign at P'ingshan in 1947.

Liu's February 1948 "Summary of Experience"—an extremely in-
sightful report—indicates that, just as in the work team episode, the
masses rose against the organization, causing disarray: "The masses
rose to struggle against the bad Party members and cadres. In many
districts Party members and cadres were arrested and beaten, causing
panic among other members and cadres." Like the work teams, the
organization reacted punitively: "The work teams insisted, rather me-
chanically, on hitting the landlords first and solving the cadre question
afterwards. They arbitrarily separated land reform from the democratic movement of Party rectification; they restrained the masses from
carrying out struggles against Party members and cadres, or removed
large groups of Party members and cadres whom the masses opposed
like 'stones.'" Like the work teams, they also attempted to divert
the wrath of the masses to innocuous scapegoats: "the work teams
abused their power by compelling the masses to carry out struggles
against the landlords who had already been struggled against in an
attempt to whip up a high tide." [60]

There are conflicting reports about the extent of the havoc wreaked
by GPCR work teams that are difficult to reconcile, given the controversial character of the materials. On the one hand, there are widespread reports of resistance: a series of incidents, such as those of June
16, 20, and 24, were reported at various schools, in which students
launched "struggles to oust cadres." On July 12, the first big-character
poster attacking the work team appeared at Peking University, whereupon the team leader was induced to submit three consecutive self-
criticisms on July 16, 17, and 18. Liu T'ao quoted her father as saying
in late June that there was opposition to work teams in thirty-nine

[59] Louis Althusser, *Reading Capital*, trans. B. Brewster (London, 1970), p. 224.
[60] "P'ingshan Sets Examples in Land Reform and Party Rectification" (February
1948), *CW* 2: 119–123.

of the more than fifty schools in the Peking municipality; [61] Mao claimed that "more than 90 percent of the work teams throughout the country have followed wrong directions and policy lines." [62] On the other hand, a sympathetic French observer writes: "The Party propaganda later exalted this opposition. With all the limitations attached to an individual witness, I must say that my impression was that this resistance, . . . was on the whole a minority." [63] On July 10, Liu told the work team at Teachers' University that "the danger has passed"; a Red Guard chronology confirms that, in the second ten days of July, "the movement calmed; some schools proposed a resumption of classwork." [64]

The question of the extent of resistance to work teams is interesting but not really germane to the crux of Mao's objection, which was not that the work teams wreaked widespread havoc (on the contrary, he said on August 23 that a few months of "chaos" would be "mostly to the good"), but that they had "strangled" the great movement he wished to incite—an objection that had undoubted validity. On July 16, Mao made his famous sixty-five-minute, nine-mile swim in the Yangtze (curiously unannounced in *PD* until July 25), and two days later he arrived in Peking. "Four days after my arrival in Peking, I was still inclined to preserve the existing order of things," [65] he said, but this may ascribe more circumspection to his decision-making process than was the case. On the day of his arrival (July 18) he telephoned a dramatic message to Tsinghua rebels, which the latter recorded for exhibition on a poster:

It seems to me that I must personally think about the end of the revolution. Am I on the right side? No! Will China be no longer proletariat, but bourgeois, at the end of the movement? Absolutely not! Why am I afraid? Haven't we seen what they want after the first period? Reviling, intimidation, threats, blackmailing—posting of "labels" everywhere, striking with sticks and pouring of reproaches of a certain "big general" [Liu Shao-ch'i] into one's ear.[66]

"It is anti-Marxist for the Communist Party to fear the student movement," he said on July 21 in a talk to a reception of regional secretaries and CCRG members. He proposed

61 Liu T'ao, "Rebel Against Liu," *CB*, no. 821.

62 *Mainichi*, October 22, in *DSJP*, October 25, 1966, pp. 15–16.

63 Daubier, *Histoire*, 1: 87.

64 "Record," *JPRS*, no. 42349, pp. 24–25.

65 "Address to Regional Secretaries and Members of the Cultural Revolution Group under the CC" (July 22, 1966), in *CB*, no. 891 (October 8, 1969): 60.

66 Blumer, *Kulturrevolution*, p. 146.

to transform work teams into either liaison teams or advisory teams. You say that advisory teams would be too powerful. Well, call them liaison teams then. In a month or so they have hampered the revolution; in fact they have helped the counterrevolution. . . . The work teams can neither struggle nor reform, not in six months or a year. The only people who can are those in the organizations in question.[67]

On July 24, Mao called a meeting of the Party Center including Liu Shao-ch'i, Li Hsüeh-feng, and the CCRG, to discuss withdrawal of work teams; it was decided to withdraw them. On July 29, at a congress of Cultural Revolution activists, Mao received all delegates; Liu, Teng, and Chou spoke, and Li Hsüeh-feng announced the decision to withdraw the teams: "You are urged to lead yourselves and carry out revolution by your own efforts," he said.[68]

Liu Shao-ch'i had put the full weight of his prestige behind the work-team policy even as Mao had earlier committed himself to the communes and GLF, and yet within a matter of days that policy had been reversed and repudiated. Given his heavy investment of "face" in the policy, one might have expected Liu to resist its reversal, even as Mao had resisted P'eng Te-huai's attempt to reverse the Leap programs at Lushan and had then tried to vindicate those programs during the GPCR. The question of Liu's reaction to this setback is of more than human interest—it bears on the accuracy of the central Maoist charge that Liu "stubbornly refused to repent" in the face of nearly universal criticism, and thus warrants close scrutiny.

According to his daughter, T'ao, this was a period of intense inner turmoil for Liu. T'ao said she had never seen her father so "vexed," that he paced from one end of the drawing room to the other. "On the evening of July 26, 1966, Ch'en Po-ta . . . and Chiang Ch'ing . . . told us at the University of Peking about the last failure of the so-called work teams and bitterly criticized that failure," she recalled. "When I told my father . . . he became exasperated and would not admit his error, saying, 'the work teams must not be blamed'." On July 28, he contacted T'ao (a leader in the student movement at Peking University) and said, "Withdrawal must be quick, otherwise it will become impossible." That evening, according to T'ao,

Liu Shao-ch'i said with emotion to me and Wang Kuang-mei: "They want me to make a self-examination, don't they? (1) If they want me to come to your school to make a self-examination, I will do so for there is nothing to

[67] "Address to the Regional Secretaries" (July 22, 1966), in *CB*, no. 891 (October 8, 1969): 60.
[68] "Report," *JPRS*, no. 42349, p. 29; "Talks to CC Leaders, July 21, 1966," *CB*, no. 891, pp. 58–59.

be feared. (2) The work group carries out its work in public. (3) Now that the work group has nothing to do, you should perform some labor and help write wall posters and sweep the floor. In this way, your schoolmates will not accuse you of behaving like officials and lords.[69]

She added that whereas Liu had always been rather laconic, he became even more so after he had "committed mistakes." At one point, when T'ao intimated that Liu's mistake was not "fortuitous," her mother "made an outburst," saying, "Your father serves on the CC, and there are things he cannot tell you. But you always exert pressure on him." Her father added: "If you feel this family hampers you, you may renounce it, and if you are not financially independent, I can give you money." By early August, "when I asked him what he thought of his own problems, he verbally acknowledged that he had made errors in orientation and in line and indicated that he was willing to remold himself." [70]

Liu was among the "responsible comrades" whom Mao encouraged to go out and observe the situation on the campuses, and Liu visited the Peking Building Construction Institute from August 2 to 4 and spoke with both Red Guards and work-team representatives there. Though his talks exhibit some of the ambivalence inherent in his suddenly untenable position, his intention to implement withdrawal and reorient the movement in the direction Mao had indicated was apparent. In his talks, he acknowledged error on behalf of the CC for dispatching work teams: "It seems . . . that it would have been better not to appoint the work teams and that it was not right to do so." He was extremely critical of the mistakes of the work teams, many of which he said he heard of for the first time, while at the same time acknowledging the responsibility of the higher leadership. ("The municipal committee should take responsibility on your behalf. The CC will take the responsibility on behalf of the municipal Party committee. You needn't push the responsibility upwards.") Accurately noting that "the basic problem is that it is permissible to oppose others but not me," Liu reproached the teams for their harsh overreaction to student indiscipline. ("You called the students reactionary without sufficient grounds! You can't make this conclusion. When the students put up big-character posters, you work teams were sure that they were reactionary students. Did the students know that?") But at the same time Liu noted, "You arrested these few [twelve "wandering fish"]. The students would have arrested many more." He continued to stress the importance of organization in implementing the GPCR ("you still

[69] Liu T'ao, "Rebel Against Liu," *CB*, no. 821.   [70] *Ibid.*

have to rely on the Party organization system") and proposed a number of organizational innovations to assure greater Party responsiveness to the masses, including reelection of Party and Youth League committees and admission of mass representatives to previously secret committee meetings in a number doubling that of the cadres in attendance.[71] Underlying his remarks was his unchanged view of the GPCR as a disturbance that ought to be conciliated rather than exacerbated, however, and in this respect he certainly differed with the CCRG, and probably with Mao as well. He admitted as much in a self-criticism delivered to the same school nearly a year later:

I believed that unity which was achieved on the basis of a desire for unity and after adequate discussions and debates—in the course of which the right was distinguished from the wrong, the truth was upheld and the mistakes were corrected—was precisely what we needed at that time. We could not say that such unity was "combining two into one." Here, of course, I should make an examination.[72]

Liu's reaction to the crisis created by the work teams—temporarily to rend the veil separating "inner-Party struggle" from "class conflict" and give the extra-Party masses a voice in the rectification of the Party —parallels his solution to the land reform crisis at P'ingshan nearly twenty years before:

Hence it is not simply a technical but a serious political problem for the rural Party branches to accept openly the masses' views and to reform and educate Party members. It was the mystery [shen-mi] of the rural Party branches in the past that made it possible for the bad elements to isolate the Party from the masses. Today [1948] we have opened the doors of the Party to the public in the old liberated areas. . . . Non-Party peasants invited to the meetings have every right to speak, give evidence and express their views. Hence, the peasants who come with grievances to vent through villification and revenge find their attitude is unconsciously changed to one of "treating an illness to save a patient." [73]

Even this relatively enlightened policy was not to win acceptance in 1966. This was partly because the organization of extra-Party radical student groups had already received not only ideological legitimation, but also elite backing, first from Mao's advisors, then from Mao himself, and quickly developed its own powerful polemical momentum,

---

[71] "Talk to the GPCR Corps" (n.d.); "Talk to the August 1 Combat Corps" (August 3, 1966), and "Talk to the Work Team of the Peking College of Construction Engineering" (August 4, 1966), in CW 3: 331–345.

[72] Liu, "Self-Examination" (July 9, 1967), CW 3: 369–377; Chinese text in LSWTC, pp. 625–628.

[73] CW 2: 121.

dramatizing any resistance it encountered to enhance its moral appeal. It was partly because Mao immediately raised such grave questions about Liu's "line" that Liu no longer felt authorized to implement policy. The Chinese political system thus found itself embarked upon a much more radical solution to the estrangement between mass and elite, one that was to engender its own problems in the form of violent mass factionalism.

On August 5, Mao posted his first big-character poster, and the concluding sentences left little doubt as to which way the "spearhead" was pointing:

However, in the last fifty days or more, certain leading comrades at the center and in the localities have taken the opposite road. Taking the reactionary bourgeois stand, they exercise bourgeois dictatorship, put down the vigorous movement of the proletariat for [the] Great Cultural Revolution, confound right and wrong and black and white, launch concerted attacks on the revolutionaries from all sides, repress dissident views, and impose a White terror. . . . Putting two and two together and recalling to mind the rightist tendency in 1962 and the erroneous tendency in 1964 that was "left" in form but rightist in essence, do we not find something that should wake one up? [74]

Given its authoritative source and national dissemination, this poster constituted a reinterpretation of the magnitude of Liu's error that was to be of far-reaching importance. "I began to understand this mistake I myself had made only after Chairman Mao's big-character poster bombarding the headquarters came out on August 5," Liu said later. "Before that, I did not know I had committed such a grave error." [75] Mao's poster did four things: it ascribed the principal responsibility for the work teams' errors to Liu; it introduced the interpretation that Liu's error was an error of "line" rather than one of mere work style; it linked Liu's error to previous errors in his career, intimating that it was not a momentary lapse but the symptom of a permanent character defect; and finally, it contained the implication that Liu's error was deliberate. Liu told Li Hsüeh-feng that, in the light of this indictment, he could "no longer interfere with the affairs" of the GPCR and withdrew. On August 22, he "reserved his opinion" on Mao's poster, stressing that in contradistinction to P'eng Chen, "It was without any purpose that I established the bourgeois reactionary line, and it involves no behind-the-scene activities." [76]

[74] "Long Live the Thought," CB, no. 891, p. 63.
[75] "Self-Examination" (October 23, 1966), in LSWTC, pp. 621–625.
[76] Sankei, April 19, in DSJP, April 19, 1967, p. 22.

Mao's reaction to Liu's mistake at P'ingshan in 1947 was a pointed and quite explicit rebuke,[77] but no organizational sanctions were imposed at that time. Mao's immediate response to Liu's errors in handling the work teams in 1966 was a much sharper *public* reprimand, followed by the imposition of organizational sanctions and finally by public criticism and purge. As to the reasons for Mao's harsher reaction to Liu's errors in handling the work teams than to his parallel error almost two decades earlier, several lines of speculation seem plausible. Mao may have considered the work-team error more serious and consequential, though similar in form. Its very similarity could have convinced him of the existence of a fatal flaw in Liu, which he had earlier dismissed as a temporary aberration. In recent conversations with Edgar Snow and André Malraux, Mao had referred to his impending death, and, as heir apparent, Liu was bound to come under sharper scrutiny now than when the prospect of succession seemed remote. Finally, Mao may have been predisposed to judge Liu harshly on the basis of personal and policy frictions that had developed between the two men over the past several years, as suggested in Chapter 3.

DECLINE AND FALL

Liu's decline and fall took a very long time and occasioned an absolutely unprecedented amount of public criticism, during which his errors became disembodied from his person and denounced as a comprehensive system of evil. The Maoist justifications for the expenditure of two years of agitational activity and more than 3,000 polemical articles were that Liu was personally blameworthy for the evils the GPCR was mobilized to renounce and that he had failed to make proper amends for them within the framework of redemption known as "criticism and sel-criticism"—i.e., that he had "refused to repent." In this section we thus examine Liu's personal reaction to the abuse accompanying the progressive redefinition of the gravity of

[77] Mao said: "Following instructions given by comrade Liu Shao-ch'i in person last spring and helped by work done by comrade K'ang Sheng . . . the Shansi-Suiyüan Subbureau held a conference of secretaries of the prefectural Party committees last year. . . . In the main, the conference was a success. The shortcomings of the conference were that it failed to decide on working policies varying with the different conditions in the old, semi-old, and new Liberated Areas; that on the question of identifying class status it adopted an ultra-left policy; that on the question of how to destroy the feudal system it laid too much stress on unearthing the landlords' hidden property; and that on the question of dealing with the demands of the masses it failed to make a sober analysis and raised the sweeping slogan, 'Do everything as the masses want it done.' " "Speech at a Conference of Cadres in the Shansi-Suiyüan Liberated Area" (April 1, 1948), *SW* 4: 231–232.

his crimes and attempt to assess the subjective factors that may have contributed to his failure to achieve atonement.

An "enlarged" session of the CC convened its Eleventh Plenum in Peking on Army Day (August 1), 1966. Although Mao resorted to the extraordinary measures of packing the galleries with radical youthful supporters and convoking only about half the total CC membership,[78] he later complained that "only after discussion was I able to get a little more than half the votes to favor me." It is doubtful whether Liu actively led this opposition, for, as we have seen, he had already commited himself to a reversal of his "line," and, in any case, the cloud of Mao's big-character poster hovered over him four days after the beginning of the session. Mao's own specification of his opponents mentioned only provincial and regional leaders, and Liu's name does not appear in available transcripts of the plenum talks. Four years later, when Edgar Snow asked Mao about Liu's role in the plenum, Mao replied, in essence, that Liu had been thrown into consternation by Mao's first big-character poster and took a very ambiguous attitude toward "The Sixteen Points" adopted by the plenum.[79]

"During the latter part of the plenum the question of our mistakes was brought up for discussion, which was followed by the election of members of the Standing Committee of the CC," Liu recounted. "At the plenum comrade Lin Piao was unanimously recommended as Chairman Mao's first assistant and successor." [80] Lin also became the sole vice-chairman, and Liu was demoted from second to eighth place in the Politiburo listings. Teng Hsiao-p'ing, apparently not yet deeply implicated in the work-team imbroglio, remained General Secretary and retained his previous ranking. Despite his eighth-place rank, Liu's status remained ambiguous. In the plenum's "Decision on the GPCR" ("The Sixteen Points."), cadres were grouped into four categories according to the gravity of their mistakes: "(1) the good; (2) the relatively good; (3) those with serious mistakes but who are not anti-Party and antisocialist elements; (4) a small number of anti-Party and antisocialist rightists." Those in the first two categories were said to embrace the "majority"; those in the third would be targets of "criticism"; and those in the fourth would be "fully exposed, pulled down, and completely discredited." [81] Liu's position in this classification system was

78 According to Soviet sources, Mao was able to bring together only 46 of 91 members and 33 of 89 candidates for the Eleventh Plenum. N. I. Kapcenko, *Peking: Politka, Cuzdaja Socializmu* (Moscow, 1967), p. 63; quoted in Dieter Heinzig, *Die Krise der Kommunistischen Partei Chinas in der Kulturrevolution* (Hamburg, 1969, no. 26).

79 Snow, *The Long Revolution*, p. 18.

80 Liu, "Self-Examination" (October 23, 1966), *LSWTC*, pp. 621–625.

81 "The Resolutions of the Eleventh Plenum of the CC of the CCP—The Sixteen Articles" (August 8, 1966), in Jerome Ch'en, *Mao Papers*, pp. 117–127.

not stated (nor was anyone else's, justifying free-floating suspicion of all authorities), but it was generally assumed at that time that the "Party persons in authority taking the capitalist road" were in the fourth category and consisted of the "P'eng-Lo-Lu-Yang group" which was segregated by a "friends-enemies" distinction from the "bourgeois reactionary line" (of Liu and Teng) in the *third* category. In other words, Liu's "bourgeois reactionary line" was still a "contradiction among the people," as an *RF* editorial later confirmed:

Generally speaking, the contradiction between those comrades who have committed the error of line and the Party and the masses is still a contradiction among the people. So long as they are able to correct the error, revert to the correct stand and carry out the correct line of the Party, they can be not just cadres of the second or third grade but can also develop to become cadres of the first grade.[82]

Liu's demotion became public knowledge on August 18 at the first of eight mass rallies; when Mao and other CC leaders gathered atop the T'ienanmen rostrum to receive the Red Guards, don *Hung wei-ping* brassards, and celebrate the GPCR, Liu's name was not mentioned. Toward the end of the radio broadcast, "various other responsible participants in the rally" were introduced; at this point, Liu's name was read in eighth place, after those of Teng and K'ang. He was not in any of the photos taken of the rally; in the documentary film produced at the time, only three men—Mao, Lin, and Chou—are shown together on the screen, while Liu is shown only once and for a moment, on a corner of the screen.

Liu, perhaps hurt by his demotion and ill-disposed toward the young rebels who precipitated his undoing, seems to have vacated his office even before the rally was held. On August 17, the new ambassador of Syria, Bachir Sadek, presented his credentials, and it was Tung Pi-wu, Vice-Chairman of the Chinese People's Republic (C.P.R.), who received him, though Liu had customarily been doing this. The Zambian Vice-President, Reuben Kamanga, arrived in Peking as head of a delegation on August 19; protocol does not require Liu to be at the airport to greet him, but he should have been present at a dinner given the same day by Chou En-lai and Tung Pi-wu. On August 21, Kamanga called on Mao, who received him with Tung, Chou, and Ch'en I; Liu was again absent; on August 22, the delegation left Peking without seeing Liu.[83]

82 *RF*, no. 14 (November 1, 1966): 1 ff.

83 *Asahi*, September 28, in *DSJP*, October 6, 1966, pp. 10–12; *CNS*, no. 134 (August 25, 1966): 4–6.

Mao Tse-tung, during this interlude, showed no inclination to endorse a full-fledged denunciation of Liu Shao-ch'i. In his final speech to the Eleventh Plenum on August 8, he said, "Our policy is 'to punish those who have committed mistakes so that others will not follow them' and 'to cure the disease in order to save the patient.' " [84] Accordingly, the Maoists tried to dissuade Red Guards from pressing their criticism of Liu. It was reported two months later:

When it was mentioned that on August 24 [1966], Chiang Ch'ing had asked Ch'en Po-ta to stop [others from] posting big-character posters against Liu, comrade Chiang Ch'ing said that was a matter of several months ago! [85]

When Liu appeared on the reviewing stand at T'ienanmen for National Day ceremonies on October 1, his position appeared to have improved. Although Japanese newsmen detected a coolness between Mao and Liu, and former Kwangtung Red Guard Dai Hsiao-ai thought Liu looked "dispirited," [86] Liu was listed third in the official name list (rather than eighth), and when Mao walked from one end of the balcony to the other toward the end of the ceremony, Liu walked with him; when Mao left the balcony, Liu took his place and reviewed the parade.[87]

At the October 5–28 work conference, the Maoists resumed their criticisms of Liu Shao-ch'i, and Ch'en Po-ta now implicated Teng Hsiao-p'ing as well. On October 23, Liu and Teng submitted self-criticisms; both acknowledged their errors in connection with the work teams, but Liu went considerably beyond this in acknowledging responsibility for a series of mistakes dating back to 1945. To wit:

February 1, 1946: After the Political Consultative Conference was closed, I issued a directive to the CC, stating that the conference marked a new stage on the road to the realization of peace. It was a mistaken view with an illusion of peace.

Summer 1947: I presided at meetings on land reform. . . . The "left" tendency discovered then was not promptly rectified. For instance, too many people were killed and middle peasants' interests were infringed upon.

Spring 1949: I talked about many things that had happened during the period of Tientsin cadres' urban work. I proposed that certain excessively

84 Jerome Ch'en, *Mao Papers*, p. 34.
85 "Minutes of a Forum with T'ung Hsiao-p'eng [Deputy Director of the General Office, CC] (October 20, 1966), in "Collections of Speeches by Central Leaders," 4, jointly compiled by the Red Guard Commune, "Mao Tse-tung's Thought," and the Combat Group of the "Defense of the Supreme Directives," December 1966.
86 Bennett and Montaperto, *Red Guard*, pp. 117–118.
87 *Mainichi*, October 2, in *DSJP*, October 1–3, 1966, pp. 16–17; also *FEER* 54, no. 1 (October 6, 1966): 5–6.

violent ways against bourgeois industries and commerce should be checked. . . . I failed to emphasize the class contradiction between capitalists and workers, thus committing a right opportunist error.

July 1951: I wrongly criticized the Shansi Provincial Party Committee, pointing out that they should not have developed the mutual-aid team into higher-level agricultural cooperatives.

1955: Comrade Teng Tzu-hui proposed to reduce the size of 200,000 cooperatives or dissolve them. The CC meeting over which I presided raised no objection, thereby giving virtual approval to this plan.

1962: I committed right opportunism. . . . At the central work conference of February 21–26, 1962, over which I presided, [we] discussed the central fiscal budget and discovered a fiscal budget deficit amounting to two billion *yüan.* As a result, I made a wrong calculation of the difficulties, thinking that "we are now experiencing in the financial realm a highly abnormal situation in an extraordinary period." The speech made by comrade Ch'en Yün on February 26 was based on my speech at the central conference. . . . On March 18, the Center distributed his talk to every provincial, city, and district committee and instructed cadres at all levels to "conscientiously discuss it, and when discussing it, you should permit everyone to bring forth all sorts of different opinions for discussion." . . . This encouraged . . . a reverse current, a spirit of going it alone (*tan kan feng*) to come up, and there were also some people who basically criticized the general line, the GLF and the people's commune. . . . So in many areas those activists who in previous years had been active in socialist reconstruction became subject to attack. When at the Ninth Plenum in January, Teng Tzu-hui proposed a "responsibility field," I did not object, thus causing this to become a legitimate proposal. After this, he spoke at several cadre meetings in various places to encourage contracting production to the individual household (*pao-ch'an tao hu*). Yet another comrade of the CC raised the possibility of redistributing land to the individual household, and yet another raised the "three reconciliations and one reduction." These proposals were based on erroneous estimates of the domestic and international situation, and furthermore directly contradicted the socialist revolutionary . . . general line. I directly heard of the plan to distribute land to the individual household, but did not reject it; this was very mistaken.

1964: I committed apparently "left" but essentially right mistakes. . . . In speeches I made in the summer of 1964, I said that the SEM was in many places not thoroughly run and in some places had even suffered defeat. I judged that in many units the class struggle was excessively severe, but judged that cadres' commission of four unclean violations was excessive. In these speeches, I emphasized that only by squatting at a point could one launch a mass struggle and clear up the situation, and considered that the method previously recommended by Chairman Mao of convening investigation meetings was insufficient, in some cases inappropriate. This . . . was 100 percent wrong, causing a bad influence. At this time, I believed excessively in Wang Kuang-mei's experience on a brigade in T'aoyüan, let her speak at several meetings . . . then let her speech be distributed all over the country. . . . Actually the T'aoyüan work method of squatting at that time had several failings. At the time of the central work conference in 1964, . . . I said that the essence of the SEM was the contradiction between the four cleans and the four uncleans, and also said that the contradictions within the Party and the contradictions outside the Party were interlocked, or that contradictions between the enemy and the people and contradictions among the people were interlocked. But as the Twenty-Three Articles stated, these two expressions failed to clarify the basic essence of the SEM. . . . Today the . . . essence is only the contradiction between socialism and capitalism.[88]

Mao responded in a long, rambling speech made at a report meeting the next day, in which he expressed various grievances with Liu and the caretaker government he had led: these men had committed mistakes, failed to consult with him, and proceeded to run the government as if he no longer counted. With specific respect to Liu and Teng, Mao observed that estimates of their high competence had been greatly exaggerated:

Liu Shao-ch'i, criticizing Chiang Wei-ch'ing, said he was stupid. However, viewed from my position, Liu Shao-ch'i is not so smart, either. He highly praised his own wife, Wang Kuang-mei, and raised her very high. However, this Wang Kuang-mei was denounced at Tsinghua University, and she blundered also when she went to the farm villages.[89]

Of Teng, Mao said, "Teng Hsiao-p'ing believes himself to be a genius. He thinks that he can take charge of everything himself. . . . Furthermore, as to what he has been doing, he has done nothing but blunder." Despite these criticisms, when K'ang Sheng interrupted to say "[Liu's] Political Report at the Eighth Congress discussed the extinction of classes," Mao retorted: "We read the report. It was passed at the general meeting. Liu and Teng alone cannot be held responsible." [90] When Lin Piao revived the coup theme with the suggestion, "Liu and Teng have already been exposed, and it has already been made clear that they are backers of the P'eng [Chen] group. We must seek out the true facts of the February coup plot and clarify why Teng and T'ao [Chu] so hastily denied its existence and protected P'eng, and investigate whether they are connected with the plot," Mao replied, "Liu and Teng have always done their work in the open, not in

88 "Self-Examination" (October 23, 1966), *LSWTC*, pp. 621–625.   90 *Ibid.*
89 *Yomiuri*, January 8, in *DSJP*, January 7–9, 1967, p. 30.

secret. They are different from P'eng Chen." [91] When Chou En-lai spoke on behalf of Liu and Teng, Mao concurred:

Chou: No matter what the small group is, all doors must be firmly closed and strictly guarded. Everything will be well if corrected, views are unanimous and all are united. We must permit Liu and Teng to make revolution, and permit them to reform. You may say I am too conciliatory, but then I am an optimistic person.

Mao: At the Ningtu Conference, Lo Fu [Chang Wen-t'ien] wanted to expel me, but Chou and Chu [Te] did not agree. At the Tsunyi Conference he played a good role. In those days, they were quite necessary. . . . Comrade Shao-ch'i opposed them. . . . Not everything comrade Shao-ch'i has done is bad. If they have made mistakes they can probably correct them! When they have corrected them it will be all right, and they should be allowed to come back and go to work with fresh spirit.[92]

But despite Mao's concluding injunction, "It is not a good thing to put up large-character posters against Liu and Teng in the streets. People should be allowed to make some mistakes," the conference had scarcely adjourned when posters against Liu began to appear in the streets of Peking. The objective reasons for this escalation of criticisms will be examined in Chapter 5; in this section we are solely concerned with Liu's subjective reaction, which was as characteristic of the man as the error that had precipitated the criticism. He continued to discharge his official duties, making a nervous, morose appearance at a centennial for the birth of Sun Yat-sen on November 12, and appearing with Mao in the remainder of eight mass rallies, the last on November 25.[93] When Red Guards called on his wife in December, she reported that her husband "is very busy the year around. He works very hard, with a mind bent on making a success of work. He may have made mistakes but has not hatched any conspiracy." Liu's last official act as chief of state was to cosign a message of greetings to Kenya on December 11; subsequent ceremonial functions were filled by Tung Pi-wu, Chou En-lai, or Ch'en I.[94]

By the middle of December, the "royalist" Red Guards who had supported Liu had been vanquished, and criticisms escalated so dramatically that Japanese reporters were led to suspect that Liu must have

[91] *Yomiuri*, February 15, 1967, and *BTA* (Bulgarian Press Agency), January 24, 1967, in *Foreign Broadcast Information Service (FBIS)* 16 (January 24, 1967): CCC-11, in Rice, *Mao's Way*, p. 262.

[92] Jerome Ch'en, *Mao*, pp. 96–97.

[93] *Mainichi*, November 13, in *DSJP*, November 11–14, 1966; *Asahi*, November 26, in *DSJP*, December 6, 1966; *Sankei*, November 28, in *DSJP*, November 29, 1966, pp. 9–10.

[94] *Yomiuri*, January 1, in *DSJP*, January 5, 1967, p. 7.

retracted his self-criticisms to incite the assault. Yet there were lingering inhibitions against criticizing the Chief of State that necessitated a
flank attack. Following Chiang Ch'ing's suggestion on December 18
that Red Guards should do "ideological work" on Liu T'ao, Ho P'eng-
fei and Li Li-feng so that they "might be won over and reveal information on their parents," Liu T'ao was persuaded to present a "self-
examination" on December 29.[95] "I am of the opinion that my father
is really the No. 1 Party person in authority taking the capitalist road,"
she announced. "For more than twenty years, he has all the time opposed and resisted Chairman Mao and Mao's Thought, carrying out,
not socialism, but capitalism." [96] However, Chiang Ch'ing did not regard T'ao's attack as sufficiently free of ambivalence, so she arranged a
rendezvous between T'ao and her mother, Wang Ch'ien (Liu's former
wife whom Liu had not permitted her to see); the latter roused T'ao
to indignation with details of her life with Liu, and three days later
T'ao submitted a second self-criticism, which was approved. At about
the same time, Liu's October self-criticism appeared on big-character
posters.[97]

An attack on Liu's wife followed immediately. "With material on
Liu Shao-ch'i far too scanty, the central authorities had granted the
Red Guards permission to check all the files on Liu's visits to foreign
countries in recent years," a Tsinghua Red Guard revealed. "There
they found that Wang Kuang-mei was a capitalist class member, a weak
chink in his armor." [98] On January 6, Tsinghua Chingkangshan rebels
decoyed Wang into a struggle meeting by persuading her daughters,
Liu P'ing-p'ing and Liu T'ing-t'ing, to report that the latter's leg was
broken and ask their mother to come to the hospital, whereupon
Wang was "captured." Notwithstanding rebel confidence that "no
matter how strong she was, we had the support of the central authorities and could certainly strike her down," the meeting was a failure
from the rebel viewpoint, for a nervous but clever Wang Kuang-mei
parried all questions, frequently hiding behind the need for security,
and the students did not know enough about previous policy to expose
her.[99]

During the January "movement to seize power," the Red Guards first
ventured to "drag out" Liu Shao-ch'i and expose him to "struggle"
(as distinguished from "criticism"—the former is the mode of dealing

[95] *JPRS*, "Samples of Red Guard Publications," (August 1, 1967), eighth item.

[96] Liu T'ao, "Rebel Against Liu," in *CB*, no. 821, pp. 1–25.

[97] Gigon, *Vie et Mort*, p. 201; T'ao's second revised self-criticism is on pp. 201–214.

[98] Ling, *Revenge*, pp. 198–199.   [99] Hinton, "Hundred Day War," p. 101.

with "enemies of the people," the latter the mode of resolving "contradictions among the people"). On January 8, Chou En-lai noted, "You and your friends have come to Chungnanhai [Liu's official residence] . . . and dragged out Liu and Teng many times."[100] Liu also participated in such meetings on January 26 and February 9, 1967. In the former:

The revolutionary masses demanded that Liu should recite the first paragraph of the first page of the Red Book. . . . Wang Kuang-mei said, "He can certainly do that." However, the result was that Liu, stammering and hesitating, could not get any farther than "the force at the core leading our cause is," and, while saying that, he still forgot the words, "at the core." Wang Kuang-mei hurried to explain to her husband that he forgot "at the core." . . . Because the attitude of Liu was not straightforward, the masses took his cap away. Thereupon Wang Kuang-mei said: "You should not do that, for he might catch cold and in that case it would not be possible to continue struggling against him." The masses asked him why he resisted Chairman Mao, which he answered by saying that he had *not* resisted the Chairman. The masses then asked why he had outlined a reactionary policy. Liu replied: "In order to oppose the *Thought* of Mao Tse-tung." When the masses were not content with these answers, Kuang-mei protected him and wanted him to leave. She proposed that the masses should wage their struggles against herself, but Liu feared that his wife would run into difficulties and did not want to leave. Then the masses pushed him out of the room. They told Wang Kuang-mei to stand on a bench and struggled further against her.[101]

In the February 9 meeting, Liu, Teng, and T'ao Chu faced mass interrogation together, again admitting opposition to Mao's line but not to Mao.[102]

The "January storm" resulted in other similar excesses that the leadership was not prepared to countenance, and, in the ensuing moderate phase, surviving conservatives among the leadership coalesced with the PLA and launched a counterattack known polemically as the "February adverse current" (*erh-yüeh ni-liu*), which allegedly included among its goals a "reversal of verdicts" on Liu and Teng. That Liu did not personally attend these or later meetings concerning his case is obliquely suggested by Wang's comment in April 1967: "We have faith in Chairman Mao. The great Chairman Mao will learn the

100 *Mainichi*, January 11, in *DSJP*, January 12, 1967, pp. 5-6.
101 Quoted in D. W. Fokkema, *Report from Peking: Observations of a Western Diplomat on the Cultural Revolution* (London, 1971), p. 60.
102 Chung Hua-min, "The GPCR in 1967," in URI, *Communist China, 1967* (Hong Kong, 1969), p. 23.

truth." [103] Yet Liu's fate had become inextricably bound with that of the GPCR, and was certainly included in the debates. In an outspoken speech at a February struggle meeting on behalf of Liu, Ch'en I denied that Liu had retracted his self-criticism:

Recently, there has been a rumor saying that Liu Shao-ch'i has fiercely resisted, wishing to argue with Chairman Mao, and has intended to withdraw his confession. In effect, no such thing has happened. Who dares to resist Chairman Mao? No one can do that, because Chairman Mao's prestige is too great.[104]

While agreeing under pressure to moderation of struggle tactics and rehabilitation of veteran cadres, Mao maintained that "criticizing and repudiating China's Khrushchev and doing it until he stinks is a phenomenon affecting the destiny of China and the world." When the GPCR shifted to the left again at the end of March, Liu was made the main target of attack in both official and Red Guard press, and the range and gravity of his errors were constantly expanded. On March 21, twenty Red Guard organizations, including Peking and Tsinghua universities and the Peking Aeronautical Institute, formed a "Preparatory Committee for Thoroughly Smashing the Liu Shao-ch'i Renegade Clique," and on April 2 a large demonstration at T'ienanmen Square marked the beginning of a month of rallies held almost daily throughout the country against the "top Party person in authority taking the capitalist road." [105]

Despite Chou's insistence that Liu should not be repudiated face-to-face, but only back-to-back (in society, through speeches, rallies, articles, broadcasts, cartoons), every "high tide" of criticism was accompanied by popular agitation for publicly dramatized confrontations. On the night of April 9, 1967, thirty-odd Red Guards stole into the couple's bedroom in Chungnanhai and forced Wang to dress and accompany them to Tsinghua, where she was subjected to a mass struggle meeting and three consecutive "trials." A sound truck had crisscrossed the city announcing the confrontation, posters were distributed far and wide, and more than 300 rebel organizations had been invited; buses blocked the roads for miles and the sea of people overflowed the university grounds so that loudspeakers had to be set up beyond

103 "Three Trials of Pickpocket Wang Kuang-mei," CB, no. 848 (February 27, 1968): 20.
104 Ch'en I, "K'an wen-hua ta ko-ming," Red Flag (Peking Aeronautical Institute) (April 4, 1967), in Chung-kung, ed. Ting Wang, pp. 641–642.
105 Nihon Keizai, April 3, in DSJP, April 1–3, 1967, p. 31; Sankei, March 27, in DSJP, March 28, 1967, p. 28.

the campus gates. Wang was forcibly clad in the glamorous *ch'i-p'ao* (dress with slit skirt) and necklace she had worn on a state tour of Indonesia and photographed, an epitome of disgraced bourgeois decadence.[106] In her trials, she again denied "subjective" opposition to Mao on behalf of Liu or herself and even retracted or qualified certain of Liu's earlier concessions:

1946: According to press reports, this was definitely not the responsibility of one person. The words "peace, democracy" were clearly written in the armistice agreement. Now he has bravely assumed the responsibility . . . ["Tell me, who were the others?"]
Is it necessary for me to elaborate?

1949: It was wrong for him to make the Tientsin speech [but] . . . one cannot do anything with no regard for the environment. For example, if you told a capitalist that exploitation was a crime, then one would commit a big crime by setting up a factory, and a bigger crime would be committed if one more factory were set up. Liu only said that so long as exploitation by factories was of advantage to the prosperity of the country and the people, such exploitation was necessary, and the workers also needed such exploitation.

1962: "*San tzu i pao*" [the extension of private plots and of free markets, the increase of small factories with sole responsibility for their own profits and losses, and the fixing of quotas based on the households] was not put forward by him. He was of the view that this was a "big retrogression in history" and was against it. His mistake lay in his not bringing it to the attention of Chairman Mao or acting too late.

1964: How much do you know about the material of the four cleans movement? . . . You have spent no more than five days at the grass-roots level while I stayed there for almost one year. I understand things better than you do. . . . T'aoyüan's experience was a good one and not a bad one. But there are shortcomings.

1966: [Wang denied recent allegations that Liu's errors during the fifty days were "ultra-left," emphasizing that their errors at that time were definitely errors of right inclination.] [107]

The spring offensive in the official press evoked rumors of "resistance" by Liu. On April 11, a wall poster alleged that Liu, Teng, and T'ao had jointly posted a big-character poster in which they attacked the GPCR, proposed that the CC hold its Twelfth Plenum

106 Hinton, "Hundred Day War," pp. 102–103.
107 "Three Trials," in *CB*, no. 848, *passim*.

in April, and presented materials to criticize the CCRG.[108] According
to a Red Guard tabloid, Liu wrote to Mao on May 14, claiming that
"the article by investigator carried by No. 5 issue of *RF* [viz., 'Hit hard
at the Many in order to Protect the Handful is a Component of the
Bourgeois Reactionary Line'] is a distortion of facts."

I have erred but am not guilty of having done something wrong. I am not
counterrevolutionary. . . . I have done a great deal that conforms to the
interests of the Party. . . . A host of mistakes in the GPCR has been committed by the CCRG, but they are all arbitrarily attributed to me.[109]

As to why Liu did not undertake a more vigorous self-defense, his wife
contended that "he has kept silent for the sake of the Party and the
revolution." [110]

On July 9, Liu submitted his second recorded self-criticism, the first
to be submitted publicly. In this document he made no mention of
"historical" crimes but confined himself to "my participation in the
GPCR at the Peking College of Construction Engineering" in early
August 1966. After a detailed analysis of his mistakes during the "fifty
days," Liu added an important concession to the principle of "line"
by which his responsibility was extended beyond his own acts: his mistakes, he admitted, might survive him in the iterative process of the
mass line:

Finally, I extend my apology to the revolutionary teachers, students, and
staff members who have been suppressed and harmed by the erroneous line
which I represent! Those revolutionary teachers, students and staff members
and the broad masses of members of the work teams who were hoodwinked
by the erroneous line and who made mistakes of varying degrees in the
initial period of the GPCR bear little responsibility. The main responsibility
rests with me.[111]

Liu's third self-criticism had the somewhat paradoxical effect of
stimulating the criticism campaign against him to take new life. In
Peking, the office which arranged for allocation of members of the
"black gang" to rebels for struggle meetings was informed in May and
June that Liu was not available,[112] but Liu's self-criticism offered suf-

[108] UPI Tokyo dispatch, April 15, 1967, quoting an *Asahi Shimbun* report based
on Peking big-character posters.

[109] "Look, These Dogs in the Water Are Not Dead Yet!" *Chingkangshan* (Canton), and *Wen-i chan-pao* [Art and literature battle news] (Kwangtung), no. 6
(August 27, 1967), in *SCMP*, no. 4032 (October 2, 1967): 6–9.

[110] Red Guard poster, reported by a Japanese correspondent in Peking, in *Hsing-
tao jih-pao*, April 15, 1967, p. 1.

[111] Liu, "Self-Examination" (July 9, 1967), *LSWTC*, pp. 625–628; trans. in *SCMP*,
no. 4037 (October 9, 1967): 1–7.

[112] Fokkema, *Report*, pp. 130–131.

ficient provocation to override this ruling, and on July 10 the August 1st Regiment of the Institute to which Liu had sent his self-criticism went to Chungnanhai to protest the fact that Liu had sent a self-criticism only to the New August 1st Regiment (an opposing faction). Between July 12 and 14, a three-day demonstration was staged in Peking with more than 300,000 people taking part; slogans calling for overthrowing Liu were openly shouted, and balloons carrying the messages "Drive Liu Shao-ch'i Out of Chungnanhai," and "Smash Liu Shao-ch'i's New Counterattack" were flown over Peking. In Shanghai similar demonstrations were held for several days, and in Wuhan contributed to the revival of armed struggle on July 20.[113]

Kuan Feng and Ch'i Pen-yü spread the word via K'uai Ta-fu that Liu was not sincere, would not admit his errors, and accused the CCRG of framing him, and "rebels" began to concentrate outside Liu's house. On July 19, a "Liaison Station of Various Revolutionary Groups in Peking to Criticize Liu Shao-ch'i in Public issued an "ultimatum" to Liu to "come out of Chungnanhai district in Peking by midnight, August 5, the first anniversary of Mao's big-character poster in 1966, and subject yourself to public interrogation by rebels." Hundreds of thousands of people permanently encamped in the streets around the west gate of Chungnanhai: banners and streamers attached to the tops of their huts and tents flooded the streets, slogans were plastered on every available wall and mat, loudspeakers blared from a hundred locations, and cooking fires sent up their smoke and aroma from make-shift kitchens.[114]

On August 2, Liu attempted to placate his assailants by submitting a response to eight accusatory questions put by Ch'i Pen-yü in his famous article, "Patriotism or National Betrayal?" Although most of his remarks were addressed to accusations raised since his first self-criticism, he also tended to qualify the blame he had assumed earlier by pointing to the collective nature of the decision-making process (cf. his statements in regard to 1946, 1962, and 1964):

1936: [Liu admits facilitating release of CCP prisoners from KMT prisons, but adds] I did not bother to find out what specific formalities they went through and it was only recently when I read a rebel newspaper that I knew they had published an anti-Communist notice.

1946: In the cease-fire order of our Party of January 20 was a reference to a "new phase of peace and democracy." On February 1, in accordance with

113 AP Tokyo Dispatch, July 16, 1967; NCNA (Shanghai), July 18, 1967.
114 Hinton, "Hundred Day War," pp. 118 ff.; FEER 57, no. 7 (August 17, 1967): 313–315.

the opinions of the CC's discussion, I wrote a directive about the "new phase of peace and democracy." This directive contains errors.

1951: [No change from October self-criticism.]

1955: [No change.]

1956: At the Eighth Party Congress in 1956, I presented to the Congress a political report on behalf of the Party CC. . . . But in another part of this report it says, "the contradiction between our country's bourgeoisie and the proletariat is already resolved," and this proposition is wrong. . . . Chairman Mao at the time expressed his opposition to these sentences in the resolution but there was no time to revise them and it was passed in this form and has still not been refuted today. Apart from this, in the Political Report and the Resolution of the Eighth Party Congress there was no mention of Mao Tse-tung's Thought as the guiding ideology for the whole Party and the whole country, and this was wrong.

1962: During the three years of difficulty I did not attack the three red flags. At one CC meeting when I heard Teng Tzu-hui say that the Anhwei field of responsibility had many good points, I did not refute him. The three reconciliations and one reduction was put forward by an individual comrade in a rough draft and was not brought up at a CC meeting. . . . Afterwards, it was removed from that comrade's safe. . . . When "How To Be a Good Communist" was reprinted, this was endorsed and revised for me by someone else. I saw that it was published in *Red Flag* and *People's Daily*. I ought to take the main responsibility.

1964: In the summer of 1964 I made statements in several cities, in some of which were tendencies which were "left" in form but right in fact. . . . The T'aoyüan experience was at the time comparatively good.[115]

Upon receipt of this document, the rebels initiated a hunger strike to force Liu out of Chungnanhai for a mass struggle meeting. Compromise arrangements were finally made to stage three rallies simultaneously on August 5 in three arenas: T'ienanmen Square, the Workers' Stadium, and Chungnanhai, to be linked by radio. Liu would appear at a "criticism rally" to be held in his garden, broadcast by loudspeaker to audiences in the other arenas. The meager results of this final confrontation were summarized in wall posters:

1949: ["Why did you ever say in Tientsin that 'exploitation has some merits?' "] I never said that.

1964: ["Why did you raise the question of contradictions between the four cleans and the four uncleans and not bring forward the question of contradiction between the two roads?"] My thought was not good.

[115] Liu, "Self-Examination" (August 2, 1967), trans. in *CL&G* 1, no. 1 (spring 1968): 75–80.

1966: ["Was the February Outline written at your house?"] I held only one meeting there. . . . I chaired the meeting and said a few words at the beginning. I heard the views of others, but did not express myself, either for or against them.[116]

Although Red Guards then began agitating to drag out Liu for a great rally in T'ienanmen Square, the request was rejected, as were all subsequent requests for "face-to-face" confrontations. Liu continued to live in his official residence, isolated from the din of the struggle against his "line," a passive observer to the public exhumation of his life. In a development reminiscent of the feudal *tsu-chu* (if one is guilty, the family is punished), Liu Yün-jo, his son, who had returned to China from the Soviet Union, and P'ing-p'ing, his youngest daughter, were reported in March 1968 to have been arrested by public security forces on charges of treason and trying to reverse the verdict on their father.[117] In July, the Hong Kong *Daily News* reported that Liu had attempted suicide "and is now being kept under surveillance"; it based its report on wall posters seen by travelers to Hong King, which did not specify the time or circumstances of the attempt.[118]

At the Twelfth Plenum (enlarged) of the Eighth CC, which met in Peking from October 13 to 31, Liu Shao-ch'i was shut out of the Party forever, removed from all offices, and cast on "the garbage heap of history." The basis for this verdict was a statement of charges prepared by a special investigation group working under the patronage of the CCRG; this document made no mention of Liu's errors during the "fifty days," which had first triggered the great criticism campaign, and in fact confined attention to errors committed prior to Liberation in 1949. The chronological shift in focus constitutes tacit ackowledgment that Liu's errors during the GPCR were not considered sufficient to warrant such extreme sanctions and also helps explain why Liu attempted to qualify his admissions of "historical" errors in later self-criticisms. Although the communiqué referred to Liu's "accomplices" (in its resolution to "continue to settle accounts with Liu and his accomplices for their crimes in betraying the Party and the country"), none was named. In fact, Liu was the only Party person in authority to be named in the communiqué, apparently the only one subject to formal disciplinary action. Teng Hsiao-p'ing was not named, even by his customary sobriquet, "that other top Party person in

---

116 Liu, "Pei tou kung-tse" [Confession made under struggle] (August 5, 1967), in *LSWTC*, pp. 629–630.

117 "Liu P'ing-p'ing, What Are You After?" *Hung-wei-ping pao* [Red Guard news] (Peking), July 1968, in *SCMM*, no. 626 (September 9, 1968): 47–48.

118 *Daily News* (Hong Kong), July 10, 1968.

authority taking the capitalist road," and has since been rehabilitated.[119]

The subsequent whereabouts and circumstances of the Lius have
been shrouded in official secrecy. In the summer of 1969, Edgar Snow
said in an interview with the Italian newspaper *L'Espresso* that he had
been told Liu was living in the Western Hills of Peking, where many
retired generals reside, but a French correspondent was told during a
later trip that Liu was undergoing "rectification in North China."
According to information given Jack Ch'en on a recent trip to China,
Liu was moved from Peking to North China because of persistent attempts by his followers to rescue him. It has since been rumored, without official confirmation (which may never be forthcoming in any case),
that he died a natural death there in 1973.[120]

CONCLUSION

We may now, on the basis of the evidence presented in the last two
chapters, reach fairly firm conclusions with regard to the following
questions: (1) Why was Liu made the target for so much condemnation? (2) Why did he respond so ineffectively to his own political
crucifixion?

(1) In the introduction to Chapter 3, two objectively possible explanations of Liu's implication were briefly presented as "ideal
types"; they may now be analyzed in greater depth. In analyzing the
validity of these two scenarios we must beware of two logical fallacies
that were commonly committed by participants in the GPCR in their
explanations of action. First, *post hoc ergo propter hoc*, or confusing
a chronological sequence of events with causation (e.g., Liu fell *after*
P'eng fell, so P'eng's fall was causally related to Liu's fall). Second,
the confusion of intention with effect (e.g., Mao's call to the Red Guards
to revolt resulted in Liu's fall, therefore Liu's fall was Mao's ultimate
intention in calling the Red Guards to revolt).

(a) The widely accepted "conspiracy" theory has it that Mao
launched the GPCR with the express prior intention of purging Liu
Shao-ch'i and his colleagues. We shall first review the evidence and

---

[119] Teng's "crimes" were never specified in any detail in official criticisms. Moreover, criticism of Teng decreased in frequency and intensity following the purge
of the senior staff of *RF* in the fall of 1967—the strongest official denunciation of
Teng appeared in the last editorial to be published before discontinuation of RF
on November 23, 1967. For an analysis of the case of Teng Hsiao-p'ing, see
Roderick MacFarquhar, "Problems of Liberalization and the Succession at the Eighth
Party Congress," *CQ*, no. 56 (October–December 1973): 617–647.

[120] *Newsweek*, November 19, 1973, p. 72; *Time*, November 19, 1973.

reasoning supporting the following chain of implication: Wu Han was a pawn protecting P'eng Chen, and P'eng was a knight protecting a king—Liu Shao-ch'i.

The evidence presented in Chapter 3 indeed supports the hypothesis of prior conspiracy on the part of Chiang Ch'ing and a small group of radical publicists. This group secretly prepared a critique of Wu Han and later coalesced to form the radical core of the CCRG. There is no evidence that Mao actively supported this group until November 1965, when he turned to them in his exasperation with the Group of Five; he did, however, give his wife's group passive support. As Chiang said, "Because he promised me to reserve my opinion it gave me courage to proceed with writing that article and to keep it secret." We may thus conclude that the original attack on Wu Han resulted from a "conspiracy," while also noting that this conspiracy was activated by P'eng Chen's prior conspiracy of silence. The conspirational activities of the Chiang Ch'ing coterie were, however, limited to the writing of radical literary criticism and not immediately connected with Liu Shao-ch'i; the conspiracy theory hence rests on the added assumption of a chain of implication linking Wu Han to Liu Shao-ch'i.

Our study of the Wu Han incident indicates that Mao had valid independent reasons to initiate a criticism campaign against Wu, that his deputization of P'eng Chen to lead the campaign was logical under the circumstances, and that P'eng's insubordination was neither necessary nor predictable—though it may not have been unforeseen, as the secret preparation of an alternative strategy of attack on Wu suggests. P'eng was forced to choose between "subordination to the higher level," his obligation under the organizational principle of democratic centralism, and protection of a protégé, his obligation under traditional principles of bureaucratic "honor" defining the patronage relationship (pao-jen, shou-chih, etc.).[121] He chose the latter, and continuing Maoist pressure induced him to conceal his choice in a web of prevarications that implicated others and magnified the gravity of his insubordination. As to the P'eng-Liu "link" in the chain of implication, the evidence supporting a binding patronage relationship is tenuous to begin with, and in any case Liu did not honor his putative commitment to P'eng, unless his absence from certain of the meetings that decided P'eng's dismissal is so construed. If the P'eng-

121 Cf. Andrew J. Nathan, "'Connections' in Chinese Politics: Political Recruitment and *Kuan-hsi* in late Ch'ing and Early Republican China," (paper delivered at the Eighty-seventh Annual Meeting of the American Historical Association, New Orleans, December 27–30, 1972).

Liu link did not exist, its suspected existence may have cast a shadow of suspicion on Liu, though this is but a surmise.

We may conclude that while Wu Han's purge was contingently linked with P'eng Chen's fall, neither available empirical evidence nor logical cogency supports the supposition that there was a causal or intentional connection between Wu's purge and Liu's implication. Such a connection seems to have been constructed *ex post facto* by Maoists who wished to perceive unity of meaning and logical inevitability in the unfolding of the GPCR, thus exalting the principles the movement had come to stand for and paying tribute to the foresight of its prime movers. The "crime" in which Liu was actually implicated, however, was not collusion in P'eng Chen's insubordination, but the suppression of "revolutionary teachers and students" during the fifty days, which may be briefly reviewed.

The circumstances defining Liu's error are reasonably clear in their essentials. By the end of May, the P'eng-Lo-Lu-Yang group's grip on the cultural superstructure had been broken, and the escalation of polemics mobilized widespread student demonstrations against local academic and Party authorities believed to be associated with this group. The CC work teams dispatched to lead the demonstrations initially received majority support but soon came under vociferous minority criticism for their "bureaucratic" leadership style, which stifled student initiative and frustrated attempts to expose capitalist-roaders in the Party. The work teams reacted to the criticism with punitive sanctions, creating polarization between work teams and "revolutionary teachers and students." When Mao returned to Peking in late July, he resolved the impasse in favor of the latter, publicly blaming Liu Shao-ch'i for the embroilment.

These circumstances seem clear enough, but the motives behind the circumstances remain elusive. The "conspiracy theory" assumes the existence of a secret Maoist network of PLA *agents provocateurs* who briefed radical students to attack the work teams and make their task impossible; without covert elite backing, it is argued, such attacks could not have occurred. However, there is no evidence that the PLA was involved, and in fact no evidence that the anti-work-team incidents were conspired (i.e., secretly organized in advance). Mao expressed delighted surprise at the risings, saying he "did not expect that as soon as the large-character poster of Peita was broadcast . . . the whole country would boil up!" And as we have tried to show, the Maoist explanation implicitly dismissed by the conspiracy theory— that the anti-work-team incidents were precipitated by the work teams' poor handling of the situation and by Liu's poor handling of the work teams—has considerable validity. The anti-work-team rebel groups then attracted the attention and sympathy of the CCRG and finally the Chairman, without whose support they could not have survived. Finally, the conspiracy theory fails to give due credence to the desire of the Maoists to launch a "cultural" revolution that would mobilize the masses to arise and throw off the vestiges of the bourgeois cultural superstructure. If Maoist objectives were limited to the purge of the Liu-Teng group, mass mobilization would be a most inefficient means of achieving this objective; Maoist ascendancy at the central policy-making level was in any case assured at the Eleventh Plenum, which marked only the beginning of extensive mobilization.

(b) Neither can the "spontaneity" theory, which suggests that the GPCR was exclusively concerned with mass education and that Liu simply fell because he frustrated this objective, be accepted in its pure form. Assuming that Mao began by wishing to transform the cultural superstructure and "touch the souls of the people," it became clear by the spring of 1966 that he wanted much more than that. Mao made no secret of this intention to subject his opponents to mass criticism. His primary objection to P'eng Chen's "February Outline" was that it failed to draw a "political conclusion" on "anti-Party and anti-socialist representatives of the bourgeoisie (there are a number of these in the CC)," and "The Sixteen Points" of the Eleventh Plenum re-iterated that "the main target of the present movement is those Party persons in authority taking the capitalist road." Even in his recently revealed July 8, 1966, letter to his wife, in which he plays down his own initiative in the purge, Mao says, "The task before us at the moment is to partially defeat (it is impossible to defeat them wholly) the rightists within the whole Party." [122] Chou En-lai and Chiang Ch'ing could in retrospect detect signs of Mao's "disappointment" with Liu in early 1965; this "disappointment" seemed apparent in Mao's immediate conclusion, publicized in his first big-character poster, that Liu was personally to blame for the errors of the work teams, that his errors were deliberate, and that they were part of consistently mistaken "line."

Thus both ideal-typical explanations have strengths as well as inadequacies, and in our attempt to formulate a more adequate characterization of the process of authoritative decision, we shall incorporate elements of both. The Chinese decision-making process functions simultaneously at two levels, the first at the level of *formal organization*, where such well-established institutional mechanisms as discussion (*t'ao-lun*), democratic centralism, and inner-Party struggle mediate

[122] Mao's letter appeared in *Hsing-tao jih-pao* (Hong Kong), November 4, 1972.

disagreements; and the second at the level of informal *loyalty groups,* which are defined by patron-client relationships and various ascriptive ties. The normal relationship between organization and loyalty group may be compared to the relationship between conscious and unconscious mental processes: loyalty groups are proscribed within the decision-making apparatus, but "opinion groups," which see a constant turnover of membership based on coincident issues and interests, are permitted; loyalty groups are normally relegated to personal friendships. Ideology regulates the relationship between these two levels of coalition formation, and if there is a policy change sufficient to provoke a crisis of legitimacy impairing ideological commitment, that relationship is thrown out of kilter.

In the case of Liu Shao-ch'i, decision making at the organizational level had become deadlocked over two issues: Mao's desire to revolutionize the bourgeois cultural superstructure, and his concern with the formation of a bureaucratic "new class," which he felt had grown away from the masses. This deadlock was more subtle than GPCR polemics have characterized it in hindsight, for Liu and the Party *apparatchiki* were always willing to compromise with Mao over substantive policies, though their compromises neatly skirted the two underlying issues, where they felt further concessions might endanger the regime's cooptation of technical and managerial intelligentsia and its control over the Party organization respectively. At the loyalty group level, Mao's withdrawal from active participation in central policy councils, his sense of frustration and growing irrelevance to the emerging drift of things in the Liu-Teng policy apparatus, and his greater attention to abstract ideological and polemical issues during this period resulted in his convocation of an informal staff of symbol specialists whose ambitions were attached to Mao's personal future rather than to any prospect of bureaucratic advancement. When Mao finally pushed his decision to launch a cultural criticism movement through the CC, only to see that movement bog down in the face of P'eng Chen's intransigence, Mao's loyalty group quickly crystalized into an organizing center for radical publicity. Though we detect no sign of a deliberate plan to entrap Liu Shao-ch'i, when mass criticism was legitimated in the spring of 1966, this group was poised to give the movement a polemical focus which coincided with the group's own rivalries with other elites and political ambitions. By discrediting as "slavism" and other errors the formal mechanisms of decision that governed the organizational level, the Maoist group opened the way for the formation at every level of conflict groups based on ideological affinity and various informal or ascriptive criteria.

To restate this conclusion in more general terms, the legitimate mode of conflict regulation is apt to break down when a dispute develops over issues transcending the ideological concensus that legitimates this mode of conflict regulation. One type of issue particularly prone to provoke such a dispute is the allocation of blame or sanctions among the leadership for an acknowledged failure, which is intrinsically a personal as well as a policy question, tending to revive particularistic loyalties as a basis for coalition formation. Such cleavages easily become stalemated, owing to the incapacity of institutionalized methods of conflict regulation to resolve or even acknowledge the underlying basis of cleavage. The temptation to break such a deadlock by introducing outside constituencies is stronger for the group of participants that has a decisive preponderance of extra-Party resources, or benefits from an asymmetry between intra- and extra-Party resources. Once the deadlock has been broken, the pattern of shifting intra-elite "opinion groups" is apt to give way to a competition between loyalty groups held together by patronage and ideological appeals.

(2) How did Liu react? He accepted Mao's reversal of the work-team policy and promptly set forth to withdraw the work teams and to institute reforms in Party organization designed to ensure greater responsiveness to the masses. When Mao's first big-character poster appeared on August 5, interpreting Liu's error in more grave and personal terms, Liu withdrew from active participation in policy, and, following his demotion at the Eleventh Plenum, he even reportedly submitted his resignation.[123] Mao turned down the resignation and accepted Liu's self-criticism at the October work conference, and it seemed Liu had regained and consolidated a reduced position in the Politburo. However, the GPCR continued to encounter opposition, in the light of which Liu's error was reinterpreted as an "antagonistic contradiction." Liu chose not to resist this reinterpretation overtly but to withdraw to his official residence, emerging only to appear at struggle meetings or to submit self-criticisms. These attempts at atonement were all met with rejection, each more indignant than the one preceding. Why?

Beginning in December 1966, rumors began to circulate that Liu had retracted his October self-criticism; they recurred in February 1967. A retraction would explain Mao's change of heart about Liu between October and December 1966, and it would also be consistent with the more guarded quality of Liu's later self-criticisms and the heightened outrage that greeted them. Yet there is no substantiation for these reports, and Ch'en I emphatically denied them in February 1967. It is true that there was a subtle shift of nuance in Liu's later

123 *Yomiuri*, October 2, in *DSJP*, October 5, 1966, pp. 1–3.

self-criticisms, consisting of greater emphasis on the collective nature of decisions for which he was previously willing to take full responsibility, but Liu never retracted his confessions to the main charges. Furthermore, the later self-criticisms were made after the decision to submit Liu to full public exposure had already been made and hence had no impact on that decision; they were also made before hostile audiences inclined to sensationalize any admissions to his disadvantage, rather than accept them as tenders of good faith.

The charges of "retraction" and "hoax" may perhaps better be understood as polemical metaphors for Mao's disappointment over the failure of Liu's first self-criticism to discredit and deter further resistance to the GPCR by Party power-holders. We may recall that Mao's reprieve was *conditional* upon unspecified acts of atonement on Liu's part: "If they have made mistakes they can probably correct them!" Mao said. "When they have corrected them it will be all right, and they should be allowed to come back and go to work with fresh spirit." Mao believed the basic obstacle to achievement of the GPCR's objectives was the resistance of "Party persons in authority taking the capitalist road," and he held Liu responsible for this resistance, arguing both by analogy (drawing a parallel between Liu's behavior during the "fifty days" and the similar reactions of lesser power-holders) and by drawing attention to the "poison" spread by Liu's "line" (e.g., in "How To Be a Good Communist").

Liu, however, understood his indictment to mean that he should "step aside": "Since the Eleventh Plenum of the CC, I have not taken part in the leadership, and therefore I am not involved in the Cultural Revolution," he said in November.[124] The desire of Lin Piao, Chiang Ch'ing, *et al.* to exploit their victory over Liu by escalating the GPCR to a new level was aided by Liu's failure to play any active role in persuading Party leaders in the various cities and provinces to accept the criticisms of the Red Guards, and Liu's attempt to detach himself from the struggle was not taken in good faith. Thus, while the Maoist indictment of Liu became more inclusive by using the principle of "line" to attribute cumulative guilt to him for problems encountered as the movement progressed, Liu's self-indictment remained consistent with his first self-criticism. Since the operational rules of mass criticism objectively define a "sincere" self-criticism as confession to *all* charges (cf. Kuo Mo-jo's model self-criticism on April 14, 1966), as expanding Maoist definitions of Liu's guilt surpassed Liu's static definition they made the latter seem increasingly "insincere"; the widening gap between charge and confession embittered both Liu and his critics and

[124] "Down with Liu Shao-ch'i," in *CB*, no. 834 (August 17, 1967): 28.

led to charges of retraction and a further escalation of charges. Yet the multiplication of charges only reduced Liu's incentive to confess.

It is uncertain whether Liu was *unwilling* or *unable* to persuade his followers to comply with Mao's designs, but the latter seems more probable. The "Liuists" were expected to preside over their own humiliation and likely purge, and it was simply not in their interest, as they saw it, to comply. That feelings of loyalty to Liu bore less weight than instincts of self-preservation is suggested by the willingness of capitalist-roaders later associated with him to turn on him before the conflict polarized.[125] It is true that Chou En-lai was able to persuade his subordinates to comport somewhat more submissively to the young rebels, as we shall see in the following chapter, but only under rather more favorable circumstances: (1) He in effect foreclosed the possibility of purge by stipulating that Red Guards could criticize and post posters as much as they liked, but that no one could be dismissed except by CC decision. (2) His men were all located in Peking, directly under his jurisdiction; the regional and provincial committees staffed by Liuists were scattered across the country and enjoyed a certain immunity from Liu's hierarchical controls. (3) Of most decisive importance, Chou enjoyed Mao's implicit support throughout the GPCR, whereas Liu was publicly discredited in August and could thenceforth influence his followers only by exemplary self-abasement. Before his demotion, he signaled his willingness to comply with Mao's new directions by reversing himself on the work-team issue and trying to persuade his followers to do likewise. After his demotion, he came under public attack (e.g., the first big-character poster calling for his retirement appeared on October 20, five days before Mao's pardon) and was hence "unable to do his job"; he became detached from the instruments of policy and appeared only at struggle meetings.

Liu's strategy of response to the criticism campaign may be evaluated on the basis of two questions: (a) What impact did it have upon public redefinition of his guilt? (b) What impact did it have upon the unfolding of the GPCR as a whole?

(a) By refusing in principle to deny his responsibility for the original suppression of revolutionary teachers and students or to target an

---

[125] "Record," *JPRS*, no. 42349, p. 39. In her "preliminary self-examination," Liu T'ao disclosed that she had written a poster condemning her mother on August 19, 1966, and showed it to Wang Jen-chung. "After he read it, he made more revisions. He also read my wall poster against Liu Shao-ch'i. In point of fact, that wall poster was basically written according to his ideas." "Rebel Against Liu," *CB*, no. 821, p. 17. During P'eng Chen's "trial" in the spring of 1967, he said: "I agree completely. Liu Shao-ch'i is the top Party person in authority taking the capitalist road," but P'eng was less certain about his own guilt. Jiji News Agency's Tokyo Dispatch, May 8, 1967.

alternative scapegoat, Liu placed his hopes exclusively on the possibility of redemption through compliance with the established norms of "criticism and self-criticism." As a strategy of survival, this was obviously a failure. It failed because those norms had been formulated to govern a closed collegial situation which no longer existed. For reasons to be discussed in greater depth in the third section of this book, expansion of the arena of criticism entailed a sacrifice of its redemptive function. In the words of Hannah Arendt:

Forgiving is always an eminently personal affair in which what was done is forgiven for the sake of who did it. Forgiving—perhaps because . . . of the connection with love attending its discovery—has always been deemed unrealistic and inadmissible in the public realm.[126]

(b) The political impact of Liu's acceptance of a passive scapegoat role in the GPCR was to leave the anti-Maoists without a leader of national stature, making Mao's eventual triumph all but inevitable. It seems clear that if it took two years and unprecedented chaos to defeat a headless opposition, if Liu had chosen actively to lead the opposition he was said to head (as Mao has threatened to do when in an analogous position), he might have plunged his country into open civil war, with ruinous consequences. In the summer of 1966, this option was arguably open to him. In declining this course of action and placing the collective interest above his own in the face of great public abuse, Liu lived up to his own ideals of "cultivation" and made his epic political destruction an ironically fitting climax to his career. Whatever one may think of the policies he stood for, Liu Shao-ch'i set an example of integrity and dignity for political dissidents under fire that may well survive him, like the example of Hai Jui before him.

Finally, we may draw two more general conclusions about politics in China from this chapter, the first concerning the institutional implications of the purge of Liu and Teng, the second concerning the method of construing the statements of Chinese political actors about their own acts. The institutional significance of the purge is that the head of an organizational unit must be responsible for everything that happens within his jurisdiction. He must without question follow the directives or even the vague intuitions of Mao, sacrificing all vested interests and organizational or personal loyalties, unless he can persuade Mao to modify his objectives. He is responsible for whatever goes wrong even if he tries in good conscience to implement Mao's wishes. In earlier periods, when there was mutual trust within the leadership, Mao's lieutenants (particularly Liu Shao-ch'i) had wide

126 Hannah Arendt, *The Human Condition* (Chicago, 1958), pp. 241–242.

latitude in the choice of means of implementation and organizational forms. Now, there could be none.

If our reconstruction of the genesis of the GPCR and its relationship to the decision to purge Liu is correct, the methodological inference is that, in the interpretation of statements by political actors about their own acts, one must maintain a distinction between "in-order-to" and "because" motives. Alfred Schutz has shown the analytic utility of such a distinction (between reasons we have for future expectations and descriptions we give to them when these situations are past), even though in practice the distinction is resolved as motives develop through time, in interaction with significant others, in terms of meaningful symbols.[127] According to Mao's "in-order-to" motives as expressed in the course of the movement, he provoked the GPCR with ambitious but indistinct notions of its purpose and emerged from the melee by dint of his skill at improvisation. To judge from his "because" motives delivered after the fact, Mao is a consummate planner who ensnared his opponents in their own sins and submitted them to prepared punishment by the masses. In seeking a meaningful explanation of the "Hundred Flowers," we meet the same contradiction: although Roderick MacFarquhar demonstrates the implausibility of a "conspiracy" interpretation,[128] Mao's own post hoc explanation supports such a construal.[129] The discrepancy between "in-order-to" and "because" results either from Mao's need to disguise his intentions before action, or from his desire to rationalize them afterward to demonstrate his clairvoyance and control over history, or to some mixture of both. We submit that for political actors the distinction between "in-order-to" and "because" often corresponds to a distinction between motivating and justificatory reasons, and that Mao's post hoc explanations should be treated with the same scepticism reserved for the memoirs of Western politicians.

[127] Alfred Schutz, "The Social World and the Theory of Social Action," in *Collected Papers, II: Studies in Social Theory* (The Hague, 1964).

[128] MacFarquhar, *The Hundred Flowers*, p. 12.

[129] In a conversation with a Hungarian Party and government delegation in May 1959, Mao explained that after the Twentieth CPSU Congress, the Chinese leadership was forced to pay attention to the Chinese right wing and that the only way to flush them out of their hiding places was to push the "Hundred Flowers" Campaign to its fullest extent. Janos Radvanyi, "The Hungarian Revolution and the Hundred Flowers Campaign," *CQ*, no. 43 (July–September 1970): 128–129.

5

LIU SHAO-CH'I IN
THE CULTURAL REVOLUTION

The last two chapters sought to explain the origins of the GPCR, Liu's demotion at the Eleventh Plenum in August 1966, and the relationship between those two events. But the riddle of Liu Shao-ch'i's fall is not yet solved. Liu was demoted at the Eleventh Plenum, and two months later he submitted a self-criticism, which was accepted. Although a measure of reconciliation between Mao and Liu appeared at this point to have been achieved, criticisms from the masses continued, and certain elites supported those criticisms, at first covertly, later openly, until finally the attack on him became virtually unanimous. Because Liu had "stepped aside" during this period, his subjective strategy of response is no longer relevant; this chapter therefore turns to Liu's "objective" meaning, as a symbol caught in the flux of a mass criticism movement. That movement was an extremely complex affair, and, in order to divide it into more easily comprehensible segments, we shall adopt a periodization of the movement originally proposed by Mao Tse-tung in a talk to the Albanian military delegation in 1967:

(1) The period from the publishing of Yao Wen-yüan's article to the Eleventh Session of the Eighth CC is the first phase, which was primarily an initiation of the revolution. (2) From the Eleventh Session of the Eighth CC to the January Storm is the second phase, which was primarily a phase of direction switch. (3) From the January Storm to power-seizure struggle, great alliance, and three-in-one combination is the third phase [January–March 1967]. (4) From the publishing of Ch'i Pen-yü's article, "Patriotism or National Betrayal?" . . . onward is the fourth phase. Both the third and fourth phases are concerned with power-seizure struggle. The fourth phase, however, is the most important one, for it marks the seizure of ideological power from the revisionists and the bourgeoisie. [Numerals added.] [1]

1 "Mao's Talk to the Albanian Military Delegation in Peking" (September 26,

Mao's periodization of the movement corresponds closely to the chronology of Liu's fall. In the first phase, the "initiation of revolution," Liu became implicated in the suppression of revolutionary teachers and students. In the phase of "direction switch," Mao's ban on big-character posters against Liu was defined and key elites were won over to the struggle against the Liu-Teng "headquarters." During the third phase, despite retreat from many GPCR objectives, a coalition now including Mao Tse-tung and Chou En-lai decided to continue the attack on Liu as a *symbol* of those objectives. The fourth phase started with the decision by the Politburo and MAC to expose Liu to criticism in the official media. Following this decision, Liu's fate was sealed; subsequent suggestions of the indeterminacy of the struggle's outcome were contrived to retain Liu's efficacy as a symbol against which the most inclusive array of revolutionary forces could unite. It was not until the conclusion of the fourth phase, however, that Liu was formally purged from all positions and his guilt officially defined. During each phase, a decision was reached to permit escalation of criticism to a new level of intensity; this decision was not necessarily made "behind closed doors," as had hitherto been customary, for the GPCR was characterized by an unprecedented expansion of the political arena, legitimating the participation of many new actors in the decision.

"Men are free to make history, but some men are much freer than others," wrote C. Wright Mills. "Such freedom requires access to the means of decision by which history is made." [2] Prior to the GPCR, access to means of decision was defined by the legal spheres of competence assigned to various offices in the bureaucratic structure of authority. The structure's legitimacy was based on belief in the vanguard role of the Party and acceptance of the organizational rules that enabled the Party to function effectively, such as majority rule, information discipline, the superior level's control of organizational sanctions, and so forth. During the GPCR, the legitimacy of the structure was undermined by Mao's Thought, which set forth ideological criteria for access to decisions and made elites liable to popular reproach or recall if they denied the validity of these criteria. The two legitimating principles for allocation of roles in Chinese society— ideology and organization—had become estranged, resulting in an ideologically vacant power structure and an arena of legitimate power

---

1967), in Wang Hsüeh-wen, "The Nature and Development of the 'Great Cultural Revolution,'" *IS* 4, no. 12 (September 1968): 11–12.

[2] C. Wright Mills, *The Sociological Imagination* (New York, 1961), p. 181.

without stable roles. This event had a broad enfranchising effect, legitimating mass participation and at the same time creating elite roles, however unstable, for leaders of the masses. The qualifications required to occupy the new leadership roles included polemical facility, access to mass media, negotiating skill, and stage presence.

In the series of decisions connected with the escalation of criticisms against Liu, the following actors seemed to play deciding roles:

(1) The Red Guards, or "revolutionary masses," constituted the only sector of the masses to exercise initiative or become decisively engaged in the struggle. They initially comprised only college and middle-school students of good class background, but, as the movement gathered momentum, its mobilizational scope included youth of other class backgrounds, demobilized soldiers, contract, rotation, and piece workers, and other disprivileged groups. The Red Guards could exercise considerable discretion both in selecting criticism targets and in promoting escalation of criticism, chiefly by tracing responsibility for work teams up the organizational hierarchy or by discovering incriminating "black materials." They exercised more initiative in the first two phases of the movement than in the latter two, and more in selecting local targets than in choosing central ones.

(2) Radical elites comprised the left-wing contingent of the Central Cultural Revolution Group (CCRG): Ch'en Po-ta (Chairman), Chiang Ch'ing (First Vice-Chairman), Chang Ch'un-ch'iao (Vice-Chairman), K'ang Sheng, Wang Li, Kuan Feng, Ch'i Pen-yü, Yao Wen-yüan, Mu Hsin, and Lin Chieh. With the exceptions of Ch'en Po-ta and K'ang Sheng, both alternate Politburo members (full members after the Eleventh Plenum), they lacked high Party-government positions and therefore had relatively little stake in political stability. The CCRG was a provisional organ whose political clout was dependent upon two closely connected factors: Mao's patronage, from which the group derived its right to render authoritative interpretation of his Thought, and the sway it held over a "revolutionary mass" constituency. The CCRG manipulated its constituency by leaking "confidential materials" to the Red Guard press, by making countless personal appearances and public speeches or by sending special delegations to various places to coordinate rebel forces,[3] and by exercising editorial control over the

[3] In October 1966, Chou En-lai decreed that no radicals should go to Tibet to "exchange revolutionary experience." Nonetheless, Chiang Ch'ing countermanded him by authorizing five Peking youth groups to enter Tibet, where they formed a coalition of "Metropolitan Revolutionary Rebels." At the request of Chang Kuo-hua, Chou issued a second directive ordering them home. The youth appealed to Chiang Ch'ing to stay, and she granted their request. Again, in early January 1967, Ch'en Po-ta, K'ang Sheng and Chiang Ch'ing dispatched a "Revolutionary

pacemaking sector of the official press between June 1966 and September 1967.

(3) Formal Party-government elites ("Party persons in authority") also had access to mass constituencies, but once Mao had stripped ideological legitimacy from the Party organization with the allegation that it harbored "capitalist-roaders," they could mobilize the masses only surreptitiously, through distribution of patronage and other "material" incentives. This was a risky defensive maneuver in the battle for personal survival and one that contributed nothing to the defense of Liu Shao-ch'i, although Maoist polemicists construed such tactics as a token of loyalty in order to discredit them. The strongest card held by the power-holders in decisions concerning escalation of criticisms against Liu (a concern that of course ranked well below personal survival) was their authority to argue their case in Party councils. However, it was feasible to call meetings only during periods of retrenchment, after the Red Guards had tarnished their mandate by their struggle tactics; during a "revolutionary high tide," conventional decision-making forums were all but paralyzed and access to Mao was cut off as each power-holder struggled for his own survival.

(4) Maoist elites (Mao, Lin, and Chou), referred to by Japanese reporters as the "mainstream faction" because they were *fons et origo* of ideological legitimacy, had high formal positions and at the same time cultivated a broad Red Guard constituency; in addition, they held authority over the PLA, the only effective hierarchical command system left relatively intact after the January power seizures. The "mainstream" elites retained their preeminence after January 1967 by a judicious balancing act: whenever the movement veered too far toward anarchy at one extreme, they shifted their support to what became a PLA-formal elite coalition (aligned with conservative Red Guard factions), and whenever the movement lost momentum and faced suppression, they moved to support a CCRG-radical Red Guard coalition.

"INITIATION OF REVOLUTION"

The nature of the conflict that broke out during the fifty days was prefigured by the disposition of elites. Mao did not return to super-

---

Rebel Regiment" to Canton to prepare for a power seizure there. On January 19, Wu Ch'uan-pin, leader of the radical faction in Canton, received a call from his Peking "agent" informing him that the CCRG now authorized the Kwangtung radicals to overthrow the provincial Party committee. Cf. Bennett and Montaperto, *Red Guard*, p. 153; also *Ko-ming kung-jen pao* [Revolutionary workers' news], Peking, January 12, 1967.

vise the rising movement he had incited but remained in Shanghai and Hangchow. This was not extraordinary, given the existing division of labor between the "first and second lines" in the Politburo, but it meant that Liu Shao-ch'i now assumed responsibility for a movement he had not originated and never really understood. "To tell the truth, I myself do not know and understand either," he admitted to Red Guards as late as July 29. "Nor do the personnel of the other organs of the Party Center." [4] On May 16, 1966, the configuration of elites was further complicated by the appointment of a new CCRG,[5] which was given a special mandate to lead the GPCR without receiving permanent offices within the Party organization. Established power-holders, with the contempt of career officials for political dilletantes, tended to dismiss the CCRG as "scholars and *hsiu-ts'ai* . . . an aggressive faction who know nothing about the business." [6]

In the course of mobilizing the masses, the work teams encountered opposition that brought to the surface a latent cleavage between the CCRG and the Party organization concerning the relative degree of elite control and mass spontaneity. Whereas Liu and the CC favored limited and controlled mobilization by Party work teams, the CCRG contended that "it is necessary to trust the masses, rely on them, and respect their initiative." Teng Hsiao-p'ing later conceded that "in mid-June comrades at the Party Center represented by comrade Ch'en Po-ta made the correct suggestion of abolishing the work groups, but we refused to listen." [7] At a CC conference convened by Liu on July 22, the CCRG again proposed withdrawal: "We never had the right to speak," they later complained, for the floor was dominated for three hours by Po I-po and T'ao Lu-chia.[8]

This inner-Party cleavage became transposed to the masses in the process of mobilization for two reasons. First, both "Liuists" and "Maoists" were sent from the center to report on activities at the grass roots and they responded rather differently to the problems they encountered. Perhaps it is going too far to say that the CCRG violated the rule of "democratic centralism," given the prevailing uncertainty about the GPCR's purpose and the nebulous allocation of supervisory authority between CC and CCRG, but the CCRG did offer encouragement and a sense of legitimacy to radicals at a few elite schools who were resisting work teams *sent* by the center. K'uai Ta-fu, a Tsinghua

[4] Cf. "Selected Edition," SCMM, no. 653 (May 5, 1969): 15–21.

[5] Blumer, *Kulturrevolution*, p. 169.

[6] "Defy Death by Ten Thousand Cuts, Dare to Unhorse Yü Ch'iu-li," *Chingkangshan*, March 18, 1967. A *hsiu-ts'ai* was a holder of the lowest (county-level) degree in the imperial bureaucracy.

[7] Teng, "Self-Examination," CL&G 6, no. 12 (September 1970): 84–90.

[8] "Record," JPRS, no. 42349, p. 28.

University rebel whom the work teams had targeted as a "counter-revolutionary," based his refusal to submit a self-criticism on his conviction that his support "reached to heaven"—i.e., that he had elite backing.[9] When K'uai's case was brought before a high-level meeting in early July, K'ang Sheng defended him and Ch'en Po-ta sent CCRG members Wang Li and Kuan Feng to Tsinghua to pay a visit to K'uai when he was placed under custody there.[10] When Peking University students wrote the first big-character poster criticizing the work teams on July 12, the CC sent Chiang Ch'ing to investigate; she went several times with Ch'en Po-ta and others, to "clarify the situation." [11] The CCRG evidently felt justified in violating the spirit of democratic centralism because of what it regarded as the work teams' more serious violation of the populist essence of Mao's Thought.

Second and more important, elite conflicts could be transposed to the masses because of the availability of alternative avenues of mobilization. Unable to gain a hearing within Party councils, the CCRG took advantage of the purge of Lu Ting-yi's Propanganda Department on June 7 to expand its control over influential mass publicity media.[12] In the editorial columns of *RF, LAD, LD,* and *PD,* Ch'en Po-ta and his colleagues introduced an interpretation of Mao's Thought that stressed mass initiative and spontaneity and encouraged the masses to rise against the established order, thereby creating contradictions between the Party organization and the masses.[13] A former Kwangtung Red Guard intensively interviewed by Gordon Bennett and Ronald Montaperto (pennamed Dai Hsiao-ai) testified to the widespread impact the CCRG was able to achieve through the media:

After the first week in June, our ideas began to change. . . . It seemed to us that, if the national leaders were guilty of mistakes and crimes, their counter-

9 Hinton, "Hundred Day War," *passim.*

10 "Down with Liu Shao-ch'i," *CB,* no. 834 (August 17, 1967): 27.

11 Bastid, "Origines," pp. 70–73.

12 On June 1, 1966, *PD* was reorganized by military personnel; in July, the Director and the four best-known Deputy Directors of the CC Propaganda Department were purged. *RF* was placed under control of the CCRG and became its propaganda organ in June 1966. Although Ch'en Po-ta was Editor-in-Chief, he became too involved in high-level policy to look after the journal, so he entrusted it to Wang Li, assisted by Lin Chieh and others. Shanghai's *Wen-hui pao* and *Liberation Daily* were taken over on January 4–5, 1967. Cf. Alan P. L. Liu, "Mass Media in the Cultural Revolution," *CS* 7, no. 8 (April 20, 1969): 1 ff.

13 A recitation of some headlines appearing during June 1966 gives some idea of the thrust of the CCRG's "line": "Tear Aside the Bourgeois Mask of 'Liberty, Equality, and Fraternity,' " *PD* editorial, June 4; "To Be Proletarian Revolutionaries or Bourgeois Royalists," *PD* editorial, June 5; "Hold High the Great Red Banner of Mao Tse-tung's Thought and Carry the GPCR Through to the End," *LAD,* June 6; "Long Live the GPCR," *RF* editorial, June 10; "Give the Masses a Free Hand, Thoroughly Oust the Counterrevolutionary Black Gang," *PD* editorial, June 16; etc.

parts in our own school were equally guilty. What we previously regarded as the prerogative of strong leadership now became in our minds pure domination for selfish purposes. It was the information from the CCRG about the mistakes of the national leaders that enabled us to see this.[14]

Available eyewitness accounts of anti-work-team incidents in Peking, Fukien, Canton, and Sian reveal no indications of clandestine organizational backing.[15] If these reports are accurate, the anti-work-team incidents were typically provoked by an observed discrepancy between the actions of the work teams and the version of Mao's Thought being disseminated through the media by the CCRG. "When we wanted information, we turned to the newspapers," Dai noted. "Anything which came from the province headquarters was immediately examined in terms of what we heard from *PD* and other rational sources. For the bulk of my classmates, the provincial apparatus existed only as the object of suspicion." [16]

Liu Shao-ch'i seemed to notice no connection between CCRG opposition to work teams in CC meetings and publicity media and grassroots anti-work-team incidents, attributing the latter rather to surreptitious backing by "high-ranking cadres of the former [Peking] Municipal Party Committee." [17] Possibly Liu was so much a prisoner of his organizing experience in the "white areas" (where access to publicity media was barred) that he failed to comprehend the independent mobilization potential of mass media.[18] It is also possible that he was aware that the CCRG was behind the anti-work-team students but, for tactical and political reasons, deliberately attributed the tenacity of the anti-work-team forces to the already discredited Peking Committee, under the assumption—or hope—that Mao would back him upon Mao's return to Peking. By July 27, this hope had been dashed, and he bitterly turned on K'ang Sheng: "I think you are behind K'uai Ta-fu," he said.[19]

As noted in Chapter 4, conflict tended to polarize along a line of

14 Ronald N. Montaperto, "From Revolutionary Successors to Revolutionaries: The Transformation of an Elite," in Scalapino, *Elites*, pp. 585, 588.

15 Cf. Hunter, *Shanghai Journal;* Ling, *Revenge;* Bennett and Montaperto, *Red Guard;* Andrew Watson's series on the GPCR in Sian, *FEER* 56, no. 3 (April 20, 1967): 123–126; *FEER* 56, no. 4 (April 27, 1967): 231–237; *FEER* 56, no. 5 (May 4, 1967): 266–269; Daubier, *Histoire;* Wang Ch'ao-t'ien, *Wo shih i-ko hung-wei-ping* [I am a Red Guard] (Taipei, 1967).

16 Montaperto, "From Revolutionary Successors," in Scalapino, *Elites*, pp. 575–600.

17 "Record," *JPRS*, no. 42349, p. 24.

18 E.g., in "Open and Secret Work" (September 1939), Liu takes to task those who fail to understand that mass movements and clandestine organizers necessarily go hand-in-hand: "They had never given any thought to the question of how, under the conditions prevalent then, the mass movements could be successfully launched." *CW* 1: 300.

19 "Record," *JPRS*, no. 42349, p. 24.

cleavage defined by the students' attitudes toward the school power structure, with the pro-work-team faction remaining in the clear majority in most schools until late fall.[20] When Mao decided that the rules under which the work teams were operating were basically misconceived and forced the teams to withdraw on July 28, he severely impaired the structural legitimacy of the Party and made his Thought the sole legitimate basis for mobilization. This was a great breakthrough for the CCRG, which now moved openly into the schools without competition from the Party apparatus, under the pretext of "learning from the masses." The formal Party organizational leadership at the central level collapsed at this point, except for a Maoist group loosely referred to as the "Party Center." But the local, provincial, and regional elites disposed of sufficient resources to survive, resist, and launch temporarily successful counterattacks even after being stripped of ideological legitimacy. The relevance of this lower- and middle-level resistance to the case of Liu Shao-ch'i is that Liu's presumed commitment to his former subordinates made him hostage to fortune, and the Maoists held him accountable for the continued resistance of the "Liuists."

"DIRECTION SWITCH"

What Mao called the period of "direction switch" may be divided into two distinct phases, divided by the October work conference. The first phase comprised a series of meetings at the elite level, where the goals of the GPCR were clarified, and a confusing transitional period at the mass level, in which different Red Guard factions formed and coalesced about the issues that were to define the next phase of struggle. After the conclusion of the October work conference, there is no record of further meetings among formal elites until the following year and initiative passed to the Red Guards and those prepared to lead them. In the first phase, Liu appeared to have been rehabilitated; in the second, he became subject to intensified attacks.

Though we have examined and dismissed the possibility that Liu actively led the opposition Mao complained of at the Eleventh Plenum, it seems that key members of Liu's political machine were openly skeptical of Mao's plans. Of the six regional Party bureaus in

---

[20] In a speech on September 25 to responsible persons representing the "Third Headquarters," Chou En-lai said, "You are the minority; . . . being a minority, only through perseverance of the truth and remedy of mistakes can you become the majority." Tsinghua University Defend-the-East Corps, ed., *Collection of Leaders' Speeches* 4 (November 1966).

China, the first secretaries of two (Li Hsüeh-feng of the North China Bureau and Liu Lan-t'ao of the Northwest China Bureau) had in the past collaborated with Liu; Li Ching-ch'üan of the Southwest and Sung Jen-ch'iung of the Northeast China Bureau were associated with Teng Hsiao-p'ing.[21] These middle-range leaders were alarmed by P'eng's fall and by burgeoning protests in their own domains (doubtlessly appreciating the import of Mao's July 21 remark, "When you are told to kindle a fire to burn yourselves, will you do it? After all, you yourselves may be burned.") and began to muster their forces to resist the GPCR. As Mao recalled in a later speech:

At that time many people were still not in agreement. Li Ching-ch'üan and Liu Lan-t'ao were not in agreement. But try to get them to talk about it and they would say, "I disagree in Peking and when I go back I will still disagree." In the end I was only able to let things go a step further and then see! [22]

In dealing with his frightened colleagues, Mao adopted a double-edged strategy to ensure compliance, combining inner-Party suasion with extra-Party pressure tactics. "There are always some who are unwilling to carry them [decisions] out," he noted. "But this time things may be better than in the past, because formerly decisions were not made public." [23] Within Party councils, he emphasized that "our policy is to 'learn from past mistakes to avoid future ones' " and assured his colleagues that they could promote the GPCR without intolerable risk to themselves:

You are too impatient. You say that the situation is sharply confused, or it is beyond control, but the masses have by no means committed a big error. They will, in short, settle down in a correct direction. If you say that they are confused, then let me continue for months. We can reach a conclusion when they have agitated to their hearts' content.[24]

Yet even while the Eleventh Plenum was in session Mao had encouraged the masses to rise against perceived inequities in the established order. On August 1, he wrote a "Letter to the Red Guards of

21 P'eng Shu-tse et al., *Behind China's "Great Cultural Revolution,"* (New York, 1967), p. 22. "Talks to CC Leaders," in *CB*, no. 891 (October 8, 1969), p. 59.

22 "Speech to Foreign Visitors" (August 1967), *Ming Pao*, July 5, 1968, p. 1. Nor had these holdouts changed their minds two months later, as the following exchange at the October work conference indicates: "The Chairman asked Liu Lan-t'ao: 'What are you going to do when you get back to your posts?' Liu replied: 'We'll take a look at things first when we are back at our posts.' Chairman Mao said: 'You are still so circumspect in your words.' " "Speech at a Report Meeting" (October 24, 1966), *JPRS*, no. 49826 (February 12, 1970): 9.

23 *CB*, no. 891 (February 12, 1970): 64.

24 *Yomiuri*, December 14, in *DSJP*, December 15, 1966, pp. 9–10.

the Middle School Attached to Tsinghua University," in which he congratulated the students for big-character posters dated June 24 and July 4, which proclaimed that "rebellion against the reactionaries is justified," and added his "warm support" for similar revolutionary activities by Peking University rebels.[25] On August 5, he wrote his first big-character poster, in which he lambasted the masterminds of the work-team policy as perpetrators of "white terror" and urged his followers to "bombard the headquarters" of "bourgeois dictatorship." [26] On August 10, he made a personal appearance to the masses on a Peking street and told them to "be concerned with state affairs and carry the GPCR to the end"; a report of his appearance was included briefly in *PD*, on the radio stations, and in a Hong Kong Communist paper:

It would be impossible to say how many hands were stretched out to him. Many eyes were filled with tears of joy. . . . Many who had shaken hands with Chairman Mao told everyone they met: "Come and shake hands with me! My hands have just touched those of the great Chairman Mao!" [27]

An examination of "The Sixteen Points" reveals the same admixture of coercion and persuasion in dealing with the Party powerholders, the same desire to reconcile the inherently contradictory goals of revolution and authority. The movement's multiple objectives were concisely formulated in point one:

At present, our aim is to knock down those Party persons in authority taking the capitalist road, criticize the bourgeois academic "authorities," criticize the ideologies of the bourgeoisie and all the exploiting classes, reform education and literature and the arts, and reform all superstructure which is incompatible with the socialist economic base.[28]

These objectives were to be accomplished by instigating mass criticism, which would destroy the legitimacy of bourgeois ideological vestiges. The "main force" in this criticism was "the masses of the workers, peasants, soldiers, revolutionary intellectuals, and revolutionary cadres"; they were encouraged to organize a permanent structure of extra-Party Cultural Revolution "teams," "committees," and

[25] "Letter to Red Guards" (August 1, 1966), in Jerome Ch'en, *Mao Papers*, pp. 115–116.

[26] *Ibid.*, p. 117.

[27] But in Peking the papers with this report were withdrawn from circulation, and new editions were printed without it. Radio stations remained silent about the event in their afternoon programs. *Die Zeit* (Hamburg) 39 (September 23, 1966): 3.

[28] "The Resolution of the Eleventh Plenum of the CC of the CCP—The Sixteen Articles" (August 8, 1966), in Jerome Ch'en, *Mao Papers*, pp. 117–127.

"congresses" in each school or work unit, whose leadership would be selected through a "system of general elections, like that of the Paris Commune." As to the CCP, the Party was to provide bold leadership to the movement:

What the CC of the Party demands of the Party committees at all levels is that they persevere in giving correct leadership, put daring above everything else, boldly arouse the masses . . . and dismiss from their leading posts all those in authority who are taking the capitalist road and so make possible the recapture of the leadership for the proletarian revolutionaries.[29]

Point three states further that "the outcome of this great Cultural Revolution will be determined" by whether the Party "boldly" aroused the masses, leaving no doubt that the Party held the mandate to lead the movement, even while leaving open the question as to whether it would in fact do so. The PLA was mentioned only briefly (point fifteen) and was apparently not expected to play an active role but was to serve as a model for revolutionary education. The CCRG was not mentioned, remaining an ad hoc body dependent on Mao's patronage. Although the Party was to be held *responsible* for the "outcome of this great Cultural Revolution," the *initiative* was given to the masses, who were encouraged to "liberate themselves," while "any method of doing things on their behalf must not be used." The Party power-holders were also inhibited by the knowledge that among them were lurking an unspecified number of "capitalist-roaders," who were the "main target of the present movement"; it was their possible inclusion in this category (on incalculable criteria) that most crimped their efforts to provide "bold" leadership.[30]

After a period of relative quiescence lasting from the end of the Eleventh Plenum until convocation of the October work conference, conflict between radical elites and veteran cadres revived. Mao abandoned the equivocal role he had adopted during the Eleventh Plenum for a stance altogether more sympathetic to the power-holders, which may well have led the latter to believe that Mao had toned down his original objectives. "Who wants to knock you down?" Mao asked. "I do not. I do not believe that the Red Guards want to do that either." Mao apologized for his "mistake" in inciting the masses to attack his colleagues by sending them letters and posting big-character posters, averred that he did not expect that "a single big-character poster, the Red Guards and the large-scale exchange of revolutionary experience would lead to the demise of various provincial and municipal com-

29 *Ibid.*   30 *Ibid.*

mittees."[31] He also acknowledged that he had underestimated the practical difficulties involved in attempting to lead a movement that might at any time target its leadership:

Some people say: "A thorough grasp of the principles does not guarantee the correct handling of concrete problems." At first I did not quite understand this. How was it possible to have a thorough grasp of principles and yet be incompetent in handling concrete problems? Now I see that there is something in that statement. . . . After [our] last conference and before meetings were convened properly in some places, seven or eight [Party] secretaries out of ten began to receive [the Red Guards]. They were thrown into a panic. . . . They did not realize that the Red Guards were annoyed by them. They lost the initiative when they were taken aback by some of the questions. But the lost initiative can be recovered.[32]

The available documents from the October work conference suggest that the debate between radicals and veteran cadres was resolved in a somewhat forced compromise: the radicals were authorized to carry the GPCR through "to the end," but Mao stipulated that errant cadres should have time and opportunity to reform themselves. Mao assured them that he would "feel sorry" if they failed to "pass the test."

Liu Shao-ch'i's fate was decided within the context of this general decision. Judging from those who most frequently interrupted his conversations, Mao's closest advisors at this point included Chou En-lai, Ch'en Po-ta, Lin Piao, and K-ang Sheng; there is no indication that Liu actively participated in discussions except to present his self-criticism on October 23. Mao's lieutenants split into two camps with respect to Liu: Chou En-lai argued that Liu and Teng Hsiao-p'ing "should be allowed to come back and go to work with fresh spirit." But Lin Piao and the CCRG were evidently not placated by Liu's self-criticism, because, on the last day of the meeting, two days after Liu had submitted it and one day after Mao had issued his "pardon," both Lin Piao and Ch'en Po-ta delivered speeches that contained long critiques of the Liu-Teng "bourgeois line of suppressing the masses."

---

31 "Speech at a Report Meeting" (October 24, 1966), in *CB*, no. 891 (October 8, 1969): 70. Mao's expression of surprise has seemed implausible to some observers, but, in terms of his difficulties in getting the GPCR underway, it was perhaps appropriate. "Last year, many comrades did not read the articles in criticism of Wu Han; they did not care. . . . The first few months of this GPCR, from January to May, I published articles on a number of occasions in the *PD* and *KMJP*, and the Center also issued a notification on May 16. But they did not attract the attention of the people. Then came the big-character poster and the Red Guards which in one stroke caught everyone's attention." *CB* no. 891: 59.

32 Jerome Ch'en, *Mao Papers*, p. 44.

"Why has the incorrect line continued to appear even after Chairman Mao laid down the correct line for the Cultural Revolution?" Ch'en Po-ta asked pointedly. "If those who have committed mistakes do not correct them after they have been pointed out there is the possibility that they might be considered counterrevolutionary." [33] Lin Piao repeated allegations of Liu's possible complicity in a "coup" plot and appealed to Mao's vanity: "Everyone has, in the last few days, come to know the attitude adopted by comrades of the CC such as Liu and Teng toward the spread of Chairman Mao's Thought. It certainly makes one indignant!" [34] K'ang Sheng raised the issue of Liu's responsibility for "extinguishing class struggle." Although Mao closed the meeting with a decree that big-character posters should not be posted against Liu and Teng in the streets, this edict seems to have done little more than paper over a deep, persisting cleavage between Liu and the Left.[35]

The October work conference was followed by a phase of mass mobilization in which the tenuous compromise between radicals and moderates fell apart and criticism against Liu escalated. The "focal point" was on the criticism against the bourgeois reactionary line in the three months of October, November, and December 1966, Mao later reflected. This "openly provoked contradictions within the Party." Among the elites, power reverted to "separate kingdoms," consisting at the central level of two coalitions: the CC-State Council, under the jurisdiction of Chou En-lai, which issued a series of directives designed to safeguard the economy; and a coalition between CCRG and MAC, led by Chiang Ch'ing and Lin Piao, which sought to escalate mass mobilization. Mao apparently left Peking with Lin Piao for the Shanghai-Hangchow region on November 26, following the last T'ienanmen Square rally, and no further word was heard from him until January.[36] At local and provincial levels, the attenua-

[33] Lin Piao, "Speech at a Central Committee Work Conference" (October 25, 1966), in *JPRS*, no. 49826 (February 12, 1970): 56.

[34] *Ibid.*

[35] In a speech to an October 12, 1966 rally, Ch'i Pen-yü criticized Liu without naming him: "In 1945 some people asked us to turn over the armed forces. At the time of cooperativization some people asked us to dissolve these cooperatives. . . . When the *"san tzu i pao"* [three selfs and one guarantee] proposal was made in 1962 and in the period of difficulties, the struggle was very violent. . . . At that time those who called for 'fixing output quotas according to the household' were not comrades below, not comrades at the basic level. The line was consistently advocated from 1962, 1963, 1964, 1965, to 1966." Tsinghua University Defend-the-East Corps, ed., *Collection of Leaders' Speeches* 4 (November 1966).

[36] *Tokyo Shimbun*, January 6, 1967, and *Sankei*, January 7, 1967, cited in Rice, *Mao's Way*, p. 249. Whereas before November 1965, Mao had occasionally received Party and government officials who were in Peking, he was not reported

tion of vertical controls left power-holders with complete autonomy in implementing the GPCR; they tended to form protective alliances with local PLA authorities and employ various active or passive defense tactics. At the mass level, ideological power was "in the streets," accessible to those with the requisite demagogical skills. The roles of the following actors in the autumn "direction switch" will be examined more closely: (1) local and provincial power-holders, (2) "revolutionary masses," (3) the CCRG, and (4) Chou En-lai and Lin Piao.

(1) The scenario set forth in "The Sixteen Points" for the "proletarian revolutionary line" called on the power-holders to combine two roles: leaders of the masses and potential targets of mass criticism. These roles are contradictory but not necessarily incompatible; the elective officeholder in Western democracies has institutionalized the two different role requirements. However, political debate in Western democracies has over long historical experience evolved implicit rules of civility, which set limits on polemics. The GPCR, on the other hand, was intended to arouse a critical spirit in a polity that had long regarded any expression of political opposition as illegitimate, and the Red Guards took advantage of their unwonted polemical license to articulate a "revolutionary" rhetoric whose action implications included sanctions the power-holders regarded as unacceptable: purge, public disgrace, even physical violence. The early examples of Wan Hsiao-t'ang, First Secretary of the Tientsin Municipal Party Committee, and several others, who submitted to the criticism of the masses and died as a result of the treatment they received in mass struggle meetings, must have confirmed their worst fears.[37] These incidents reinforced the power-holders' anticipatory "counterrevolutionary" instincts, which in turn exacerbated their difficulties with the Red Guards.

To accord with the altered "rules of the game" that had been promulgated at the Eleventh Plenum, the power-holders shifted their method of control from democratic centralism, based on the structural legitimacy of the Party, to bottom-to-top mobilization, relying on social forces sharing their interest in the status quo. They quickly

---

to have received any Chinese officials from then through the end of 1966, although there were several accounts of his meeting with foreign guests during the same period.

[37] Even P'an Fu-sheng, First Secretary of the Heilungkiang Provincial Committee, who had confessed errors and pledged loyalty to Mao immediately after the Eleventh Plenum, was violently struggled against by Red Guards, and had to be rushed to a hospital after being deprived of food for four days. RF no. 6 (May 8, 1967): 35, in Parris Chang, "Strategies for Survival," in Scalapino, Elites, pp. 512–515.

discovered a community of interest with "five-good" **Red Guards** under the leadership of cadre children. "It was not difficult for the [Amoy] Municipal Party Committee to convert the Red Guard General Headquarters into a protective organization," Ken Ling, a not always reliable Red Guard chronicler of the GPCR, observed.[38] Even allowing for Red Guard polemical exaggeration of the power-holders' responsibility for a now autonomous factional opposition, it seems that power-holders did contribute in at least some measure to the rise of "counterrevolutionary" forces. After August 20, Peking was flooded with big-character posters accusing power-holders of organizing counteroffensives; reports of resistance also came from Tsingtao and Tsinan in Shantung Province, Ch'angsha in Hunan, Chengchow and Loyang in Honan, Kweilin in Kwangsi, and from Canton, Shanghai, et al. Mao noted on September 7:

The situations which have developed in Tsingtao, Ch'angsha, and Sian are all the same. In all instances, organized workers and peasants have been opposing the students, but they are all wrong and things must not be allowed to continue in this way.[39]

To protect themselves, the power-holders were also quite skillful in manipulating the organizational resources still at their disposal. Although they were relieved of command over the local PLA units on September 1,[40] in many provinces, power-holders deposited 'black materials" in PLA Headquarters for safekeeping, or persuaded local PLA leaders to deploy troops to guard the premises of the Party against rebels. Some civilian Party leaders even donned PLA uniforms and worked in the offices of the PLA headquarters, using it as

[38] Ling, *Revenge*, p. 65. When T'an Li-fu, a leader of moderate Red Guards, gave a speech in August supporting the mobilization of the "5-red" categories, it was reported that the Party distributed his speech at all levels. The Peking Party committee openly supported his position, and, when radicals assailed it, the committee encouraged him via telephone to stand firm. *Chung-hsüeh wan ko-pao* [Middle school revolutionary evening news], April 1, 1967; I owe this citation to Hong Yung Lee.

[39] From August 12 to 20, 1966 there were street fights between Red Guards and "Workers' Scarlet Guards" [*kung-jen ch'ih-wei-tui*], which were resolved only by the intervention of the military. (Radio Hunan, June 3, 1968). From August 25 to September 1, "white terror" was reported in Tsingtao (*PD*, January 30, 1967). On September 11, 1966, *PD* alleged that the "Sixteen Points" were being "openly defied" by "responsible persons in some localities and units" who "created various pretexts to suppress the mass movement . . . and even provoked a number of workers and peasants . . . to antagonize the revolutionary students." Ch'en Po-ta endorsed this allegation in a speech in early December. *Tung-feng chan-pao* [East wind battle news] (Peking), December 11, 1966.

[40] On that date, the political department in charge of troops in each province was removed from the provincial Party committee and control was vested in the MAC. Blumer, *Kulturrevolution*, p. 209.

their "shelter." [41] The power-holders also continued to use their leverage with sympathetic central figures (such as T'ao Chu) to solicit covert support. Although they could no longer use ideological appeals to mobilize countervailing mass organizations after Mao had shifted his support from the Party to the CCRG, they did use their patronage to induce officials and relatively satisfied strata of workers and peasants to support them, promising promotions, raises, bonuses, and other incentives. Finally, the power-holders exploited the fear that "once the butcher is dead, [we] will have to eat pork with bristles on," [42] in some cases allegedly contributing to the economic disruption in order to discredit the revolutionaries and make a case for their own indispensability.

As a survival strategy, the power-holders' use of evasion, suppression, cooptation, and preemption must be considered temporarily successful; each time the radicals escalated the conflict by expanding the movement's mobilizational scope, the power-holders responded with the countermobilization of relatively satisfied groups. But like P'eng Chen, who forced Mao's target definition to expand by continually frustrating the attack on Wu Han, the power-holders unwittingly provoked a radical redefinition of Red Guard objectives to include the entire Party apparatus, led by Liu Shao-ch'i. To be sure, the intransigence of the power-holders was not the sole, perhaps not even the chief, cause of the escalation against them. Escalation in the intensity of criticism or the range of targets was a highly effective mobilization device, and the reinterpretation of power-holders' errors in ever graver terms was in some measure a reflection of the ambitions of the Left, which rested on the power of their mobilized mass base.

(2) The Red Guard movement [43] went through three stages in the summer and fall of 1966, which may be distinguished on the basis of the type of external control and range of criticism targets.

(a) Before the Eleventh Plenum, the activities of "revolutionary teachers and students" were confined to school campuses and strictly controlled, first by the local Party committees and educational authorities, later by work teams. Criticism targets were defined by the authorities on the basis of their pedagogic-cultural output, their classification during previous campaigns, and their attitude toward the authorities.

41 *Ta p'i-p'an t'ung-hsün* [Mass criticism and repudiation bulletin] (Canton), East Is Red Corps, cited in Parris Chang, "Strategies for Survival," in Scalapino, ed., *Elites.*
42 Jerome Ch'en, *Mao Papers*, p. 47.
43 In this section I owe much to the work of Hong Yung Lee, who is completing a dissertation for the Department of Political Science, University of Chicago.

(b) Following repudiation of the "bourgeois reactionary line" at the Eleventh Plenum, Red Guards "sallied forth to the streets" (*shang-chieh*) in an attack on the "four olds" (viz., culture, habits, customs, ideas). The attack involved desecrating various symbols of traditional culture and ransacking the homes of China's residual bourgeoisie. It was carried out by moderate (i.e., "five good") Red Guards with the support of local Party authorities, who welcomed any divertissement from the dangerous issues of responsibility for the work teams and the identity of the "Party powerholders." [44] This stage reached its acme in Peking in the second and third week of August; thereafter it began to slack off due to protests from the center.[45]

During September Red Guard "link-up" (*ch'uan-lien*) delegations from Peking began converging on district capitals to "exchange revolutionary experience" with local Red Guards. It is said that the transportation expenses of revolutionary exchanges for August and September totaled 20 percent of the yearly transportation budget. This lateral mobility tended to radicalize the movement, since Red Guards were chosen for liaison on the basis of their militance and became all the more militant in strange places where no one knew them.[46] The tendency was to begin accusations at lower levels and rise to the top; by early September, Red Guards had attacked provincial leaders, and in mid-October, the regional bureaus came under fire, including Liu Lan-t'ao and Li Ching-ch'üan. The attacks consisted of demonstrations, sit-ins, and big-character posters, which used brief slogans to compensate for skimpy concrete knowledge of policy at this early stage.[47]

(c) When the National Day "armistice" on attacks against central elites ended, there was an apparent net reversal of migration patterns as Red Guards took advantage of the extension of free public transit to the rest of the country in early October to send link-up teams to Peking to view Chairman Mao on the T'ienanmen rostrum.[48] Re-emphasis on the work team issue resulted in attacks on central elites, which quickly escalated to include the upper strata of the central gov-

[44] For example, Hunter reports that Chao Tzu-yang, First Secretary of the Kwangtung Party committee, congratulated the Red Guards in late August for vandalizing the homes of the bourgeoisie. *Shanghai Journal*, p. 209.

[45] E.g., *PD* admonished on August 28 that civilized methods should replace force.

[46] As Chou En-lai was to note in a speech on September 17, 1967: "[Red Guards] who go to places outside Peking always support the faction which opposes the leadership. . . . Your liaison stations have also brought the factionalism of Peking to outside places."

[47] *Mainichi*, October 28, in *DSJP*, October 28, 1966, p. 13; *Mainichi*, November 25, in *DSJP*, November 28, 1966, pp. 12–13.

[48] Ling, *Revenge*, p. 99.

ernment ministries, taking a zigzag course due to protests from central and local Party leaders, and to a split in the ranks of the Red Guards. The first wall poster criticizing Liu as "Li Hsüeh-feng's wire-puller" was posted in front of the Peking Municipal Committee on October 10, together with another poster saying, "Wang Kuang-mei, you must go back to Tsinghua University and undergo self-examination." [49] Yet the tentative nature of the initial attacks on Liu suggests that they did not have authoritative approval at this stage. According to Japanese newsmen, open criticism of Liu and Teng first surfaced in Tientsin and Shanghai, not appearing in Peking until late October. Toward the end of that month, posters attacking Liu appeared in increasing numbers, but there were none supporting him; on the other hand, every time critical posters appeared others were posted on top of them or the posters were quietly removed.[50]

In November, criticisms of Liu became increasingly forthright as the conflict between radical Red Guards and their "royalist" opponents polarized. In mid-November, posters began to link together Liu, Teng, and Li Hsüeh-feng as leaders of the "bourgeois reactionary line." This conception (which justified attribution of guilt to Liu for mistakes *analogous* to his prototypical mistake even if they had no *empirical* connection to it) was a logical extension of the characterization of his error as an error in "line." The struggle between two "lines" was first publicly mentioned in a *Red Flag* editorial on October 1 and given much publicity on October 19 in the official report of the fourth reception of Red Guards at T'ienanmen Square, which appeared in all the newspapers. A second extrapolation of the "line" concept was the idea, first used in Mao's August big-character poster, that Liu's error was associated with a history of analogous errors. This implication also became public in November, when Red Guards began distributing a twenty-page pamphlet that accused Liu and Teng of "having a long history in their opposition to Mao Tse-tung" and quoted corroborating passages from speeches made by the two men to the CCP Seventh Congress in 1945 and the Eighth Congress in 1956.[51]

The conservative Red Guards who had been shunted aside split off and formed a "United Action Group" (*Lien-ho hsing-tung wei-yüan-hui*, abbreviated Lien-tung), and the conflict escalated to focus on the presumed leaders of the opposing groups: the CCRG on the left and the Liu-Teng "Headquarters" on the right. The consistent tendency

49 *Sankei*, November 4, in *DSJP*, November 9, 1966, pp. 10–13.

50 *Mainichi*, November 25, in *DSJP*, November 26–28, 1966, pp. 12–13; *Nihon Keizai*, November 21, in *DSJP*, November 22, 1966, p. 8.

51 Keesing's Publications, *The Cultural Revolution in China: Its Origins and Course up to August, 1967* (Keynsham, Bristol, 1967), p. 22.

to escalate criticism to the top leaders was in keeping with one of the basic premises of the GPCR: it is wrong to "hit hard at a great number to protect a small handful," for the "masses" are by definition incapable of guilt and subject only to being "hoodwinked" by bad leaders. On November 20, while attacking the Maoist "Third Headquarters," the "Second Headquarters" implicitly criticized Chiang Ch'ing, Ch'en Po-ta, Kuan Feng, et al. On November 24, in the Peking Aeronautical Institute, the children of high-ranking cadres organized an "August 1 Column" and put up the poster, "Questioning the CCRG"; on November 29, they posted "Again Questioning the CCRG." The debate escalated during the first two weeks of December, and the loyalists were strong enough to produce a "December black wind" (shih-erh-yüeh hei-feng).[52] On December 5, Lien-tung declared, "The new form of bourgeois reactionary line [the CCRG] is the greatest menace in the current movement." The loyalists accused the CCRG of implementing an ultra-left line that was "left" in form but right in essence: "Let the masses liberate themselves," they cried, according to one not always reliable source. "Kick aside the CCRG, we don't need a nursemaid."

The CCP decided on Liu Shao-ch'i as Mao Tse-tung's successor more than twenty years ago. Who the Hell is Lin Piao? Lin Piao should step aside. Chiang Ch'ing is only a stinking old woman. Wang Kuang-mei is not guilty. Mao Tse-tung is being kept from the facts, and he is a senile old fool![53]

By the middle of December, the "black wind" had been reversed and a leftist triumph assured. Of most critical importance in deciding the victory was the open intervention of the CCRG on behalf of the Left, to be examined below. An ancillary factor, ironically enough, was the termination of link-ups. On November 16, the CC and State Council issued a directive stipulating that following the last mass rally on November 25 (at which Liu and Teng also made their last public appearance in an official capacity), all Red Guards should return home to help with the autumn harvest; to enforce the directive, free transport for liaison was rescinded as of December 20. Japanese reporters noticed that, with the departure of most of the Red Guards, criticisms of Liu in Peking became more outspoken.[54] The reason for this paradox was that the majority of Tsinghua University militants had returned to their campus by mid-December in compliance with this regulation, making it possible to form the "United Chingkang-

---

52 Hinton, "Hundred Day War," p. 97.
53 Quoted in Ling, Revenge, p. 160.
54 Sankei, November 28, in DSJP, November 29, 1966, pp. 1–2; Mainichi, December 27, in DSJP, December 28, 1966, pp. 25–26.

shan Regiment" there and turn the spearhead against Liu; Tsinghua thereafter became a concentration point for the exposure of Liu. For example, on December 24, the "United Chingkangshan Regiment" put up posters listing ten "crimes" of Liu; on the next day, they held a great rally at T'ienanmen Square to criticize the "bourgeois reactionary line and the bourgeois headquarters headed by Liu Shao-ch'i and Teng Hsiao-p'ing" and posted great quantities of posters and mimeographed leaflets criticizing him in downtown Peking. The struggle meeting and later "trials" of Wang Kuang-mei were also held at Tsinghua, as were the self-examinations of Liu T'ao; Liu's first self-criticism first appeared on a *Chingkangshan* wall poster, and was then published in the faction's tabloid.[55]

(3)The CCRG saw its role not as a fair broker between heterodox factions, but as the leadership of the "revolutionary masses," a role it sought to play in accord with its interpretation of Mao's Thought. That interpretation emphasized that two basic questions must be answered before conflicting claims to legitimacy could be resolved: (a) Which side favors maximal participation in the movement? (b) Which side is relatively deprived (in the minority, oppressed, and so forth)? It identified the side that stood for setting "frames" on mass mobilization and backed relatively satisfied groups as the opposing "side" and the promulgators of the "bourgeois reactionary line." This opposition was later described as the (more blameworthy) "Party persons in authority taking the capitalist road," and the CCRG eventually concluded that Liu Shao-ch'i's spirit motivated the resistance, that the key to this line's defeat was Liu's public repudiation. These ideological objectives meshed perfectly with the CCRG's power-political interests, so it is difficult to say whether the ideological or the power-political motive was the more dominant. The radical younger CCRG members were middle-level elites (e.g., Chang Ch'un-ch'iao and Yao Wen-yüan were subordinate officials in the Shanghai Party Committee, while Wang Li, Kuan Feng, et al. were radical publicists) and whenever veteran cadres were forced to withdraw, the younger men stood ready to assume the vacated positions. For example, after Deputy General Secretary P'eng Chen fell (in June) and General Secretary Teng Hsiao-p'ing was implicated (in October), the CCRG assumed the powers of the CC Secretariat, according to Chiang Ch'ing:

55 *Nihon Keizai,* January 1, in *DSJP,* January 5, 1967, p. 9; *Chingkangshan,* (Peking), January 1, quoted in *Sankei,* January 3, in *DSJP,* January 4, 1967; *Mainichi,* December 27, in *DSJP,* December 28, 1966, pp. 25–26; *Asahi,* January 1, in *DSJP,* December 31–January 5, 1967, p. 8.

I have a little bit of additional work since last year. I am also Secretary of the Standing Committee. As a matter of fact, the entire CCRG is nothing but a Secretariat for the Committee. All they do is make suggestions and provide references for Chairman Mao, Vice-Chairman Lin, Premier Chou En-lai, and members of the Standing Committee.[56]

CCRG intervention seemed to arise in response to local initiatives by Red Guard groups, which escalated the struggle to include a new issue and then drew higher echelons into the fray when the issue could not be resolved at lower levels. In resolving these issues, the CCRG played a decisive role in determining the movement's direction. The three issues confronting the movement in the fall—the same issues that had stymied it during the "fifty days"—were now brought into the arena of open contestation: criteria for participation, leadership, and criticism targets. The last issue is the only one directly concerned with Liu Shao-ch'i, but it was inextricably intertwined with the other two: the selection of participants in the long run determined the leadership of the movement, and the leadership selected the targets.

The first issue to arise was that of *criteria for participation*. Beginning at the end of July and in early August, the slogan, "When the father is reactionary, the son is a scoundrel" appeared in some higher and middle schools in Peking.[57] When the strict use of blood lines to define class membership was first introduced, it was radical in intent, directed against P'eng Chen, who had used "emphasis on performance" in order to coopt "bourgeois academic authorities" into the Party and to permit children of the "five black" categories to carve out professional careers in the school system.[58] But by August, the use of blood lines tended not only to set "frames" on the mobilization of the masses, but also to inhibit further expansion of the range of targets. The retention of blood-line criteria was often linked with the survival of a Red Guard leadership sympathetic to the work teams well after the latter withdrew, because the Red Guards who insisted on blood-line criteria became dominated by a work-team-appointed leader-

[56] Chiang, "Speech at Enlarged Session of MAC" (April 12, 1967).

[57] Most of the posters written in August that have become available begin by proclaiming that the writers were members of the "5-red" categories and therefore had a right to revolt against the old world; only leftists and not rightists (defined by blood lines) had this right.

[58] In 1964, P'eng had introduced a new policy on CYL membership—the CYL could absorb youths of bourgeois background and even those of rich peasant and landlord origin. In 1965 the CYL consequently accepted more than 8 million new members, more than in any year since 1949. In some cases, a good academic record was all that was necessary for admission. Bennett and Montaperto, *Red Guard*, p. 133.

ship that often included children of high cadres (*kao-kan tzu ti*), such as Liu T'ao (Liu's daughter), Ho P'eng-fei (son of Ho Lung), or Li Li-feng (son of Li Ching-ch'üan). Survival of the original Red Guard leadership created a basis for continuity of a pro-work team "line," as Liu Shao-ch'i conceded in his October self-criticism:

> When work groups withdrew, their functions and powers were turned over to the Cultural Revolution committees and provincial preparatory committees of various schools. Since most of them were directly or indirectly assigned by work groups, the members of those committees were unable to implement the correct line of the Party.[59]

The grievances of the "five-good" or "five-red" categories had to do with the prestige or power held by certain members of non-"five-red" categories (teachers, landlords who still collected rents, ex-capitalists who still received fixed interests, and the like). When the spearhead of the movement threatened the basis of their privileges, "they [the provisional preparatory committees] protected the work teams in order to protect themselves."[60] This was of course particularly true for children of cadres, whose dilemma was cruelly satirized by the radicals: they "don't want to become children of Party power-holders taking the capitalist road."[61]

By taking an early and outspoken stand against the theory of "natural red" (i.e., red father, red son), the CCRG facilitated the mobilization of the more radical nonproletarian elements not compromised by their earlier collaboration with the Party. As early as August 14, Ch'en Po-ta had denounced this exclusionary principle, urging that performance be given consideration equal to that granted to class background. Ch'en's position was quickly endorsed by Chiang Ch'ing, Lin Piao, and even (more qualifiedly) by Chou En-lai and Liu Shao-ch'i.[62] Finally on October 5, a MAC directive stated that Mao's

[59] Liu, "Self-Examination" (October 23, 1966).

[60] K'uai Ta-fu, "An Open Letter to the Premier" (August 6, 1966), in Chingkang-shan Red Guard Propaganda Team, Tsinghua University, comp., *Selected Big-Character Posters of Tsinghua University.*

[61] "More recently, let us look at the revolutionary leftists who brought forth their fearless rebellious spirit in the first stage of the Cultural Revolution. . . . Have not some of them since turned into henchmen to defend the bourgeois reactionary line? Have not the little warriors of the middle school affiliated to Tsinghua University, who wrote, 'Long live the revolutionary rebel spirit!' turned into active promoters of the 'work team line,' extinguishing the fire and supporting the 'monarchy' everywhere, and declaring that they would 'wipe out the Red Guards of Chingkangshan in three months'?" Red Wind Combat Team, Red Flag Combat Brigade, "Whither the Revolutionary Minority?" *RF* (Peking Aeronautical Institute), no. 3 (December 26, 1966): 3–4, in *JPRS*, no. 40234 (March 13, 1967): 23.

[62] As one might expect, the support expressed by Liu Shao-ch'i and Chou En-lai for an "open-door" admissions policy was somewhat more restrained. Chou said on

Thought should be the sole criterion for class membership. Largely because of this elite support, the Eleventh Plenum was followed by progressive mobilization of those who had been classified non-"five-red," either on the basis of parentage or opposition to work teams.[63] The non-"five-red" categories were not integrated into the original Red Guards, however, but formed their own factions, later coalescing to form their own radical "headquarters."

The radical solution to the controversy concerning appropriate criteria of participation led immediately to a struggle for *leadership* of the Red Guard movement. The establishment of three Red Guard headquarters (all set up in early September in Peking) launched a process of polarization that led to clear-cut victory of the Left. Whereas the "First" and "Second Headquarters" were still led by "children of high cadres" and others compromised by their collaboration with the work teams during the "fifty days," the "Third Headquarters" was led by K'uai Ta-fu and radical minorities comprising Tsinghua's Ching-kangshan Regiment, Peking Aeronautical Institute's Red Flag Combat Team (Hung-ch'i chan-tou tui) and Geological Institute's East is Red group (Tung-fang-hung) who had borne the brunt of work team "restriction, suppression, and control." Enjoying the patronage of the CCRG, the "Third Headquarters" boldly leaped to the forefront of the movement, and when the CCRG again raised the issue of the work teams as a means of stigmatizing the "bourgeois reactionary line," the "Third Headquarters" was prepared to dramatize the issue, unencumbered as it was by compromising connections with that line.

The CCRG's support for the radical "Third Headquarters," which contributed incalculably to the latter's eventual triumph, was manifest in several ways. First, the CCRG gave publicity to radical ideological slogans: Ch'en Po-ta's October 3 editorial in RF (No. 13) and Lin

---

September 1: "Those students, though having poor family background, may also join the Red Guard organization, providing they have turned against their original class and behaved well, because they could not choose their class when they were born. But, the 'Red Guards' organizations should chiefly admit students of the 5 red categories." "Premier Chou En-lai's Speech to the Representatives of Peking 'Red Guards' in the Annex of the People's Great Hall in Peking on September 1," in CB, no. 819 (March 10, 1967): 17. Lin Piao and Chiang Ch'ing, on the other hand, stated forthrightly, "There is no relationship between standpoint and class origin. . . . We consider whether one is superior to another or not lies neither in his class origin, nor in his personality, nor his age, but his performance and holding of Mao Tse-tung's Thought." *Wen-hua ko-ming t'ung-hsün* [Cultural Revolution bulletin], December 11, 1967.

[63] *E.g.*, by early October, 20 percent of the membership of the Red Guard Military School was drawn from "nonrevolutionary" classes and about 10 percent of the teachers and staff had also been admitted. *Nihon Keizai*, October 12, in *DSJP*, October 12, 1966, p. 22.

Piao's speech of October 6 designated the main target of criticism as the "Party persons in authority taking the capitalist road," [64] and the CCRG kept the explosive work-team issue alive. Second, CCRG members attended and addressed "Third Headquarters" rallies and meetings but boycotted meetings by the other two headquarters.[65] At an "oath-taking" rally on October 6, the first public occasion on which rebels formerly labeled "counterrevolutionary" by the work teams appeared on the speaker's platform, Chou En-lai for the first time joined the CCRG in support of the "Third Headquarters." Thanks in large part to this elite support, but also to the radicals' enterprise in exploiting publicity media (the three newspapers published by "Third Headquarters" factions, Tsinghua's *Chingkangshan*, Aeronautical Institute's *Red Flag*, and Geological Institute's *East Is Red*, had circulations greatly exceeding those of any moderate rival), the radicals swept the field. In October, a power struggle in the "First Headquarters" resulted in a leftist takeover, and in late November the Left finally captured control of the "Second Headquarters." [66]

Capture of leadership by the Left in turn led to the criticism of more prominent targets. As noted above, the triumph of the Left alienated the Right, which split off, formed Lien-tung, and launched a vigorous, temporarily successful counterattack. Taking its cue from the CCRG, Lien-tung shifted polemical focus from its rivals' less pure class backgrounds to the errors of their leadership, thus prodding the CCRG to make an open and direct counterattack on the putative leadership of the bourgeois reactionary line, Liu and Teng. On November 28, Chiang Ch'ing gave an important speech in which she denounced "a few comrades [who] sent work teams hastily which suppressed the revolutionary masses without asking Mao's permission." [67] On December 13, the No. 15 *RF* editorial supported the CCRG in the dispute, and on the same day T'ao Chu announced that

64 When "loyalist" Red Guards sent a delegation to the CCRG to request clarification on the shift in targets, they were told that, since the "Party organization resisted the orders, failed to implement the orders, the Party CC published the editorial [*RF* no. 13 (October 3, 1966)] directing the primary offensive forces of the Cultural Revolution directly at the Party persons in authority taking the capitalist road." *CB*, no. 819 (October 8, 1969): 79–84.

65 "The CCRG supports the Third Headquarters, and it regards the Third Headquarters as synonymous with itself," protested a loyalist Red Guard. "In order to smash the Third Headquarters, it is necessary to break down the CCRG." *Hung Wei Ping*, December 13, 1966.

66 *Mainichi*, November 25, in *DSJP*, November 26–28, 1966, pp. 12–13; *Nihon Keizai*, November 21, in *DSJP*, November 22, 1966, p. 8; Hinton, "Hundred Day War," p. 117.

67 Chiang, "Speech at Peking Cultural Revolution of Literature and Art Workers" (November 28, 1966), in *SCMP*, no. 3908 (March 30, 1967): 9–16.

any who criticized Mao, Lin, Chou, or Ch'en Po-ta were "counter-revolutionaries" (amending his earlier statement that anyone but Mao or Liu could be criticized); by this ruling, more than thirty Lien-tung leaders were promptly arrested by public security forces. The triumph of the Left seemed complete.[68]

When Red Guard resistance to the radical faction collapsed, strong pressure built up among Red Guards to carry the attack directly to the men who had now been identified as leaders of the bourgeois reactionary line. As a result, posters calling for the public trial of Liu and Teng flooded the city. To judge from its public statements, the CCRG was split by this pressure: T'ao Chu's faction apparently resisted pressure from the Left and was purged to a man.[69] Even in the more radical contingent of the CCRG, enthusiasm about the decision varied considerably. "Liu Shao-ch'i and Teng Hsiao-p'ing are the truest and biggest Party persons in authority taking the capitalist road," Ch'i Pen-yü told Red Guards on December 24. "You should aim at big figures if you are to attack any at all." [70] Yet, although Chiang Ch'ing in a December 18 speech proposed that Red Guards should grill Liu's children, she also said that the time to seize Liu and Teng had not arrived, that the problem was a Party problem that the CC was capable of solving: "Remember the wall posters about Liu Shao-ch'i at Tsinghua University and at Peking University? Chairman Mao personally sent comrade Ch'en Po-ta to stop them," she recalled.[71] At late as December 25, Lin Chieh stated (to his subsequent embarrassment): "Liu Shao-ch'i is a contradiction among the people [who] cannot be knocked down." [72] Chiang and Ch'en Po-ta warned Red Guards

[68] *Yomiuri*, December 14, in *DSJP*, December 15, 1966, pp. 13–14. Lien-tung was publicly denounced in *PD* on March 27, 1967, after 139 of its members had already been arrested by police for their role on February 12 in restoring to Party cadres leadership in organizations captured in the January power seizure. Chou En-lai subsequently secured their release from jail, however. Jean Esmein, *La Révolution Culturelle Chinoise* (Paris, 1970), p. 151.

[69] T'ao's resistance may be inferred from statements he made on December 8 and 11, in which he agreed that "comrades" Liu and Teng represented the bourgeois reactionary line" but refused to call them "Party persons in authority taking the capitalist road," insisting that their errors were still "contradictions among people." *Yomiuri*, December 14, in *DSJP*, December 15, 1966, pp. 13–14; "Record," *JPRS*, no. 42349, p. 60.

[70] *Nihon Keizai*, January 1, in *DSJP*, January 5, 1967, p. 9; *Yomiuri*, January 1, in *DSJP*, January 5, 1967, p. 7.

[71] *JPRS* pamphlet, "Samples of Red Guard Publications," 1 (August 1, 1967), 8th item.

[72] Revolutionary Rebel Commune, Peking College of Iron and Steel Industry of the Red Guard Congress of the Capital, comp., "The Exposure of a Hu Feng-type Counterrevolutionary Conspiratorial Clique," in *CB*, no. 844 (January 10, 1968): 15.

at a forum on December 27 against "a growing tendency toward anarchism." Ch'en even advised the students not to take over the administration of their schools and universities but to learn from the military.[73]

Despite this apparent ambivalence on the part of its leadership, on Mao's birthday, December 26, the movement achieved a polemical breakthrough, which was marked by two events. The first was the announcement, in a *PD* editorial, that the GPCR would be extended to the mines and factories, preparing the way for the January wide-scale attack on the power structure.[74] The second event was the release of Liu's first self-criticism of October 23: the text first appeared on a Chingkangshan poster, probably having been obtained by the CCRG. Whereas publication of a self-criticism normally signals an end to public attack on the individual making the self-criticism, an accompanying note made it clear that this was not to be the case.

At the Eleventh Plenum, although the line of the power-holders taking the capitalist road led by Liu Shao-ch'i and Teng Hsiao-p'ing was defeated, they have devised new methods of misleading the masses to attack the proletarian revolutionary line represented by Chairman Mao, to attack Chairman Mao and Vice-Chairman Lin, and to provoke the "December black wind." . . . The self-criticism Liu Shao-ch'i made at the October Work Conference was only superficial.[75]

No documentation was provided to support the alleged connection between Liu and continuing resistance to the GPCR, nor is such a connection at all plausible, in view of Liu's retirement; the connection referred to was one of analogy. The analogy was double-edged: Liu was attacked because others had followed his example and repressed the revolutionary movement, and, at the same time, those others (typically provincial and local power-holders) were attacked because the evil rooted in Liu Shao-ch'i was now blooming in them. The analogy gave meaningful unity and a common name to an attack on political figures organizationally unconnected.

(4) In talks with visiting Liberal-Democratic Party dietmen in September 1968, Chou En-lai explained his strategy of survival during the GPCR with remarkable candor: one's "personal opinions," he said, should "advance or beat a retreat" according to the decision of

---

[73] "Minutes Compiled by K'uai Ta-fu and Ch'en Yu-yen of Tsinghua University and Put up on Wall Posters on December 31, 1966," in Gargi and V. P. Dutt, *China's Cultural Revolution* (New York, 1970), pp. 130 ff.

[74] "Carry the GPCR through to the End," *RF-PD* editorial, December 26, 1966.

[75] Quoted in Fan Shu-cheng. "Tzu-wo chien-ch'a pao-kao," pp. 30 ff.

the majority. In other words, one should "shift with the wind."
"The one danger is a tendency to turn conservative." [76] Chou's basically pragmatic outlook and his paramount interest in preserving the
continuity of essential governmental operations during this period
made him a natural ally of Liu Shao-ch'i, and indeed, he defended Liu
whenever he deemed it feasible and consistently took positions opposed to the extensive mobilization of the masses. If Chou adopted
policies resembling Liu's "bourgeois reactionary line," why did he
neither win, in which case Liu et al. might have been salvaged, nor
lose, in which case Chou should have fallen victim to the same
coalition of forces that destroyed Liu? One reason is that although
Chou appeared to defend Liu on several occasions before February
1967, in each case he did so on procedural grounds, repudiating rebel
struggle tactics but never risking association with Liu's policies. Second, Chou avoided victory or defeat by declining to commit himself
fully to any issue; his survival and that of his State Council were *sine
qua non,* and he abandoned one position after another as it became
untenable.

Chou's tactics during this period contrast with those of Lin Piao,
as is indicated by a comparison of their positions on two basic issues:
scope of mobilization and range of targets. With regard to the former,
Chou consistently tried to prevent Red Guards from "sallying forth
to the streets" and from dispatching "liaison teams," with the evident
intention of restricting intercity mobility and increasing central control. In his speech to the first mass rally on August 18 (at which Lin
Piao encouraged Red Guards to "remove all stumbling blocks"), Chou
said, "The main task of the revolutionary teachers and students both in
Peking and in other parts of the country is to carry out the Cultural
Revolution in their own schools." At a Peking rally on September 15,
at which Lin Piao urged Red Guards to "bombard the headquarters"
of the capitalist-roaders in the Party, Chou advised Red Guards to
curtail activities until after the autumn harvest and directed that "the
broad masses of workers, commune members, scientific and technical
personnel and functionaries of the Party, of government and public
organizations and enterprises should remain firmly at their jobs,"
adding that Red Guards "are not to go to the factories and enterprises and to Party, government, and public organizations of county

76 *Yomiuri Shimbun,* September 26, in *DSJP,* September 27, 1966, pp. 10–11. For
a perceptive analysis of Chou's role in the GPCR, see Thomas W. Robinson,
"Chou En-lai and the Cultural Revolution," in T. W. Robinson, ed., *The Cultural
Revolution in China* (Berkeley, Calif., 1971), Chapter 4.

level and below the people's communes in the rural areas to establish revolutionary ties." [77] On October 3, he announced a series of restrictions on Red Guard activities:

Red Guards cannot enter organs guarded by the PLA, and Red Guards cannot carry arms or wear military uniforms, because you are not a regular reserve force. Second, judicial power belongs to the law courts. Third, propaganda organs, Party newspapers, the NCNA, and radio stations cannot be used by any Red Guard organizations.[78]

With regard to targets of criticism, Chou consistently attempted to limit criticism to "tigers" who were already "dead" and to deter the movement from moving from criticism to the actual deposal of power-holders. On August 22, when he and Yeh Lin visited Tsinghua, Chou spoke out against the pursuit of work teams (a pursuit that would lead not only to Liu Shao-ch'i but to members of his own State Council):

The Peking Municipal Party Committtee committed a new mistake in failing to carry out the activities of work teams from above and the revolutionary movement from below at the same time and also in parallel with each other. However, individual work teams should not be denounced for their following wrong, universal directions on a national scale.[79]

Chou sought to define the work-team error as a "contradiction among the people" and to deflect attacks from Liu and Teng and redirect them at P'eng Chen.

Even if they have made such mistakes, are they the black gang? We cannot say that. For instance, the sending of work teams is a mistake in orientation, but are those a black gang? No. . . . The black gang mentioned in the papers means people like P'eng Chen of the old Peking Municipal Committee who formed an independent kingdom. . . . Are all those who have made mistakes in orientation nonrevolutionaries? We cannot say that. . . . Don't turn a contradiction among the people into one between the enemy and ourselves.[80]

In contrast to Lin Piao, Chou also tended to play down the "struggle between two lines." In their joint appearance on August 30, Lin

[77] Both speeches are in PD, September 15, 1967, and RF, no. 12 (September 17, 1966), in JPRS, no. 39235 (December 22, 1967): 90–91.

[78] "Speech by Premier Chou at Reception of Red Guard Representatives at Chungnanhai on October 3," in CB, no. 819 (March 10, 1967): 58.

[79] "Premier Chou En-lai's Speech at Tsinghua University on August 22," in Collection of Materials Pertaining to the GPCR (Canton, October 28, 1966): 42–46, in JPRS, no. 41313 (June 1967): 14–21.

[80] "Speech by Premier Chou En-lai at Altar of Agricultural Park on September 13, 1966," in CB, no. 819 (March 10, 1967): 40–48.

emphasized that the "main target of attack is those Party persons in authority who are taking the capitalist road," whereas Chou discussed the GPCR as an attempt to destroy the "four olds" and foster the "four news"—a theme at that time favored by "five-good" Red Guards. Again in speeches at the National Day rally and reception, Lin stressed the "struggle between two classes," whereas Chou enthused about how the GPCR had "given a powerful impetus to socialist construction" in industry, science and technology, agriculture, and national defense.[81]

Most of the CC-State Council directives issued through the fall of 1966 were also meant to restrict the scope of mass mobilization and to protect central targets from attack, in contrast with the (relatively few) MAC and CCRG directives that were issued during this period. On September 8, the CC and State Council jointly issued a regulation to protect the security of Party and state secrets, thus attempting to prevent Red Guard raids on government offices for "black materials." On September 14, a CC regulation prohibited communication between units, telling Red Guards to make revolution by themselves; cadres were in no case to be "discharged from office" directly by the masses. On November 16, a Joint State Council-CC circular announced termination on December 20 of free transport.[82]

Conservative though the drift of such documents was, most of them had but slight effect, as indicated by the repeated reissue of essentially identical directives. This was in part because the Red Guards were non-Party masses who hearkened to the mass media rather than to Party circulars, and the media during this period were coordinated by the CCRG. But the main reason for their lack of effect was that Chou En-lai, unlike Liu Shao-ch'i before him, made no serious attempt to enforce the directives but quietly abandoned each position without a fight, avoiding involvement in the sort of polarizing conflict spiral that destroyed Liu.

FROM "JANUARY STORM" TO "TRIPLE COMBINATION"

The first phase encompassed Liu's implication in his prototypical error, the second phase encompassed the re-evaluation of the gravity of that error by the revolutionary Left upon meeting unremitting opposition from Party power-holders and conservative Red Guards associated with them. But the third is in many respects the most decisive of all,

[81] *CB*, no. 838 (October 13, 1967): 10–14; NCNA, September 30, 1966.
[82] URI, *CCP Documents of the GPCR*, 1966–1967 (Hong Kong, 1968), pp. 72, 79, 109 (hereafter URI, *CCP Documents*).

for during this period the highest-level leadership, including Mao Tse-tung and Chou En-lai, first committed themselves to the criticism of Liu, and their decision opened the way to a massive public campaign through the official media the following spring.

The January "movement to seize power" was stimulated by publication of two *PD* editorials, one on December 26 (mentioned above), and a joint New Year's *PD-RF* editorial entitled "Carry the GPCR Through to the End." The import of both was to expand the movement's target range from the original "small handful" of capitalist-roaders to include China's entire "middle class" of technical-managerial officials. The slogans, "grasp revolution, promote production," and "everyone should carry out the GPCR within their own units," the editorials explained, were being used "as a pretext to repress the revolution," and unless production could be disrupted by outside agitators, local officials would simply coopt any rebellion within their units through what became known as "sham power seizures." "If the revolution stops at the offices, schools, and cultural circles, the GPCR will be abolished half way." [83] The idea of a "power seizure" was still only implicit in these editorials, and its actualization seems to have occurred on Red Guard initiative, with the CCRG acting as a conduit to transmit information and coordinate rebel movements in different cities. On December 31, the CC and State Council issued a circular calling for PLA cadres to give "short-term military and political training to all the revolutionary teachers and students of universities and middle schools," [84] indicating how far power seizure was from the mind of Chou En-lai at this time. When Mao Tse-tung and Lin Piao returned to Peking in early January, Mao gave his approval to the idea in a January meeting with the CCRG. "This stands for the overthrow of one class by another; it is a great revolution," he exulted. "Don't . . . think that we cannot get along without them." [85] Lin initially supported the power seizures with equal enthusiasm, but Mao's decrees of January 23 and 28 authorizing PLA intervention on behalf of embattled rebels exposed Lin for the first time to criticism on the basis of his responsibility for autonomous decisions reached by his subordinates, putting him in an analogous position to Chou En-lai. Although a Japanese correspondent said he "often" heard the view that had the PLA not supported the rebels the latter might have been "defeated miserably," intervention brought to light deep rifts within

83 Cf. n. 74, above.

84 URI, *CCP Documents*, p. 150.

85 "Speech at a Meeting of the CCRG" (January 9, 1967) in *CB*, no. 892 (October 21, 1969): 47–48.

the PLA; in fact, in only six provinces did the PLA actively support Maoist power seizures.[86] Leftist criticism of the PLA for failing to support the rebels or for backing local power-holders forced Lin to take a more conservative stance with regard to the permissible range of targets, resulting in strains in his relations with the GPCR and in the formation of a tacit coalition with Chou En-lai, a realignment that contributed to the temporary triumph of the Right in February and March.

The movement to seize power was initially accompanied by a corresponding intensification of criticisms of Liu Shao-ch'i as the symbolic leader of the opposition forces. This criticism continued to originate from lower-level (or at least from unofficial) sources, however, and a January visitor to Canton reported that a great majority of the Red Guards he questioned refused to comment on Liu, saying "One cannot say he is good, nor that he is not good." [87] On January 8, Chou En-lai, claiming to speak at Mao's bequest, turned his back on the audience when there were shouts of "Down with Liu Shao-ch'i and Teng Hsiao-p'ing" and only turned around again when there was a call to overthrow the reactionary line of Liu and Teng. "Liu and Teng are still members of the Standing Committee of the Politburo, and your calling for the overthrow of these two makes my position very difficult," he said.

The task Chairman Mao assigned me is to persuade you not to do that. You can thoroughly criticize the bourgeois reactionary line which these two persons represent, but you cannot drag them out and struggle against them. . . . This question has been discussed by the Party CCRG. . . . As regards your plan to drag them out by besieging Chungnanhai, we in the Party Central and Chairman Mao recommend you do not take such action, for criticism must be made within the Party Central. . . . As you are besieging Chungnanhai from early morning till late at night and speaking angrily over the microphones, our great leader and comrades who are working under his guidance cannot devote themselves to work calmly. Groups have dashed at the gate of Chungnanhai several times in the past.[88]

If Chou's remarks in early Janaury accurately represent Mao's position, by the middle of the following month both men seem to have undergone a change of heart. This change occurred in the context of

86 In five more, the local commanders were benevolently neutral toward the leftists; in nine, they adopted strict neutrality; and in another nine, they did not support the Maoist power seizures at all. Jürgen Domes, "The Cultural Revolution and the Army," AS 8, no. 5 (May 1968): 356.

87 Neville M. Merrett, "Impressions of a Canton Glimpser" (unpub. paper), January, 1967, p. 6.

88 Mainichi, January 11, in DSJP, January 12, 1967, pp. 5–6.

the conservative reaction to the excesses of the power seizure movement that later became known as the "February adverse current" [erh-yüeh ni-liu], whose outlines we shall attempt to reconstruct.

By the end of January, the Red Guards and Revolutionary Rebels had succeeded in "toppling" provincial Party committees in about half of China's provinces, and yet several factors made the consolidation of power much more problematic. First, the regime was stricken with "demand overload." Chiang Ch'ing and the CCRG received a delegation of temporary and contract workers on December 26, agreed that they had been exploited, and supported their demands for restitution. This was but one of many disprivileged groups, however, and by legitimating its grievances the CCRG set in motion a long train of economic demands. Von Groeling undoubtedly exaggerates in saying the regime was faced with a serious prospect of a nation-wide anti-Communist uprising,[89] for even when worker or peasant groups were anti-revolutionary they remained pro-Maoist, but all available accounts indicate that worker-peasant notions of their class interests, varying though they did according to relative position on the socio-economic scale, were consistently more narrow, concrete and short-term than CCRG definitions of their interests.[90] Chou En-lai was first to repudiate these demands, ingeniously justifying his decision in terms of the same rationale used to legitimate them: Mao's Thought. The CCRG had justified restitution on grounds of relative deprivation; Chou denounced it as a form of "economism"—an immoral concession to self-indulgent consumerism. The slogan, "oppose economism" first appeared in PD on January 12, and by the next day, a poster campaign was unfolding in the streets of Peking.[91]

Second, the escalation of criticism without effective organizational controls created intolerable regime instability, as vertical alliances between rebel factions and various elite cliques exacerbated schismatic tendencies at both central and mass levels. The radicalization of the

---

[89] Erik von Groeling, China Langer Marsch—Wohin? (Stuttgart, 1972), pp. 79–80.

[90] On Jaunary 26, the official press reported a confrontation in Harbin between 300 war veterans, armed with daggers and clubs, and the local garrison. The veterans were involved with the so-called Red Flag Army, which Chou in a January 19 speech called a "counterrevolutionary organization"; several commanders of the Red Flag Army and another "counterrevolutionary organization," the "National Headquarters for a Takeover by Workers, Peasants, and Soldiers," had been arrested, he said. There were reports from nearly every province or region, notably frontier areas, of peasant raids on state granaries, refusals to pay the grain tax, withdrawals of commune funds from the banks, demands for a greater share of the unit's collective profits, etc. CN (New York) 5, no. 2 (April 1967): 1–15; also von Groeling, ibid.

[91] Merrett, "Impressions," p. 34.

CCRG resulted in the dismissal of its moderate contingent (T'ao Chu, Wu Te, Wang Jen-chung, Chang P'ing-hua, and Liu Chih-chien), and in recriminations between the radicals and surviving formal elites (e.g., Lin Piao denounced Chu Te and Ho Lung, Chiang Ch'ing denounced Hsiao Hua). News of such disputes was frequently "leaked" to the masses, who promptly advertised them in big-character posters, making reconciliation difficult. During the early weeks of 1967, only six members of the State Council, which normally included more than twenty, remained at work, and they were under constant attack. "We are short of hands," complained Chou En-lai. Revolutionaries even struggled against Yao Wen-yüan and Chang Ch'un-ch'iao for more than six hours on January 28, calling them "arch criminals for leading troops to subdue the student movement." [92]

Once power had been seized, the most pressing exigency was thus to reconstitute political authority and create order. Two different organizational forms for the consolidation of the power seizures were proposed nearly simultaneously at the end of January: the "Paris Commune," which represented the interests of the "revolutionary masses," led by the CCRG; and the "Revolutionary Committee" (RC), representing the interests of the rump officialdom, led by Chou En-lai.

The ideological case for the Paris Commune was advanced in an editorial that appeared on January 31 in PD and on February 3 in RF; it envisaged a full-scale appropriation of offices by rebel forces and a transformation of the state structure, citing Marx's assertion that the original (1871) Paris Commune had demonstrated the necessity to smash, rather than simply re-man, the pre-revolutionary organs of power.[93] The first Paris Commune was established on February 6 in Shanghai, and on February 13 and February 16 respectively, Peking and Harbin followed suit.[94] The most immediately apparent weakness of this new form of regime was rebel inexperience with the political institutions conventionally used to socialize political elites in China, the Party-state administrative apparatus and the PLA military hierarchy, and their concomitant inability to institute order and unity. In the words of one observer,

92 "Yao Wen-yüan—New Blood in the Mao Regime," IS 8, no. 6 (March 1972): 80–85.

93 "On the Proletarian Revolutionaries' Struggle to Seize Power," PD, January 31, 1967, in RF, no. 3 (February 3, 1967), and trans. in PR 10, no. 6 (February 1967): 10–15.

94 Radio Shanghai, February 6, 1967; Radio Harbin, February 16, 1967; cited in John Bryan Starr, "Revolution in Retrospect: The Paris Commune Through Chinese Eyes," CQ, no. 22 (January–March 1972): 118–119.

According to plan, the revolutionary mass organizations should have united in the struggle for power. In fact, the small groups in many places formed themselves into two large opposing associations. Sometimes one seized power and excluded the other. In other cases, both claimed to have seized power. Occasionally while one group seized power at the top, the other seized power at the lower levels. Stalemate and conflict ensued.[95]

Thus, although thirteen power seizures had been proclaimed by the end of January, the Center recognized only four of them, dismissing the remainder as "shams." Even where bona fide power seizures succeeded in establishing Paris Communes, their attempts to realize the anarchist ideals implicit in the CCRG popularization of Mao's Thought aroused misgivings among incumbent elites. As Mao noted in February:

The Shanghai People's Council offices submitted a command to the Premier and the State Council in which they asked for the elimination of all chiefs. This is extreme anarchy; it is most reactionary. . . . Actually, there always have to be chiefs.[96]

The organizational genius behind the formation of the RC seems to have been Chou En-lai, who already expressed reservations about the feasibility of the Paris Commune in late January.[97] Comprising a "triple combination" of revolutionary mass representatives, PLA men, and "liberated" civilian cadres, the RC represented an attempt to "parcel out" the revolution to smaller units more capable of subduing factional tendencies and maintaining production; in every unit, from school or factory to province, there was to be a seizure of power in the name of the proletariat through "struggle—criticism—reform." [98] In practice, the PLA and civilian cadres (particularly the former) rapidly assumed a position of dominance. The ascendancy of these veteran elites was reinforced by Mao's coterminous injunctions against rebel excesses in criticism tactics. On February 1, he wrote a letter to Chou En-lai:

Recently many revolutionary teachers and students and revolutionary masses have written to me asking whether it is considered armed struggle to make those Party persons in authority taking the capitalist road and freaks and

95 Jack Chen, "Biting the Bullet," *FEER* 73, no. 32 (August 7, 1971): 21–23; also *Asahi Shimbun*, March 1, 1967.

96 *JPRS*, no. 49826 (February 12, 1970): 10.

97 "Chou En-lai t'an tou-ch'uan wen-t'i" [Chou En-lai on the question of power seizure], *Hung-se chan-pao*, February 17, 1967; reprinted in *Hsing-tao jih-pao*, April 21, 1967; cited in Starr, "Revolution in Retrospect," p. 119.

98 Oskar Weggel, *Die Chinesischen Revolutionskomitees, oder der Versuch, die Grosse Kulturrevolution durch Parzellierung zu Retten* (Hamburg, 1968), pp. 58–60.

monsters wear dunce caps, to paint their faces, and to parade them in the streets. I think it a form of armed struggle. . . . I want to stress here that, when engaging in struggle, we definitely must hold to struggle by reason, bring out the facts, emphasize rationality, and use persuasion. . . . Anyone involved in beating others should be dealt with in accordance with the law.[99]

In the "adverse current" that followed the decision to establish RCs and moderate criticism, conservative cadres either misjudged Mao's intentions or overstepped the limits of his tolerance in pushing for a sweeping "reversal of verdicts." In a series of meetings of the Party Center held at Huaijent'ang around the middle of February, surviving power-holders gave vociferous expression to their grievances. Pounding the table to punctuate their remarks ("Yeh Chien-ying even broke his finger as a result of pounding.") these men evoked bonds of loyalty based on common experiences often dating from the Long March to protest the public humiliation of veteran cadres.[100] As the most prominent symbol of the GPCR's violation of principles of just desert based on prior service, these cadres apparently rallied around Liu Shao-ch'i as a banner of unreconstructed opposition to the GPCR, heedless of Liu's own attempts to recant the bourgeois reactionary line he had originated through self-criticism. Nowhere is this more evident than in Ch'en I's pungent defense of Liu before a February Red Guard rally:

In my opinion the wall poster criticizing Chairman Mao may also be justified. Chairman Mao is also a cog. . . . Chairman Mao became a dictator in directing the GPCR. Lin Piao is also of no importance. He used to be under my command. . . . You should study well Chairman Liu's thought. Liu Shao-ch'i is my teacher, my master, my king. His level is quite high. . . . There is a rumor running that Liu Shao-ch'i has been deprived of his post, isn't there? That needs to be decided by the National Party Congress. Despite the fact that Liu Shao-ch'i and Teng Hsiao-p'ing committed some political mistakes, they still hold their positions. . . . Someone said that P'eng Chen's backbone was Liu Shao-ch'i. How can this be tolerable? . . . Liu Shao-ch'i's criminal charges, some of which were concocted and some of which were only slaps in the face, were all purposely created for disgracing the Party and Chairman Mao.[101]

[99] "Chairman Mao's Instructions" (February 1, 1967), in *JPRS*, no. 49826 February 12, 1970): 22. Again on February 2, Mao reiterated that the "standard of struggle" should be raised, that such slogans as "smash dogs' heads" would "not be understood by the people." *Tokyo Shimbun*, March 3, in *DSJP*, March 4-6, 1967, p. 8.

[100] "Chou En-lai Talks About the 'February Adverse Current,'" *IS* 5, no. 12 (September 1969): 103-104.

[101] Ch'en I, "K'an wen-hua ta ko-ming," in *Chung-kung*, ed. Ting Wang, pp. 651-652.

Ch'en puts his plea on behalf of Liu in the context of a deprecation of both Mao and Lin Piao, though he later tries to rectify this slip by saying that criticism of Liu is a "disgrace" to Chairman Mao. It is also placed in the context of scorn for the CCRG ("Some people hide behind the curtains, simply ordering some 'children' to write big-character posters," he sneered. "What poor taste they have!") and general opposition to the GPCR:

I have always insisted that big-character posters should not appear in public. My insistence was the basis of the criminal charges against me for my use of the bourgeois reactionary line. Now it seems that their destructiveness is getting more and more serious. I . . . would rather die than let you drag my wife into the street. What crime did she commit? She was just the chief of a work team.[102]

Inasmuch as Liu was responsible for formulating the bourgeois reactionary line and Ch'en I et al. only for implementing it, rehabilitating Liu would have logically entailed that the reversal of verdicts be made general. Such a sweeping reversal of verdicts would certainly have been construed as an exoneration of the power-holders and a repudiation of the version of Mao's Thought that had first emancipated ideology from organization, permitting the formation of extra-Party Red Guard groups; it would quite likely have also implied purge or demotion of the CCRG for inciting rebellion against the Party. As Hsieh Fu-chih put it, "The object of the February adverse current was to overthrow the CCRG that held high the great red banner of Mao Tse-tung's Thought." [103] On February 18, the confrontation reached a climax as Mao offered his opponents a Hobson's choice between accepting his leadership and truncating the nation:

You may call back Wang Ming [Ch'en Shao-yü] and Chang Kuo-t'ao and I and comrade Lin Piao, together with Yeh Ch'ün, will go to the south. Comrade Chiang Ch'ing will be left with you as well as the comrades of the CCRG. You may behead Chiang Ch'ing and banish K'ang Sheng. All this you may do.[104]

Mao's opponents declined the gambit, and it was at this time that the vindication of Liu Shao-ch'i seems to have been definitively ruled out. Circumstantial evidence suggests, however, that Mao had to make a number of concessions in order to maintain the forward momentum of the criticism campaign. For example, on February 15, Chou En-lai met with Mao and received permission to retain all State Council members who could still be salvaged; two days later, Chou made his

---

102 *Ibid.*   104 See above, note 100.
103 Quoted in Rice, *Mao's Way*, p. 443.

first public denunciation of Liu Shao-ch'i. On the same day, Chou met with representatives of rebel factions in the Finance and Trade Ministries and set forth some guidelines: henceforth, neither invasion of government ministries by outsiders nor seizures of power would be permitted without prior consent of the Center; when Vice-Minister Tu Hsiang-kuang defied Chou and led a seizure of power in the Ministry of Finance, dissolving its Party committee, Chou had him arrested.[105]

This episode suggests that Mao purchased the GPCR's survival at the cost of narrowing its polemical objectives: no longer would wholesale assaults on the power structure be permitted; criticism would henceforth be concentrated against Liu Shao-ch'i and a "small handful" of authoritatively designated targets. The new allocation of blame was officially announced in a February 23 (no. 4) RF editorial, "Revolutionary Cadres Must Be Treated Properly," which keynoted a three-month campaign to show tolerance to errant cadres; it stressed that "the overwhelming majority of cadres at all levels" were "good or comparatively good," and that criticism should be aimed rather at "China's Khrushchev." [106] Also with regard to Liu, Mao told Chang Ch'un-ch'iao during a series of meetings on February 12–18 that the quality of criticism should be elevated and should focus on Liu's pedagogic influence rather than on his person:

Liu Shao-ch'i's book How To Be a Good Communist is a typical representative piece of revisionism. This book has spread its pernicious influence at home and abroad. The criticism and repudiation of it now poses the Red Guards a difficult question. . . . Our method of struggle ought to be more intelligent than it is now. . . . I think university students should make a better study of the book and write articles in repudiation of some paragraphs in it.[107]

In the actual implementation of the decision, the criticism of Liu Shao-ch'i remained at a constant and exclusively unofficial level for the rest of February and March, whereas the suppression of Red Guard indiscipline and curbing of cadre criticism was carried out with thoroughness and ardor. On February 17, members of work teams who had been dragged out were excused from further struggle and ordered remanded to their units: "Schools, factories, organs, and various units

---

105 Nihon Keizai, February 24, 1967; cited in Rice, Mao's Way, pp. 329–331.
106 "Revolutionary Cadres Must Be Treated Properly," RF, no. 4 (February 24, 1967).
107 Liaison Center of the Peking Railroad College, "Red Flag Commune," comp., "Thoroughly Smash Liu's Black 'Cultivation' " (April 1967), SCMM, no. 582 (July 3, 1967): 20.

should refrain from dragging out . . . work teams in the future." On the same day (and again on August 31, this time with CCRG support), the CC and State Council reissued a September 8, 1966 directive to vouchsafe the security of confidential files and dossiers.[108] In declaring work teams and confidential files off limits, the CC-State Council was attempting to block the two most important channels through which Red Guards had hitherto been able to secure incriminating materials, thus effectively curtailing mass initiative in the selection of targets and putting teeth in the verdict that the "overwhelming majority" of cadres were "good or comparatively good."

In the interest of reducing factionalism, a number of measures were also adopted that effectively reduced the scope of mobilization. A CC circular was issued February 8 terminating the exchange of revolutionary experience and directing Red Guards to return to their units; this request was repeated in directives dated February 17, 21, and April 20, testifying both to the importance attached to the measure and the difficulty of enforcing it. Nationwide rebel liaison stations were ordered disbanded, and the heterogeneous miscellany of Red Guard units in the capitol were consolidated into a single "Congress of the Red Guards of Universities and Colleges in Peking" [Hung-ta-hui]; speeches at the February 24 rally proclaiming this congress suggested an intent to establish similar congresses in all major provinces, culminating in a national organization more accessible to central co-ordination.[109]

With rebel initiative so severely restricted by the imposition of such prohibitions, even power seizures were increasingly coopted by forces of the status quo. Rebel power seizures had by the end of the first week of February resulted in the establishment of four provincial (Heilungkiang, Shansi, Kweichow, and Shantung) and two municipal (Peking and Shanghai) RCs. Although the six chairmen had close links with the PLA,[110] the standing committees manifested relatively strong rebel representation: of the eighteen provincial RC vice-chairmen, five were PLA men, five mass representatives, and six revolutionary cadres.[111] In those provinces deemed too "politically immature" for

108 URI, *CCP Documents,* pp. 309, 503.

109 NCNA, March 2, 1967. Central authorities also called conferences to consolidate the fissiparous revolutionary organizations of poor and middle peasants (on March 19) and industrial workers (on March 22); on March 18, workers were instructed to make revolution in their spare time and work an eight-hour day.

110 Of the six RCs that came into existence between January and May, three were headed by cadres supporting Mao who also held military posts, and the other three were PLA officers.

111 Rebel representation was even more impressive numerically if one counts membership in the plenums: in Peking, where the municipal RC took office in April, of the seventy-seven members of the committee, 31 percent were Red Guards,

RCs (i.e., those that withstood the January–February "revolutionary high tide"), the Party Center authorized formation of a "Military Control Commission" (MCC) which, by enforcing military rule, rescinded the powers of the provincial Party and governing organs. By July 6, Chou En-lai issued a statement disclosing that the PLA had taken control of the provinces of Fukien, Yünnan, Kiangsu, Shensi, Anhwei, Tibet, Ch'inghai, Kwangtung, and parts of Sinkiang; a PLA takeover was imminent in Tientsin, in Inner Mongolia, and in Szechwan; preparations for military takeover had been initiated in Kwangsi, Honan, Hopei, Hunan, Kiangsi, and Chekiang. After July 1, 1967, CC directives were no longer even addressed to the regional Party bureaus and provincial Party committees. In those provinces in which MCCs seized power, the army took charge of industrial and agricultural production, finance and trade, famine relief, the press, the public security forces, People's Court and Procuratorate.[112] Establishment of a Military Control Commission was normally followed by establishment of a "preparatory team for a Revolutionary Committee," likewise supervised and staffed by the PLA.[113]

Unlike earlier power seizures in which RCs were based on a genuine or superficial unity of rebel forces, the entire process of RC formation thus became dominated by local military authorities. Though this practice avoided the chaos of a rebel power seizure, it also froze the rebels out of the political process and resulted in the creation of a new local establishment. "Taking advantage of the CC's order that old Party cadres be treated 'correctly,' the counterrevolutionaries are attempting to reappoint and reintegrate anti-Mao elements," a joint PD-RF editorial alleged on March 30. "They also threaten 'true revolutionary organizations' and speak of a 'settling of accounts.' "[114] In response to reviving Red Guard protests, Mao agreed to a "second great upheaval," this time attempting to maintain unity among the revolutionaries by utilizing the official media network to coordinate a nationwide campaign against one man: Liu Shao-ch'i.

---

25 percent were workers, 13 percent peasants, 17 percent PLA men, and 13 percent revolutionary cadres; in Shansi's RC, 118 of a total committee membership of 248 were "rebels." These statistics are somewhat deceptive, however, in view of the plenums' relative lack of real policy-making power.

112 Ch'in T'i, "The Government in Mainland China in 1967," in URI, *Communist China, 1967,* pp. 120–121, 138.

113 *Nihon Keizai,* September 1, 1967 (reporter Samejima quoting Chou); Radio Kunming, July 14, 1967; Radio Hofei, October 1, 1967; Radio Ch'engtu, October 5, 1967. Wallposters of March 30, 1967, stated that the PLA would also take over the Central Trade Bureau and the Telegraph Bureau in Peking (Radio Tokyo, March 31, 1967).

114 Quoted in *Nihon Keizai,* September 7, in *DSJP,* September 7–9, 1968.

"SEIZURE OF IDEOLOGICAL POWER"

Like the compromises that led to the "February adverse current" and
the March "black wind," the decision to launch a full-fledged campaign against Liu in the official media was made through regular
policy channels, but whereas veteran cadres held sway in the February–
March interlude, the "latest series of moves to criticize Liu were proposed by the CCRG" (according to T'ang P'ing-chu, former chief
editor of *PD*). Besides relying on their representatives in the Politburo (viz., K'ang Sheng and Ch'en Po-ta) to state their case, the CCRG
used their control of the media and contacts with Red Guard groups
to exert pressure on the decision makers. *RF* warned on March 9 that
the "big question now confronting the people of the whole country"
was whether the GPCR should be "carried through to the end, or
abandoned halfway." While the meeting that decided Liu's fate was in
session, the CCRG reportedly launched a "general offensive" outside
the building calling for the decision that Liu and Teng were the
"biggest counterrevolutionary revisionists." [115]

In reconstructing the context of the decision, we have recourse to
two forms of evidence: the first consists of wall-poster reports on the
actual committee meetings, while the second, more reliable, concerns
the decision's social effects. According to posters sighted by Japanese
newsmen, the decision was reached after a "furious struggle" in meetings of the Politburo-MAC from March 14 to 18 and of the Politburo
Standing Committee in the last two weeks of March. The latter meeting was attended by eleven members who split into two groups: a six-
man group consisting of Mao, Lin Piao, Chou En-lai, Ch'en Po-ta,
K'ang Sheng, and Li Fu-ch'un, and a five-member group consisting of
Liu, Teng, T'ao Chu (*sic*), Chu Te, and Ch'en Yün. The Maoists per-
sistently criticized Liu's faction for their "revisionist line," whereupon
the latter defended themselves, saying the GPCR did not seem to be
achieving its purpose. During the meeting it was decided to launch a
nationwide campaign against Liu.[116]

Indirect but more reliable is the evidence concerning the outcome of
the meetings: on April 1 and 6, the CC and MAC issued orders forbidding the PLA to arrest and persecute the "revolutionary masses" or to
label mass organizations "reactionary" and suppress them.[117] Although

115 *Asahi*, April 12, in *DSJP*, April 13, 1967, p. 22; *Yomiuri*, April 10, in *DSJP*,
April 8–10, 1967; *Yomiuri*, April 10, in *DSJP*, April 8–10, 1967.
116 *Nihon Keizai*, April 3, in *DSJP*, April 1–3, 1967, p. 31; *Sankei*, March 27, in
DSJP, March 28, 1967, p. 15.
117 "Order of the MAC of the CCP CC," in *CB*, no. 852 (May 6, 1968): 115–116.
The April 6 document even warned that a "small handful" of officers was pur-

military suppression was relaxed, the altered tone of the propaganda made clear that this was not meant to imply reversion to factionalism and attacks on the power structure. As a *Wen-hui pao* editorial put it, "All revolutionary mass organizations that are 'fighting a civil war' (*ta nei-chan*) should immediately stop the 'civil war,' throw themselves into this great criticism-struggle, and through this struggle achieve unity and solidarity." [118] Evidently, military control of the criticism movement was to be replaced by ideological control: the chorus of criticisms would be directed by the mass media, permitting even more extensive *participation* while at once reducing the scope of popular *initiative,* thus reverting to the pattern typical of earlier mass campaigns.

Most active in implementation of the decision were the CCRG and PLA. In late March and early April, CCRG members delivered no less than ten public speeches denouncing Liu (in comparison with only one in February) to herald the initiation of the campaign. They focused their attacks on his book, *How To Be a Good Communist,* in keeping with Mao's desire to raise the "standard of struggle," and included explicit instructions to Red Guard polemicists outlining other criticism themes.[119] The central propanganda apparatus was now wholly in the hands of the CCRG, with Ch'en Po-ta as editor-in-chief of both the *NCNA* and *RF,* and Wang Li Director of the CC Propaganda Department (since T'ao Chu's purge in January). On April 27, Ch'en Po-ta convened a meeting of the CCRG, in which he stressed that articles criticizing Liu must be analytical, vigorous in style, and of high caliber. Most articles denouncing Liu were thereafter submitted to a writing group consisting of thirty writers, working under the CCRG. The Group would periodically publish "keynote" articles on various topics, which were reproduced in various forms in newspapers and magazines throughout the country.[120] The PLA also gave strong support to the anti-Liu drive, holding local rallies in regions under military control and publishing critical articles on April 11, July 17,

---

suing a "bourgeois reactionary line" and warned of the possibility of a purge in the PLA.

118 *Wen-hui pao* (Shanghai), April 2, 1967.

119 There were three speeches criticizing Liu by Ch'en Po-ta, two each by K'ang Sheng and Wang Li, and one each by Chiang Ch'ing, Kuan Feng and Yao Wen-yüan. In addition to attacks on his book a persistent theme was Liu's alleged perduring opposition to Mao. Cf. *SCMM,* no. 582 (July 3, 1967): 23–30, *inter al.*

120 *Wen-hua ko-ming t'ung-hsün* [Cultural Revolution Bulletin] (Lanchow), May 11, 1967, quoted in Chang Man, "The GPCR in 1968," in URI, *Communist China, 1968* (Hong Kong, 1969), pp. 8–9.

21, 23, 24, September 4, 23, October 12, 25, November 3, 5, and 18. Many of the *PD* critiques were also written by military personnel, such as that by Fu Ch'ung-pi on June 7.[121] That Mao was now fully behind the campaign there could be no doubt. According to Wang Li, the May 6, 1967 joint *RF-PD* editorial, "Treason to the Dictatorship of the Proletariat Is the Essence of the Book on 'Self-Cultivation of Communists'," was "corrected and revised" by the Chairman himself.[122] In his April 29 instructions on reorganization of the Party, Mao again referred to Liu's famous book, attributing the progressive alienation of the Party from the masses to its elitist influence.[123]

The attempt to detach Liu from the criticism process gave the struggle a somewhat abstract quality, and the relationship of the "Liu Shao-ch'i" symbol to empirical referents became fraught with ambiguity. On the one hand, the campaign was meant to reduce resistance from middle- and lower-level Party and government officials by temporarily easing pressure on smaller targets and shifting it to the biggest ones. This intention is clear in the March 1967 *RF* article accusing Liu of hitting at a "large number of good or comparatively good cadres" to protect a "handful" during the "fifty days." It was Liu, the article maintained, who was responsible for inciting the cadres to oppose the Red Guards and the new interpretation of Mao's Thought they heralded, and even now he continued to exert his mysterious influence to block "revolutionary cadres" from seats on the RCs.[124] Thus the Maoists sought to drive a wedge between Liu and those hitherto identified with his "line" by suggesting that he was to blame for their present disgrace and that they could recover their positions by turning against him:

Cadres who have committed mistakes must pause and think: Who told you to suppress the masses? Who pushed you to take the front line? Who told you to be docile slaves? Can they be other than the handful of top Party persons in authority taking the capitalist road? You should direct all your class hatred against this handful of people.[125]

121 *PD*, June 7, 1967.

122 "Document of the CCP CC" (May 11, 1967), in URI, *CCP Documents*, p. 440.

123 "Since 1952, the masses have turned cold toward us. Party members in the past were isolated from the masses because of the influence of *How to Be a Good Communist*, held no independent views, and served as subservient tools of the Party organs. The masses in various areas will not welcome too quick a recovery of the structure of the Party." *Asahi*, May 20, in *DSJP*, May 23, 1967, p. 22.

124 "'Hit Hard at the Many in Order to Protect a Handful' Is a Component of the Bourgeois Reactionary Line," *RF*, no. 5 (March 1967), in *SCMM*, no. 571 (April 10, 1967): 1–17.

125 *Wen-hui pao*, May 14, 1967.

At the same time, in keeping with the saying, "kill the chickens to scare the monkeys" (*hsia chi ching hou*), the attack on Liu was intended to eliminate lingering loyalties and to *warn* local cadres who might imagine they could be reinstated by a superficial self-criticism and then revert to their old ways. Although local power-holders were no longer to be deliberately investigated and targeted, the possibility was foreseen that they might continue to adhere to the bourgeois reactionary line, in which case they must participate in Liu's ignominy: "The general orientation of the Cultural Revolution at the present stage is to link up this campaign of mass criticism and repudiation with the tasks of struggle, criticism, repudiation, and transformation in local areas, departments, and units.[126]

Available statistics (cf. Chapter 9) suggest that the criticism campaign against Liu Shao-ch'i, which reached a crescendo between April and June 1967 in both official and Red Guard presses, was temporarily successful in its attempt to unite fractious revolutionary forces against a common opponent. The critical momentum could not be sustained, however, and as the campaign declined in intensity in the summer of 1967 from its zenith in April, criticism of Liu Shao-ch'i was deflected to his local counterparts and the revolutionary united front began to fragment once more into myriad "civil wars." Competing elite groups actively courted the allegiance of mass organizations in order to defend themselves or attack their adversaries; the emerging pattern seemed to be one in which locally based mass organizations (such as the "Alliance Command" in Kwangsi or "East Wind" in Kwangtung) coalesced with local militia units that were armed and backed by the provincial PLA against leftist insurgents supported by the CCRG. The rise of hostilities between these vertical factional structures culminated in Ch'en Ts'ai-tao's insubordination in Wuhan in July (he backed the rebel faction opposed by the CCRG) and in pitched battles between heavily armed groups in August, as leftist factions across the country tried to "drag out" the local PLA equivalent of Ch'en Ts'ai-tao. Needless to say, this was not a favorable climate for the construction of RCs, not one of which was established between late April and early August 1967.[127]

The factional strife was curtailed in September, in a repudiation of the left reminiscent of the "February adverse current." Chiang Ch'ing disavowed the "attack with nonviolence, defend with force" policy she had earlier advocated, and, in an effort to dissociate themselves from this policy the Maoists held CCRG members Wang Li,

[126] *Ibid.*   [127] Chung, in URI, *Communist China, 1967*, p. 65.

Kuan Feng, Hsieh T'ang-chung, and Mu Hsin (later polemically referred to as the "May 16 Group") responsible for proposing in the
August RF to "drag out the power-holders in the army" (as a result
of which "practically every military region suffered attacks," according
to Chiang Ch'ing) and purged them for this error, while RF suspended
publication until July 1968. Following a suggestion by Chou En-lai,
Mao undertook a tour of North, Central-South, and East China in
September to observe conditions; upon his return on September 24,
he reportedly rebuked Ch'en Po-ta and Chiang Ch'ing and had them
submit self-criticisms. Beginning in November 1967, Chiang Ch'ing
took a seven-week "rest," as a revindicated PLA-liberated cadre coalition ushered in a second Thermidorean interlude.[128]

As we have noted, the mass criticism of Liu was an inherently ambiguous symbolic action. On one level, it was meant to give lesser
power-holders a convenient scapegoat for their errors without excusing
the errors per se; on another, it was meant as a warning to those same
power-holders. As Liu's credibility as a threat declined, the Red
Guards understood the criticisms of Liu increasingly in the latter
sense—as warnings to their opponents and authoritative vindications
of their own positions. When their opponents refused to heed these
warnings but only hurled back similar imprecations, internecine disputes intensified into warfare rather than becoming channeled into
common opposition to Liu. When Mao said the GPCR was a continuation of the fight between the CCP and the Kuomintang, for instance,
each faction denounced the other as today's KMT.[129] Although Mao
expressed steadfast public optimism during his tour, in private remarks to Chou, he revealed his dismay. "I think this is a civil war,"
he said; the country is divided into "800 princely states." [130] His solution was not yet to curtail mass criticism, however, but to restrict its
spillover from the abstract attack on Liu Shao-ch'i (which was good) to
criticisms of the objective correlatives of Liu's "line" whom local
revolutionaries perceived in their factional opponents. "Personally, I
sense the portents of giving up the struggle against the enemy, the
struggle against the highest authorities in the Party taking the capitalist road," Mao warned in September. Factional cleavages were the-

128 Parris Chang, *Radicals and Radical Ideology in the Cultural Revolution* (New
York, 1972), p. 44 (prepublication text).
129 Hinton, "Hundred Day War," p. 111.
130 "So many cadres have collapsed," he remarked in Kiangsi, as if previously
unaware of the magnitude of the purge. "Is this good or bad? Have you ever
studied this problem? At any rate, we should give the cadres time to recognize their
mistakes. We should criticize the idea of overthrowing everything." *SCMP*, no. 4070
(November 30, 1967): 6; *FEER* 66, no. 40 (October 2, 1969): 34–35; *IS* 4, no. 12
(September 1968): 11–12.

oretically incomprehensible and hence unjustified: "There is no fundamental clash of interests within the working class. Why should they be split into two big irreconcilable organizations?" he asked. "I don't understand it." [131]

Thus, at the beginning of October, the criticism of Liu was coordinated with a new campaign against "anarchism, small-group mentality, sectarianism, individualism, and pragmatism in our ranks," and Liu's works were now culled for evidence that he supported a "small-group mentality" or "mountain-top-ism" (*shan-t'ou-chu-i*). "We hope you will be models in waging struggles against the No. 1 Party person in authority taking the capitalist road and models of opposition to anarchism, small-group mentality, economism and selfishness," Mao said on October 5.[132]

Considerable headway was made in the reconsolidation, as fourteen RCs were established between November 1967 and April 1968, but the PLA evidently exploited the muting of the rebels to expand its power, for these RCs had a lower proportion of mass representatives than did the six RCs that had been established during the revolutionary high tide from January 1967 to April 20, 1967.[133] With the establishment of RCs, the factional conflict acquired an institutional focus, and in late 1967 "new wave" (*hsin szu-ch'ao*) Red Guards launched attacks on RC leaders in Shanghai and in such provinces as Heilungkiang and Kweichow; Chiang Ch'ing noted a tendency as early as September to demand that the CC "dissolve" all the RCs it had sanctioned.

The suppressive implications of the consolidation policies became painfully apparent in January–February 1968. In January, the emphasis was shifted from RCs to Party rectification; in the Party structure, mass representatives were consigned to an even more meager role than in the RCs.[134] On January 17, Chou En-lai stated that "the working class is now to take the lead in revolution, just as the intellectuals and students did at an earlier stage." And on January 28, *LAD* published an editorial denouncing "petty bourgeois factionalism"

[131] *CL&G* 2, no. 1 (spring 1969): 8; "Instruction Given During Inspection Tour," in *PD* editorial, September 14, 1967.

[132] Cf. *CB*, no. 885 (July 31, 1969): 36–37, 41–43; also *FEER* 66, no. 40: 34–35.

[133] Oskar Weggel, *Die Partei als Widersacher des Revolutionskomitees* (Hamburg, 1970), pp. 4 ff.

[134] Whereas *Wen-hui pao* had earlier called for quick admission of "large numbers" of revolutionaries into the Party, the joint New Year's editorials in both Peking papers said only that "a number" should be admitted. Editorials in the Shanghai papers said that "those advanced elements within the proletariat who have distinguished themselves during the revolutionary struggle should be gradually absorbed." *Wen-hui pao* noted on December 28 that "Party consolidation is a profound class struggle which requires a considerable amount of time." *CS* 6, no. 4 (March 1, 1968): 1 ff.

which called on the PLA to "support the Left, but not factions" (*chih tso, pu chih p'ai*)—a slogan usually interpreted to mean form opportunistic coalitions with any factions willing to cooperate in the formation of an RC. Those factions not included in the PLA-dominated RCs (usually the more radical ones) came under renewed attacks for refusing to cooperate.[135] This charge may have applied in some cases, but in others it was self-serving cant:

Some of the militia departments monopolize everything without . . . any consultation with the masses, and without cadres properly making public appearances. "You need not care who the RC members are. Those who go up on the platform at the inaugural meeting will be committee members." . . . Some people did not even know they had been named to the committees until inaugural day.[136]

In March 1968, Red Guard forces, apparently encouraged by the purge of PLA leaders Yang Ch'eng-wu, Yü Li-chin, and Fu Ch'ung-pi at the end of that month, rallied for one last offensive against reconsolidation tendencies, which they labeled "rightist reversal of verdicts." The forbidden posters and tabloids reappeared, and CCRG leaders again appeared before Red Guard rallies.[137] Liu Shao-ch'i was again invoked in the renascent criticism campaign; but it is interesting to note that whereas CCRG denunciations of Liu reached an all-time high during this period, both in terms of frequency of speeches and severity of charges (he was now for the first time accused of treason), Liu was not mentioned at all in the Red Guard press. One possible interpretation of this discrepancy is that the CCRG, having been coopted into the establishment, now felt obliged to camouflage its warnings to ensconced rightist opponents as attacks on Liu; it is also possible to interpret the invocation of Liu as a diversionary tactic (to divert rebel factions from attacks on each other). In any case, the attempt to "point at the mulberry bush while cursing the locust" (*chih sang ma huai*) was even less effective than it had been the previous spring, for the rebels knew very well that Liu was a "dead tiger" and

135 Chou's January 17 speech is in *SCMP*, no. 4148 (March 28, 1968): 3–10; *LAD* editorial is reprinted in *PR*, no. 5 (February 2, 1968): 8–9.

136 *Chan Kwangtung* [Fighting Kwangtung] (Canton), July 10, 1968, in *SCMP*, no. 4388 (April 2, 1969): 4–8.

137 Cf. Pearl River Film Studio East Is Red, comp., "Important Speeches by Central Leaders at 100,000-man Rally in Peking" (March 27, 1968) (Canton), April 1968, in *SCMP*, no. 4168 (May 27, 1968): 1–5. A *PD-RF* editorial on April 12 stated, "In class society, there is no factionalism which is abstract and above classes . . . we must adhere to the factionalism of the proletarian revolutionaries." Those rebels who had been excluded from the RCs or otherwise "oppressed" seized on this as justification for counterattack. *FEER* 60, no. 19 (May 9, 1968): 285–289.

used their new freedom to attack their real targets. The claim was generally made that the main contradiction was now between the RCs and the masses, that the former represented the "new bourgeois authority" that suppressed the masses. Serious "struggle by force" between opposing rebel groups or with the PLA was reported in Kwangsi, Yünnan, Kwangtung, Fukien, and Peking. In Kwangtung, factional fighting spread to fifty-six cities, counties, and towns in the summer of 1968 and both sides used modern weapons.[138]

By August, Mao had lost all patience with the rebels and "worker-peasant Mao Tse-tung Thought propaganda teams" were dispatched to China's schools and universities to restore order, resulting in a wave of "voluntary disbandments" of revolutionary mass organizations and widespread rustication of radicals. The interpretation of Mao's Thought was restored to an authoritative organizational context, as the worker-peasant propaganda teams held "Mao Tsetung Thought study classes" (*Mao Tsetung ssu-hsiang hsüeh-hsi pan*) to demonstrate its correct application to concrete problems. Although the mass criticism of Liu reached one more high-water mark following Liu's formal purge at the October 1968 Twelfth Plenum, mass initiative had by this time been brought back under organizational control no less pervasive (though different in significant other respects) than Liu's network of work teams.[139]

CONCLUSION

The GPRC placed the hierarchically stratified structure of authority roles on a public "stage" where stabilized intra-elite communication patterns were disrupted and elites were obliged to seek new patterns of communication with a mass audience to legitimate their authority. These elite-mass communication patterns typically developed through the mass media, providing charismatically gifted symbol specialists among the audience with a brief opportunity to mount the stage and play significant parts. The legitimacy of organization was subverted, and tenure was, of course, highly uncertain. Nevertheless, the processes of mass criticism proceeded according to a discernible order. As in a play, the action fell into "acts," each marked by the resolution of a particular conflict, and "scenes," each marked by its setting. New role definitions of extraordinary sharpness and rigidity became articulated

138 Hinton, "Hundred Day War," *passim;* John Gittings, "Inside China: In the Wake of the Cultural Revolution," *Ramparts* 10, no. 2 (August 1971): 10–20.

139 Richard Baum, "China: Year of the Mangoes," *AS* 9, no. 1 (January 1969): 1–18.

through the repetitive process of mass criticism. There was no "script" ("great strategic plan"), but action was governed by a tacit set of ground rules. First, action was assumed to be norm-oriented: every group was believed to act according to a system of ideas, or "line." Second, while "struggle" was encouraged, violence was not (i.e., *wen-tou*, not *wu-tou*); any group violating the taboo on physical violence acquired a moral onus. In the absence of mutually acceptable umpires to dispense penalties, the "victims" tended to retaliate, resulting in conflict of a see-saw-like escalatory character, but the overall level of physical violence remained below what might have been expected had it been officially sanctioned. Third, it was assumed that the "masses" could function only in supporting roles, led by central elites. While this rule belied the frequently professed faith in the initiative of the masses, it also meant that the masses were never to be blamed for their errors: they were perforce "hoodwinked" by "black backers."

Liu's fall occurred in four acts, and the parts played by various actors in the escalation of criticism varied from act to act, even between scenes within acts. The first act, the "fifty days" from June 1 to the end of July 1966, involved "Chinese box" conflict: the officially sanctioned conflict was between the anti-Mao elements of the Peking cultural establishment on the one hand and the Party and masses on the other, but within this conflict another conflict grew up concerning the Party's procedures for leading the masses, an issue that eventually preempted the original cultural issues. The second act, from August to the middle of January 1967, involved conflict between those wishing to expand the movement's mobilizational scope and range of targets (the CCRG and MAC) and those wishing to restrict them (the Party power-holders) and was resolved by the clear-cut victory of the former. The third act, from late January through March 1967, involved conflict between surviving veteran cadres and representatives of the CCRG and was resolved in a compromise that exempted the majority of cadres from further criticism and concentrated attacks on Liu Shao-ch'i. The final act consisted of another "Chinese box" conflict; the official conflict was between a revolutionary coalition of PLA, CCRG, and masses on the one hand and Liu's "small handful" on the other, but this situation camouflaged myriad unsanctioned conflicts between factions within the anti-Liu coalition. The official conflict was resolved by Liu's purge at the Twelfth Plenum in October 1968, while the factional conflicts among the masses were suppressed by Mao's Thought propaganda teams.[140]

140 Cf. Jean Daubier, "Les Problèmes actuels du PCC," *La Nouvelle Chine*, no. 6 (February 1972): 6–9.

In the resolution to the first act, the original cultural issues dwindled into relative insignificance, whereas the conflict over means of implementation was provisionally resolved by Liu's demotion at the Eleventh Plenum. Liu's demotion is subjectively accountable to Liu's errors in supervising the work teams during the fifty days, analyzed in Chapter 4. The three objective ingredients in Liu's failures consisted of (1) latent cleavages among central elites (i.e., between Liuists and the CCRG) concerning the scope and purpose of mobilization; (2) in the existence of alternative avenues of mass mobilization, through which these cleavages could be transposed to the masses and become interlocked with latent social cleavages; and (3) in a pervasive climate of elite suspicion, which had been generated by the 1965–66 campaign against the "black gang," and followed by unexplained purges of the P'eng-Lo-Lu-Yang group. This conspiracy of circumstances, particularly the operation of alternate avenues of mass mobilization bearing conflicting messages, aggravated the socially disruptive consequences of Liu's subjective errors. The surprisingly harsh evaluation of Liu's culpability publicly indicated in Mao's big-character poster (followed, however, by mild organizational sanctions at the Eleventh Plenum) reflected Mao's foregoing "disappointment" with the making of policy during Liu's six-year stewardship.

The second act subsumes two scenes: in the first, at the October work conference, Liu seemed to have redeemed himself through self-criticism; in the second, in the streets of China's major cities, a "direction switch" ensued in which the movement switched from "cultural" targets to a full-scale attack on the "bourgeois reactionary line" attributed to Liu and Teng (the latter always a secondary figure). The two main reasons Liu's verdict was reversed in the public arena were that Liu no longer commanded the resources in that arena that he had previously exercised through his office, and that his elite backing turned out to be highly tenuous in the face of mass disaffection.

The influential participants in the October work conference were central, regional, and provincial elites; senior members of the CCRG were present by dint of their official positions, but were in the minority on the Liu Shao-ch'i question, and indicated their disagreement with the conciliatory verdict in their speeches and obiter dicta. Upon adjournment of the October work conference, action shifted from the conference hall to the streets. As the publicly stigmatized mastermind of a "bourgeois reactionary line" that allegedly sought to minimize mass initiative and protect the existing authority structure, Liu was placed in a vulnerable position. Mao's opposition to Liu's work team line became widely publicized in the ensuing months, whereas Mao's positive reaction to his October self-criticism did not achieve the same currency, possibly partly owing to the radicals' controlling influence over the mass media. The *public* nature of Liu's rebuke and demotion and the *private* nature of his redemption already assured that mass feedback would be predominantly critical. Left unimpeded, critical feedback inherently tended to build up escalatory momentum through the iterative process of the mass line; this momentum was so strong and so ruthlessly consequential that although several criticism drives began "spontaneously," not one is known to have stopped spontaneously—that some stopped short of purge was due solely to the intercession of elites on behalf of the would-be victim. In Liu's case, not only was there no such intercession, there were repeated intercessions on behalf of those attacking him, ideologically justified by an interpretation of Mao's Thought that emphasized enfranchisement of those groups who had suffered most under the previous regime and now demanded redress.

In the face of mass agitation against Liu, one segment of the elites joined his assailants, while his erstwhile supporters were placed on the defensive and temporarily muted. As action shifted from the conference hall to the streets, Liu sequestered himself in his official residence to wait out the storm, while his supporters dispersed to their regional seats of power and became preoccupied with fending off challenges to their own authority. Lin Piao and the CCRG, of course, actively encouraged Red Guard attacks against Liu; although the rule of democratic centralism formally bound them to heed Mao's injunction that posters should not be posted against Liu and Teng, neither ideological nor expedential considerations committed them to enthusiastic implementation of that ruling. Organizational rules of this sort, which the CCRG had most recently seen used to "strangle" the fledgling Red Guard movement "in the cradle" (and which they were later to criticize as the "theory of docile tools"), were clearly not high on their list of priorities. If after his demotion to 8th place Liu no longer posed a threat to Mao, he remained a potentially formidable opponent for these former subordinates, who could not rest until his power to retaliate had been utterly destroyed. An insecure and relatively inexperienced minority among seasoned officials, Lin and the CCRG members were nevertheless better equipped to dominate this new arena than their more "bureaucratic" colleagues—their adventurist rhetoric caught the imagination of the masses, they enjoyed privileged access to key national mass media, and most important, they became popularly identified as the voice of Mao Tse-tung. Whether Mao was in fact directing the anti-Liu forces from behind the scenes is more difficult to determine; one may observe, however, that Mao never went to any particular trouble to conceal his intervention in the movement in the spring and summer of 1966, but that he made no public statements of any kind during the fall of 1966, that he included Liu among the dignitaries who appeared with him in eight mass rallies between August 18 and November 26, and that Chou En-lai claimed his private support for Liu as late as January 1967. On the other hand, it cannot be denied that Mao alone held the power to halt the escalation of criticism, and that he made no effort to do so.

It would seem that the selection of Liu Shao-ch'i as the campaign's polemical focus during this phase occurred as the result of a complex value-added process [141] rather than as the end consequence of an elaborate prior conspiracy by a coherent group of elites. Mass mobilization and elite cleavage seemed to have had a mutually reinforcing effect, causing the thrust of the movement to diverge from its initial cultural targets to political ones, and finally to concentrate on the chief of state.

In "Act III" (January–March 1967), the scene shifted from the poster-decked city streets to the conference halls of Huaijent'ang. As rebel excesses by now made the possibility of a consequential "power seizure" seem quite remote, there was an important realignment of forces among elites: the "revolutionary masses" were excluded from the meetings, the CCRG went into eclipse, Lin Piao was put on the defensive by rebel friction with PLA forces, and the "power-holders" reappeared in force to press their advantage. The Maoist elites were at this point convinced of the need to make Liu the central target by the tendency of those who remained adamantly opposed to the mass criticism movement to adopt Liu (in his polemical role as unreconstructed nemesis of the GPCR) as their standard-bearer—by releasing the Liu Shao-ch'i case to the forces of public opinion, Liu's image had become frozen for friend and foe alike beyond all hope of alteration through self-criticism. In the compromise that emerged, the criticism of Liu was almost the sole plank in the radical platform that survived the "adverse current"; he became, *faute de mieux*, a symbol of all the forcibly abandoned, often contradictory, movement objectives.

The final decision—the March 1967 decision to criticize Liu in all official media—was a concession to the Left, which was designed to permit the resumed mobilization of the masses while keeping the movement united in opposition to a central symbol. The decision was reached in formal political councils, upon which the CCRG was none-

141 Cf. Neil Smelser, *The Theory of Collective Behavior* (New York, 1962), pp. 13–14, 18–20.

theless able to bring extraparliamentary pressure to bear, and implemented by a CCRG-PLA coalition. The criticism of Liu Shao-ch'i
seemed to be the minimal program all could agree upon; given the
disarray of the Party-state organizational control network, ideological
control through mass criticism had to be given a central focus or the
movement would disintegrate in factionalism. Thus, while the initiative in bringing the attack to Liu Shao-ch'i seemed originally to arise
from the grass roots, the impetus for sustaining the offensive against
him now came from the center.

At this point, Liu's purge came to resemble previous major CCP
purges somewhat more closely: "one, two, or a few" leading figures
(P'eng Te-huai, Ch'en Shao-yü, Ch'en Tu-hsiu) are made condensation
symbols against which all grievances may coalesce, hypostatizing a
monolithic evil to rationalize organization of a monolithic good. Liu
was incessantly criticized without ever being "overthrown" from
March 1967 until October 1968 because his "overthrow" would mean
the end of central direction over the movement. Liu had to be spared
physical injury or incarceration and the myth of his lingering potency
preserved in order to sustain the plausibility of a "struggle between
two lines." [142] It is perhaps for this reason that he was not required
to submit to "struggle" after August 1967; as K'ang Sheng pointed out
(in another context), "If you strike him to death, you will lose a living
target of attack. . . . After 'traveling by airplane' (a form of struggle
in which the accused must respond to questions while crouching with
arms extended behind him) Lu Ting-yi is not required to make further
confession." [143] As the more utopian substantive goals of the GPCR
had to be diluted or compromised away, the symbolic goals assumed
increasing importance as the mute embodiment of those frustrated
goals, until by October 1968, the struggle against Liu Shao-ch'i and
what he stood for was what the GPCR had come to mean, and his
overthrow was its greatest and most ineluctable achievement.

142 Allowing Liu to retain his office also placed the Red Guards in a favorable
symbolic light by ascribing the "ratio of apparent forces" to Liu (as the "authority")
and evoking public sympathy for the "rebels" who "dared to topple the emperor at
the risk of suffering death by a thousand cuts." Had Liu's political impotence been
publicly announced, the intent of the GPCR to foster a "revolutionary" spirit by
encouraging the nation's youth to criticize him would have been exposed to be somewhat artificial. See Orrin E. Klapp, Symbolic Leaders (Chicago, 1964), pp. 173 ff.

143 "Speech to Red Guards" (January 23, 1967), in Hsin Pei-ta [New Peking Uni-
versity], January 28, 1967.

PART II
Two Roads

> Two roads diverged in a yellow wood
> And sorry I could not travel both
> And be one traveler, long I stood
> And looked down one as far as I could
> To where it bent in the undergrowth;
> —ROBERT FROST, "The Road Not Taken" *

> Every great experience presents life to us in a different aspect; only then the world is seen in a new light: while such experiences repeat themselves and coalesce, we form attitudes toward life. . . . They will change, as life reveals new facets to man, but in different individuals there prevails certain attitudes according to their own character. One man will hold on to the tangible, material objects and will live fully enjoying each day, another will pursue through chance and fate the great purposes which constitute stability for his existence.
>
> —WILHELM DILTHEY, *The Types of World Views and Their Unfoldment Within the Metaphysical Systems.*

* From *The Poetry of Robert Frost,* edited by Edward Connery (London: Jonathan Cape). Reprinted by permission of the publisher.

6

LIU SHAO-CH'I AND MAO TSE-TUNG: A COMPARISON OF CHARACTER, POLITICAL STYLE, AND POLICY

The conclusion to the last section conceded that Liu's errors during the "fifty days" were causally adequate to explain his demotion at the Eleventh Plenum, granting that Mao's allocation of responsibility between subjective and objective factors may have reflected his prior disappointment with Liu. The increase of Red Guard criticisms during the second phase was a value-added social process that Mao might have halted, but to which he did not directly contribute. Yet, when the rebel tide overreached itself in the January power seizures, making Liu's rehabilitation feasible in terms of the objective balance of forces, Mao resisted the "adverse current" and insisted on making Liu the principal target of attack. He no longer referred to Liu's errors during the GPCR to rationalize his decision but began to make a more general indictment of the cumulative "revisionist" impact of Liu's life and teachings, primarily as expressed in his writings. Either objectively or subjectively considered, the events of the GPCR alone seem inadequate to explain Mao's decision at this phase, and we must now examine the contention, reiterated ad infinitum in the criticism campaign, that the GPCR brought to light fundamental and long-standing differences between the two men that made further cooperation impossible.

For purposes of analysis we divide the politically relevant action patterns and predispositions of the two actors into three aspects: character, political style, and policy. In the body of this chapter, we attempt to delineate the basic character structure of both actors, relying for the most part on their voluminous published works, but also resorting on occasion to credible Red Guard documents, personal reminiscences, and anecdotal data. From these sources we select a series of what appear to be character-revealing episodes, which fall into networks of meaning called *thema*, a composite of which makes up that actor's "operational code." The following *thema* seemed both psychologically basic and politically relevant: (1) "Display" refers to the actor's way of organizing his life into public and private realms, to his mode of self-expression and repression. (2) "Contact" refers to his way of mediating self-other relationships, including his style of organization and leadership. (3) "Interest" refers to his conception of such material inducements as status, wealth, and power. (4) "Reality" refers to the actor's primitive ontology: what is "real" in life, and how does man relate to reality? (5) "Evaluation" refers to the actor's moral classification of reality. (6) "Work" refers to his mode of interacting with his usable environment, to how he does his "job." In the conclusion, we attempt to show how character was translated into policy within a stable authority structure and how changes in role and milieu ultimately brought the two characters into a conflict involving the entire political system.

DISPLAY

It is helpful in understanding a person to know which aspects of himself he displays and which he conceals. It is apparent to those who have met both men that Liu reveals much *less* of himself than Mao, but this observation begs the question of what is displayed and what is concealed. Generally speaking, Mao seems to be a more spontaneously emotional person than Liu; in meetings with subordinates he has been known to weep or to become violently angry and curse his antagonist in blunt, colorful language. "I never saw him angry, but I heard from others that on occasions he has been aroused to an intense and withering fury," notes Snow. "At such times his command of irony is said to be classic and lethal." And again:

Mao impressed me as a man of considerable depth of feeling. I remember that his eyes moistened once or twice when speaking of dead comrades or recalling incidents in his youth.[1]

Liu, on the other hand, is emotionally withdrawn—a "cold fish," according to former Foreign Service Officer John S. Service, who interviewed him in 1944 at Yenan.[2] In his only published poem (*supra*, pp. 10–11), it is interesting to note that Liu's expression of "wistfulness" is

---

[1] E. Snow, *Red Star Over China* (New York, 1961), pp. 76, 78.
[2] I am grateful to John Stewart Service for telling me of his interviews with Liu and Mao in Yenan.

put in the *second* person (nearly all of Mao's poems are written in the first person) and immediately followed by mockery of his own self-indulgence: "Your aspirations are foolish and your sentiments silly." Chang Kuo-t'ao characterized him in Confucian terms:

Confucius said, "The ardent will advance and get what they want; the stoical will refrain from doing what they do not want." Liu Shao-ch'i belongs to the latter category. . . . All his successes and failures are closely connected with his stoical character.[3]

Liu speaks with a heavy Hunan accent and a slight stammer, and his thin, sharp appearance and reserved bearing are said to convey a "forbidding" air:

When he begins to speak, he stammers, so that his speech is indistinct and even his Hunan friends do not hear him clearly. . . . People who talk to him, shake hands, interview him, feel that he has a forbidding air. . . . Liu's speech is sharp, concise, and rigorous—with little sentimentality. Without stopping talking, Liu ceaselessly puffs Russian cigarettes. . . . In speaking to him, no one can move his heart-strings. No externals distract him —his entire heart and mind are concentrated on the internal work of the CCP. Even Confucius . . . would commend this present-day Communist Party sage.[4]

It is correct but insufficiently specific to say that Mao is more "emotional" than Liu, however. Mao does not convey the full gamut of his moods to the public but rather tends normally to repress his combative qualities and display calm benevolence; the countenance that beams down from the ubiquitous reproductions is a serene one. In Mao's occasional moments of self-criticism, he has expressed the (not entirely unfounded) judgment that his gravest political errors have arisen from his *excessive* magnanimity, his guileless faith in human nature. Thus, when chiding Liu and Teng for their mistakes over the past six years, which in his view led to the June–July 1966 work team crisis, Mao allocated responsibility in this way:

It seems that the comrades on the first line haven't done their work well and some of the things they ought to have done were left undone. The blame, however, is not entirely theirs; I am also responsible. Why do I say that I am also responsible? First, to divide the Standing Committee into the first and second lines and to let them take charge of the Secretariat was my idea. Furthermore, [I] had too much trust in them.[5]

[3] Chang Kuo-t'ao, "Introduction," Liu, *CW*, p. i.
[4] Chao Kuang-yi, "Liu Shao-ch'i," *Chung-kung jen-wu ssu-miao* (Hong Kong, 1952), pp. 7–8.
[5] "Talk at the Work Conference of the Center" (October 25, 1966), in Jerome Ch'en, *Mao*, p. 96.

When he found it necessary to purge Liu, he did so with severe disappointment over Liu's betrayal of his confidence, according to Chou En-lai: "At that time, Chairman Mao expressed his . . . disappointment with Liu Shao-ch'i. Despite his help for twenty years, Liu had not lived up to expectations." When Lin Piao shortly went the way of his predecessor, the same dismay was expressed: though the Chairman "showed extreme patience and magnanimity" and gave Lin "many opportunities" to correct himself, he still "did not repent," Chou explained.[6]

Liu Shao-ch'i's political errors, on the other hand, according to his own self-criticisms as well as the criticisms of others, usually consisted of excessive rigor in the enforcement of justice. He tries to display rationality and unbending rectitude (Wang Kuang-mei testified during her "trials" that she had never known him to lie in twenty years) [7] and to repress sentiments of tenderness.

The following incident is characteristic of Liu. His older sister and brother, who had become small landowners in Hunan in the years prior to the revolution, sought special consideration from their newly prominent younger brother during land reform. Liu's response was didactic and uncompromising:

In the past your family lived on rent, it was others who supported you. Therefore, you should be grateful to those who paid you rent, those who farmed your land. . . . People say that you exploited others. That is right. You in the past did exploit others. Now it is also right to demand that rent be reduced and deposits returned in the rural areas. You should reduce rents and return the deposits as required. You cannot reproach others, calling them a union of small boys or a team of rascals. No. They are the great benefactors who have supported you and many others. You should respect them. . . . A long time ago I had told you that you should not collect rent and issue loans. But you didn't listen to me, but said that I was wrong. Now you come to me in your suffering, but it is already too late. I can do nothing for you. As I see it, these hardships you have asked for. You cannot blame others.[8]

But although Liu coldly declared that he could "do nothing for you," he then in fact proceeded to point out provisions in the law that would enable his relatives to comply with the new regulations at minimal loss:

Should you be unable to return the rent now, you may ask the *hsiang* peasants' association to allow you to return the rent in the autumn of this

6 *NYT*, August 13, 1972, p. 3.

7 "Three Trials," in *CB*, no. 848 (February 27, 1968): 11–12.

8 "Down with Liu Shao-ch'i, Filial Son of the Landlord Class," *Hsin Pei-ta*, February 10, 1967, in *SCMP*, no. 3916 (April 11, 1967): 1–19.

year when you will have collected your rent. You may give a debit note to the peasants' association and ask it to forgive your mistake in not having reduced rent last year. . . . It is probable that after the autumn harvest this year you may still collect a year's rent, and this will still be allowed by the law. . . . With regard to the matter of return of rent, you have already returned a part of it. If you are unable to return a further part, you may apply to the peasants' association for exemption. The Party CC has instructed all areas to stop the return of rent. . . . I have become the Vice-Chairman of the Chinese People's Government and you are tilling the land in your hometown. That is my glory. If, now that I am Vice-Chairman, you are still collecting rent and doing nothing but eat, that will be my shame.[9]

Despite this explicit repudiation of favoritism, Liu did exploit his position to secure minor favors for his relatives. The Red Guards reproduced the following note to the Hunan Province chief:

My seventh older brother Liu Tso-heng will pass through Ch'angsha on his way home from Peking. Will you please take care of him for several days before he goes home? He told me that the grain levy in the countryside was excessive in some cases and that some were unable to pay up. I am afraid that this is not entirely the rumor of the landlords. Some thought may be given to this. . . . My sixth older brother is short of labor power in his family. . . . Now the several old and young people in the house have to eat and they are unable to pay the grain levy. Can you see your way to reducing it? . . . My seventh older brother has a grandson who wants to go to school in Ch'angsha. I wonder if there is a free school for him. If so, please help him.[10]

This episode shows that Liu engaged in petty nepotism, but this is in itself not that remarkable; it is common in Chinese politics for the wives of high-level leaders to achieve high positions as well, for example, and during the GPCR Mao and Lin Piao even appointed their daughters to key political posts. What is notable is that Liu did not claim credit for his help but rather haughtily informed his relatives that he could "do nothing for you," then helped them behind their backs, applying a sort of inverted hypocrisy.

Liu reacted the same way when his son Yün-jo, who had fallen in love with a Russian girl while studying in Moscow, tried to get permission to return to the Soviet Union to marry her. The widening Sino-Soviet schism made this move politically inopportune. Liu's instructions to those charged with reconciling his son to the "realities of life in China" were stern: "Don't be afraid I may not be satisfied, because I stand on your side. . . . Don't spare him, give him no privileges. . . . The problem of corresponding with a foreigner should be considered a violation of discipline." But although Liu suggested

9 *Ibid.* 10 *Ibid.*

sending his son to the field for productive labor, when the Minister of Public Security accepted this proposal, he immediately reneged. Arrangements were reportedly made to introduce Yün-jo to eligible and desirable young women, to give him work suited to his "special qualifications," and Liu specifically requested "commending him for work done (when commending him, be sure he is given encouragement or favorable criticism)." [11]

CONTACT

Like many professional revolutionaries, Liu values his secondary associations (i.e., his relationship to such abstract categories of humanity as the "masses," "proletariat," and so on) above his primary associations; during his unusually peripatetic career, his intimate relationships have been frequently interrupted, usually (according to his own account) because they interfered with his overriding commitment to the interests of the "masses." "Liu Shao-ch'i suffered many setbacks on the question of marriage," Wang Kuang-mei put it delicately. He was betrothed by his parents as a child in Hunan but (like Mao) abandoned his bride before consummating the marriage. He is said to have married a Russian girl during his 1920–21 sojourn in Moscow, abandoning her when he returned to China. Thereafter, in 1924, he married Ho Pao-ch'en, who was arrested and killed by the KMT in 1933 after a period of imprisonment. Unwilling to let their son become a "burden" on his Party work, Liu reportedly arranged for his adoption during the Long March. In 1935 he married Hsieh Fei, with whom he lived until January 1939, when he divorced her. In the New Fourth Army, he befriended a nurse named Wang Ch'ien, said to be sixteen years old at the time, whom he later married. He divorced her in March 1947 because she "interfered with his Party work," after she bore him two children, son Yung-chen and daughter T'ao (both of whom were to become minor celebrities during the GPCR, when they in turn publicly "divorced" their father). He then married Wang Chien but only two or three months later sent her to a sanitarium in the Northeast for treatment of "neurosis." In 1948, he married Wang Kuang-mei, scion of one of the "eight big houses" of North China, who worked as an interpreter for the Communist side at General Marshall's mediation headquarters after the war.[12]

11 "Liu Shao-ch'i's Reactionary Nature as Seen from His Indulgence of His Son's Betrayal of His Country," *Na-han chan-pao* [Outcry battle news], February 1968, in *SCMP*, no. 4140 (March 18, 1968): 4–16.

12 "Appendix 2: A Biographical Sketch," in C. P. FitzGerald, ed., *Quotations of Chairman Liu.*

Liu's emotionally inhibited personality undoubtedly has much to do with the fact that his relationship to the anonymous "masses" has not only overshadowed but seemingly established a pattern for his other relationships: his dealings with people are invariably courteous but impersonal. Liu's cool approach to human contact and his reserved, dignified presentation of self in public lend surface plausibility to the charge that his attitude toward working people was one of arrogance, that he thought he was Chu-ko Liang (a wise man) and that they were A-tous (fools). This charge is belied by Liu's career, however, much of which was spent working for and with workers as a trade-union organizer, an experience in which he took great pride. Even after rising to prominence, Liu made a point of "joining in productive labor" whenever possible during his frequent "inspection trips" to the countryside [13] and his life style remained "simple and frugal": in a display of conspicuous nonconsumption, he had his shirt collars and cuffs turned, mended his socks with "patches over patches," and relegated his children to hand-me-down clothing.[14] On one occasion he allegedly caused his retinue of security personnel inconvenience by insisting on boarding an ordinary passenger car "with hard seats" to mingle with the masses, rather than boarding his special train to Peking.[15] Later decried as "economism," the sincerity and consistency of Liu's concern for the material welfare of the masses cannot be gainsaid. Referring to the time they worked together, Chang Kuo-t'ao recalls:

We developed an attitude of respecting the interests of the masses and taking action on the basis of practical conditions. This was an attitude of realism, not opposed to amelioration and progress, striving for legal benefits and legal activities.[16]

Chang distinguishes Liu in this regard from those who felt that "any amelioration . . . would only be an obstruction of the revolution," and from those who "ignore the interest of the masses to the extent of exploiting them for the Party's personal ends." Nor do Liu's works betray any sense of arrogance toward the masses; on the contrary, they

13 Wang Ying, "A Sketch of Liu Shao-ch'i's Daily Life," in *Chung-kuo ch'ing-nien* [China youth], no. 3 (February 1, 1959), in *Extracts from China Mainland Magazines*, no. 172 (June 15, 1959): 45–46 (hereafter *ECMM*).

14 Yen Shang-hua, "A Most Impressive Lesson," in *Chung-kuo ch'ing-nien* [China youth], no. 3 (February 1, 1959), trans, in *ECMM*, no. 115 (January 20, 1957): 1–5.

15 "A History of Crimes of Opposing the Party, Socialism, and Mao Tse-tung's Thought," *Pa-i-san hung-wei-ping*, no. 68 (May 13, 1967), in *SCMM*, no. 588 (August 14, 1967): 14 ff.

16 Chang Kuo-t'ao, "Introduction," Liu, *CW*, pp. ii–iii.

are filled with tributes to the wisdom and courage of the masses, admonitions to learn from them, and the like.[17] These seem to be more than ritual accolades; they indicate a well-articulated conception of social progress in which the masses play an indispensable role. For example, he said in 1945:

In the campaign for reducing rent and interest, they publicly appear to have been reduced but remain the same privately. This is a result of the fact that the masses themselves have not yet risen to lead the campaign. In a mass movement it must be understood that we can only take one end of the bread. This means that it is up to the masses themselves to carry out the struggle.[18]

Perhaps part of the reason for the Maoist belief that Liu did not care about the masses is that Mao and Liu seemed to have different constituencies in mind when they used the term: when Liu speaks of masses, he means workers, whereas when Mao speaks of masses, he means peasants. Liu's preference is clear, for instance, in his 1941 essay, "The Class Character of Man," in which he characterizes peasants in words redolent of Marx's remarks about "the idiocy of village life":

The peasants have for a long time been tied to the land and have been engaged in production in a form that is scattered, independent, simple, self-sufficient, and with little mutual cooperation. Their way of life is simple and individualistic and they bear the burden of land rent and unpaid services, etc. Thus, the ground is set for their lax ways, conservatism, narrow-mindedness, backwardness, outlook of private owners, revolt against the feudal lords and their demand for political equality, etc.[19]

A few paragraphs later, Liu gives this description of the workers:

The proletariat are concentrated in big industries, carrying on production with a minute division of labor: all their actions are governed by machines and mutual dependence. . . . They rely on wages as a means of livelihood and their basic interests do not conflict with those of other toilers. Hence, the ground is prepared for their great solidarity, mutual cooperation, sense of organization and discipline, progressive outlook and demand for public ownership of property, revolt against all exploiters, militance, tenacity, etc.[20]

Mao, on the other hand, in a corresponding section of his own writings, had nothing but praise for the peasants, while qualifying his praise for the workers: "It's size is smaller. . . . It is still young

---

[17] E.g., *CW* 1: 46; *CW* 2: 44; and *CW* 2: 454.
[18] Liu, "A Summary of Several Basic Understandings of Women's Work" (April 1945), *CW* 2: 6.
[19] *CW* 1: 323.   [20] *Ibid.*

in age. . . . And cultural standard is low." [21] In Mao's *Selected Works* and *Selected Military Writings*, the word "peasant" (including "peasant masses," "rich," and "poor peasant") appears on 287 of a total 2,022 pages, while "worker" (including word connections) appears on only 51 pages.[22]

Of greater importance than this semantic difference in determining the rapport each man has with the common people is the emotional mediacy of the relationship. Mao's conception of the proper relationship between leader and led is unmediated contact, and he deplores "bureaucratism" (*kuan-liao-chu-i*). "This great evil, bureaucratism, must be thrown into the cesspool, because no comrade likes it," he said in 1933.[23] More than thirty years later, during the GPCR, he commented with regard to the public security, procurative, and judicial organizations, "People seem to think that these organizations are indispensable. But I shall be glad if they will collapse." [24] The admonition not to become "divorced from the masses" recurs frequently throughout Mao's *Selected Works,* and such a "divorce" is the integral feature of his definitions of "revisionism," "bureaucratism," and other vices. In his 1965 comments on medical reform, he went so far as to object that "When making an examination, the doctor always puts on a gauze mask, regardless of what kind of patient he is dealing with. . . . I think the main reason is that he is afraid of being infected by other people." [25] Mao's ideal of an unmediated relationship between elites and masses may have achieved its highest state of realization during the GPCR, when China became in effect a vast "media village," and Mao's numerous "latest instructions" were transmitted to the nation almost instantaneously. To be sure, this was an exceptional episode, and in fact Mao spends no more time mingling with the masses than anyone else of equivalent rank—he may actually be the most conspicuous victim of the bureaucratic "divorce," since he often secludes himself for such long periods that rumors of his death arise. But if Mao's attempts to facilitate unmediated contact between

21 Cf. Mao, "On the Coalition Government" (1945), *SW* 4: 295; "Report on an Investigation into the Peasant Movement in Hunan" (1927), *SW* 1: 22, for positive evaluations of the peasantry. His negative evaluation of the industrial proletariat is from Mao, *Chinese Revolution and the Chinese Communist Party* (Bombay, 1950), p. 24, as quoted by Yung Ping Chen, *Chinese Political Thought: Mao Tse-tung and Liu Shao-ch'i* (The Hague, 1966), p. 32.

22 Klaus Mehnert, *Peking and the New Left: At Home and Abroad* (Berkeley, Calif., 1969), p. 45.

23 "Pay Attention to Economic Work" (August 1933), *SW* 1: 129–137.

24 *Cheng-fa hung-ch'i* [Politics and law red flag], nos. 3–4 (October 17, 1967), in *SCMP*, no. 4070 (November 30, 1967): 1–4.

25 "Instruction on Health Work" (June 26, 1965), in *CB*, no. 892 (October 21, 1969): 20.

elites and masses have been rather episodic, and too disruptive to be institutionalized on an on-going basis, one can at least argue that he has devoted more attention to the problem of enfranchising the disadvantaged, "uncultivated" sectors than has Liu Shao-ch'i.

Liu has a contrasting tendency to mediate and formalize relationships between people. For example, when his son wrote to him from his dormitory at the University of Moscow, complaining that his Soviet roommate was "gambling through a whole night, always keeping himself drunk and rowdyish so other students of the same abode are unable to study and rest," Liu offered this paternal advice:

However, in handling the disputes between Chinese students and Soviet students, you must follow an even more well-organized method: you must first refer to the Communist Youth League organization to which you belong, then the CYL organization or Party organization will refer to the League organization or Party organization under its subordination, and then the Soviet League organization or Party organization will criticize him, educate him.[26]

As this quotation suggests, Liu's propensity to isolate potentially delicate relationships is reflected in his approach to organization. Incalculable and potentially disruptive personal feelings are repressed in an emphasis on functionally specific roles, defined by a complex web of written rules; personal responsibility is diffused through a bureaucratic division of labor. In a word, Liu was a bureaucrat. He even told an audience of young workers once that there was room at the top for them as "district leaders, *hsien* leaders, province chiefs, ministry heads in the government," but that "if you want to have an important duty, you have to be able to do a big job, to manage a big office." [27] Whereas Mao considered bureaucracy an unmitigated evil, Liu's condemnation of bureaucracy is more qualified:

Bureaucracy is the opposite of democracy. . . . It is one kind of formalism, paying particular attention to forms of things, not to the content and essence of things. . . . Bureaucracy exists today and it will continue to exist in the future. Therefore, liquidating it will take several decades. . . . Today we cannot liquidate all bureaucracy, otherwise we will have to liquidate all our organs, and that will be going too far.[28]

When he addressed himself to the problem of curbing bureaucracy a quarter-century later, Liu's views showed no change. "Bureaucracy exists all the time," he assured graduating seniors.

26 "Three Letters to His Son" (May 6, 1955), *CW* 2: 318.

27 "Tsai hua-pei shih-kung tai-piao-hui i-shang kuan-yü kung-hui kung-tso went'i ti pao-kao" [A report delivered before the North China workers' representative meeting on the problems concerning the work of labor unions] (May 1949), in *LSWTC*, p. 207.

28 "Democratic Spirit and Bureaucracy," *CW* 1: 85.

Wouldn't you show any bureaucracy at all when you go out to work? I don't believe that you wouldn't. It may even be more serious. Therefore, anti-bureaucracy is a long-term campaign. There will be a struggle against it so long as it exists.[29]

Inasmuch as the purpose of Liu's tendency to mediate and formalize human contact is to isolate disruptive emotions, during periods of crisis, the need to mediate and formalize seems all the more impera-tive. During the frantic "fifty days," for example, Liu thought in terms of resolving disputes through such organizational devices as the "tem-porary convener":

At the time of election, some may express their approval and others their disapproval. If different opinions persist, you will find a temporary convener. . . . If a committee cannot be selected, a temporary convener may be ap-pointed. Today I convene the meeting, tomorrow he will convene the meet-ing. In this way, the masses will not have any objection.[30]

The withdrawal of the work teams did not placate but rather aggra-vated student agitation. Liu responded to the new grievances with more organizational solutions. "You still have to rely on the Party organizational system," he insisted, and proposed reelection of the school Party and Youth League committees and participation of the masses (on a quota basis) in previously closed Party conferences.[31]

Although Liu contrasts bureaucracy with democracy, condemning the former in the light of the latter, his conception of democracy also betrays his formal, mediational approach to contact. Whereas Mao's conception of democracy emphasizes immediate contact between lead-ers and led, Liu stresses personal freedom from governmental inter-ference ("bourgeois privacy") and access to elites through institutions. Liu indicates his commitment to "freedom" in his 1954 "Report on the Draft Constitution," which lays strong stress on civil liberties:

The Draft Constitution calls for freedom of speech, of the press, assembly, association, procession, and demonstration, and lays down that the state shall provide the necessary material facilities to guarantee to citizens the enjoyment of these freedoms. . . . No citizen may be arrested except by decision of a people's court or with the sanction of a people's procuratorate. . . . The homes of citizens in the People's Republic of China are inviolable, and privacy of correspondence is protected by law.[32]

A chief institutional medium through which the non-Party masses are granted access to policy decisions was the system of people's rep-resentative conferences, and later the people's congresses. Liu was a

---

29 "Address to the 1957-Class Graduates of the Peking Institute of Geology" (May 1957), *CW* 2: 423.
  30 (August 3, 1966), *CW* 3: 335.   31 *Ibid.*, pp. 350–355.   32 *CW* 2: 299.

prime mover in organizing these institutions: he headed the Electoral Law Drafting Committee and delivered its report to the First National People's Congress in 1954, and in the government reorganization that took place with the inauguration of the new Constitution, he was elected chairman of the Standing Committee of the Congress. Communication from the masses would be mediated by letters to specialized organs set up to receive them, and by electoral representation (in 1951, 83 percent of the representatives to the national conference had been elected by the people, Liu proudly reported):

The People's Government and consultative committees at all levels should establish special and competent organs to deal appropriately with every demand submitted by the people, reply to their letters and make themselves easily accessible to the people. By this means the Party government . . . will be closely linked with the people and will serve them in a practical way, while at the same time the broad masses will be enabled to manage their own and state affairs through the conferences.[33]

Like many other aspects of Liu's political style, his distinctive approach to the masses had its most marked impact on China's institutional structure in the early 1960s. Intricate policy-making and implementing institutions were interposed between those at the top and the masses, making it almost impossible for Mao to get the kind of direct mass participation he wanted; the masses could only participate differentiatedly, more on some issues and less on others, and indirectly, through a hierarchy of specialized organizations. If institutions failed to meet expectations, the leadership would seek a remedy through organizational reforms rather than ideological rectification and would attempt to coopt diverse elements into organizational networks.[34]

Liu's approach to people is also reflected in his deferential and scrupulously correct leadership style. "Unlike Mao, Liu is frequently present at important conferences and, moreover, says very many important things. . . . Whatever is or is not said—he is clearly informed." "He listened to reports with deep concentration, sometimes taking notes; he wanted the person making the report to make the situation perfectly clear, and didn't like vague talk, a careless (ta-kai pa) way of talking." "Comrade Shao-ch'i had a lot of views and bright ideas for every problem, but he would always say, 'This is my view, but please go out and study the situation for yourselves.' "[35] So scrupu-

---

33 (February 28, 1951), *CW* 2: 235–246.

34 Ahn, "Adjustments in the GLF," p. 299.

35 Chao Kuang-yi, "Liu Shao-ch'i," pp. 5–13; Yang Chin-ch'eng, "Mien mang chu shih" [Always busy with important affairs], *HCPP* 13: 65; "Shao-ch'i t'ung-chih tsai Huai-pei" [Comrade Shao-ch'i north of the Huai], *HCPP* 13: 72.

lous was Liu about adhering to the norms of collective decision-making
that during the GPCR it was hard to pin him with personal responsibility for past mistakes. In his three self-criticisms, his admissions were
typically phrased: "Comrade Teng Tzu-hui proposed. . . . The CC
meeting over which I presided failed to raise objection." "The conference therefore approved comrade Ch'en Yün's speech." "I heard
directly about . . . but did not stop him from advocating it."

While Liu's leadership style is formal and routinized, Mao's is
episodic and provocative. Liu exerts influence by setting conference
agendas, selecting speakers, or drafting reports; Mao conducts a guerrilla war with the bureaucracy, short-circuiting regular "channels" to
call ad hoc meetings of more complaisant subordinates, or evading the
apparat altogether by suggesting a plan to the public before it has
been presented to the leadership, confronting his colleagues with a *fait
accompli*. Mao exhibits a flexibility in switching positions or allies
that prevents any stabilization of expectations and leaves his colleagues
in perpetual uncertainty.[36] Bored with the routine of formal conferences, he invests long periods of time in the private study of philosophy, history, and literature and informally proposes his ideas to
his colleagues in the form of marginalia on reports submitted to him,
short notes to various political figures, or the convention of different
political bodies. When on July 31, 1955, Mao called for increasing the
pace of agricultural collectivization, he did so in a speech to secretaries of provincial, municipal, and autonomous regional committees,
flouting the formal authority of the CC. The people's commune apparently originated as a result of Mao's offhand response to a reporter
during a tour of Shantung:

When I was in Shantung, a correspondent asked me: "Is the people's commune good?" I said, "Good," and he published a report on the strength of
this in a newspaper. From now on I must shun reporters.[37]

By the time the Politburo met on August 18 to consider the question,
several provinces had already organized peasants into communes, so

36 One of the most bitterly disappointed of his erstwhile allies, Lin Piao, reportedly summed up his experience: "At no time has [Mao] stopped trying to
pit one force against another. Today he may try to win over this force to deal with
that, but tomorrow he may put that force against this. . . . Looking back over the
past decade, how many do you see who were raised to power and fame by him
but later escaped political death?" *NYT*, July 23, 1972, pp. 1, 16. By the time
of this writing, Lin had presumably lost all objectivity about Mao, but even during the GPCR he took note of Mao's tactic of "using one faction to hit another"
[la i p'ai, ta i p'ai]. *Ming Pao*, July 5, 1968, p. 1; see also Chow Ching-wen, *Ten
Years of Storm* (New York, 1960), pp. 255–257.

37 Parris Chang, "Struggle Between the Two Roads in China's Countryside," *CS*
6, no. 3 (February 15, 1968): 1 ff.

the August 29 Politburo resolution to establish communes amounted to a pro forma endorsement of Mao's decision.

Whereas Liu's institutional strategy of policy formulation results in exhaustively detailed directives like the "Sixty Points for People's Communes," the "Seventy Points for Industrial and Mining Enterprises," the "Sixty Points for Higher Education," and so on, Mao's directives tend to be schematic, under the apparent apprehension that precision in definition may obstruct flexibility in action. This produces administrative havoc but at the same time allows play to what appears to be one of Mao's central values: the creative spontaneity of the masses. When in 1958 a group of journalists asked whether they could report on contradictions among the people, Mao thought for a moment and said, "Try it. Then let us see." [38] He has fittingly been called a "great experimenter":

He often does not plan in a rational way in advance. He suggests something and lets the propaganda drums roll—and then waits to see what will happen. If the experiment fails entirely or partially, then he always makes the necessary retractions.[39]

Such a technique is obviously more suited to the campaign, where popular participation and the mass media play a more important role, than to orderly bureaucratic implementation. A drive based on a cryptic slogan is organized, and when it has been developed for some months, its merits and demerits are examined and debated and a "summary of experience" is made.

As the debacle of the GLF demonstrated most clearly, Mao's direct, personal approach to policy leaves him open to personal blame if the policies fail. To defend himself against this contingency, Mao "ghosts" his proposals, releasing them under a pseudonym to the media, revising them in the light of the ensuing campaign, and finally releasing an appropriately revised edition under his own name several months or years afterward. For example, in 1958, Chang Ch'un-ch'iao wrote an article in *Chieh-fang* [Liberation] (the theoretical organ of the Shanghai Party Committee) based on Mao's comments at the Peitaiho Politburo conference, advocating restoration of the suppply system and abolition of the current wage system. Mao ordered the reproduction of Chang's article in *PD* and personally wrote an accompanying "Editor's Note" affirming its theses.[40] Mao's role in this affair, however,

38 *Wen-hui pao*, April 28, 1958, in Dick Wilson, *Anatomy of China* (New York, 1968), p. 57.

39 Lily Abegg, *Ostasien Denkt Anders*, p. 368.

40 Wu Leng-hsi, "Confession," *Hung-se hsin-hua* [Red new China], no. 43 (May 1968), in *CL&G* 2, no. 4 (winter 1969–1970): 63–87.

was not known until eight years later. Since his interview with Malraux in 1965, he has, with perhaps the single exception of Edgar Snow in 1970, permitted no foreign newsman to interview him, and none to quote him directly.

INTEREST

For both Mao and Liu, collective interests are absolutely paramount, and both have had some difficulty reconciling themselves to the existence of inconsistent personal interests. Mao, basing his leadership on ideological legitimacy, tends to resolve this problem by insuring the integrity of the symbols to which collective interests are committed; individual lapses in attaining the form of behavior prescribed by the symbols might be overlooked so long as the integrity of the symbol is preserved intact. For instance, at Lushan Mao said it mattered little if 70 percent of the communes collapsed, so long as 30 percent continued to operate successfully. It seems fair to say that Mao's concept of interest, at least in his later years, has tended to become somewhat abstract and idealized. He even said in 1958 that "the outstanding thing about China's 600 million people is that they are 'poor and blank.' . . . On a blank sheet of paper free from any mark, the freshest and most beautiful characters can be written." [41] And he seemed genuinely nonplused by his discovery of the apparently irreconcilable heterogeneity of mass interests during the GPCR.

Liu, as the administrator of affairs, deals in goals that must be practically attainable; he bases the reconciliation of collective and personal interests less on the invocation of inspiring ideological appeals than on the explicit acknowledgment and manipulation of personal interests. Part of the reason for the different styles of the two men is perhaps personal—Liu lacked Mao's emotionally appealing charismatic and literary qualities—but it is also partly due to the differing experiences of the two men at formative periods in their careers.[42] Mao was the leader of a revolutionary movement and later a nation at war who could mobilize the support of the populace against the threat of a common enemy; Liu was the manager of underground Party organizations in the "white areas" where the "we-they" distinction was never as clear-cut as in the "red areas," and Liu therefore could not define the collective interest through ideological appeals against a

---

[41] "Where Do Correct Ideas Come From?" in *SRWM*, pp. 502–504.

[42] James Barber emphasizes the formative influence of early career experience in the development of political character in *The Presidential Character: Predicting Performance in the White House* (Englewood Cliffs, N.J., 1972).

common enemy. Furthermore, the possibility of infiltration was an ever-present worry and the use of ideological appeals was likely to be imprudent, even foolhardy:

Hence, so far as secret work is concerned, empty "revolutionary" shouts which have no practical meaning must never be made (verbal or written), for such shouts would only spur the reactionary forces to alertness, heighten their attentiveness, undermine the secret work and carry no revolutionary significance.[43]

In the course of his work in the "white areas" Liu elaborated an intricate program for the reconciliation of collective and personal interests that did not regard the masses as "poor and blank" but took explicit account of personal interests in all their diversity. In exchange for services to the collective interest, he was willing to satisfy personal interests, fulfilling those needs of client groups that he in no way condoned as well as those he approved of. Thus in a 1938 lecture he recommended that *booty* be awarded to bandit groups who aided the CCP:

[We] may fight better jointly with a certain guerrilla team. If we win the battle through cooperation, we may give them the victor's spoils to make them feel the benefits of cooperating with the Eighth Route Army. After cooperating successfully two and three times, they will naturally bring forward the question of long-term cooperation.[44]

As a second illustration of Liu's tolerance of ideologically heterodox interests, he noted with approval that:

In a few regions, fairy tales can play a very useful role among the underground societies. In a certain locality, it is widely said that Chu Te is the descendant of the First Emperor of the Ming Dynasty, and the underground societies in the locality have maintained particularly good relations with the Eighth Route Army.[45]

Liu was not content with this policy of trade-offs that bought cooperation from a congeries of ideologically incompatible personal interests at the seller's price, and he articulated a program of progressive mass mobilization that had the goal of educating people to a "higher" conception of their interests. This program began by organizing the masses around heterodox personal interests.

Among the masses, there are various kinds of people (workers, peasants, merchants, small craftsmen, teachers, students, etc.) and thus also various

[43] "On Open and Secret Work" (1939), *CW* 1: 293.
[44] "Work Experiences in the North China War Zone" (1938), in Schwarz, *Liu Shao-ch'i and "People's War,"* pp. 33–34.
[45] (July 1, 1938), *CW* 1: 74.

different demands. For organizing the masses, various methods and forms shall be applied based on the masses' various demands. For instance, we will organize political parties for the masses who have political demands, organize study societies, libraries, singing teams, athletic clubs, etc., for those with cultural demands, organize economic units for those with economic demands, such as labor unions, peasant associations, etc.[46]

The objective of all these "front" organizations was what Liu called "raising the level." As he put it in 1953, "We must . . . raise their political consciousness, so that they realize that the interests of the community, of the state, and of themselves are one." This "raising" (*t'i-kao*) involved not simply an increase in altruism, but an insight into a broader, more inclusive conception of self-interest. This "class" consciousness, Liu said, was the most important characteristic distinguishing socialist morality from the individualistic hedonism of the "landlord-bourgeois class": "For the enjoyment of material life, a Communist Party member takes, not an individual, but the whole class as his aim. His concern is the material life of the entire proletarian class." [47]

Liu's clearest formulation of the organizational tactics of "raising the level" is presented in his 1939 essay, "Some Basic Principles for Organizing the Masses." In this essay, he makes it clear that while the highest form of organization is the political organization, the most "important" is the economic organization. "Why? The reason is that the masses—workers, peasants, students, women, and merchants—all have economic demands." Although it is "highest," the political organization can "never" be the most extensive form of mass organization, because "only people with a high political consciousness can join a political party." Therefore, "all the economic demands of the masses must be integrated with political or cultural demands. When the masses begin to take action on one simple demand, we must lead the masses in fields related to their actions on this simple demand so that they can understand better a series of problems and further push their actions to a still higher stage." Thus, by "raising the economic demands to political demands, raising partial and temporary demands to whole and permanent demands, and raising local demands to state and national demands," the masses are "cultivated" to a higher conception of their interests.[48]

"Cultivation," as Liu conceived it, was a slow and arduous process, and the masses did not "raise" their level of understanding the way an

46 "Work Experiences," in Schwarz, *Liu Shao-ch'i and "People's War,"* pp. 51–52.
47 "On Enjoyment and Happiness," *CW* 1: 89–94.
48 (May 1, 1939), *CW* 1: 99–115.

army storms a city, but in the manner of an endless procession. Liu makes this clear in a later discussion of the method of increasing production, still using the "levels" analogy:

The broad masses of people are the creators of history. The history of human society is at base a history of production, a history of the workers in production. Production is always in a state of constant development and change, and new production techniques are always replacing the old ones. Therefore in all times and in all departments there are always a minority of pioneer workers who adopt comparatively more advanced production techniques and create comparatively more advanced working norms. Following them more and more workers will come to learn their techniques and reach those working norms until, at last, the production level of the few advanced workers becomes the level of the whole of society.[49]

At the highest "level" in this process was the Communist Party, where personal and collective interests perfectly coincide:

It must be understood that the interests of the Party are identical with the interests of the people. Whatever benefits the people also benefits the Party and must be carried out by every Party member with heart and soul. Likewise, whatever injures the people also injures the Party. . . . The Party has no special interests of its own beyond the people's interests.[50]

This assertion of an identity ("merging") of interests is central to Liu's rationalization of personal interests, but it is in fact a prescriptive statement masquerading as description; what Liu meant was that if the interests of the people and those of the Party differed, the former should take precedence. The same is true regarding the identity between the interests of the Party and those of the individual: the individual should sacrifice his interests to those of the greater whole, and the Party would see to it that the sacrifice was made good:

You must not be double-minded and pay attention to both ends. Only in this way can you master your own destiny. You must have faith in the Communist Party and exert your efforts in this direction. As to the other end, we'll take care of it, and if it is not taken care of, you should point this out to us.[51]

What emerges is a vision of society as a vast, corporate hierarchy, ordered according to recognition of collective interest and moral efficiency in service to that interest. The "corporate" aspect of the hierarchy is in its web of mutual obligations and tacit contracts to satisfy personal interests. The ultimate objective was elimination of all con-

49 "Message to Outstanding Workers" (April 30, 1956), *CW* 2: 330.
50 "On the Party," *CW* 2: 41.
51 "Report (August 18, 1964), in "Selected Edition," *SCMM*, no. 652.

flict of interest, and competition for private interest was specifically disallowed, as Liu explained in a speech to People's University in 1950:

Our university does not set up such departments as physics, chemistry, mechanics, and electricity. Why? Because other universities can also set up these sciences. . . . Competition for students has been a common occurrence in the history of China; for instance, when Confucius was head of the judiciary, a post he held for only three months, he had XX killed because he thought the latter had competed for his pupils. By the way, anyone who competed for pupils with a saint should be beheaded. It is due to this very reason that the People's University has only set up these few classes and departments. Such a way of dividing work is to the benefit of the country.[52]

As Liu implies in this statement, a division of labor could be, and was, incorporated within this hierarchy; in fact, the taboo on competition necessitated a rather "minute" division of labor:

People are different and have different qualities. Some are clever and some are stupid; some are tall and some are short; some are strong and some are weak; some are men and some are women; men are born different. . . . Moreover, as men's social conditions vary—such as some men have the opportunity for schooling and some have not—their functions differ. There is a division of labor and differences in work and career. For instance, in our army there are the commanders and the fighters, and among the commanders there are the high-level commanders and the lower-level commanders. . . . Within the Party there are those who are the responsible persons and those who are not; those who are the leaders and those who are the led.[53]

What we begin to perceive here is that Liu's hierarchy of moral efficiency had a tendency to incorporate other hierarchies and become an interdifferentiated multi-value, yet all-embracing "establishment," still legitimated by the assumption that these increasingly diverse interests and skills may be arranged to contribute to an overarching collective interest, so long as they adhere to certain meritocratic formal values. The tendency to absorb other hierarchies was given its greatest impetus by the Party's conquest of national power, which gave it simultaneous jurisdiction over the vast resources of government, economy, cultural affairs, science, education, medicine, and so forth. From the beginning, the ideology of moral efficiency was an incipient legitimation of status and political power as well: "Irrespective of his position, every member of the Party has an opportunity to express his

---

52 (October 3, 1950), *CW* 2: 238.
53 "Democratic Spirit and Bureaucracy," *CW* 1: 81.

opinion *if he is up to a certain intellectual level and is able to understand the revolution."* [Emphasis added.] The Party's seizure of the state apparatus gave it a monopoly of political power, vastly increasing the political rewards it could offer. The introduction of the division of labor made it a hierarchy of skill as well. Finally, Liu accepted a differentiated wage scale to correspond to the divison of labor, making it a hierarchy of income also.

The incorporation of these other meritocratic value hierarchies within the original legitimating framework of moral efficiency created the possibility that young men might seek entry into the hierarchy to maximize personal interests, such as power, wealth, prestige, and so on, and not out of dedication to the collective interest. Liu's confidence in the ultimate compatibility of all interests led him to view this prospect with increasing tolerance if not equanimity, even to foster a certain functional autonomy within peripheral hierarchies (e.g., medicine, culture, science) conducive to the maximization of their respective values, and to encourage ambitious youth to work out a satisfying compromise of personal and collective interests. In the following two quotations Liu appeals to political and economic ambitions respectively:

If a university graduate after five years of study goes to work on the farm for another five years, he would be a laboring peasant with many good conditions. He would then know farming, be a cultivated man close to the masses. The masses would choose you as a commune chief and a village-group chief. . . . After you have worked on the farm for several years and became a commune chief, then a village-group chief, you will be a county chief.[54]

We do not have enough housing. This difficulty the nation is trying to solve, but you should also think of a way to solve it yourselves. . . . You may contribute some money with which to build houses. When houses are built, you can move in and not pay rent. Or, you can sell it to the government when you leave, and build another house, or buy or rent a house, when you reach a place. . . . You should put aside some money, so that you may some day build a family dependents' dormitory or set up a family dependents' cooperative. Get the money together and the state will build the house for you. When you do not want them, you can sell them back to the state. This will be no different from depositing money in the bank.[55]

Liu asserted that "despite all the differences in nature, in work, in duty, and in authority, mankind is basically equal. There is no inequality in human rights." How was he able to reconcile the existence of this hierarchy with the values of democracy and equality he pro-

[54] "Address to the 1957-Class Graduates," *CW* 2: 424–425.   [55] *Ibid.*

fessed? Aside from defining these values in formal, rather than substantive terms (i.e., in terms of rights, rather than goods), Liu assumed that the imposition of socialist morality could offset material differences. "In the United States, an engineer may receive higher pay and be more capable, but he is in no way superior to the workers," he opined.[56] Implicit in this statement is an assumption that differences in wealth and income per se do not violate democratic values, but rather the adoption of these differences as a criterion for the invidious treatment of other people. "Democracy" consists of everyone treating everyone else with a certain modicum of consideration, and this state of affairs could be brought about by common adherence to a set of shared values and is compatible with the continued existence of inequalities in wealth, power, and prestige, so long as these inequalities produce some actual benefit for the less advantaged groups.[57]

By the time of the Cultural Revolution, Mao had become profoundly disturbed by the hierarchical implications of a conceptual framework he originally found no reason to fault. Apparently he came to feel that, in his concern for form, Liu had lost sight of a growing discrepancy between formal and substantive justice; in order to call attention to this discrepancy in a sufficiently dramatic way, Mao has called for the complete effacement of personal interest, for "annihilation of the self" (hsiao-mieh tzu-wo). Mao's intention to restore Liu's multi-value hierarchy of interlocking interests and mutual obligations to its pristine condition, in which the sole motive for upward mobility is dedication to the collective interest, became clear in an "instruction" of mid-September 1967 (which is surely one of his most radical pronouncements on the subject):

Why should we practice the wage system? This is a concession to the bourgeoisie and would discredit us by ridiculing the "style of the countryside" and the "habits of the guerrilla" and lead to the development of individualism. . . . How about letting the military lead in restoring the supply system? The bourgeois conception of law should be relinquished. For example, rank, extra pay for extra working hours, and the theory that mental labor should be more highly paid than physical labor, are all remnants of the bourgeoisie. . . . Our Party members in general lived a life of egalitarianism, worked diligently, and fought bravely up until the period of liberation. They did not depend on material stimulation at all but were inspired by the revolutionary spirit.[58]

56 "Democratic Spirit," CW 1: 82–83.
57 Cf. John Rawls, Theory of Justice (Cambridge, Mass., 1972), pp. 66–70, cited in Tsou, "The Values of the Chinese Revolution," in China's Developmental Experience, ed. Michel C. Oksenberg (New York, 1973), pp. 30–34.
58 "Mao's Latest Instruction," in Chinese Communist Affairs: Facts and Features, no. 1 (November 1, 1967): 18–19.

Mao holds the division of labor chiefly responsible for growing discrepancies in wealth and power and has subjected functionally autonomous skill hierarchies, such as medicine, education, et al., to criticism on this basis. He has also criticized the principle of the division of labor and proposed new institutions or reforms of old institutions that would aim at its dissolution. On May 7, 1966, he wrote a famous letter to Lin Piao:

The PLA should be a great school. In this great school, our army men should learn politics, military affairs, and culture. They can also engage in agricultural production and side occupations, run some medium-sized or small factories and manufacture a number of products to meet their own needs or to exchange with the state at equal value. They can also do mass work and take part in the SEM in the factories and villages. . . . They should also participate in the Cultural Revolution and criticize the bourgeoisie.

While the main activities of the workers is industry, they should at the same time also study military affairs, politics, and culture. . . .

While the main activity of the peasants . . . is agriculture, they, too . . .

This holds good for the students too.[59]

This "instruction" was made the basis for the widespread establishment of "May 7 schools," which functioned as reeducation centers for disgraced or surplus personnel at a time when most offices were closed. As we shall see in the following chapter, the reform of the regular education system was also informed by the desire to reduce functional specialization, as were post-GPCR reforms of the medical delivery system and other institutions.

REALITY

Like many emotionally repressed persons, Liu Shao-ch'i tends to deny the reality of internal feeling states; reality is for him external, hard, and clearly defined. Like the characters in Alain Robbe-Grillet's novels, he seems to attribute paramount reality to what is *seen,* for vision places distance between subject and object and permits "objectivity," defined as detachment and the feasibility of precise measurement; the other senses obscure the subject-object distinction and cannot gauge reality precisely enough for intersubjective agreement. In *How To Be a Good Communist,* Liu proposed to "adapt ourselves to reality and know reality, and seek existence and development in reality." Liu

[59] Quoted in Liu Mao-nan, "The Sixth Anniversary of the 'May 7th' Road," *IS* 8, no. 10 (July 1972): 65–73.

conceives of the constraints of reality on human action in strict deterministic terms:

Objectively, a Party member cannot have liberty. . . . Only by understanding the nature of inevitability, grasping the objective law and moving within the limits of fixed regulations [and so on.] . . . We the revolutionaries should strive vigorously for what can be attained and stop trying to accomplish what cannot be realized.[60]

Liu's denial of internal reality is also reflected in his repudiation of "preconceived ideas." In 1963, preparatory to her stay in T'aoyüan, Wang sought her husband's advice, and he told her, "You must not have any preconceived ideas. When a problem crops up, solve it." [61] An exchange took place between Wang and her Red Guard interrogator during her April "trials" that highlights the difference between Maoist and "Liuist" perceptions of reality:

Wang Kuang-mei: Facts are facts. Conclusions should be drawn according to facts. This is the thought of Mao Tse-tung.

Interrogator: No, the standpoint is most important. Taking the reactionary stand, you see only the seamy side of the revolution.[62]

Implicit in the interrogator's reply is the Maoist belief that reality is not "hard," but plastic, protean; one can change reality simply by changing the way one thinks about it ("taking a proletarian standpoint"). Because the subject is the deciding factor in determining the nature of reality, "As long as there are people, every kind of miracle can be performed. . . . All pessimistic views are utterly groundless." Mao is suspicious of adaptation to reality and, like Polonius, regards action as authentic only insofar as it accurately expresses "preconceived ideas":

He who pays no attention to ideology and politics and becomes immersed in daily work can turn into an economist or technician who has lost his bearings, which is very dangerous. Ideology and politics are the leader and the soul.[63]

Mao evidently believes in his emotions as indicators of a more compelling truth and in the same article evinces his willingness to draw inferences about reality on the basis of feelings: "Just as there is no love without cause in the world, so there is no hatred without cause."

---

[60] "Training in Organization and Discipline," *CW* 1: 405.
[61] "Selected Edition," *SCMM*, no. 652 (April 28, 1969): 36.
[62] "Three Trials," in *CB*, no. 848 (February 27, 1968): 23.
[63] "Who Is the Chief Culprit?" Chingkangshan Corps of Tsinghua, in *KMJP*, Peking, April 4, 1967. The article goes on to charge that Liu wants people to "lose their political bearings and become walking corpses with no soul."

These differing assumptions about the relative "reality" of internal and external experience resulted in differing practical consquences in the political and economic realms. Whereas Mao tends to be "unrealistic" (i.e., to underestimate objective constraints), it may be said that Liu inclines to what Sartre calls "seriousness," [64] in that he is sometimes guilty of "overestimating the importance of objective forces and underestimating the importance of subjective forces." [65] Because of Liu's underevaluation (from the Maoist viewpoint) of the potential of internal energies, Liu shows undue solicitude about the possible depletion of energies. In 1957 he said at a graduation address:

As zeal is essential, so is sobriety. When zeal rises high, it is necessary to see that it does not go beyond limit. Life is a long way to go, and there is no need for haste. Hastiness leads to trouble. Full-spiritedness is important but there is always a limit. . . . Shock attacks are necessary but avoid them where possible. You must do what your capacity permits and do it carefully and cautiously. Enthusiasm without care for your health is undesirable.[66]

Even during the GLF, when his role and the situation required that he encourage the high expenditure of energy, Liu betrayed his concern about its possible depletion in his assurances that nonexpenditure ("slowing down") actually involved invisible expenditure: "Some say it's better to slow down the tempo. But are things not going to get tense if the speed of construction is slowed down?" His concern was most clearly (and most justifiably) manifested in retrenchment from the Leap, when he showed a constant preoccupation with the "costs" of things (which had been blithely ignored during the Leap, under Mao's assumption that human potential is boundless, its generous expenditure heroic).

With regard to agricultural production, farming systems are changed at random. Some technical measures which are impractical and unscientific are adopted indiscriminately. Some water conservancy projects which are not only useless but harmful are built. With respect to industry, rules and regulations are abolished at will and some impractical and unscientific technical measures are adopted indiscriminately, with the result that equipment has been damaged, the quality of certain products has declined, the cost have increased, and labor productivity has dropped.[67]

[64] Cf. Joseph P. Fell, III, *Emotion in the Thought of Sartre* (New York, 1965).

[65] Mao, "Letter to Lin Piao" (1930), in *SW*, 1947 ed., supp., pp. 98–99, quoted in Stuart Schram, ed., *Quotations from Chairman Mao Tse-tung* (New York, 1967), p. xvii.

[66] "Address to the 1957-Class Graduates," *CW* 2: 426.

[67] "Enlarged Work Conference" (January 1962), *SCMM*, no. 652 (April 28, 1969): 24–25.

It is telling that, before joining the Communist Party, Liu chose to study engineering (as it is also telling that Mao was first a teacher), for he always paid attention to the material preconditions for undertakings, such as the fact that "it is not possible to run many schools in cities due to the consumption of commodity grain." In his promotion of the part-study part-work system in 1964, he mentioned as one prominent point in its favor the system's cost-effectiveness: "How can there be any loss at all when these students work throughout their four or four-and-a-half years with nothing like wages except merely their board?" [68] Mao for his part has been so repelled by such "calculation" that each time he has personally intervened in the economy, considerations of costs have been suppressed to the extent of dismantling the statistical system and discouraging cost accounting. In evaluating projects like the commune, he remarked as Lushan, "It seems to be impossible to judge the result if economic accounting is applied." [69]

What can be said of the reality against which Liu is dedicated to testing himself so relentlessly? Like Max Weber (who replied, when asked the purpose of his researches, "To see how much I can endure"), Liu seems to consider reality a basically discouraging aspect, so discouraging that he constantly urges steely-eyed resolution just to look upon it clearly. As Wang Kuang-mei says to her interrogator (the writer notes parenthetically that she is "peering through narrowed eyes," which figuratively suggests the appropriate stance for gazing upon reality), "One should call a spade a spade if one really cherishes the revolutionary young fighters. One cannot cherish the revolutionary young fighters by distorting facts.[70] When, during the "three years of natural calamities" of 1960–62, the nation's news media tactfully avoided any discussion of the domestic economy, Liu reproached them for "habitual lying." At the January 1962 cadre conference of 7,000, he called for "bravery" in facing reality: "We are unwilling to admit or tend to discount our difficulties for fear that giving a true picture of our difficulties would make our cadres lose confidence. . . . This is obviously not true bravery." [71]

Liu's model of learning is informed by the same dogged, almost masochistic spirit. "Self-cultivation" is described in figures of speech, such as "steeling" and "tempering" which suggest relentless confrontation with a distressing, obdurate reality. In *How To Be a Good Com-*

[68] "Report on the Work of the CC of the CCP to the 2d Session of the 8th National Congress" (May 5, 1958), *CW* 3: 22–23.

[69] "Mao Tse-tung's Speech at the 8th Plenary Session of the CCP 8th CC" (August 2, 1959), in *CL&G* 1, no. 4 (winter 1968–1969): 60–63.

[70] "Three Trials," in *CB*, no. 848: 14.   [71] Cf. n. 67.

munist, Liu quotes with approval the injunction from the Confucian *Book of Odes* that one should cultivate oneself "as a lapidary cuts and files, carves and polishes." [72] What is being "cut and filed, carved and polished" is the (instinctual) self, by controlled, sustained exposure to "hard" reality. Liu's model of learning is one of ego-adaptation and emotional repression.

In Mao's model of learning, the emotions play a more active role, stimulating sudden insights or basic reorganizations of cognitive structure. The participation of the emotions is intended to raise "consciousness" by bringing together the perception of mistreatment and injustice with the repressed emotion, thus overcoming the separation of thought from emotion that "cultivation" deliberately fosters. Mao illustrates the process in a long passage from his own experience:

I began life as a student and at school acquired the ways of a student. I then used to feel it undignified to do even a little manual labor, such as carrying my own luggage in the presence of my fellow students, who were incapable of carrying anything, either on their shoulders or in their hands. At that time I felt that intellectuals were the only clean people in the world, while in comparison workers and peasants were dirty. But after I became a revolutionary and lived with workers and peasants and with soldiers of the revolutionary army, I gradually came to know them well, and they gradually came to know me well too. It was then, and only then, that I fundamentally changed the bourgeois and petty-bourgeois feelings implanted in me in the bourgeois schools. I came to feel that compared with the workers and peasants, the unremolded intellectuals were not clean and that, in the last analysis, the workers and peasants were the cleanest people and, even though their hands were soiled and their feet smeared with cow dung, they were really cleaner than the bourgeois and petty-bourgeois intellectuals. This is what is meant by a change in feelings, a change from one class to another.[73]

This passage contains no reference to the forces or relations of production to justify its reference to "bourgeois and petty-boureois." The "transformation" Mao discusses is rather an emotional transformation of the fear of "dirt" (which he, apparently in common with many in his audience, was accustomed to use as a metaphor for "workers and peasants") [74] into feelings of admiration and respect through willed contact with the feared thing.

72 *CW* 1: 165.

73 "Talks at the Yenan Forum on Literature and Art" (May 1942), *SW* 3: 73.

74 Evident in the foregoing quotation is Mao's propensity at times to confuse a proletarian life style with a Bohemian one. His boyhood friend Siao-yü also remembers his "invariably untidy" room and personal disarray: "Not only was he content with being dirty himself, but he objected to my cleanliness. For instance, I always brush my teeth after meals and he would mock me. . . . He started to

The implications of these differing models of perception—Liu conceiving it after the model of *sight*, emphasizing a detached, accurate rendition of "objective" reality, Mao conceiving it on the model of *feeling*, implying selective sensitivity to colorful, dramatic aspects of reality—may also be traced to different conceptions of the role of the communications media, as the following chapter makes clear. To Liu, perception and motivation are distinct processes; to Mao, they are integrally linked. Thus, Liu's notion of the role of the media has tended to be limited to reality-testing, while Mao seems to lay greater stress on the media's mobilizational role; given Mao's refusal to recognize any clear distinction between cognitive and emotive faculties, "objectivity" is impossible anyhow, since all news can excite feelings of some sort.

It is tempting to generalize from these divergent learning models that Liu was a "materialist" and Mao was an "idealist," but this would be an oversimplification. It is true that Mao attributes greater importance to ideal (superstructural) factors in the causation of history and pays less attention to the material infrastructure, and his relative emphasis on the former seems to have increased with time. As he said in 1957:

Some people think that China scored a genuine success in the socialist revolution in 1956, but I think this actually took place in 1957. The system of ownership was changed in 1956, and this was easier to carry out. The success of the socialist revolution in the political and ideological fields was not scored until 1957. The rightists have now been toppled.[75]

As is well known, Mao later reversed this optimistic early verdict on the defeat of the "rightists." Liu's different perspective on the problem of the traditional cultural legacy is reflected in his 1959 remark:

It is true that the bourgeoisie will make use of this policy of "letting a hundred flowers blossom" to engage in anti-socialist activities. However, under present conditions in China, the proletariat has the upper hand in every respect. We have nothing to fear from the bourgeoisie.[76]

The attempt to classify Mao an "idealist" founders on his experiential empiricism. "Where do correct ideas come from?" he asks.

---

nickname me 'son of a rich father'; later he was to call me 'bourgeois,' but at this time he had not yet learned that word. There was no doubt that for him, cleanliness implied a bourgeois type of mentality." *Mao Tse-tung and I Were Beggars* (Syracuse, N.Y., 1959), pp. 68–69, 122.

[75] "Talk at a Meeting with Chinese Students and Trainees in Moscow" (November 17, 1957), in *CB*, no. 891 (October 8, 1969): 26.

[76] "The Victory of Marxism-Leninism in China" (September 14, 1959), *CW* 3: 62.

"They come from social practice, and from it alone." At one point in his writings, Mao concedes that some knowledge does come from "indirect experience," only to show that since indirect experience is only someone else's direct experience, "knowledge of any kind is inseparable from direct experience." Mao's attack on "idealism" thus tends to focus on a Confucian elevation in the status and influence of those who work with symbols ("indirect experience") above those who work with things. As he wrote in 1959:

The primary condition enabling idealism to become a philosophical thought is the separation of physical labor and mental labor, which is the result of the development of social productive forces. Division of labor occurs in the society and the further development of the division of labor produces people who specialize in mental labor.[77]

Mao would not necessarily regard his thought as idealist, because his thought is never to be allowed to become alienated from (manual!) practice and was meant to emancipate previously inarticulate and powerless segments of the polity, not simply to legitimate authority. Indeed, Liu might be considered "idealist" according to the Maoist definition, because of the functional autonomy he permitted certain disciplines in achieving self-sustaining accumulation of expertise and the supervisory role he allotted to technocrats in the industrial sector.

EVALUATION

Liu's choice of a "bridge" as the leitmotiv of his only poem is perhaps thematic, for mediation between opposites forms the basis for Liu's evaluative categorization of experience. One of his habitual stylistic devices is to show the correct way balanced between "leftist" and "rightist" errors. For example, in 1939 he defended the simultaneous use of legal and illegal organizing methods by denouncing "rightist liquidation ideology—legalism" (i.e., cancelling illegal activities) on the one hand and " 'leftist' liquidation ideology—illegalism" (i.e., cancelling all legal organizations) on the other. In 1941 he wrote:

Our inner-Party struggle must be directed . . . against both right opportunism and "left" opportunism. . . . If we merely carry on a one-sided struggle . . . then the enemy not only can but assuredly will attack . . . from that very side which we have neglected.[78]

77 "Outline of Dialectical Materialism" (1959), in "Selections from Chairman Mao, Part 2," *JPRS*, no. 50792 (June 23, 1970): 3.
78 *CW* 1: 294.

Again in 1945, Liu speaks in terms of a "right-opportunist line in Party-building" (i.e., open-door recruitment policy, loose discipline), and a " 'left'-opportunist line in Party-building" (i.e., excessive centralism, "mechanical" struggles).[79] The conception of rectitude implicit in these classifications superficially resembles the Confucian "golden mean" (chung-yung):

A. "Left" Opportunism | (Rectitude) | Right Opportunism

Mao has also discussed rectitude in these terms, but "there is in the thought of Mao a tendency to polarize all things into two opposites,"[80] which militates in favor of a different conception of rectitude. During the GPCR, the Maoists employed a classification schema, ironically derived from "united front" terminology, to conceptualize the polarization of rectitude: the pertinent parties are first divided into friend and enemy (usually 90 percent and 10 percent, respectively) and then the "friends" are further subdivided into three groups: those who are good, those who are relatively good or not too bad, and those who have serious problems but can still be redeemed if they sincerely repent, but who otherwise must be reclassified. This schema can be depicted as follows:

B. Good | Relatively Good | Serious Problems |
Friends | Enemies

This schema is obviously conducive to movement, since rectitude is inhibited on only one side by the possibility of deviation, and one is more certain of maximizing rectitude the farther left one moves on the continuum. Schema A is conducive to balance, since one is inhibited on either side by the possibility of error. During periods of heightened concern about the possibility of committing deviations (as during a rectification campaign), the deviant categories in both schema would be seen to expand and include a wider range of possibilities; an actor using schema A would be frozen into immobility as inhibitions grew on either side, but an actor using schema B would be strongly impelled to move to the left.

There has been a post-GPCR modification of schema B back to what Mao has called "center-leftist":[81] the terms "phony 'left,' " "ultra-left," and "anarchist," have appeared to characterize the "May 16

[79] CW 1: 329; CW 2: 22.

[80] Tang Tsou, "Revolution, Reintegration and Crisis in Communist China," Tang Tsou and Ping-ti Ho, eds., China in Crisis, I, bk, 1 (Chicago, 1968), p. 296.

[81] Ross Terrill, 800,000,000: The Real China (Boston, 1972), p. 68.

Group," Ch'en Po-ta, and Lin Pao. This is only an "apparent" reversion back to schema A, however, for these people are only "apparently 'left' but essentially right," and are also referred to as "people like Liu Shao-ch'i," to emphasize their essential rightness. Lin Piao and his "gang," initially defined as "ultra-left," were officially reclassified "ultra-right" in a December 1972 *RF* article. These evident scruples about conceptual consistency suggest that the GPCR's "imprinting" of schema B has introduced a certain terminological rigidity into the violent polemical oscillations of Chinese politics: in the countryside, cadres have reportedly concluded that "to be left is a question of work style; to be right is a problem of political orientation" and have sometimes displayed reluctance to comply with moderate directives, apparently assuming that Mao disapproves of them and may reemerge to strike down all "revisionists." [82] Possibly the GPCR has accomplished one of its objectives, which was to create a permanent taboo on right deviation.

A second stylistic device Liu uses to deal with contradictions is paradox; i.e., simple juxtaposition of the two terms of the contradiction. He accepts a paradoxical relationship between ends and means and even between different ends. The Party itself consists of contradictions:

What is the Party's organizational structure? Like everything else, it is a structure of contradictions . . . containing leaders and led, the Party leadership and Party members.[83]

This acceptance of paradox reflects Liu's resignation to the continued coexistence of evil in the world, his willingness to work with evil to do good, to persevere in moral ambiguity and "keep . . . bearings and distinguish right from wrong in complex situations." [84] Only with the advent of Communism will contradiction be wiped out and harmony reign:

In that world, there will be no exploiters, oppressors, there will be no landlords, capitalists, imperialists and Fascists, etc., and there will be no one who is exploited or oppressed. . . . In that society, people will all have a high cultural level, there will be all public and no private. . . . People will all have plenty, will help each other, and love each other. There will be no . . . hurting each other, killing each other and struggling with each other.[85]

---

[82] *CNA*, no. 839 (April 23, 1971): 1–5; *CNA*, no. 876 (April 7, 1972): 1 ff.

[83] "Training in Organization," *CW* 1: 369–411.

[84] Hsü Kuan-san, "Tang-ti ta chien kung-shih," *Jen-wu*, no. 40 (July 15, 1970): 8–15.

[85] *CW* 1: 174–175.

Mao has become opposed to these views and now makes two seemingly contradictory assertions about "contradictions": first, contradictions and struggle will not end with the advent of Communism but will continue indefinitely thereafter. Second, Mao has shown an increasing tendency to assert that the thesis of the contradiction must be "swept away," as he put it in a 1963 poem to Kuo Mo-jo:

> We must sweep away all the harmful insects
> Until not a single enemy remains.[86]

In the past, Mao maintained (in greater consistency with his view on the persistence of contradiction) that in the dialectic, the antithesis does not simply annihilate the thesis, but rather that a synthesis is formed in which the thesis is also contained. In 1959 he expanded on this point, using the sexes as an example: "If there were only men and no women, if women were negated—what would happen then?" But by 1965 Mao had changed his mind. In a conversation with Ch'en Po-ta and K'ang Sheng, he said:

What is synthesis? . . . It is eating something up . . . one eating another. Synthesis is the big fish eating the small fish. This is not written down in any book. My writings do not describe it this way either. . . . One class is eradicated and the other emerges; one society is eradicated and another rises.[87]

WORK

The prototypical mode of action in Mao's world-view seems to be combat. "Everything that Mao learned of life—theoretical or practical—bore out that truth: all is struggle," writes Frederic Wakeman. "Mao's entire structure of thought and action [is] based on it." [88] The corresponding mode of action in Liu's world-view is labor:

. . . the world of man and even man himself are the creation of labor. Labor is the foundation on which human society exists and develops. Workers are the creators of civilization. Therefore, labor must command the highest respect in the world.[89]

Just as Mao has extended his favorite action mode into the Communist millennium, Liu's utopia will feature four hours of "manual labor," even "play" seems rather laborious:

---

86 "Chairman Mao's Latest Directive" (September 13, 1967), in *Ko-ti t'ung-hsün*, no. 4 (December 15, 1967), in *SCMP*, no. 4081 (December 15, 1967): 1.

87 "Chairman Mao's Conversation with Comrades Ch'en Po-ta and K'ang Sheng" (1965), *JPRS*, no. 49826 (February 12, 1970): 28.

88 Frederic Wakeman, Jr., *History and Will: The Origins of Maoism* (Berkeley, Calif., 1973), p. 299 (prepublication text).

89 "May Day Address," *CW* 2: 192.

Tell them that with the advent of Communism, things will also be like this. They have to perform four hours of manual labor in the least, and can spend the rest of their time at play. They can devote themselves to business management, painting, opera, or research work. In the future, everybody can carry out research work.[90]

By all accounts, Liu worked very hard. "He ascended step by step, not by obvious talents, but by solid hard work," recalls Chang Kuo-t'ao. "Papa is so very busy that he can spare no time for rest," his wife told his daughter in 1959. "Chairman Mao does not attend to the concrete major affairs of state and has assigned them to papa. You must not disturb him." [91]

A foreigner who knew Liu in the 1940s described him as a man of narrow mentality, with little knowledge of, or interest in, events outside China.[92] The scope of topics covered in criticism of Liu—foreign affairs, education, the economy, the legal system, cultural affairs, and so on—certainly belies this impression, but it is easy to see how such an impression might arise: Liu showed an apparent preference for routine, technical tasks for which most people showed neither interest nor aptitude. He seemed to specialize in writing constitutions, through which he could impose orderly systems on others: he wrote the revised Party Constitution in 1945, the "Report on the Draft Constitution" of the C.P.R. in 1954, and the CC's political reports to both the first and second sessions of the Eighth Party Congress in 1956 and 1958, all of which are comprehensive, exhaustively detailed documents. Liu prided himself on his self-discipline and disliked ostentation, adjuring "every comrade" to "do more daily trifling and troublesome work but utter less smart words." [93] In a rare access of dry humor, he observed:

Some of the intellectual elements with a stronger tinge of heroism . . . always feel that they are not the kind of person to deal with this kind of "trifling" and "troublesome" things. They always feel as if in addition to these concrete but revolutionary works, there seem to be existing in a certain mysterious place an abstract, general, and magical kind of work which is not so troublesome, and would insure their posthumous names. They ask the Party to assign them such a mysterious type of work, so that they could be contented and the work could be done in no time. The Party is unable to locate such a kind of work for them, however, nor can they. But they do not

90 "Speech in Hopei" (July 5, 1964), in "Selected Edition," *SCMM* no. 652 (April 27, 1969): 35.

91 Chang Kuo-t'ao, "Introduction," Liu *CW*, p. i; "Drag Out Liu Shao-ch'i and Show Him to the Public," *SCMP*, no. 3946, pp. 1–16.

92 Harold C. Hinton, *Leaders of Communist China* (Santa Monica, Calif., 1956), pp. 120–123.

93 "Training in Organization," *CW* 1: 402–403.

believe it. There must be such a kind of work kept somewhere by someone from the knowledge of everybody. They are puzzled and frustrated; they show their discontent, and further complain that the Party is not treating them well.[94]

In earlier years, Liu foresaw a bright future for the form of work he most respected:

Technical work gives one the brightest future. After the enemy is wiped out and no more fighting is to be done, technical work will become the central task. . . . When we build a new China, we want everybody to take part in the administration. Technical work will then assume the primary importance. The military commanders will go to factories to work at that time. Technology will decide everything.[95]

Later, during his period of stewardship, Liu was to restructure the ladder of success to fulfill his own prophecy. If Mao was concerned about the absence of revolution as a fiery *rite de passage* for China's future elites, Liu seemed quite ready to accommodate himself to its absence:

Not a few of our comrades have gone through the test and discipline of such revolutionary struggles as guerrilla warfare and land reform. But there is no more guerrilla warfare and no more land reform. In the training of and selection of cadres hereafter the one principle to be observed is: only those who have been workers or peasants can be selected to be leadership cadres.[96]

Liu's dedication to a lackluster "underlaborer" role contributed to his public reputation as China's *éminence grise*. Harold Hinton comments in 1956 that Liu has "no distinguishable characteristics," and Donald Klein wrote in 1967 that Liu is a "dour and rather colorless man." [97] But this "greyness" may account in part for his long tenure of peaceful coexistence with Mao. Mao personally dislikes routine work, yet realizes it must be done; Liu was glad to do it and did not crowd the spotlight.

Mao's feelings about work seem to be quite different. According to Emi Siao, in his boyhood Mao's father called him lazy and worthless for sitting around reading novels rather than working. Mao appeased his father by doing an extraordinary amount of work in a short time and

94 "Fan-tui tang-nei ko-chung pu-liang ch' ü-hsiang" [Opposing various evil trends existing in the Party], in *LSWTC*, pp. 115–127.

95 *CW* 1: 403.

96 Yen Shang-hua, "A Most Impressive Lession," *Chung-kuo ch'ing-nien*, no. 21 (November 1, 1957), in *ECMM*, no. 115 (January 20, 1958): 1–5.

97 Donald W. Klein, "The Party and the Leaders," in *The China Giant*, ed. C. P. FitzGerald (Glenview, Ill., 1967), pp. 47–50; Harold C. Hinton, *Leaders*, pp. 120–123.

then returning to his novels.[98] Since that time, his own life has tended to oscilate between periods of intense activity and periods of solitary reflection and study. This pattern was well adapted to his life as a guerrilla leader, which alternated between campaigns and periods of studious retreat and prolific writing. These habits mark his policies as well: he has consistently opposed the relentless, methodical work style that characterized his father, warning that one who "becomes immersed in daily work can turn into an economist or technician who has lost his bearings, which is very dangerous." It is perhaps not adventitious that both of his interventions into the economy have occurred at times when five-year plans were under discussion (1957 and 1966), throwing those plans awry. For Mao, it seems, work must be intense, dramatic, of limited duration, and preferably organized as a form of "struggle," a "campaign" against something—five-anti, three-anti, four-clean, and the like. "What is work? Work is struggle," he wrote in 1945.

If for Mao work was only acceptable as a form of warfare, warfare was for Liu a form of work. Though he participated in the first and second civil wars and the intervening Sino-Japanese War in many high leadership posts, his activities were always described, by himself as well as others, as "work." Work became for Liu an avenue for the covert and rule-governed expression of aggression, as the activities of the work teams he sent in the SEM and GPCR were to demonstrate. Liu "worked" at warfare as he worked at everything else—he was patient, practical, and thorough. It is hardly surprising that during the GPCR he objected to the heaven-storming purge style of the rebels, protesting, "Changing bad people into good people remains a long-term task."

Liu was known as the Party theorist, and he had a formidable reputation for competence. "Liu Shao-ch'i is a very intelligent man," said Khrushchev,[99] but we need not rely on the word of his namesake. According to Edgar Snow, foreign diplomats who spoke to Liu considered him "a first-rate politician—shrewd, practical, clear-thinking, unemotional, and exceptionally able in the quick analysis of complicated problems in simple language clear to all." An Indian ambassador told Snow:

Liu Shao-ch'i at first gives a superficial impression of mediocrity. Five minutes of conversation reveals a man with an extremely logical mind capable of

98 Cf. Emi Siao, *Mao Tse-tung: His Childhood and Youth* (Bombay: People's Publishing House, 1952), pp. 5–20.

99 Strobe Talbott, ed., *Khrushchev Remembers* (Boston, 1970), p. 478.

quickly penetrating to the heart of a question and organizing his answers simply yet with great force and thoroughness.[100]

Liu's speeches are studded with references to water conservancy projects, commodity grain consumption, and various other "systems," indicating a detailed grasp of the terminology of the social sciences. He proudly told a class of university graduates:

I, for one, have never attended any university; I was only a middle-school student. Many of my schoolmates studied in universities or abroad, but their knowledge in the fields of economics and social sciences is not deeper than mine; it is even more shallow in some cases.[101]

Mao seems to have more global interests than Liu, as is reflected in his wide-ranging conversations with close associates like Ch'en Po-ta and K'ang Sheng. As Chiang Ch'ing said, "Sometimes when he begins to talk, he talks primarily about politics, economics, culture, the international and domestic situation, whatever comes to mind." Although Mao more than once said, "One who goes to school for several years becomes more stupid as he reads more books," he has seen fit to expose himself to the "poisonous weeds" from which he paternalistically shields his people. "At the time I read newspapers, although I was not influenced by them," he reflected, betraying his awareness of the contradiction involved. "I read *The Dream of the Red Chamber* five times without being influenced." [102] An "omniverous reader," according to Snow, "he may spend as much as a whole week reading." In a name-dropping chat with a visiting French delegation, he remarked, "I've read Diderot and in fact all your encyclopedists. I even read a French author of the eighteenth century who wrote that remarkable book, *L'homme machine* [*L'homme méchanique,* by La Mettrie]. I've read Fourier. But above all I am a great admirer of Napoleon. I know every one of his works." In a conversation with Ch'en Po-ta and K'ang Sheng, Mao boasted, "I have studied Confucius, the *Four Books* and the *Five Classics.* . . . Later on I spent seven years in a bourgeois school learning everything they had to teach—natural sciences, social sciences, and even some education. All I believed in was Kant's dualism, particularly his idealism." [103] The references in his most recent speeches suggest that Mao has of late become im-

100 Snow, *Red China Today*, p. 336.

101 "Address to the 1957-Class Graduates," *CW* 2: 421.

102 "Conversation with Ch'en Po-ta and K'ang Sheng," (1965), *JPRS*, no. 49826 (February 12, 1970): 28.

103 "Selections from Chairman Mao; Part 2," *JPRS*, no. 50792 (June 23, 1970): 1 ff.

mersed in classical Chinese philosophy and literature, but he also read Red Guard publications during the GPCR and commented favorably on their vivid style. As he freely admits, he knows little about economics: "Take me for example, there are many questions of economic construction which I don't understand: industry, commerce I don't much understand. With regard to agriculture I understand a bit." [104] Yet this dearth of knowledge has obviously not inhibited his participation in policy-making for this field—this is one instance in which "redness" preempts "expertise."

CONCLUSION

The time has come to "squeeze the universe into a ball," in the mocking words of T. S. Eliot's Prufrock, and to venture an explanation of how two such different men as Liu Shao-ch'i and Mao Tse-tung were able to unite in common cause for so long, and why the alliance they formed ultimately disintegrated. Such an explanation involves a preliminary theory of how character interacts with role constraints in response to political change within the high-level Chinese policy-making process.

The characters of the political actors seem to fit rather neatly into a typology proposed by Lasswell, indicating the feasibility and potential fruitfulness of applying cross-culturally social-science models first formulated in a Western context. In Lasswell's most recent formulation, there are two "types," the compulsive character, who "relies upon rigid, obsessive ways of handling human relationships," and the dramatizing character, whose "unifying feature is the demand for immediate affective response in others":

The compulsive inclines toward carefully defined limits and the well-worked-out ordering of parts; the dramatizer excels in scope and abundance of loosely classified detail. The hallmark of the former is the imposition of uniformity, while the latter tolerates diversity and excels in nuance. The compulsive desubjectivizes a situation, while the dramatizer remains sensitized to psychological dimensions; the one denies novelty, while the other welcomes it; one squeezes and compresses the dimensions of the human situation which the other complies with and allows to spread. The compulsive monotonizes the presentation of the self to the other, while the latter multiplies the faces and facades which can be presented to other persons.[105]

104 "Mao Tse-tung tsai ch'i-ch'ien jen ta hui shang-ti tzu-wo chien-ch'a" [Mao Tse-tung's self-criticism at the meeting of 7,000], Jen-wu, no. 40 (July 15, 1970), pp. 27–33.

105 Harold D. Lasswell, *Power and Personality* (New York, 1948), p. 62.

Liu Shao-ch'i, clearly a compulsive character, exhibits conscientious-ness, parsimony, thoroughness, rationality, and orderliness. His de-votion to norm-governed action is evident in his consistent attention to "principle," to planning, and to the formulation of policies and schedules qualified for every conceivable contingency; it is also oc-casionally manifest in a tendency to accord priority to adherence to the letter rather than the spirit of the law ("obedience must be unconditional and absolute") and to red tape rather than creative achievement. His mind is complex, with a meticulous grasp of de-tail,[106] but the underlying premises that order this maze of detail are simple and highly stable over time. Liu's overriding concern in an un-stable setting is with balance, and his writings contain intricate formula-tions designed to reconcile contradictions ("combine two into one," as his critics put it), qualified by references to exceptions, conditions, and so forth that are strung together with "buts" or "on the other hands." His writings are lucid, technical, prosaic, sometimes repetitious in style. Their subject matter is almost exclusively concerned with two issue areas: the "unity, predictability, and effectiveness of organiza-tion" [107] (usually the CCP, but also guerrilla base areas, trade unions, mass organizations, et al.), and the "cultivation" of a universalistic official morality among elites. His attention span has great historical longitude—he has good memory, is consistent, and perceives events with a sense of perspective (and is therefore patient and persevering)—but narrow spatial latitude—his attention is narrowly focused and insulated from irrelevancies, creating systematic blind spots in his vision. He is equable in temperament, emotionally repressed, and phobic—i.e., his attitude toward conventional pieties tends to be deferential. The common feature of this family of traits is that *control* is valued more highly than *expressiveness*.

106 One of Liu's colleagues remembers a somewhat amusing episode from the midst of the Sino-Japanese War: "I invited Liu Shao-ch'i to come into my house for a rest. On entering the house, we saw a heap of old newspapers on the desk. Swiftly he walked toward the desk and picked up the newspapers to read, in a state of joy. I did not disturb him, for I was aware that both he and the Chairman had a common habit, namely, paying serious attention to newspapers. . . . Suddenly he raised a sheet of newspaper and asked me: 'Where was it pub-lished?' 'By the Shansi-Suiyüan Sub-Bureau!' I replied, looking at the news-paper. The newspaper carried an article by comrade Liu Shao-ch'i entitled, 'On Inner-Party Struggle.' Looking at it, comrade Liu Shao-ch'i shook his head: 'Well, there are some misprints here.' He took out a pencil and made corrections on the paper." Lt. Gen. Yang Hsiu-shan, "Escorting Comrade Liu Shao-ch'i to Shansi-Suiyüan," *Chung-kuo ch'ing-nien pao* [China youth daily], June 6, 1961, in *SCMP*, no. 2529 (July 3, 1961): 7.

107 Ying-mao Kau, "The Organizational Line in Dispute," *CL&G* 5, no. 1 (spring 1972): 8.

Mao Tse-tung, a dramatizing character, permits his feelings far greater play in his decisions, and although he cultivates a placid public image, he exhibits relatively intense affective reactiveness, his moods ranging from enthusiasm to fury, from indignation to depression. Whereas Liu's politics are characterized by tactical flexibility and strategic rigidity ("principle"), Mao's seem to be characterized by strategic flexibility as well, resulting in a "general line" of sometimes startling zigzags. Mao's attention span has limited longitude—he tends to "forget" selectively and is both forthright and inconsistent in his policy stands over any extended period (hence Teng T'o's satire, "A Special Treatment of 'Amnesia' ")—but wide spatial latitude—he is intuitive and sensitive to nuances of mood and seems to have a highly perceptive if emotion-tinged grasp of the situational Gestalt of any given time frame. He is stubborn,[108] but the underlying premises that order his thinking undergo periodic reevaluation, throwing his judgmental faculties into temporary disequilibrium. Mao's interests are more varied than Liu's, his writings more wide-ranging, both in their intended audience and in their subject matter; they include classical poetry, military-political strategy, Marxist epistemology and theory of socioeconomic development, and simple, hortatory essays addressed to the masses at large; his prose style is alive with metaphors of both scatological and classical derivation, reflecting his peasant background and literary aspirations. His vision is broad, his imagination vivid and original; his comprehension of qualifying detail seems to have fallen into desuetude, however, in his more recent concern for more general trend forecasting ("big empty talk" to Teng T'o).[109] He tends to attribute exaggerated efficacy to the repetition of set formulas and gestures, to colorful pageantry and mass spectacles. His attitude toward conventional restrictions and institutional regularity is iconoclastic.[110]

While this typology seems to fit the available data rather well, we must in fairness note incongruencies in both characters that the model fails to encompass. Mao's writings (particularly those on military strategy) often demonstrate sound judgment and balance, patience, grasp of detail, and analytical ability. Liu has on occasion made radi-

108 "As stubborn as a mule, and a steel rod of pride and determination ran through his nature," according to Agnes Smedley. "I had the impression he would wait and watch for years, but eventually have his way." Battle Hymn of China (New York, 1943), pp. 168–169.

109 Oksenberg notes the apparent attentuation of the "incisiveness and brilliance so obvious in Mao's speeches in the 1950's" in "Policy Making Under Mao," p. 108.

110 Cf. Otto Fenichel, "The Counterphobic Attitude," Collected Papers (London, 1966), pp. 163–174.

cal departures from his characteristic prudence: joining the CCP in 1920 and dedicating his life to the implausible prospect of the Party's success was certainly a high-risk venture; subsequent Maoist criticisms to the contrary notwithstanding, Liu remained among the staunchest supporters of "Maoism" up to and during the GLF. He exhibits greater tolerance and open-mindedness than is typical of his character type, particularly toward cultural notables.

According to Chang Kuo-t'ao, the differences between Mao and Liu were so vast as to make the two men incompatible:

Basically, the characters of Mao and Liu were antithetic, and Liu was never much of an admirer of Mao's. He once told me that, in his opinion, Mao was somewhat illogical in his approach to problems, stubborn, indiscriminate in his choice of means, and lacking in self-cultivation.[111]

And yet, for about thirty years, Mao and Liu were to form a highly effective political team and their relationship was reportedly friendly: according to a Chinese Communist source, only Liu in the Party was able to speak unreservedly with Mao; their close association lasted until 1959, when Liu became Chief of State and Mao retired to a less active role in politics.[112] In many respects, their characters appeared to complement one another: Mao was more capable than Liu both in mustering enthusiastic public support behind initiatives and in formulating broad programmatic strategies to maintain the polity's forward momentum. Liu, with his grasp of detail and painstaking, unflagging attention to "trifling and troublesome work," devised plans and mechanisms that took account of personal interests and other objective conditions and supervised day-to-day implementation. The two functioned in tandem without apparent friction for more than twenty years, during which time the CCP seized power and launched the nation into an economic and social reconstruction program of impressive dimensions. If the two men had incompatible character differences, as Chang contends (and as this chapter tends to confirm), these must have been circumvented through an agreement on policy and an arrangement of roles that prevented those differences from becoming salient.

Previous formulations of the relationship between character and policy tend to "psychologize"; i.e., to assume a direct relationship between private motive and political act, which is only "masked" by ideological rationalizations.[113] This approach consigns the ego's role

111 Chang Kuo-t'ao, "Introduction," Liu, CW, p. ix.
112 Quoted in Yomiuri, December 16, in DSJP, December 22, 1966, pp. 1–4.
113 E.g., Lasswell's well-known formula states that "private motives rationalized in terms of the public interest" beget political acts. Power and Personality, p. 38.

to the relatively minor functions of censorship and disguise, attributing insufficient importance to role structure and other situational variables. The Mao-Liu case suggests the following revisions in this formulation. (1) It is useful to distinguish analytically between "character," which includes the actor's assumptions, values, and general predispositions; "political style," which has to do with his preferred means of implementing policy; and "policy," or his choice of political ends. (2) The relationship between "character" and "style" tends to be direct, but the relationship between "style" and "policy" is mediated by ego functions. (3) Ego functions are informed by the immediate social milieu, particularly by the structure of roles.[114]

The dissolution of the alliance between Mao and Liu seems to have been caused by two factors: a shift in role structure, and the change in policy that ensued from that shift. In the CCP division of powers between "policy" and "operations," Mao's role as Supreme Leader was to preside over the formulation of general policies, and Liu's role, corresponding to that of a chief of staff in a military unit or a prime minister in a traditional constitutional monarchy, was to supervise implementation of those policies. Mao gave his staff wide latitude in implementation of policy, the mechanics of which did not greatly interest him, and the staff in turn accepted implicitly Mao's preeminence in policy formulation. In 1959, Mao retired from the Chairmanship of the C.P.R., allowing Liu to take his place.

As leader of the "first line," Liu used his authority to convene conferences and secure passage of the measures he supported. While he did not necessarily change his ultimate goals during this period, the diverging action-implications of his political style, which had not been visible in his previous subordinate role, now had an unimpeded opportunity to manifest themselves, resulting in a subtle modification of policy. For example, the 1960s confronted China with what both Liu and Mao agreed was a problem: the migration to the cities of farm workers who were seeking higher-paying factory jobs faster than the industrial sector could employ them and faster than houses could be built for them to live in. In the countryside, agriculture suffered because departing manpower, however underemployed it had been, was not replaced rapidly enough by mechanization and improved land use. The departure of youth to the cities left a residual peasantry and created "contradictions" of age, income, and education between

114 This formulation is prefigured in contributions by the psychoanalytic school of "ego psychology." See Heinz Hartmann, *Ego Psychology and the Problem of Adaptation*, trans. D. Rapaport (New York, 1958), also the well-known works of Erik H. Erikson.

town and countryside. Liu resorted to impersonal economic mechanisms to resolve this "contradiction," creating a wage disparity between unskilled contract workers and skilled workers in order to reduce the pecuniary incentives for unskilled farm hands to migrate (except during seasonal slack periods); Mao has resorted to the more direct, political solution of transferring surplus urban labor, deviant cadres, idealistic or troublesome youth, and the like to the countryside. As a second example, the Leap's failure and subsequent retrenchment resulted in "demand-pull" inflation caused by the shortage in commodities. Rather than appealing to the idealism of the masses to persuade them to invest rather than consume, Liu proposed in 1963 that commodity prices be raised by 50 percent and also advocated increasing the volume of currency in circulation. A rise in the selling price of commodities would have drained off from the factories and urban consumers a greater volume of cash, part of which the state could have then used to raise output in the villages through higher purchase prices for commodities. Rural living standards would have risen at the expense of the towns' real incomes.[115]

Mao seemed finally to conclude that, despite the apparent coincidence of ultimate goals, Liu's preferred means of implementing those goals through impersonal bureaucratic or market mechanisms violated his own ideals of substantive justice, informal and functionally diffuse fraternity, and "face-to-face" responsibility between leaders and led. Liu's political style, with its emphasis on institutional mediation, interlocking interests, and functionally specific division of labor, systematically increased the hiatus between elite and masses that the GPCR was specifically designed to alleviate. Thus, Mao turned to Lin Piao and the PLA for aid in recovering the face-to-face conviviality and "one-for-all" spirit of a military unit, in which the collective interest as defined by a common foe subdues all considerations of personal interest, in which men respond to direct orders rather than to calculated manipulations of complex institutional or market mechanisms that were fully understood only by "experts." This vision was effective at Yenan, as Mao remembered it, and Lin Piao had recently demonstrated its feasibility in the PLA; why could it not be realized in society at large?

115 *KMJP*, March 14, 1970, in Leo Goodstadt, *Mao Tse-tung*, p. 156.

7

THE "CAPITALIST ROAD": CRITIQUE AND METACRITIQUE

So sweeping was the Maoist critique of Liu, who was revealed to have had a far more profound impact on the institutionalization of authority and on the formulation and implementation of policy in China than had hitherto been suspected, that to assess the charges against him entails no less than a reevaluation of the history of the Chinese Communist movement. Despite the enormity—even futility—of such a task, only through careful analysis of the criticisms can the rationale of the Maoist repudiation of Liu's "road" be understood and assessed and the rectified direction of the "proletarian revolutionary road" projected. In fewer words, such an analysis should help us to see what difference Liu's fall makes to China.

In comparing the two "roads," we have found it useful to make analytical distinctions among: (1) general political assumptions and values ("character"), (2) methods of organizing and implementing policies ("style"), and (3) the formulation of policy ("policy"). In Chapter 6, we attempted to establish a nexus between (1) and (2) and to portray the differences between the two men as deriving from a fundamental divergence of character. In this chapter, we seek to determine the nature of the relationship between (1) and (3). As pointed out in the conclusion to Chapter 6, it should not be assumed without careful empirical investigation that the close relationship between character and political style implies an equally close relationship between character and policy. Such an assumption would derogate the importance of the shifting structure of roles and other environmental variables, neglecting history and politics for an inadmissibly monocausal psychologism.

In our assessment of the "truth" of the criticisms, we shall apply four criteria: "confessed" (i.e., Liu admitted committing the "error" in one

214

of his three self-criticisms), "accurate" (i.e., verifiable on the basis of reliable independent evidence), "valid" (i.e., at discernible variance from Mao's Thought as it was understood at the time), and "sincere" (i.e., there has been a good-faith attempt in the post-Liu period to rectify the "erroneous" policies). In addition to these four criteria are two whose bearing on the truth of the criticisms could not always be calculated. The first is the question of Liu's proportional responsibility for the error in question: when personal responsibility could not be demonstrated, we have tended to fall back on the assumption that Mao's semiretirement and Liu's promotion made the 1959–66 period one of Liuist "stewardship," during which Liu bore more responsibility for the general drift of policy than did Mao; if Mao controlled the policy apparatus during this period, why should he have had to resort to such extraordinary measures to "seize power"?[1] Yet it is possible that this assumption oversimplifies the power balance during the "stewardship" period, and that further research will show Mao's responsibility to have been greater than assumed.[2] The second is the question of internal consistency: the critics conceive Liu's guilt to be deliberate, comprehensive, and utterly consistent; hence any inconsistency in the criticisms would seem to damage their credibility. But this was a political contest, not a Platonic dialogue, and people from all walks of life participated, each with his own grievance; inconsistencies may reflect cleavages in the ranks of the critics but do not in themselves invalidate the criticisms.

To sum up the gist of the Maoist criticisms in advance, Liu's attempt to combine revolution with order and equality with efficiency within a lasting institutional framework tended ultimately to subvert the values to be institutionalized. The criticisms have been subsumed under four general categories: philosophical, political, economic, and cultural. The first consists of the Maoist conception of the core values underlying Liu's political, economic, and cultural errors; the second and fourth categories illustrate different aspects of Liu's attempt to combine revolution and order; the third, his attempt to combine

---

[1] This characterization of the division of power during the "stewardship" period has been officially endorsed by Chou En-lai in his report to the 10th National Congress: "There were many tendencies in the past where one tendency covered another and when the tide came, the majority went along with it, while only a few withstood it." "Report to the 10th National Congress of the CPC" (August 24, 1973), *PR*, nos. 35–36 (September 7, 1973): 21. Wang Kuang-mei referred to this characterization in her third "trial" with implicit scorn: "The achievements of the past seventeen years belonged to Chairman Mao, and since Liu Shao-ch'i was on the first line, all mistakes were his." *CB*, no. 848 (February 27, 1968): 27.

[2] J. D. Simmonds takes this "revisionist" position in *China: Evolution of a Revolution*.

equality with economic efficiency. Each section includes an exegesis of the criticism followed by a "meta-critical" analysis (i.e., criticism of the criticism).

PHILOSOPHICAL THEMES

CRITIQUE

Criticisms of Liu's "philosophy of life," to which Mao seemed to attach preeminent importance in his own critical remarks (following his change of heart), concentrated on Liu's "selfishness" and were principally founded on quotations from *How To Be a Good Communist*, easily Liu's most influential work. "Any man can become a Yao or a Shun," Liu wrote, quoting Mencius in support of bureaucratic careerism; "as long as he has ability," a young cadre will be given an important post, for "the Party will promote him." On one occasion he told students:

After leaving school, you will encounter difficulties in everyday life, such as providing yourself with food, clothes, and housing, and getting married. Life is full of difficulties. If you don't exert yourselves, struggling and improving your lot, you won't live well.[3]

This willingness explicitly to accept and even to rationalize self-enhancement drives is manifest in a "calculating" attitude toward losses and gains. Liu's advice is to "forebear minor disadvantages so that I can gain major advantages," "suffering hardship first in order to enjoy comfort later." In a conversation with his brother-in-law Wang Kuang-ying, he reportedly said:

Lose a little to gain a lot is a law of the development of things turning into their opposite. If you think of yourself all day long you will have gained nothing in the end. You will have a partial loss in terms of personal gain. But if you work for the people, others will bear your well-being into consideration.[4]

Liu's legitimation of personal interests assumes the ultimate compatibility or "merging" of personal and collective interests. To the Maoists, "merging" contaminates the purity of altrustic motives; their evident objective is to forge an "ethic of intention" (*Gesinnungsethik*) unsullied by considerations of consequences. The ultimate decadence of personal interests is demonstrated by following them to their sequel in a "bourgeois life style," motivated by greed for "material incentives"

[3] *Tung-fang-hung* [East is red], in *KMJP*, April 24, 1967, in *SCMP*, no. 3934 (May 8, 1967): 4–8.

[4] "Selected Edition," *SCMM*, no. 653 (May 5, 1969): 2–3.

and rank self-indulgence: "You ought to enjoy yourselves; take life easy walking in the parks and looking after the children," Liu said. "Eat good food, that's something worthwhile." Liu himself was alleged to have lived "like a belly god," eating "bird's-nest soup in the morning and white fungus soup in the evening." [5]

A second false premise (closely related to "selfishness") is Liu's "philosophy of survival" ("What is the use of principle if one dies?"), which lies at the root of the "betrayals" of dozens of "renegades" and ultimately led to Liu's personal "treason." In 1936, Liu permitted Communists in KMT jails to sign what he called "contrived confessions" to "deceive the enemy" and purchase their freedom; some of these "turncoats," such as Po I-po, Liu Lan-t'ao, and others, "wormed their way" into high positions under Liu's auspices. "When filling in the forms, just skip the details and put 'brought to safety by the Party organization,' " Liu told them. Liu himself, it was discovered toward the end of the campaign, had defected to the enemy no less than five times and sold Party secrets, while his wife was an agent for "American Strategic Intelligence Service" (*mei-kuo chan-lu ch'ing-pao*).[6]

A third false premise (at the heart of the assumption of ultimate compatibility of interests) is the philosophy of "two into one": "Our principle is to make use of the unity of a contradiction (not to heighten its struggle)." Liu's "stoop to compromise in order to accomplish something" and "suffer wrong in the general interest" are contrasted with Mao's "Promethean spirit of daring to unhorse the emperor at the risk of suffering death by a thousand cuts." The debilitating influence of Liu's philosophy is illustrated by the "personal story" of a Tsinghua Red Guard:

She was cheated by the work team into regarding the violent struggles between the two lines as a "hollow debate" and "improper way of looking at problems"; she took "no interest in unprincipled debate," demanded to "deal with them equitably." [7]

Liu's love of harmony and compromise are said to lead to the appeasement of "capitalist imperialism" abroad and to the "extinc-

5 " 'Get Rich Through Labor' Is a Slogan for Development of Capitalism," *PD*, September 16, 1967, in *SCMP*, no. 4033 (October 3, 1967): 5–7; *Pa-erh-wu chan-pao* [August 25 battle news] (Canton), February 14, 1967, in *SCMM*, no. 574 (May 1, 1967): 1–8.
6 "A Report by the CCP CC's Special Panel on Renegade, Traitor and Scab Liu Shao-ch'i's Crimes," *Fu-chou kung-jen chan-pao* [Fuchow workers' battle news], no. 33 (November 23, 1968), in *SCMP*, no. 4334 (January 9, 1969): 6–11; "Red Guards Repudiate Renegade Philosophy," in *SCMP*, no. 3980 (July 14, 1967): 13–16.
7 "Who Is the Chief Culprit?" *KMJP*, April 4, 1967, pp. 10–14.

tion of class struggle," "inner-Party peace," and so forth at home, permitting enemies to survive and prosper who should in principle be destroyed.

ANALYSIS

The criticisms of Liu's "philosophy of life" provide a good test for the validity of Maoist charges, because most of the charges can be checked against his writings. The criticism that Liu condoned "selfishness" seems to be a misrepresentation: he prescribed *subordination* of individual interests to the collective. "It is incumbent on him [the Party member] to sacrifice his personal interests and unconditionally subordinate them to the interests of the Party; under no pretense or excuse may he sacrifice the Party's interests by clinging to his own." This theme is steadfast throughout Liu's writings.[8]

Liu did make concessions to "self"; these did not constitute the major thrust of any of his writings, but it seems fair to say that Liu was more "liberal" with regard to self-interest than Mao. Certainly he did not call for martyrdom or for dramatic self-renunciation, in the Lei Feng style. As the following quotation (from a 1957 address to graduating seniors) suggests, he called for optimum altruism consistent with a modicum of self-interest:

You are young and have just started your life. People do not have much faith in you. You must in every way possible prove to them by action, do well in everything you take up and show people you are not selfish. When you make friends with them you must be prepared to help them, even to your own disadvantage, of course, not to too great an extent, which is also not good.[9]

Second, Liu did acknowledge a sphere of personal privacy, within which legitimate personal interests existed. Whereas Mao's moral injunctions are exclusively addressed to the group, Liu's ethic is an *individual* (but not individualistic) one. Quoting Tseng Tzu ("I reflect on myself three times a day") and Mencius, he tells the cadre to be "watchful over himself when alone"; leaving the impression that if the Party demands implicit obedience, it permits the individual to "cultivate" his conscience in private.[10] "Party members do have their

---

[8] Some of Liu's denunciations of selfishness are often cited as oblique criticisms of Mao; e.g., "Conceit, the idea of individualistic heroism, ostentation, etc., are still to be found. . . . They like to show off and to have people sing their praises and flatter them. . . . They are extremely vain, and are unwilling to immerse themselves in hard work," and so forth. Liu, "How to Be a Good Communist," *CW* 1: *passim.*

[9] *CW* 2: 423.

[10] Liu counterbalances this impression, however, with the statement that "of course" it is "absurd" to withdraw from struggle to strive for moral improvement

personal problems to attend to, and, moreover, they should develop themselves according to their individual inclinations and aptitudes." For "personal problems," Liu made two provisions. First, he placed certain restrictions on the claims of the public on the individual: "So long as the interests of the Party are not violated, the Party member can have his private and family life, and develop his individual inclinations." [11] Second, although Liu believed that public and private interests could usually be arranged to coincide, he acknowledged a *reciprocity* of obligation that would cover cases when they could not. He used the tacit promise of reciprocity to promote "altruism": "If you suffer hardships to let others have a better life, they will appreciate it and look after you." [12]

Finally, Liu undeniably fostered a form of bureaucratic careerism. Moreover, he offered *two* validating principles for upward mobility, reflecting a certain moral elitism. As indicated in Chapter 6 (pp. 187–193), within the political elite (the CCP), upward mobility was validated by moral efficiency in service to the people, which is conceived as a good in itself. To the Party cadre, Liu promises liberation from "self" through identification with an organization that conceives of interest in terms of "the lofty socialist ideals of all the people" and yet will also look after his personal needs, but the rewards that reciprocal obligation remits to the masses are more tangible and are premised upon the masses' failure to transcend a materialistic, individualistic conception of interest. In 1956 he said:

It is perfectly justifiable and necessary to demand, on the basis of developed production, an increase in one's income and improvement in one's living standards. Only in this way, can the enthusiasm of the workers be continuously promoted and the outstanding workers' movement acquire a solid foundation.[13]

Implicit in the words "solid foundation" is Liu's view that economic demands are the "foundation" upon which "higher" demands may be built; only through "self-cultivation" and "tempering in the revolutionary struggle" can one learn to renounce material needs and subsist on moral rewards ("members of the Communist Party . . . can endure any difficulty of living where material life is concerned"). Thus

---

through individual self-reflection. "We are revolutionary materialists; our self-cultivation cannot be separated from the revolutionary practice of the masses." *CW* 1: 334 ff.

11 "The Party will use every possibility to help members develop their individual inclinations and aptitudes in conformity with its interests, furnish them with suitable work and working conditions and commend and reward them. . . . The Party will attend to and safeguard its members' essential interests." *Ibid.*

12 "Address to the 1957-Class Graduates," *CW* 2: 406.

13 *CW* 1: 334.

there are two legitimations for upward mobility: material accumulation for the masses, and self-cultivation for the elite. It is within the context of such a status hierarchy that worker protests against the "insult" of material incentives (indignation at the thought that money can "buy us over") may be understood—assuming they are genuine.

The frequent allegations that Liu revised his 1962 edition (and timed its appearance) to make it more critical of Mao can be shown to be objectively false. In fact, the 1962 edition contains six additional paragraphs from Mao's works, although it is shorter in total length. The passage beginning, "We have had not a few people of this type in the Communist Party. We had certain representatives of dogmatism at one time who were even worse," which was frequently cited as an instance of implicit criticism of Mao, was contained in the original 1939 edition, as were all other passages cited as implicit criticisms. Would Mao have allowed an implicit critique to stand uncorrected for twenty-seven years and promoted its author to be his successor? Revisions of the text uniformly indicate a desire to make it more, rather than less in tune with Mao's thought: the words "revolutionary" and "masses" were occasionally added, and a long paragraph citing classical references ("To examine oneself by self-reflection," etc.) was omitted, together with a section on the value of keeping a personal diary. The only point on which Maoist criticisms are accurate is that there was indeed an omission of six paragraph-length quotations from Stalin, leaving only two of his quotations; the title of Chapter II, "Be Worthy Pupils of Marx, Engels, Lenin and Stalin" became "Be Worthy Pupils of Marx and Lenin." But the assumption that deletion of Stalin's writing implies a covert attack on Mao is premised on an identification of Mao with Stalin, which Liu did not necessarily share.

As to the allegation of "treason," Liu's involvement with the release of prisoners from KMT jails is confessed with minor qualifications. The charges of personal treason have been painstakingly investigated elsewhere and shown to be without foundation.[14]

POLITICAL THEMES

CRITIQUE

Criticisms of Liu's political blunders embrace accusations that he undermined the dictatorship of the proletariat and was permissive to

14 *Chinese Communist Affairs: Facts and Features* 2, no. 7 (April 22, 1969): 6–8; also Li Tien-min, "Examination Report on Liu Shao-ch'i's Crimes," *IS* 5, no. 7 (April 1969): 11–18.

class enemies on the one hand, and that he oppressed the masses and demanded "absolute and unconditional obedience" of Party members on the other. This not-often-noted contradiction might lead one to suspect ambivalence toward authority on the part of the critics, but some of the more logically meticulous articles argue that liberalization and oppression were applied differentially—that Liu was liberal toward the bourgeoisie while oppressing the proletariat, instituting "bourgeois dictatorship." The former group of criticisms refers to Liu's advocacy of the "parliamentary road" to socialism, the "extinction of class struggle" following successful socialization of the means of production, opposition to the "cult of personality," perpetuation of the "united front" in relations with minority religions and nationalities, and a "capitulationist" foreign policy. The latter refers to Liu's overemphasis on organizational control and mechanical discipline in relation to both lower-level cadres and non-Party masses, a fault exemplified in his handling of the Socialist Education Movement and the first fifty days of the GPCR.

The Liberal—(1) The allegation that Liu committed "Treason to the Dictatorship of the Proletariat" was inaugurated in a *Red Flag* article of that title which appeared on May 8, 1967, after being "corrected and revised" by Mao himself. The article criticized *How To Be a Good Communist* for failing to mention class struggle or the dictatorship of the proletariat, noting that Mao had always stated that democratic centralism was exercised over the people and dictatorship over the enemy, whereas Liu discussed democratic centralism without any mention of dictatorship. In opposition to the "dictatorship of the proletariat," Liu posed the "democratic spirit," a "spirit of total equality for all mankind": "that is, no man has a right to oppress or exploit another man." [15]

The most frequently mentioned historical instance of Liu's "democratic" tendencies was his advocacy of cooperation with the KMT during the war against Japan and of cooperation in a national parliament upon the war's successful conclusion. In 1946, Liu wrote that "the principal struggle in the Chinese revolution has turned into peaceful and parliamentary struggle" and recommended that the Party subordinate the Red Army to a coalition government made up of the CCP, the KMT, and a loose coalition of bourgeois democratic parties. "We must learn to do propaganda, to make speeches, to conduct election campaigns, and to ask everyone to cast his vote in favor of us." This was necessary because "it is impossible to stipulate juristically that some

15 NCNA, July 14, 1968, in *SCMP*, no. 4221 (July 19, 1968): 19–24.

people should constitute the majority and have a leading position in the government. The leading status of the CCP members . . . can only be maintained and consolidated through legal struggle." [16]

(2) Liu's willingness to join in a parliamentary arrangement that failed to discriminate between bourgeoisie and proletariat was said to be but one of many indications of his consistent tendency to deny the reality of classes in the name of "equality" and "democracy" and to "extinguish class struggle." Whereas Mao wrote in February 1957:

Although the large-scale and turbulent class struggles of the masses charac- teristic of the previous revolutionary periods have in the main come to an end, there are still remnants of the overthrown landlord and comprador classes, . . . and the remolding of the Party bourgeoisie has only just started. The class struggle is by no means over . . . [but] will continue to be long and tortuous and at times will even become acute.[17]

Liu reportedly said in an (unpublished) speech in Shanghai on April 27, 1957, "Class struggle has in the main ended, counterrevolu- tionaries have become fewer and so have criminal cases, so the state apparatus of the dictatorship can be reduced in size. . . . From now on, the most important task of the state is to organize social life." He envisaged a "state of the whole people" in which all classes lived to- gether in peace, each "respecting one another and getting what he wants." [18] Formal equality and democratic access to authority would be routinized through a structure of institutions arranged to keep one another in check. Liu advocated establishment of a "perfect legal system" to dispense "equal justice," even "protecting the legal rights of counterrevolutionaries" (i.e., allowing them a "fair trial"), thus "opposing leadership of the Party over . . . legal work" and subvert- ing the role of law as a "powerful weapon for exercising dictatorship over the exploiting class." He encroached further on the Party's pur- view by sanctioning the expansion of the Procuratorate, a parallel control network: "The Procuratorate must see to it that the rights due

16 *PD*, November 26, 1967, in *SCMP*, no. 4071 (December 1, 1967): 18–27. Three "historically unprecedented conditions," he argued, made a "parliamentary road" a feasible one in China: three countries (Britain, the United States, and the Soviet Union) and three political parties (KMT, CCP, and Democratic League) favored cooperation, and three principle classes (working people, middle-of-the-roaders and middle bourgeoisie, and part of the big bourgeoisie) "demanded democracy" in China. Furthermore, "As soon as we participate in the government, a $200 million loan will come from the United States."

17 "On the Correct Resolution," *SRWM*, pp. 445–447.

18 "Proletarian Dictatorship and the Renegade China's Khrushchev," *PD*, August 26, 1967, in *SCMP*, no. 4012 (August 31, 1967): 21–25; "Top Ambitionist," *PD*, May 25, 1967.

to offenders are guaranteed," he said in 1957. "The Party must also abide by the law. If the Party acts unlawfully, are you going to bring up the matter?" In 1962, he stipulated that "from now on, cases of a political nature should not be dealt with in office," thus further restricting the role of ideology by defining rectitude in legal rather than political (class) terms.[19]

The Maoist objection to Liu's "theory of the extinction of class struggle" was that he overestimated the efficacy of reeducating members of nonproletarian classes through thought reform. The criticisms heap scorn on Liu's assumption that landlords and capitalists were "gradually turning themselves into laborers in name and in fact" and are "no longer willing to oppose socialism." In view of the assumed quasi-permanence of class designations, Liu's attempts in the name of the "united front" to endow non-Communist elites with consultative or nominal leadership positions are seen as outrageous mollycoddling of the bourgeoisie. Liu's "liberalism" extended well beyond the bourgeoisie, however, to include tolerance for a "loyal opposition." In 1962, he reportedly said "there should be an open opposition among the people and within the Party"; in 1966, he even admitted the conceivable fallibility of socialism:

So far as all humanity and the whole world is concerned, the taking of the socialist road is still in an experimental stage. We too are experimenting, uncertain of what is in store for us in the future. We may have to go through twists and turns, and no conclusion can yet be reached.[20]

From a Western viewpoint, this might seem admirably open-minded, but such comments violate doctrinal claims to a monopoly of truth and are hence considered heretical and indicative of Liu's failure to understand the nature of political power and the meaning of the dictatorship of the proletariat.

(3) Implicit in the Maoist criticisms is the assumption that the only way to ensure such a monopoly of truth is to make one man the final arbiter of all doctrinal issues; in other words, dictatorship of the proletariat becomes equated with the "cult of the personality." This assumption provides the moral basis of the criticisms of Liu's "opposition to Mao Tse-tung." Indications of Liu's opposition are found in anonymous references to boastfulness, to the fallibility of the auto-

---

19 NCNA, July 14, 1968, in *SCMP*, no. 4221 (July 19, 1968): 19–23; "Drag out Liu," *SCMP*, no. 3946 (May 25, 1967): 1–16.

20 "Strongly Refute the Fallacy of 'No Conclusion Yet' for the Socialist Road," *PD*, October 16, 1967, in *SCMP*, no. 4048 (October 26, 1967): 7–10.

crat,[21] to the faults of projects with which Mao had become publicly associated,[22] or to his own competence (felt to be invidious).[23] That Mao's monopolization of doctrinal authority is based on the same principle that legitimated Stalin's rule is tacitly acknowledged in criticisms of Liu for participating in the Chinese de-Stalinization effort that followed Khrushchev's secret speech in 1956: any aspersion on Stalin is taken to be an oblique attack on Mao.

The criticisms of Liu's opposition to Mao's *Thought* are, of course, closely connected with criticisms of his opposition to Mao himself, but whereas the latter are based on a defense of China's hierocratic or "Caesero-papist" authority structure, the former rest on different premises. It is apparent that the popularization of Mao's Thought serves three functions. The first is to elevate the power and prestige of Mao, the second to supply a set of revolutionary clichés that may be "creatively applied" (*huo-yung*) to diverse everyday problems (in much the same way that Confucian and folk clichés were applied earlier); the third to legitimate political action by the masses. This third function liberated ideology from organization and enfranchised non-Party masses, leading Red Guards to call Mao's Thought an "invincible weapon" (*chan-wu pu-sheng ti wu-ch'i*), which had "armed" them. Liu Shao-ch'i failed to recognize the political or psychological gains that accrue to the masses as a result of their incantation of such abstract formulas, however, and repudiated any attempt to emancipate ideology from organization in the name of the vanguard Party; Liu saw only a relationship between popularization of Mao's Thought and Mao's personal prestige. When he approved deletion of reference to Mao's Thought from the Constitution at the Eighth Congress in 1956, he explained:

When the Seventh Congress was in session, Chairman Mao's leadership over the whole Party had been firmly established, and even though no mention

21 "Marx, Engels, Lenin, Stalin, and Chairman Mao have made mistakes," he allegedly said in 1963; in June 1966 he allegedly said, "Marxism-Leninism must of course continue to develop and does not stop at the stage of Mao Tse-tung's Thought."

22 When he heard the report from Tach'ing, Liu remarked, "Effort was made to integrate industry with agriculture. As a result, a number of people invested their wages in farming and grain. Problems will arise if this practice is allowed to go on permanently." "Drag out Liu," p. 7. Liu apparently preferred that capital be invested in industry.

23 In 1963, he said to a relative, "To become famous and expert, you must first bury yourself in study and work. You must not always think of getting famous. The more you want to become famous, the harder it will be for you to become famous. . . . When I joined the revolution, I didn't have any idea of becoming Chief of State. Yet, am I not Chairman now? I am known throughout the country and all over the world." *Ibid.,* p. 6.

is made of it now, this is understood by everybody. Moreover, no useful role is made by repeating the same thing again and again.[24]

Liu disliked the popularization of Mao's Thought, not only because it contributed to the impious deification of his immediate superior, but also because he felt that it fostered an excessively rigid and mechanical approach to problems, which he called "dogmatism," "oversimplification," or "Philistinism." [25]

(4) Liu's foreign policies are said to exhibit the same irenic permissiveness toward foreign powers that he displayed in dealing with domestic class enemies. His errors were formulated in the slogan, "three reconciliations and one reduction" (san ho i shao): reconciliation with capitalist imperialism, social imperialism (the Soviet Union), and reaction, and reduction of aid to national liberation movements— in other words, he favored a "united front from above" with the world bourgeoisie (foreign ruling elites) to the neglect of a "united front from below" with the (theoretically) oppressed masses. Specifically, he "created illusions" about the benign nature of U.S. imperialism, noting in 1963 that "within the U.S. ruling group there are also fairly determined people who are gradually coming to realize that the policy of war is not necessarily beneficial to the U.S." [26] He also advocated cooperation with the Soviet Union, claiming in a June 1962 talk that Khrushchev's opposition to imperialism was "genuine" and "we want to unite with them" and "rescue our friendship" and "stand in united opposition to imperialism." Much was made of his courtship of Sukarno and the "executioner Nasution" during his 1963 state tour of Indonesia (which became acutely embarrassing in the wake of the wholesale slaughter of overseas Chinese following the abortive Communist coup), and his friendship with Ne Win of Burma was also deplored.

Consistent with his belief in the feasibility of cooperation with the world's bourgeois or social "revisionist" governments was his advocacy

24 CW 2: 164.

25 "One must not regard Marxist-Leninist theory as dogma, nor must one regard Mao Tse-tung's works and speeches as dogma. . . . Today, there are people within the Party who look upon the Thought of Mao as dogma," he noted in a 1964 letter to Chiang Wei-ch'ing. "We should learn from all those inside and outside the Party who know the truth, regardless of whether their positions are high or low; we should not learn only from those who hold high positions." "A Hundred Examples of Liu's Speeches Opposing Mao's Thought," Chingkangshan (Peking), February 1, 8, 1967.

26 In a March 1963 talk with foreign guests he said China "wished to develop friendly relations with the United States" and was prepared to do so once the latter withdrew troops from Taiwan (a precondition which has of course since been discarded). NCNA, October 17, 1967, in SCMP, no. 4045 (October 23, 1967): 13–15.

of peaceful transition, coexistence, and a "parliamentary road" to socialism. Thus, in 1959, he hedged the international applicability of Mao's model of national liberation with several qualifications.[27] In his 1962 state tour of Burma he recommended that the Burmese Communist Party "bury its weapons, reorganize its army into the [government's] 'defense forces,' and cooperate with Ne Win in the building of socialism." In his April 1963 visit to Indonesia, he suggested that the Communist Party (PKI) "have more Party members in positions of minister in the government, to accumulate some experience in governing the country." The Maoist criticisms of Liu's willingness to cooperate with bourgeois governments seem to assume that, as in the case of domestic reactionaries, class character is ascribed, and that the only effective policy toward "bourgeois" nations is one of uncompromising hostility. One article asserts that "peaceful transition" in Indonesia and Iraq had brought about the slaughter of revolutionary forces; another claims that because revisionists in postwar France and Italy (viz., Maurice Thorez and Palmiro Togliatti) had forfeited revolutionary violence for the "parliamentary road," they had necessarily "come to grief." [28]

(5) A number of criticisms of Liu's Party-building policies also assail his "liberalism." First, his critics charged that Liu opposed inner-Party struggle or sought to mitigate its intensity by denying its class character: "The *differences among Party members in the approach to problems* leads to different ways of handling problems, to divergences and controversies in views, and this provokes inner-Party struggle." [Emphasis added] To preserve "inner-Party peace," it is alleged that he taught Party members to be "forebearing and tolerant" and to "make concessions in the general interest." By proposing to "let everybody speak, so that everybody will be satisfied," a "do-as-you-please" liberalism, he is said to have given full currency for erroneous ideas while hampering efforts to criticize them. Second, Liu was accused of having discarded class criteria for admission to the Party in favor of "open doors," a "Party of the masses": the CCP should not be "afraid of our leadership being seized by others, of ourselves being used by others," he said, thus opening the Party to "opportunists,

---

27 In "states which are not adjacent to socialist countries, with developed means of communication; countries without numerous forests and mountainous areas situated far away from the cities, and where the enemy is strong," the outlook for guerrilla warfare is slim. "The bankruptcy of China's 'Devotee of Parliament,'" *PD*, August 12, 1967, in *SCMP*, no. 4006 (August 22, 1967): 13–18; *NCNA*, September 13, 1967, in *SCMP*, no. 4022 (September 15, 1967): 19–22.

28 Ch'en Hsiang-tung, "Shameless Renegade, Black Sheep of the Nation," *PD*, December 12, 1968, in *SCMP*, no. 4328 (December 31, 1968): 1–6.

renegades, and other nonproletarians" and limiting the admission of workers, peasants, and soldiers. Third, Liu allegedly advocated a "theory of many centers," which attenuated the authority of the CC and fostered "sectarianism, mountain-stronghold mentality and splittism for the purpose of usurping Party leadership." [29]

(6) The clearest case cited of Liu's liberalism is his policy toward China's minority nationalities and traditional religions. Criticisms of this policy are all variants of one essential criticism: Liu grants independent validity to nationality, ethnic background, or religious creed for the integration of groups, whereas the only legitimate criterion is said to be class. Under the assumption that ethnic or religious ties are valid criteria for integration, and that integration is in turn a sufficient condition for self-government, Liu honored indigenous traditions and worked through and with established traditional elites in a "united front" rather than replacing them.[30]

The Dictator—As noted earlier, Liu was accused not only of subverting "proletarian dictatorship" but of "commandist" or "bureaucratic" tendencies. The antiauthoritarian strain in the criticisms alleges that Liu is autocratic and peremptory in his administration of the Party bureaucracy, repressive and punitive in dealing with the masses. Within the Party, Liu is said to advocate a "slave mentality" that requires cadres to obey an order "even if it is incorrect": "Any subordination with conditions attached is incorrect. It should be unconditional and absolute subordination." In answer to a question about the correct "aspiration of a Communist," he replied, "Should one be a docile tool or an unruly tool? . . . Naturally one should be a docile

---

[29] "A Complete Reckoning of China's Khrushchev's Crime of Splitting the Party," *KMJP*, May 16, 1968, in *SCMP*, no. 4197 (June 13, 1968): 4–10; NCNA February 21, 1968, in *SCMP*, no. 4125 (February 26, 1968): 23–26.

[30] Whereas Mao wrote, "struggles between nationalities is in the final analysis a question of class struggle," Liu wrote that "linking national struggle with class struggle is entirely correct, assuming the independent reality of nationalism. With regard to national boundaries, Liu wrote that Communists "advocate complete equality and free union or division internationally . . . for all nationalities, and through different concrete ways of such free divisions and free union, gradual transition toward a united world." He included in his 1954 "Report on the Draft Constitution" a "guarantee that all places inhabited by various minority nationalities can really exercise the right of self-rule," thus undermining proletarian dictatorship. With regard to religious groups, Liu wrote in 1956, "we must . . . adhere to the policy of religious belief. . . . We should help those who live by religion as a profession to find a proper solution to any difficulties of livelihood." "Completely Purge Liu Shao-ch'i for His Counterrevolutionary Revisionist Crimes in United Front, Nationalities, and Religious Work," comp. "Red Army" Corps of K'angta Commune of the Central Institute for Nationalities, April 1967, in *CB*, no. 645 (March 3, 1969): 17–23.

tool, a tool easy to control." This emphasis on organizational compliance is said to militate against Mao's emphasis on ideological control, as represented by the Mao's 1942 statement: "Communists must always go into the whys and wherefores of anything, use their own heads and carefully think over whether or not it corresponds to reality and is really well founded; on no account should they follow blindly and encourage slavishness." [31]

Liu's repressive reaction to the "revolutionary masses" first triggered and then sustained the fury of the criticism campaign against him during the GPCR. Inasmuch as the events of the "fifty days" have already been examined in chapters 4 and 5, we now turn to a second instance of repression, the Socialist Education Movement or "four cleans" (ssu-ch'ing). On the basis of his eighteen-day stay at a brigade in Hunan in 1964 and his wife's year-long "squat on a spot" (tun-tien) at T'aoyüan in 1963–64, Liu pessimistically reported (in 1964) that "in the past year or more, we did not win but lost in the revolutionary struggle."

In 1961, a comrade of the CC brought a work group to T'ienhua Brigade in Hunan and spent two months there to make investigation and study, but he failed to find any problem. I discovered the problems after eighteen days of stay. Following this, I went to the hsien magistrate and told him to convene a meeting of poor and lower-middle peasants and strike root through the exchange of revolutionary experience. . . . He spread the rumor that I had upset things and procrastinated production. Hearing this I knew that he wanted to drive me away. I am the Chairman of the state, and since the grass-roots cadres wanted to drive me away, which of you would he not want to drive away? . . . The grass-roots cadres have a way to deal with us.[32]

Liu analyzed the causes of this unhappy situation in terms of the "contradiction between clean and being dirty on four questions: political, economic, organizational, and ideological questions," transforming the "essential" contradiction from one between poor and rich (which placed the onus on the "rich") to one between the backward and the advanced sectors (which placed the onus on the "backward").[33]

---

[31] "Bury the Slave Mentality Advocated by China's Khrushchev," PD, April 6, 1967, in SCMP, no. 3920 (April 17, 1967): 1–8; "A Complete Reckoning," pp. 4–10; Hung Yü, "Vigorously Destroy the Slave Mentality," KMJP, April 29, 1967, in SCMP, no. 3934 (May 8, 1967): 9–12.

[32] "Report at a Forum of District Committee Secretaries" (July 2, 1964), "Selected Edition," SCMM, no. 652, p. 35.

[33] PD, July 19, 1967, in SCMP, no. 4015 (September 6, 1967): 22–27. As one article put it, "During the three bad years, a lot of expropriated landlords and rich peasants wormed their way into positions of power. Instead of attacking these, China's Khrushchev and his wife attacked the good and relatively good cadres."

"We must not define the classes, we must investigate the bad elements," Liu said. In his view, "class struggle" was not feasible because complex cross-cutting cleavages had obscured distinctions: "The contradictions inside and outside the Party are interlocked, or the contradictions between the enemies and ourselves are interlocked with contradictions among the people." Mao's conception of the SEM as class conflict implied encouraging the poor and lower-middle peasants to direct punitive measures against those who had been amassing surplus wealth, but Liu allegedly saw the campaign as a police effort to eliminate the corruption that had become endemic in the disillusioned aftermath of the Leap. As the foregoing quotation suggests, he thought that variations in corruption were independent of class membership and that the culprits had grown capable of outwitting the system and concealing their violations. "The enemies have become wiser. . . . They have done better than we Communists." He spoke of enemies "who are organized and have connections on the top and the bottom and the Left and Right." [34]

In dealing with these enemies, Liu said, "A high standard demands: first, that we fully arouse the masses to action; second, there be less chaos," but in practice, these priorities seemed to become switched. In a talk on October 7, 1964, he said, "All rotten ones must be transferred away first. After that, it will be easy to mobilize the masses." Liu opposed Mao's call "boldly" to let the masses "educate and liberate themselves" by maintaining tight Party control of the "degree of tempering of the movement" rather than working through extra-Party organizations of poor and lower-middle peasants, warning that "the masses are like wild horses and will cause trouble when mobilized." Liu's line placed first priority on rectification of the Party: "It is better to make concentrated use of a superior force to fight a battle of annihilation, operate on a smaller scope, make concentrated use of the strength of the cadres, and wait for the training of one group to finish before we train another group," he said in July 1964. This emphasis on institutionalization and professionalization resulted in a conception quite different from Mao's more spirited and voluntaristic notion of a mass movement:

This is not a question of one or two groups to work for several months. It is a question of several years and even several decades until work is finished. We must have some professional revolutionaries. There are three types of

---

"Crimes of China's Khrushchev in the SEM," in *SCMP*, no. 4017 (September 8, 1967): 20–23.

[34] *KMJP*, December 27, 1969, in *SCMP*, no. 4571 (January 4, 1970): 77–83; *PD*, September 6, 1967, in *SCMP*, no. 4024 (September 8, 1967): 20–23.

forces for the prosecution of the four-clean movement: (1) professional revolutionaries; (2) work teams; and (3) those under training. . . . It is impossible to beat the bad people without having leading cadres and work teams.[35]

Liu's penchant for accurate intelligence about the situation at the
grass-roots level and for more precise targeting of purge victims led
him to propose replacement of conventional investigatory techniques
with undercover investigations (like that of Wang Kuang-mei at
T'aoyüan), associated in CCP historical experience with clandestine
operations in wartime "white areas." Noting that "many shortcomings
emerged during the Great Leap Forward in the past because the responsible comrades of the CC, provincial committees, and district committees did not themselves go to the grass-roots level . . . and they gave
credit to the nonsensical reports of those at the grass-roots level," Liu
directed that the setting up of organizations of poor and lower-middle
peasants must be preceded by visits and interviews with the peasants
and the establishment of mutual contacts; peasant organizations could
then increase in size and gradually develop in accord with the development of the movement. Due to the "interlocking" distribution of contradictions within the unit's authority structure, "the poor and lower-
middle peasants have a lot of misgivings." Due to their "misgivings"
about the eventuality of retribution by local authorities, workers and
peasants "would not tell us the truth," making it "impossible to find
out problems by holding investigation meetings." Consequently, Liu
recommended "relying on a few hand-picked activists to collect information through secret contacts," for "it is only by striking root and
linking up with the villages that they will have their fears allayed and
dare to speak out." [36]

ANALYSIS

The Liberal—The political criticisms comprise a confusing melange
of truths and falsehoods. Most of the criticisms of Liu's "liberal"
policies are accurate in their essentials but invalid, since they do not
deviate from Mao's Thought or from central policy at the time.

(1) For example, one may search in vain for any sign of difference
between Liu's and Mao's policies toward a united front with the KMT.
Although the first edition of *How To Be a Good Communist* did not
mention dictatorship of the proletariat, it appeared in 1939, shortly
after formation of the Second United Front, when it was prudent to

---

[35] *Pa-i-san hung-wei-ping* [August 13 Red Guard], no. 68 (May 13, 1967); "The
Reactionary Line of 'Hitting Hard at Many,'" *PD*, April 2, 1967, in *SCMP*, no. 3918
(April 13, 1967): 17–21.
[36] "Selected Edition," *SCMM*, no. 652 (April 28, 1969): 32–39.

stress unity. Mao's contemporaneous writings also omitted mention of a "dictatorship of the proletariat," [37] but stressed unity and expressed deference to Chiang Kai-shek; [38] expressions of deference by both Liu and Mao seem to occur during periods of high CCP vulnerability to KMT forces, and were replaced by increasing intractability as CCP troops expanded their control. Chapter 3 suggested that Liu originated the united-front policy of "unity and struggle" and in 1941 recommended resistance to the KMT: "We must severely criticize all policies and methods carried out by the KMT diehards and point out what harm these policies and methods will do to the War of Resistance, and that they will bring about disastrous failure." [39]

Following the end of the Sino-Japanese War, there was a brief period when the CCP leadership apparently believed that cooperation with the KMT within a parliamentary context offered a good prospect of CCP success—and not without reason. In an interview with John Service on August 23, 1944, Mao insisted on forcing the KMT "at once—to convene a provisional (or transitional) national congress" that "would have full charge of the preparations for full democracy and constitutionalism. It would supervise the elections and then convene the national congress." [40]

When Mao flew to Peking on August 28, 1945, he was optimistic: "It was when there was so much hope in the air, when we trusted the Generalissimo," he recounted to Robert Payne the following year.[41] A CC resolution issued three days before his departure (and included in his *Selected Works*) put forward the "three great slogans of peace, democracy, and unity." For a time, these hopes seemed well founded. On January 10, 1946, Chiang convened the Political Consultative Conference and immediately granted certain fundamental democratic rights, including freedom of speech, assembly, press, and equal legal rights for all parties.[42] Thus, on February 1, Liu wrote a report heralding a "new phase of peace and democracy," in which he sought to prepare

37 Mao Tse-tung, *Hsin min-chu-chu-i lun* [On New Democracy] (San Francisco, Ho-tso ch'u-pan-she, January 1940), pp. 8–9: Mao refers to a "joint dictatorship of several classes," and not once to a "proletarian dictatorship."

38 In 1938, Mao wrote, "The Kuomintang has a brilliant future," in a report to the Sixth Plenum (omitted from *SW*): "It enjoys the historic heritage of the Three People's Principles; it has had two great leaders in succession—Mr. Sun Yat-sen and Mr. Chiang Kai-shek." Stuart R. Schram, ed., *The Political Thought of Mao Tse-tung*, rev. ed. (New York, 1969), p. 228. See also Mao Tse-tung and Ch'en Po-ta, *Lun san-min-chu-i* [On the three people's principles] (n.p., n.d.).

39 *CW* 1: 308, 314.

40 John S. Service, *The Amerasia Papers: Some Problems in the History of U.S.-China Relations* (Berkeley, Calif., 1971), p. 168.

41 Payne, *Portrait of a Revolutionary*, p. 225.

42 U.S. Department of State, *The China White Paper* (Stanford, Calif., 1967), pp. 136–145.

"all of our organizations" to "evolve toward struggle without weapons": the army would become part of the national army, and "our
Party organizations in the army must be disbanded." [43] However, in a
report on the constitutional congress written by Mao on the same date,
the same points were made more briefly: "Henceforth the national
political system of China will follow the fundamental principle of
democratization, the general military agreement has determined the
fundamental principle of nationalization of the nation's armed forces.
. . . China will travel into a new period of peace and democracy." [44]
The subsequent Military Reorganization Agreement of February 25,
1946, envisaged a mutual reduction of armed forces and a process of
integration into a national armed force, based on the principle of
separating the army from politics. [45]

Liu has since frequently indicated his commitment to "proletarian
dictatorship," but he also professes devotion to democratic values, and
the policy implications of the latter commitment seemed to diverge
subtly from Mao's notions of democracy. Mao has favored periodic
"movement" democracy, as in the "Hundred Flowers," the Great Leap
Forward, or the GPCR, in which maximal participation-mobilization
of the masses is encouraged. Liu participated in all these campaigns
(the last in an unexpected role), but his independent attempts to
realize democratic ideals are represented in sections of the constitution
guaranteeing civil rights, or in the establishment of institutions for
mass representation of a formalistic "cultivated" form. [46] It is also
true that, in the first decade of CCP rule, an effort was made to develop comprehensive codes of law and that the prime movers behind this effort were Liu Shao-ch'i and P'eng Chen; from the GLF to
the GPCR there has, however, been a steep decline in China's legislative output. [47]

(2) The criticisms of Liu's "theory of the extinction of class struggle" are also accurate but invalid, as Mao himself indicated at the
October 1966 work conference: "We read the report. It was passed at
the general meeting." Liu's statement at that conference that "the
question of who will win the struggle between socialism and capitalism
in our country has now been decided" was not inconsistent with Mao's
statement in 1955, "By the end of this year the victory of socialism

43 "Shih-chü wen-t'i pao-kao" [Report on the current situation], LSWTC, pp.
182–185.
44 Mao Tse-tung Chi [Mao's works] (Tokyo, 1971), vol. 10, pp. 27–28.
45 U.S. Department of State, China White Paper, pp. 136–145.
46 E.g., CW 2: 60, 63.
47 Jerome A. Cohen, "Drafting People's Mediation Rules," in The City in Communist China, ed. John W. Lewis (Stanford, Calif., 1971), pp. 48–49.

will be practically assured," nor with Mao's 1957 statement in "On the Correct Resolution of Contradictions Among the People": "In our country, the contradictions between the working class and the national bourgeoisie belong to the contradictions among the people" and may therefore be handled either by the method of "peaceful transition" or by "unity, criticism, and education." [48] Both Liu's and Mao's statements bespoke an unrealistic optimism about the ideological progress of the intelligentsia that was perhaps current among CC members during the interregnum between the unexpectedly swift completion of collectivization and the rightist closure of the "Hundred Flowers." After the anti-rightist campaign abruptly ended the "Hundred Flowers," textual indications of optimism about the extinction of class struggle vanished from the writings of both men.

Although the criticisms are invalid from a strict point of view, one can still detect subtle differences in the way the two men sought to promote class struggle following Mao's invocation of this slogan in 1962. This question will be examined at greater length when the critique of the SEM is analyzed, but it seems fair to say that Liu's attempt to mediate class struggle through a network of institutions and to define class contradictions according to organizational or legal rather than ideological criteria resulted in a subtle transformation of class struggle into bureaucratic struggle and police action. Since Liu's fall, class struggle has again been muted in a renewed emphasis on solidarity, but this new form of class collaboration seems to be based on ideological conformity rather than organizational discipline and "merging" of interests.

(3) Despite their frequency and undoubted importance, allegations of Liu's "opposition" to Mao are difficult to test objectively. Liu always denied "subjective" opposition to Mao. Only two of the statements cited to indicate opposition explicitly *name* Mao, and these are short, out of context, and appear only in the less reliable Red Guard press.[49] Other purported instances of opposition refer only to "those who" behave in a given reprehensible manner; although the selected quotations obliquely indicate what Liu's critics consider Mao's most conspicuous vulnerabilities (e.g., braggadocio, impulsiveness, contentiousness), they fail to establish that Liu had Mao in mind when he wrote the passages. If the statements were so clearly aimed at Mao, why should Mao have allowed them to stand for so long? Why should

[48] *SRWM*, p. 434. As late as February 19, 1958, Mao wrote that "the nature of struggle and revolution is different from the past; it is not a class struggle, but a struggle between the advanced and the backward science and technology." "Sixty Articles on Work Methods: Article 22," *CB*, no. 892 (October 21, 1969): 6.

[49] Both in "Drag out Liu."

Liu be permitted continuously to slander Mao in public speeches? In fact, one may read the three-volume *Collected Works* of Liu Shao-ch'i from cover to cover without detecting a sign of opposition.

As an empirical measure of Liu's feelings toward Mao, we submitted an unofficial edition of his *Collected Works* to content analysis, counting the number of positive references to Mao per page as well as the total references per year. As Figure 1 indicates, there is no decrease either in average references per page or in total references per year between the seven-year 1959–66 period (the period of putative opposition) and the previous seven-year period (a period climaxed by Liu's promotion, with Mao's apparent blessing, to Chief of State). As is immediately evident, however, beginning in 1965, Liu was completely outbid in his expression of deference by Lin Piao. A qualitative analysis of the same documents confirms the conclusion reached by quantitative methods: not only were Lin's professions of deference truly effusive, but, in comparison to Liu, his thinking seems to have remained more closely attuned to Mao's concerns in the early 1960s; for example, no less than seven pages of Lin's well-known 1965 article, "Strategy and Tactics of the People's War" are devoted to the topic "Khrushchev Revisionists and Betrayers of the People's War." [50]

As for "opposition to Mao Tse-tung's Thought," Liu confessed "objective" opposition on certain occasions while maintaining that his opposition had been unintentional and nonconspiratorial. However, Mao himself had previously registered disapproval of the sort of indiscriminate repetition of quotations in place of rational problem-solving that the widespread dissemination of his Thought seemed to involve.[51] In a post-GPCR interview he admitted that the "cult of personality" had been created "in order to stimulate the masses to dismantle the anti-Mao Party bureaucracy" and regain "effective control," entirely neglecting to mention its efficacy in revolutionizing the thinking or enhancing the power of the "people," a goal that has perhaps been relegated to lower priority in the post-GPCR consolidation period. It had "of course . . . been overdone," he added.[52] Recent visitors to the mainland have noted such a muting of the cult that Mao buttons have become collectors' items, and the public criti-

50 *Lin Piao chuan-chi* [Lin Piao's collected works] (Hong Kong, 1970).

51 "There are not a few people who still regard odd quotations from Marxist-Leninist works as a ready-made panacea which, once acquired, can easily cure all maladies. . . . It is precisely such ignorant people who take Marxism-Leninism as a religious dogma." *SW* 3: 43. See also, "On the Historical Experience of the Dictatorship of the Proletariat" (a critique of Stalin's personality cult written under Mao's personal supervision), *PD*, April 5, 1956, in *CB*, no. 403 (July 25, 1956).

52 Snow, *The Long Revolution*, p. 71.

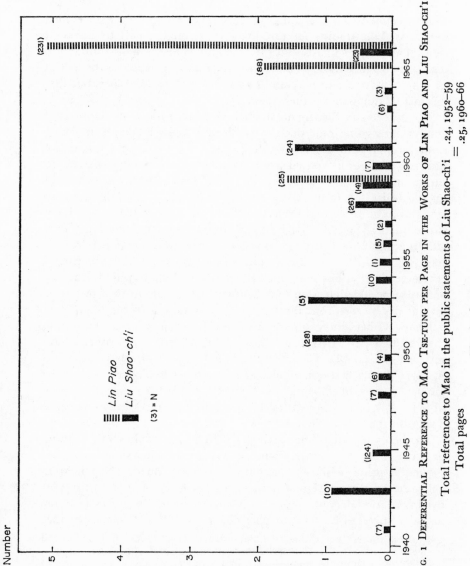

FIG. 1 DEFERENTIAL REFERENCE TO MAO TSE-TUNG PER PAGE IN THE WORKS OF LIN PIAO AND LIU SHAO-CH'I

Total references to Mao in the public statements of Liu Shao-ch'i
$$\frac{\text{Total references to Mao in the public statements of Liu Shao-ch'i}}{\text{Total pages}} = \begin{cases} .24, 1952-59 \\ .25, 1960-66 \end{cases}$$

Total references = 9.0, 1952-59
Seven years = 9.0, 1960-66

cisms accompanying the purge of Ch'en Po-ta and Lin Piao chided these erstwhile Maoists for pushing the personality cult to excess. It seems that the personality cult can wax and wane for short-run tactical purposes and that those who are instrumental in promoting the cult at an auspicious moment may use it as a ladder to higher office, but that this tactic cannot ensure their tenure.

(4) "No, this is Chairman Mao's line. You're too crazy. You don't know what's going on," declaimed Ch'en I to Red Guards attacking Liu's foreign policies. The evidence confirms that the criticisms of Liu's advocacy of a "united front from above" were only partially accurate and were also invalid and utterly insincere. Moreover, Liu's responsibility for formulating policy during the period in question seems to have been greatly overstated. As John Gittings has noted, the entire 1949–59 decade is ignored in the Maoist criticisms; the only serious accusations apply to the years following the Leap, particularly 1963, when Liu is said to have put forward his capitulationist line of "three reconciliations and one reduction." [53] Yet, it was during the post-1959 period that Mao took his most active role in foreign policy, making a generous contribution, as already noted, to the Sino-Soviet polemics. Others more directly responsible for foreign policy during the disputed period (such as Chou En-lai, Ch'en I, and others) have survived the GPCR. For example, following the Ninth Congress in April 1969, the first ambassador sent out from Peking to assume the important post in Albania was Keng Piao, the man directly responsible for Peking's close relationship with Rangoon as China's ambassador to Burma from 1963 to 1967. [54]

To the extent that Liu participated in foreign policy formulation, he seems indeed to have promoted moderate policies; he expressed particular pride in the border settlements with Burma, Nepal, Mongolia, Pakistan, and Afghanistan. Although he was the first to suggest the international applicability of Mao's national liberation formula, his later speeches do tend to play down the role of violence in that

[53] John Gittings, "The Crimes of China's Khrushchev," *FEER* 59, no. 16 (April 18, 1968): 176–179. Daniel Tretiak has checked the criticisms of Liu's trip to Indonesia in 1963 against the public record of his statements there, finding that of eight charges, five are demonstrably false, one moot, and two correct. "The Chinese Cultural Revolution and Foreign Policy," *CS* 8, no. 7 (April 1, 1970): 1–14.

[54] The four ministries in the State Council most involved with foreign affairs (Foreign Ministry, Ministry of Foreign Trade, Commission for Cultural Relations with Foreign Countries, and Commission for Economic Relations with Foreign Countries) seem to have survived the GPCR with relatively low attrition. Donald W. Klein, "The State Council and the Cultural Revolution," *CQ*, no. 35 (July–September 1968): 78–95; see also Peter Van Ness, *Revolution and Chinese Foreign Policy: Peking's Support for Wars of National Liberation* (Berkeley, Calif., 1970), pp. 240–248.

formula. Yet he employed his pacifist rhetoric with sufficient flexibility to include encouragement of national liberation wars and threats of war in protective reaction against those who would suppress them. Due to a particularly militant speech in support of Ho Chi Minh on July 22, 1966, some Western commentators have even characterized him as a "hawk" with regard to the prospect of Chinese intervention.[55]

The insincerity of the foreign policy critique seems patent in the light of post-Liu foreign policies, which have pursued the same moderate line for which Liu was condemned—with striking success, in terms of conventional national interest. Peking has made commercial and diplomatic overtures to a number of Western powers, resulting in recognition by Canada, Italy, Austria, Belgium, Ethiopia, Japan, and Western Germany (among others), and in China's admission to the United Nations. As for "reduction of aid to wars of national liberation," a focal criticism of Liu, the Chinese have subsequently tolerated the blockade of North Vietnam and intensive bombing of North Vietnamese cities while hosting a visit from the U.S. President and vocally supported West Pakistan's unsuccessful attempt to subjugate Bangladesh as well as Mrs. Bandaranaike's more successful suppression of the quasi-Maoist JVN uprising in Sri Lanka (Ceylon). When General Goafar al-Nimeiry of the Sudan crushed a Communist-backed coup, executing the top conspirators, the Chinese even endorsed his actions, apparently because leaders of the Sudanese Communist Party leant to the wrong side of the Sino-Soviet schism.[56]

(5) Criticisms of Liu's "liberal" Party-building policies are only partially accurate and largely invalid but seem to be sincere. The criticisms of Liu's advocacy of a "whole people's party" and "open doors" seem to be accurate, but these policies did not diverge from Mao's at the time.[57] The charge that he proposed a "theory of many centers" is inaccurate and based on expedient distortion of his writings on "base areas." Allegations that Liu favored "inner-Party peace" are based on a one-sided interpretation of his 1941 essay, "On Inner-Party Struggle" (which had been quietly removed from publication in the 1950s).[58] Though Liu did oppose "excessive" or "mechanical" struggle in that work, Mao's works also contained passages denouncing "excessive

[55] Cf. Uri Ra'anan, "Peking's Foreign Policy 'Debate,' 1965–1966," in China in Crisis, ed. Tang Tsou, 2: 27; also Schurmann, Ideology, pp. 555–556. For a critique of this argument, cf. Michael Jahuda, "Kremlinology and the Chinese Strategic Debate," CQ, no. 49 (January–March 1972): 45–48.

[56] Curtis Ullerich, "When the Pot Calls the Kettle Black," Journal of Contemporary Asia 2, no. 3 (1972): 297–300.

[57] SW 2: 114–115, 181–182; 4: 271, 274–275.

[58] Blumer, Kulturrevolution, pp. 110–111.

and sectarian intra-Party struggles" (which were, however, deleted from the post-1965 editions).[59] Liu distinguished between "principled" and "unprincipled" disputes; only the latter could be compromised, and the former must be settled through "struggle": "We should not adopt the point of view of liberalism, but should struggle uncompromisingly with ideas and proposals which are mistaken in principle and with all evils in the Party, so that these mistakes and evils can be overcome once and for all." How long would inner-Party struggle be necessary? "As long as these evils still exist in society, as long as classes and the influence of exploiters still exist, these evils will certainly continue to exist . . . in the Communist Party." [60] It is true that Liu did not stress the class character of inner-Party struggle, but, in theory, all Party members were proletarian, either by birth or through thought reform, making the application of class labels theoretically problematic.

(6) The criticisms of Liu's nationalities and religions policy are accurate, invalid, and sincere. That he granted legitimacy to nationalism or religious creed as criteria for integration and self-rule may be verified on the basis of his 1948 essay, "Internationalism and Nationalism," and in his 1954 "Report on the Draft Constitution." [61] But he did not differ in this regard from Mao, the author of a formula for wars of *national* liberation, who wrote in 1934, "Soviet China recognizes the complete self-determination of the minorities, who may go so far as to secede and form independent free states." [62]

The GPCR brought the entire united-front concept under attack as capitulationism; those singled out for most vehement attack were not national elites, but Han Chinese associated with the policy—not a single Han Chinese survivor of the Party elite is engaged in minorities

59 Mao condemned the "sectarian organization policy of attacking comrades"; "factional activities against the Central leadership"; those who acted "as if they were dealing with criminals and enemies" and "attacked, punished, and dismissed from the Central and local organizations large numbers of veteran cadres." *SW* (1965 ed.) 3: 182, 87, 209. See also *SRWM*, p. 516.

60 *CW* 1: 327–369.

61 *CW* 2: 123–153, 275–317.

62 In 1957, Mao said, "When we continue to strengthen the unity of the whole Party, we must at the same time continue to strengthen the unity of all minority nationalities, all political parties and all people's organizations, continue to consolidate and further expand our people's democratic united front." "Opening Address at the Eighth National Congress of the CCP" (September 15, 1956), *Jen-min shou-tse*, comp. *Ta-kung pao* [Daily worker] (Peking, 1957), p. 8. And again: "Some people actually disagree with Marxism, although they do not openly say so. There will be people of this sort for a long time to come, and we shall allow them to disagree. . . . The same holds true for the patriotic people in religious circles. They are theists, and we are atheists. We cannot force them to accept the Marxist world outlook." "Speech to the CCP's National Conference on Propaganda Work" (March 12, 1957), *SRWM*, p. 499.

work.[63] Though the 1969 Party Constitution passed at the Ninth Congress specified that "all nationalities have freedom to use their written and spoken language," it departed from the 1956 Party Constitution of the Eighth Congress in omitting mention of the minorities' special needs, nor did it give guarantees for their protection against discrimination.[64] This departure from the federalist implications of Liu's united front policy seems to be based on long-standing resistance in those regions (particularly among the Mongols, Kazakhs, Uighurs, and Tibetans in North and West China) to radical socioeconomic reform campaigns.[65]

The Dictator—Generally speaking, the criticisms of Liu's alleged autocratic tendencies toward lower-level cadres and masses seem to have greater validity. It is true that Liu demanded "absolute obedience" and also true that he made organizational compliance imperative independent of the ideological "correctness" of the command.[66] However, in his typically "balanced" style, Liu also reprimanded those "who knew nothing but blind obedience" and made a number of provisions to allow for flexibility in application ("changing conditions may even warrant change of program"), to "allow appeals and encourage arguments on principles," and to permit the minority to "hold their own opinion" and "carry on their effort of persuasion." To draw attention to Liu's "slavishness" while failing to concede these provisions for flexibility and appeals seems to be a considerable distortion.

The criticism is nonetheless sincere, for there have been determined

[63] June Dreyer, "Traditional Minorities Elites and the CPR Elite Engaged in Minority Nationalities Work," in *Elites*, ed. Scalapino, pp. 416–451. According to a 1973 visitor, roughly a third of the national ministries still had no permanent ministers, which raises the question of the future of the united front. A. Doak Barnett, "There Are Warts There, Too," *NYT Magazine*, April 8, 1973, pp. 36–37, 100.

[64] *The Ninth National Congress of the CCP* (Peking, 1969), pp. 109–129.

[65] *CNA*, no. 831 (February 12, 1971): 1 ff.

[66] "It is wrong for them to put up such a condition [i.e., ideological correctness], for it destroys the system of democratic centralism," Liu wrote. *CW* 1: 327–369. "Once a decision is made by the majority, the higher-level leadership, or the CC, it must be carried out even if the decision is wrong." Without expressing himself in such uncompromising terms, Mao has also supported this formulation: in 1938, he wrote, "(1) That individuals must subordinate themselves to the organization; (2) that the minority must subordinate itself to the majority; (3) that the lower level must subordinate itself to the higher level; (4) that the entire membership must subordinate itself to the CC." "The Role of the CCP in the National War," *SW* 2: 203–204. Since 1970, with the reconstruction of the CCP, this quotation has reentered circulation in the nation's media, to the bemusement of many.

attempts to shift from Liu's emphasis on organizational compliance to ideologically motivated compliance. "Never again . . . will the decision of a majority in committee be taken as gospel," asserts Neale Hunter, with somewhat short-sighted optimism. "Only decisions which accord with the thought of Mao Tse-tung will be considered correct." [67] The essence of the Maoist dissatisfaction with democratic centralism had to do with its lack of representativeness and its "mechanical," amoral character, which made it possible, for example, for the Party to suppress the revolutionary teachers and students during the "fifty days" without the full awareness or intention of its leadership. In the emerging organizational structure, there has accordingly been an attempt to incorporate ideological citeria (Mao's Thought) to complement if not replace organizational criteria (democratic centralism, majority rule) for obedience, and also to make Mao's Thought a popular ideology that the masses may invoke outside the organizational apparatus to legitimate grievances. Because of the ideology's lack of precise content, these experiments have provoked doctrinal controversy and factionalism and there has been a noticeable recession back to more easily calculable procedural criteria, as the leadership shifted its concern from political representation to administration and economic regulation. The RCs have become subordinate to the Party committees at each level on a basis of "democratic centralism," for example, and the role of mass representatives has been progressively reduced. There has, however, been a noticeable simplification of the bureaucratic structure both vertically (in the wholesale dismissal of secretarial and staff personnel) and horizontally (in the replacement of the functionally specialized "branch principle" by the "committee principle"), and the emancipation of ideology from its organizational context has not been entirely reversed, for there are occasional reports of "rebels" invoking Maoist principles to attack the local Party organization.[68] Important changes have also been undertaken in elite socialization and in ongoing community control of elites in an effort to prevent any recurrence of bureaucratic alienation: Liu's cadre schools were replaced by "May 7 schools," which em-

---

67 *FEER* 56, no. 9 (June 1, 1967): 478.

68 For instance, in the fall of 1970, after peasants had been urged to increase their investment funds by expanding sideline occupations and industries, radicals began attacking the commune system. They agitated for the commune as the unit of accounting, for abolishing the right of teams, brigades, and communes to retain title to property, and for relating wages to need rather than to work. (Radio Shensi, September 9, 1970). During the winter, criticism continued in Shantung (Radio Shantung, September 9, 1970, March 5, 1971) and Shansi (Radio Shansi, October 12, December 23, 1970), until on February 18, 1971, *PD* issued an edict from Mao forbidding further alteration of the commune system.

phasize manual labor and association with local workers, and periodic "open-door rectification" provides the masses with an opportunity to vent grievances and participate in decisions. *Hsia-fang* has been placed on a regular footing (e.g., one of the rotation schedules is the "3-3-3 system," whereby a third of the administrative personnel of a unit is responsible for routine office work, one-third carries out inspections of basic-level units, and the remaining one-third engages in labor at "May 7 schools") in a further effort to promote more fluid relations between elites and masses.[69]

Criticisms of Liu's suppression of the masses, as exemplified in the SEM, include two accusations: first, that the Party, through a process of alienation and *embourgeoisement,* had become a "new class" which suppressed and exploited the masses; second, that Liu was to blame for this development. Both accusations seem to be accurate and valid, though the second is more disputable than the first. The retrenchment program Liu introduced to recover from the Leap had two important consequences: first, increasing stratification in the countryside set in, as certain strata were better equipped to profit from the material incentives and broadened entrepreneurial freedom than others, because of greater ability or resources. Second, corruption became endemic, both among peasants and low-level cadres. Given Mao's overriding concern with egalitarianism, the first phenomenon was salient; given Liu's concern with orderly economic growth, the second assumed highest importance.[70] But both agreed that the situation was critical, that the social forces set in motion by the retrenchment policies must now be curbed; so the SEM was formally introduced in 1962, and intensified the following year.

Although Mao and Liu agreed that the loosening of controls had gone too far, they disagreed on how to check it, Mao favoring upsurge from below, Liu favoring Party reform and the imposition of Party controls. In May 1963, Mao secured CC adoption of his "First Ten Articles" which resulted in formation of many poor and lower-middle peasant associations in the summer and early fall of 1963. But in September 1963, the "Second Ten Articles" were adopted, which were apparently drafted by P'eng Chen; this document dropped all refer-

---

[69] Weggel, *Die Partei als Widersacher,* pp. 73–84.

[70] E.g., on December 11, 1965, Liu said: "The achievement of this movement must find expression in better service for the countryside . . . in the increase in production and expansion of the scope of production, so that laborers may gain greater income and heighten their standard of living." The Lien-chiang documents confirm that both were right—there was both cadre corruption and a "spirit of individual enterprise" among peasants. C. S. Chen, *Rural People's Communes in Lien-chiang,* pp. 99–102.

ences to poor and lower-middle peasant associations and assigned a leading role to work teams formed by provincial or county-level cadres to direct the movement; it also instructed cadres to be lenient to deviants and to coodinate SEM work with production, in effect ignoring Mao's call for class struggle. Mao was displeased and asked Liu to write a revision. Liu released the revised "Later Ten Articles" in September 1964; he formulated this document on the basis of Wang Kuang-mei's T'aoyüan experience and his own short stay at a brigade in Hunan, and it was more "left," or pessimistic, in its estimate of the situation than P'eng had been the year before. Liu's revised draft indicated that the "major conflict" was between the peasants and the basic-echelon cadres, more than 80 percent of whom, he estimated, had been guilty of corruption or law violation. It contained two new items aimed at enhancing the mobilization and direct participation of the masses: first, direct transmission of information from the masses to the center was called for, and second, there was to be direct participation of the masses in meetings called to criticize cadres. Thus, throughout the fall of 1964 the cadres were severely attacked by the newly-formed poor and lower-middle peasant associations. Cadres became demoralized, and their authority was undermined.[71]

In January 1965, Mao called a work conference and promulgated the "Twenty-Three Articles," in which he made his dissatisfaction with Liu's performance clear. Liu's undercover investigation tactics were repudiated, and a vague threat to "Party persons in authority taking the capitalist road" within the CC was included. Press and radio criticism of cadre corruption ceased abruptly, but the scope of the SEM was broadened, as the document now defined as "fundamental" the antagonistic contradiction between socialism and capitalism and described as nonantagonistic the contradiction between corrupted cadres and peasants. Toward the end of 1965 (at the time of Mao's attack on the Peking Municipal Party Committee), the struggle turned upward, focusing on "bureaucratism, conservatism, and commandism" of cadres at county and even provincial levels.[72]

The evidence thus suggests that Liu was indeed guilty of "hitting the many" lower-level cadres; that he did this in order to "protect a handful" was not alleged until Liu came under criticism more than

[71] Baum and Teiwes, *Ssu-ch'ing;* also Baum and Teiwes, "Who Was Right?" *FEER* 57, no. 12 (September 14, 1967): 562–567.

[72] The struggle thus shifted from criminals back to accumulators of surplus capital. In May 1965, *PD* declared an expansion of targets to the "struggle between the socialist direction of the poor and lower-middle peasants and the capitalist tendencies of the upper-middle peasants." Cf. K. C. Yeh, *Agricultural Policies and Performance* (Santa Monica, Calif., March 1970), pp. 61–62.

two years later. There is no indication that any rightists at higher levels were being consciously "protected" in the autumn of 1964; the "Later Ten Articles" contained a specific injunction to expose higher-level "protectors and instigators" of errant cadres no matter how exalted their positions. "Protection of the handful" was not purposeful, but it was a functional consequence of the hierarchical organization of the movement. As Tang Tsou has pointed out, Liu's conception of leadership led him to trace blame down the chain of command to the levels responsible for implementation, whereas Mao's ideological conception of leadership led him to blame the initiators of unsuccessful policies.[73]

What may we conclude from this bewildering congeries of fiction and truth: was Liu Shao-ch'i a "bourgeois dictator"? In the split between "liberal" and "dictatorship" themes, the former seemed to be largely accurate but invalid, since Mao was also "liberal" at times in question; the latter seem to be fairly accurate, valid, and sincere. Even if all the criticisms were generally valid, however, they fail to show that Liu discriminated in his application of "liberalism" and "dictatorship" on the basis of *class*. Criticisms of his opposition to "proletarian dictatorship" cite passages to show his support for "equal justice," a "whole people's state," and the like, without showing any particular discrimination against workers and peasants or favoritism toward the bourgeoisie. Criticisms of his foreign policy ascribe class character to foreign governments solely on the basis of their friendship with China, with the result that Liu is considered "bourgeois" because (inter alia) he allegedly favored reconciliation with "fraternal socialist states." Criticisms of his blunders in the SEM show that he sought to *avoid* class categories under the assumption of "interlocking contradictions," not class discrimination. The "bourgeois dictatorship" accusation rests on the unproved assumption that "there is only class dictatorship"; hence, if there is no proletarian dictatorship, there must be bourgeois dictatorship. It seems more accurate to define Liu's "state of the whole people" as a rational-legal bureaucracy operating in tandem with an incipient technical meritocracy.

ECONOMIC THEMES

CRITIQUE

The essential criticism of Liu's economic policies was, of course, that he promoted economic "revisionism" and sought thereby to lead China

[73] Tang Tsou, "The Cultural Revolution and the Chinese Political System," *CQ*, no. 38 (April–June 1969): 63–91.

down the "capitalist road." These policies had both defensive and offensive dimensions: the former encompassed Liu's "shielding" of ex-capitalist elements and otherwise obstructing the socialization process, the latter his introduction of various "revisionist" elements into the socialist economic system. The GLF seems to be the watershed that divides the defensive and offensive strategies chronologically. First, then, we turn to an examination of Liu's alleged protection of capitalism (which was polemically defined simply as the amassing of an invidious proportion of wealth, without much regard for the mode of production by which wealth is acquired), and then proceed to an examination of his active promotion of "revisionism."

Opposition to Socialization—Indications of Liu's tendencies to "shield" bourgeoisie are found in writings dating from as early as 1924 (in the article, "Save the Hanyehp'ing Iron and Steel Company"), but certainly the most frequently cited indications of shielding are culled from his 1949–50 speeches to laborers and capitalists in Tientsin, immediately following Communist capture of the city. "Exploitation has its merits," he said, defending managerial discretion to hire and fire and set pay and working hours. When asked how workers should act, he replied, "basically as in the past." He admitted that "taxes were heavy" and encouraged capitalists to "consult together and share responsibility" to devise new tax scales, or even to reopen the Tientsin Stock Exchange, adding, "If you have any good and feasible plans, you may let me know. I have a 50 percent say in these things." But in regard to the attempts of workers to set up and run their own factories without expert assistance, Liu expressed skepticism:

Some workers would say, "We can run factories even without capitalists. Let us get organized to run cooperative factories." What about the cooperative factories? Many have been set up, but not a single one is run with success.[74]

In his analysis of post-Liberation class structure, the critics point out, Mao said the fundamental contradiction would be between the proletariat and the bourgeoisie and that it would emerge in the form of struggle between "restriction and opposition to restriction" of capitalism. Within the purview of "restriction," the "biggest agent of the bourgeoisie" perceived "vast room for private enterprise to de-

[74] "Firmly Uphold the Taxation Policy of the Proletariat," *PD*, December 28, 1968, in *SCMB*, no. 4347 (January 28, 1969): 3–9. Tientsin capitalists prospered under Liu: in 1949 the value of imports for private merchants amounted to 66.6 percent of the total and the value of private exports was 77.7 percent of the total; the rate of private industrial profit in 1949 was more than twice that of local state-owned enterprises. *PD*, November 8, 1967, in *SCMP*, no. 4059 (November 14, 1967): 25; *Pa-erh-wu chan-pao* [August 25 battle news], February 7, 1967.

velop alongside the state-owned enterprises." In fact, he proposed restrictions of the proletariat and protection of private industry under the slogans "joint public-private operation" and "mutual development." "Mutual development" meant not only that half-private enterprises might continue to operate, but that bourgeois experts and enterprisers might be incorporated into the socialist managerial elite, in a mutually profitable relationship with representatives of the proletariat. Even after basic completion of socialist transformation of ownership of the means of production in 1957, Liu reaffirmed his paternalistic solicitude for the welfare of progressive capitalists: "As long as the industrialists and businessmen follow the lead of the People's Government and promote socialism with heart and soul . . . we will hold ourselves responsible for them to the end, regardless of whether they are young or old, in sickness or in health." [75]

Why was Liu so solicitous of the bourgeoisie? He justified his cooptative strategy by alleging that the bourgeoisie were making progress in "transformation" through thought reform to a "proletarian" standpoint, which the Maoists deny in their generally more skeptical view of thought reform. But Liu's decisive reason seems to have been his high appraisal of the contribution capitalists could make to industrialization regardless (or even because) of their class backgrounds: they had the training, capital, and experience that the proletariat lacked. To him the threat of a bourgeois "rebellion" was both real and serious. The Maoists dismiss this threat, pointing out that the bourgeoisie may be subjected to coercive constraints if they refuse to cooperate, that in any case the competence of bourgeois experts has been vastly exaggerated, and that proletarian innovators can without much specialized training make significant contributions to industrial technology.[76]

75 "So-called 'Mutual Development' Meant Development of Capitalism," PD, December 28, 1969, in SCMP, no. 4347 (January 28, 1969): 10–11; KMJP, July 21, 1967, in CB, no. 836 (September 25, 1967). "Perhaps private production could exceed state production, but the state is not afraid of this. Our chief object is to develop production, and we have no objection to which kind of production can expand on a larger scale," Liu told Tientsin capitalists. He proposed that private and public personnel should "sit and stand" together as equals in an industrial united front. "On your part, you should make all industrial and commercial men take the socialist road, follow the CCP, advance their ideology . . . and work for the state. . . . What we should do is to take care of the livelihood of the industrial and commercial men. Either side may criticize the other if there is any shortcoming. Let us have this verbal agreement." Many enterprises then drafted "regulations of cooperation between public and private personnel" formalizing the terms of this agreement. "Struggle Between Two Lines in the Transformation of Industry and Commerce," PD, April 15, 1968, in SCMP, no. 4159 (April 17, 1968): 13–20; Shao Pai, "Refuting Several 'Bases of Agreement' for Theory of 'Class Cooperation,'" KMJP, June 29, 1967, in SCMP, no. 3987 (July 25, 1967): 1–14.

76 "Defender of the Capitalist Economy," KMJP, July 21, 1967, in CB, no. 836 (September 25, 1967): 31–38.

Whereas evidence of Liu's "shielding" of capitalism is culled for the most part from 1949 talks in Tientsin, his obstruction of the socialization of the Chinese economy was said to be concentrated at three "crucial points" in that process: the period of land reform, 1950–51; the period of socialist transformation of industry and agriculture, 1955; and the "three years of temporary economic difficulties," 1960–62. At the first "crucial point," Liu argued that mechanization must precede collectivization to provide the material wherewithal to sustain cooperation ("without machines, no collective farm can be consolidated"), that if mutual-aid farming teams were built on the basis of bankrupt peasants they would collapse; only after they had all become middle peasants could they be run well. Liu's priorities, assert his critics, derive from his overestimation of machinery and technical expertise and his underestimation of "limitless human potential"; they deny the possibility of revolution in the Third World and ultimately imply that people in developing countries cannot but tolerate exploitation while those in developed countries undergo peaceful transition to socialism. At the second chronological "point," besides opposing transformation of capitalist industry and commerce into a state of joint public-private ownership, Liu approved the dissolution of 200,000 cooperatives. This decision was based on the theory of "three surpassings": the movement had "surpassed the actual possibility," the "level of awakening of the masses," and the "cadres' level of experience." [77]

Revisionism—During the third period of heightened obstructive activities following the Leap's debacle, Liu took advantage of "temporary economic difficulties" and Mao's semiretirement to shift from a defensive to an offensive posture, introducing "revisionist" economic policies of a type that have also made their appearance in Yugoslavia, Dubcek's Czechoslovakia, and other socialist states. Criticisms of these policies will be examined as they were applied to agriculture, business, and labor.

(1) Three broad criticisms of Liu's revisions in agricultural policy centered about the issue of mechanization. The first issue concerned introduction of mechanization under state supervision versus local (i.e., commune-level) control. After the Leap, Liu decided that "since the

[77] "In the future, when China has industrial overproduction, and there are more factories and more products, that will be the time to embark upon socialism," he said in 1949. But "throughout the phase of New Democracy, it is necessary to preserve the rich peasant economy." When there were spontaneous attempts in July 1951 to move from agricultural mutual aid teams to APCs, he protested that this was "erroneous, dangerous utopian agricultural socialism," and reversed the initiatives. *LAD*, June 26, 1969, in *SCMP*, no. 4448 (July 3, 1969): 13–17.

sending of tractors to the grass roots does not work they should be re-called and state tractor stations should be set up." His support of tractor stations was based on three advantages: (a) superior facilities and personnel (i.e., "university graduates and college technicians") for training in the use of machines and modern agricultural techniques; (b) higher efficiency in machine utilization (Liu spoke of the "contradiction between centralized leadership and decentralized use," claiming that whereas one machine station could service several communes, decentralized use, as when each commune owns its own machinery, is inconvenient to manage, disturbs unified coordination, and is unable to bring the effectiveness of machines and tools into full play, resulting in more rapid equipment deterioration); (c) greater financial resources (Liu spoke of the "contradiction between the need for sizable funds to realize agricultural mechanization and the weak economic strength of communes," claiming that "only 5 percent of the brigades can promote mechanization themselves").[78]

In the Maoist view, these advantages are spurious. The assumption that tractor stations can provide superior educational facilities is based on a bourgeois conception of education that forces the masses to learn from engineers, agro-technicians, and economists rather than inducing the experts to learn (as they teach) by working among the masses. Machine stations may enhance machine utilization efficiency, but they reduce farming efficiency because of the difficulty in linking the mechanized plans of the stations with the production plans of the communes and teams.[79] Concerning the capability of communes to finance their own mechanization, the masses can indeed afford to buy machinery

[78] "Thoroughly Wipe out the Pernicious . . . over the Agricultural Mechanization Front," *Nung-yeh chi-hsieh chi-shu* [Agricultural Mechanization Technique], nos. 2–3 (May 23, 1967), in *SCMM*, no. 585 (July 24, 1967): 10–14 (hereafter *NYCHCS*).

[79] Since a station cannot easily obtain a concrete understanding of production conditions and farm work arrangements in every commune or team, it may fail to coordinate its operation with production requirements. Furthermore, the division of labor exacerbates the contradiction between the working class and the peasant class; because mechanized plowing is done by the stations on the basis of contracts signed with communes and teams, this creates "two sets of hearts and two sets of books." "Collective Strength . . . of Mechanized Farming," *NYCHCS*, no. 2 (1968), in *SCMM*, no. 620 (July 22, 1968): 1–5. E.g., in one *hsien* the chief of the provincial agricultural machinery corps said, "No machines will be assigned to those who sustain heavy losses. Those who are incompetent must hand over control to other parties. If this still does not work, both the machines and the personnel must leave." Though this *hsien* reportedly sustained losses year after year, the tractor station neither analyzed the cause of the loss nor gave concrete assistance. "In future, we shall plow land when there is money to be made, otherwise we shall just stand aside," he said. "If we have no land to plow, we shall take up sideline occupations." "Thoroughly Eliminate . . . Material Incentives," *NYCHCS*, no. 4 (July 8, 1967), in *SCMM*, no. 605 (December 11, 1967): 26–29.

by sacrificing more and working harder and Liu's contrary assumption shows once again his disesteem for the masses and their resourcefulness.

The second issue in the mechanization controversy concerned farm implement development and manufacture. Mao favored "self-reliance," which meant mass participation in the development of indigenous, small-scale farm implements, but Liu and his cohorts preferred "bigness, modernity, and completeness." Emphasizing the need to meet quality standards and to recover from a large business deficit, in 1961 Liu suppressed the mass movement for reform of farm implements. Farm implement research stations were "chopped down" and scientific experiments of a mass character were abandoned in favor of bourgeois expertise. Liu gave up the attempt to create an intermediate technology by manufacturing a congeries of labor-intensive "small and indigenous" farm implements and concentrated on establishing "large, modern, and comprehensive" enterprises that would permit economies of scale.[80]

The third issue concerns the scale and source of funding for mechanization. Liu sponsored systematic state-organized introduction of machinery at experimental points, selecting "a hundred key *hsien*" for full-scale mechanization in a "war of annihilation." The Maoists objected that it would take a long time at this rate before all 2,000 *hsien* were mechanized, and the sequence would entail uneven development, giving "key *hsien*" a head start in capital accumulation.[81]

(2) In the area of business and commerce, Liu made two important revisions. First, he revived the market. Referring to its superior "diversity and flexibility" in allocating means of production and adjusting to consumer demands, Liu fostered a market socialism that tolerated a private sector of manufacturers, handicraftsmen, peddlers, and traders. In a talk with Minister of Commerce Yao I-lin as late as October 1960, he said:

[80] The double-wheel and double-blade plow popularization campaign was termed a "mess" and after 1961 local farm machinery enterprises engaged in the manufacture of small-scale indigenous implements were faced with "closure, suspension, merger, and change of lines of production." Liu smothered mass enthusiasm in favor of expertise, "crawling" to "learn, buy and steal" foreign farm implements allegedly ill-suited to Chinese terrain. *NYCHCS*, no. 4 (July 8, 1967), in *SCMM*, no. 605 (December 11, 1967): 26–29.

[81] "We must equip whole *hsien* one by one and not equip them on a piecemeal basis," Liu directed. In October 1965 he advocated sending a group of persons "to a place to work five solid years" so that peasants might learn to use, overhaul, and administer new equipment. "When the peasants have learned to handle things themselves, five years afterward, this group of persons can go to another *hsien* to train the peasants there for five years. The state could invest a large sum of money within ten years, and when this money is recalled ten years later, the state can use it to equip another area." *NYCHCS*, nos. 2–3, in *SCMM*, no. 585 (July 24, 1967): 10–14.

It is also good to have some bourgeoisie in a society. These people are most energetic, and they are capable of crawling through cracks. . . . They are able to crawl through a crack to make money because they have discovered our shortcomings in planning. Our cracks are thus filled. When they start anything, we should also start the same thing.[82]

Increased use of the market revived discussion among professional economists over the "law of value," including proposals to adulterate the labor-cost price with considerations of scarcity or capital outlay and to use the profit index as a measure of economic efficiency. This was the first time such liberal proposals had received a hearing in the professional journals, and the debate continued for several months before being suppressed, giving rise to speculation that the revisionists had higher backing. In support of the supposition that he backed such revisions, Liu is quoted as saying, "We must work on what makes money." The prospect of a resort to the profit index evoked nightmares of greed-driven individualism: profit would not result in a rational distribution of capital investment, either in terms of the public interest (e.g., there would be no mechanization of agriculture because returns would be low and require a long period of investment) or national defense (e.g., factories would not be geographically dispersed in preparation for air attack and people's war); profit would also undermine the socialist relations of mutual help between enterprises under unified state planning and replace it with cut-throat competition, and so on.

In his second revision in business and commerce, in 1963 Liu introduced "socialist trusts" for the purpose of "improving quality, increasing the variety of products, cutting down production cost, raising labor productivity, and elevating technique to meet the needs of the people." Trusts would also "probably lessen bureaucratism," he predicted, confining local governments to supervisory functions such as collection of surtaxes and supervision of municipal projects, permitting trusts to purchase materials and sell their products on the market. Four industrial trades were selected as experimental units in 1964; shortly afterwards, trusts were spread to twelve industrial trades connected with national economy, people's livelihood, and

---

[82] Shang Hua, "Criticism of Liu Shao-ch'i's . . . on the Commercial Front," *KMJP*, February 1, 1969, in *SCMP*, no. 4363 (February 25, 1967): 1–3. In a directive written for a conference of October 22, 1961 on prevention of commodity black marketeering, Liu went so far as to say, "It is good to have underground factories where these do not cheat their customers; the things they produce are useful." "Selected Edition," *SCMM*, no. 652 (April 28, 1969): 4; Ting Hsüeh-lui, "Class Struggle Essential to Communist Party," *PD*, May 6, 1967, in *SCMP*, no. 39, 44 (May 23, 1967): 1–8.

local finance, including the pharmaceutical, rubber, aluminum, tractor, salt, and other industries. Within a few months after introduction of trusts to the pharmaceutical industry, 40 percent of the total number of pharmaceutical plants, many of which had been built in indigenous ways during the Leap, were "chopped down." The head office "monopolized the powers" of branch companies and basic-level factories in various localities, regulating the supply of commodities, allocation of funds, and distribution of cadres.

Liu's introduction of "trusts" is taken to be a paradigm of "scientific management" and its objectification of men for the sake of "specialization, standardization, and systematization." The trusts brought management and "technical work" to the fore and introduced rules and systems to manage the masses, while letting cadres and political personnel "shut themselves up in the office reading statistical returns and reports and studying 'business methods.'" Granting trusts "enterprise autonomy" (i.e., allowing them to buy raw materials and sell their products on the market) contributes to the dissolution of proletarian dictatorship, making "politics" (or state planning) redundant and placing "rationalization on the principle of economic management" in command. It purportedly promotes "bourgeois dictatorship" by granting "highly centralized" monopolies and by untrammeling trust managers from "local interference" of Party committees. Implementation of trusts exemplifies the "crawling philosophy" of a "foreign slave": rather than rely on Mao's Thought and the native, creative abilities of the masses, Liu said, "We should learn from the . . . capitalist management of enterprises, monopoly enterprises in particular," and "we must learn from the Soviet Union and other fraternal countries their experiences in socialist construction." [83]

(3) In labor policy, Liu's major revisionism is "economism," which means reliance on material incentives and creation of a labor "market" that regulates itself by trading skills for commodities. Incentives were distributed on the basis of a graduated scale of pecuniary rewards, scrupuously geared to the social utility of the output and to a precise measurement of labor input. In agriculture, the system meant "work points in command," a steady reduction in the size of the unit of accountability in an effort ever more accurately to correlate rewards and penalties with labor input, and application of the infamous "three selfs and one guarantee" (san tzu i pao): "extension of plots for private

83 Ching Hung, "The Plot of the Top Ambitionist to Operate 'Trusts' on a Large Scale Must Be Thoroughly Exposed," KMJP, May 9, 1967, in SCMP, no. 3948 (July 25, 1967): 1–10; NCNA, March 25, 1968, in SCMP, no. 4148 (March 28, 1968): 23–26; "Down with Foreign Slave Philosophy," KMJP, March 22, 1969, in SCMP, no. 4395 (April 15, 1969): 4–7.

use, the rural free market, increase of small enterprises responsible for their own profits and losses," and "fixing of output quotas based on the individual household." Liu's responsibility for this policy is traced to an *in camera* statement he allegedly made in 1962:

All methods conducive to the mobilization of the peasants' enthusiasm for production during the transition period may be adopted. . . . Industry must retreat to a sufficient extent and so must agriculture, by fixing quotas based on the household and allowing individual farming.[84]

To create a labor "market" subject to the fluctuations of supply and demand, there was a general transformation of the relationship between worker and producer in production units from compulsory assignment of employees to organization units to contractural commitment. In agriculture, the earlier method of management at brigade level was formally replaced by a contractual relationship between brigade and team, with the team permanently in possession of the means of production. In industry, it meant piece-rate wages wherever possible and a "double-track labor system" of higher-paid, unionized, permanent workers on the one hand, and a "peasant-worker" program whereby migratory contract workers undertook "work and farming by [seasonal] rotation" on the other. Liu claimed the latter arrangement would narrow the difference between city and countryside, benefiting industry by reducing labor costs and benefiting communes by increasing income in rural areas.[85]

The criticism of more highly differentiated wage scales was that they enabled some people to "get rich through labor" and thus resulted in the reappearance of invidious (if not technically "class") distinctions, a prospect Liu evidently considered perfectly legitimate so long as rewards were based on labor rather than property or exploitation of others' labor. "The Soviet Union is free of exploitation; one who dresses himself beautifully . . . is one who labors well," he remarked in 1958. His critics, however, argued that distribution according to "quality and quantity" of labor input disproportionately rewarded those who had "capital assets, were technically competent, and had strong labor power" while placing "poor and lower-middle peasants, particularly those who had small children and little labor power and capital assets" at a marked disadvantage, systematically widening income disparities and impeding the transition to Com-

84 "Settle the Crimes of China's Khrushchev for Restoring Capitalism to the Countryside," *PD*, August 28, 1967, in *SCMP*, no. 4021 (September 14, 1967): 9–14.
85 "Liu Shao-ch'i Is the Chief Culprit Involved in Institution of System of Temporary Workers and Contract Laborers," *Hung-kung chan-pao* [Red workers' battle news] (Shanghai), February 6, 1967.

munism. For example, under the "three selfs and and guarantee" rich- and middle-peasant households in one area reportedly received 70 percent of the land in the form of "responsibility fields," although they made up only 53 percent of the populace, since efficiency took prece- dence over equity in the allocation of resources.[86]

In Liu's labor policy, unions were to serve two complementary functions: expand production in the public interest, and promote welfare in the workers' interest. The task of trade unions was "to struggle to raise labor productivity without cease through socialist emulation and the movement of advanced workers," Liu said after Liberation, and he allegedly felt "political slogans and political de- mands" were irrelevant. Thus, he advocated "class assimilation" and a whole people's union" so that "all those who have common economic demands can unite and get organized." In the same connection, he also advocated "syndicalism" (*kung-hui chung-hsin lun*), stressing that during the democratic revolutionary period unions were "indepen- dent" organizations and that "the Party and all mass organizations should be placed on an equal footing." "Be it the Party, the govern- ment, the army, or any popular organization, when it carries out mass work, it should accept the leadership of the mass organizations," he said; the Party "can only assist, but not exercise leadership over" the trade unions, which should have their own "systematic leadership." Furthermore, in an effort to "tempt and benumb us, make us forget about class struggle," Liu and the union leaders promoted "culture and welfare" for the workers, building theaters, workers' cultural palaces, and sanatoriums, to which workers were sent to "eat well, play well, and rest well." [87]

ANALYSIS

Opposition to Socialization—The two major economic criticism cate- gories, the accusations that Liu "shielded" capitalists and otherwise obstructed the socialization of the Chinese economy, are relatively easily testable on the basis of historical evidence. First, the "shielding" accusations are accurate but invalid. In his 1949 Tientsin speeches, two of which have been recently published, Liu was indeed quite out- spoken, as he apparently recognized at the time: "Recently I went to Tientsin; the capitalists were very happy, some of the workers were perhaps not so happy, but no matter, I sincerely planned for the work-

86 Cf. n. 84.
87 *PD*, June 18, 1968, in *SCMP*, no. 4201 (June 19, 1968): 17–25; *LD*, August 18, 1968, in *SCMP*, no. 4259 (September 17, 1968): 7–15; *PD*, November 20, 1968, in *SCMP*, no. 4309 (December 2, 1968): 1–8.

ers, they will see this in the future," he said. Liu soothed the apprehensions of the industrialists, assuring one Sung Fei-ch'ing, who had expressed concern lest he be accused of "exploiting," that he could thus "solve the problem of employment for many workers." "You are now exploiting more than 1,000 men; if you exploit more than 2,000 men that's even better, we want you to exploit more laborers!" To workers who proposed opening cooperative factories, he gave skeptical approval: "If you say you can run it, I will certainly let you run it, if you run it well." But although he advised the workers temporarily to subordinate themselves to private capitalists, he also defended the right of the workers to collective bargaining and redress of grievances, pointing out to the capitalists: "You capitalists have status . . . if the workers scold you a bit, you think you've lost face; but don't workers have status? Workers also have status, their political status is a little higher than yours. You think if you scold the workers, they don't feel the insults?" [88]

Liu's remarks, however unfelicitous, do not seem at any time to be out of step with the Party's General Line, as articulated by Mao. Kenneth Lieberthal provides convincing evidence that when the Red Army entered the cities, the initial policy was "revolutionary" to the point of threatening economic disaster; a major shift to the right occurred in both rural and urban areas following Mao's publication of "The Present Situation and Our Tasks" in December 1947.[89] In other speeches during the same general period, Mao bade workers to honor private labor contracts, encouraged the development of private capitalism, supported the cooptation of bourgeois managerial and technical personnel into the socialist sector, and even welcomed the investment of U.S. venture capital in China, often in the same phraseology Liu used.[90] The Party's General Line "shielded" private capi-

---

[88] "Tsai hua-pei chih-kung tai-piao-hui" [Work conference in North China], *LSWTC*, pp. 200–207.

[89] Cf. Kenneth Lieberthal, " 'Mao Versus Liu?' Policy Towards Industry and Commerce, 1946–1949," *CQ*, no. 47 (July–September 1971): 494–521.

[90] Mao stipulated in 1940 that workers should keep contracts with capitalist employers (*SW* 3: 220 ff.). In his interview with John Service in 1944, he proposed the industrialization of China by "free enterprise and with the aid of foreign capital." See n. 40. In a "CCP Directive on Diplomatic Work" issued within a few days of the Service interview, the third point stated: "With regard to economic questions—under conditions involved in the observance of mutual advantage we welcome international capital investments and technical cooperation." *Problemy Dal'nego Vostoka* (Moscow), No. 1, signed to press March 24, 1972. Barbara Tuchman published previously classified documents in 1972 indicating that in August 1945 Mao and Chou even offered to visit Washington to confer with Roosevelt to promote Sino-American cooperation. *Notes from China* (New York, 1972), pp. 77–78. In 1948 Mao proposed to "advocate the development of capitalism" under given

talist enterprises at the time of Liberation in order to prevent national economic collapse, because the pre-Liberation industrial and commercial system was, after all, based upon private property. For several years after Liberation the private sector continued to produce and export more than the public sector, not only in Tientsin, where Liu gave his notorious speeches, but nationwide.[91]

The allegation that Liu obstructed the socialization of the Chinese economy can be confirmed with regard to certain episodes, but his record is on the whole no more consistently conservative than that of, say, Chou En-lai. And it is interesting to note that these episodes all occurred in the agricultural, not the industrial, sector. Liu's early statements stressing the priority of mechanization over socialization and forecasting a rather slow pace of agricultural collectivization were perfectly consistent with Mao's contemporaneous statements on these issues, as well as with Mao's broader theoretical position, which characterized the 1949–54 period as a transitional stage of "people's democratic dictatorship," which was essentially different from "proletarian dictatorship" in that private property would continue to be an important part of the means of production, bourgeois political parties would be tolerated, and so forth.[92] The two confessed and empirically

conditions, echoing a similar statement in 1945 (*SW* 3: 281): "Foreign imperialism and native feudalism are things unneeded in China today but native capitalism is not; on the contrary, there is too little of it." *SW* 4: 275–276. A PLA directive issued in April 1959 (at the time of Liu's Tientsin speeches) states, "Protect the industrial, commercial, agricultural and livestock enterprises of the national bourgeoisie. All privately owned factories, shops, banks, warehouses, vessels . . . will without exception be protected against encroachment. It is hoped that workers and employees . . . will maintain production as usual and that all shops will remain open as usual.'

Liu's policy of socializing industry by coopting entrepreneurs into the state managerial sector is also consistent with central policy at the time. As early as 1939, Mao wrote "Recruit Large Numbers of Intellectuals" (*SW* 2: 301–305). In his Report to the Second Plenum in March 1949, he said that the proletarian dictatorship should "unite with as many as possible from the petty bourgeoisie and national bourgeoisie" and "We must learn to do economic work from all those who know how, no matter who they are, we must esteem them as teachers." *SW* 4: 423.

91 From 1949 to 1952, privately owned industries throughout China increased their gross output value by about 54 percent, while retail sales at privately owned commercial firms rose by about 20 percent. Franklin W. Houn, *A Short History of Chinese Communism* (Englewood Cliffs, N.J., 1967), p. 174.

92 In "On the People's Democratic Dictatorship" (1949), Mao wrote: "The steps toward socialization of agriculture must be coordinated with the development of a power industry using state enterprise as its backbone." *SW* 4: 419. In his June 6, 1950 speech to the Second Session of the People's Political Consultative Conference Mao said, "there should be a change in our policy toward the rich peasants, a change from the policy of requisitioning the surplus land and property of the rich peasants to one of preserving a rich peasant economy in order to further the restoration of production in the rural areas." He added that "The view held by

documented cases of Liu's obstructionism do not seem to be based on opposition to socialism per se but rather are concerned with the tactical issue of the appropriate degree of Party control (as opposed to mass spontaneity) in mobilization of the masses, the same issue that was to embroil Liu with the Maoists in the 1966 controversy over work teams. Liu perhaps overreacted to Mao's reproof that he had raised the "sweeping" slogan, "Do everything as the masses want it done," in his administration of land reform at P'ingshan in 1948, and he thereafter became much more circumspect in responding to mass initiatives. In his June 1950 speech, "On the Agrarian Reform Law," Liu said:

We request that, in those areas where it is decided not to carry out agrarian reform this year, it shall not be carried out. Even if the peasants should spontaneously go ahead with agrarian reform, they should be dissuaded from doing so. . . . Chaotic conditions must not be allowed to occur and no deviation or confusion may be allowed to remain uncorrected for long in our agrarian reform work in the future. Agrarian reform must be carried out under guidance, in a planned and orderly way, in complete accordance with the laws and decrees.[93]

Thus, when the Shansi Party Committee opted on its own initiative to "raise the mutual-aid teams another step" and organize agricultural producers' cooperatives (APCs), Liu wrote a document "erroneously criticizing" this act in July 1951. And again in 1955, when Teng Tzu-hui (then Director of the Party's Rural Work Department in charge of cooperation) made a convincing case that acceleration in collectivization had resulted in setting up many APCs without sufficient preparation to stand much chance of survival, a central work conference chaired by Liu approved Teng's proposal to dissolve 200,000 cooperatives.[94]

---

some people that it is possible to eliminate capitalism and introduce socialism at an early date is wrong and not in accordance with our national conditions." In his closing speech on June 23, Mao endorsed Liu's remarks on the rich peasant economy: "You have all endorsed Vice-Chairman Liu Shao-ch'i's report and the Draft Land Reform Law recommended by the CC. . . . This is good." K. Fan, ed., *Mao Tse-tung and Lin Piao: Post-Revolutionary Writings* (Garden City, N.Y., 1972), pp. 108, 93.

93 *CW* 2: 217.

94 By the fall of 1954, the number of APCs had reached 100,000 exceeding the original plan for 36,000. A Party resolution in October 1954 called for development of 600,000 APCs within one year, but, by the end of June 1955, 670,000 APCs had already been formed. According to an NCNA report of February 18, 1955 (*PD*, February 19), many of these had been established with little preparation; of the newly established ones, only 20–30 percent were comparatively good, while 50 percent were beset with problems, and the remaining 20 percent were on the verge of bankruptcy. According to information collected by Adrian Hsia, the number of pigs fell from 101,718,000 in July 1954 to 87,920,000 in July 1955, and to 84,400,000

There seems to have been a "consensus" (not unanimity) among Politburo members that opposed rapid collectivization at that time, but in a speech shortly afterward, Mao bitterly denounced the " 'drastic compression' policy":

Throughout the Chinese countryside a new upsurge in the socialist movement is in sight. But some of our comrades are tottering along like a woman with bound feet and constantly complaining, "You're going too fast." Excessive criticism, inappropriate complaints, endless anxiety, and the erection of countless taboos—they believe this is the proper way to guide the socialist mass movement in the rural areas.[95]

After Mao articulated these views on July 31, 1955, Liu reportedly made a self-criticism and fell into line. He then shifted to the left, becoming one of the staunchest backers of the Leap (which Chou apparently opposed); his subsequent misgivings with regard to the Leap were due not to the ambitious scale and speed of the undertaking but to the lack of disciplined organization and leadership in implementation. As he summarized his views in a speech to the conference of 7,000 cadres in January 1962:

We failed to conduct adequate investigations and studies or to carry out full consultations with the masses of workers and peasants and with basic-level cadres and technical specialists. We failed to do things strictly in accord with democratic centralism in Party organizations, state organizations, and the organizations of the masses, and yet we arrived at decisions rashly and implemented them in wide areas. Moreover, things were done in short order. This was a violation of the traditional styles of the Party in seeking truth from facts and of the mass line.[96]

Revisionism—The second major economic criticism category comprises Liu's "revisionist" innovations, most of which were instituted in 1960–64; these are confessed (with certain minor qualifications), for the most part accurate, and probably valid, though Stuart Schram has

---

in July 1956. Many provincial papers reported a drastic reduction in draft animals as well; fields were not well worked; and the scarcity of food supplies was so serious that provincial first secretaries criticized planning errors. Adrian Hsia, *The Chinese Cultural Revolution* (New York, 1972), pp. 114–118. Another student of this period states, "Reading the full and frank reports published in China on the campaign, it is impossible to avoid the conclusion that like its predecessor in 1952 it was marred by widespread violations of basic principles, only they were on a grander scale and carried more serious consequences." Kenneth R. Walker, "Collectivization in Retrospect: The 'Socialist High Tide' of Autumn 1955–Spring 1956," *CQ*, no. 26 (April–June 1966): 18.

95 "On the Question of Agricultural Cooperation" (July 31, 1955), in *SRWM*, pp. 389–420.

96 "Selected Edition," *SCMM*, no. 652 (April 28, 1969): 24–26.

suggested that differences between Mao and Liu did not become clearly manifest until after Mao initiated the "class struggle" theme in 1962.[97] The general validity of these criticisms bears out Franz Schurmann's 1964 judgment that "individuals in very high places in China have been giving serious thought to a basic approach to economic development that is neither a return to the Soviet model of centralized planning nor a return to the Great Leap Forward guerrilla-type mobilization and production." [98] The dimensions of Liu Shao-ch'i's "revisionism" will be analyzed in the same sequence as their previous exposition.

(1) The critical characterization of Liu's agricultural mechanization policies seems to be accurate: for example, mass research was downgraded after 1960 and replaced by expertise, careful testing, and prudent popularization of farm tools. Mao's county and special district "mass research institutes" were indeed "chopped down": only ninety-two of several hundred of these GLF artifacts remained by 1961. In the same year, Liu directed that "improvement of farm tools should not be undertaken by factories in counties or districts but by experimental engineers in factories at the provincial level." [99] It should be pointed out, however, that these decisions came in reaction to clear failures of GLF policies, which Liu had initially supported, and do not necessarily indicate a long-term "revisionist line." With regard to state-run tractor stations versus commune ownership, for instance, Liu concurred with Mao's 1958 decision at Chengtu to transfer tractors to commune ownership and operation. "The state has to spend sums of money to build the tractors, and another sum . . . has to be lost in the end," he reasoned. "It is better to send them to the grass-roots level." Not until the National Conference on Tractor Station Work in 1962 did Liu propose tractor stations, arguing that "the original set of rules and regulations has gone to pieces, and the machines are utilized at a lower rate and severely damaged." [100] Liu's record with respect to mass participation in development of indigenous, small-

97 Stuart R. Schram, "Mao Tse-tung and Liu Shao-ch'i, 1939–1969," AS 12, no. 4 (April 1972): 275–294.

98 Franz Schurmann, "China's 'New Economic Policy'—Transition or Beginning?" CQ, no. 17 (January–March 1964): 65–92.

99 NYCHCS no. 9 (1968), in SCMM, no. 633 (November 4, 1968): 1–45.

100 NYCHCS, no. 6 (September 18, 1967), in SCMM, no. 610 (January 15, 1968): 5–10. By the end of 1958, 70 percent of all tractors were operated by communes, but peasants were "unprepared," and, because the Agricultural Mechanization Ministry was dissolved in order to rely more fully on the initiative of the masses, the peasants were left without leadership or instruction and allowed the machinery to deteriorate. "Equipment which originally could be used for ten years lasted only five years," Liu reported in 1962. "While equipment was often damaged, no attention was paid to repair and maintenance."

scale farm implements was also quite flexible; the essential difference between Mao and Liu on this issue seemed to be that in the pursuit of maximum participation Liu was somewhat more constrained by considerations of economic feasibility.[101]

The criticisms do not deal with the question of economic feasibility, condemning Liu rather for his lack of faith in Mao's Thought and the masses and for his amoral regard for expediency. Yet the generally moderate nature of post-Liu reforms suggests that this question has not been ignored. The financial burden of agricultural mechanization has been shifted back to the communes, and district propaganda teams have been sent down to persuade peasants to invest their collective income in machinery rather than consumption; both moral pressure and tax assessments have also been used to induce the cities to contribute to agricultural mechanism. In contrast to the pre-GPCR industrialization strategy, which was based on an assumption that "resources or manpower, material, and funds for capital construction are necessarily limited [and if] they are spread out then development will be slowed down and manpower, materials, and funds will be wasted," [102] the GPCR repudiated the "theory of conditions" (t'iao-chien lun) and averred that many things can be done with simple things. This policy resulted in the greatest upsurge of mass entrepreneurship at the county level and below since the GLF, a flowering of "small local industries" producing such things as cement, lathes, nitrate fertilizer, and so on and depending on local manpower and funds, indigenous equipment and skills.[103] The production of agri-

101 From 1950 to 1956, with Liu's apparent concurrence, the introduction of seven-inch or eight-inch walking plows, three-tined tillage hoes, iron water-wheels, animal-pulled farm implements (double-wheel and double-blade plows, animal-pulled sowers, shaker-type harvesters) led to overproduction of new-fangled farm tools in 1956 (particularly double-wheel and double-blade plows), and the question of adaptability was overlooked in the course of popularization. Thereafter, Liu and others (including Chou) protested against "adventurism" in the disregard for "sources of materials, the balance between supply, production, and marketing, and the formulation of practical material plans." Yet, in 1958, at the Ch'engtu Conference (chaired by Mao), it was decided again that farm mechanization should proceed by "self-reliant" methods and by "mass movement for the reform of farm implements." This movement, however, fizzled for lack of popular enthusiasm. "History of Struggle Between Two Lines," NYCHCS, no. 9 (1968), in SCMM, no. 633 (November 4, 1968): 1–35.

102 Ta-kung pao (Peking), May 7, 1965.

103 An NCNA report from Kwangsi on February 27, 1970, reported operation of 174 factories by twenty-two communes and 428 small factories and workshops in production brigades on the outskirts of P'inghsiang. The total output of these farm-machinery and farm-implement factories, small cement works, insecticide plants, lime kilns, and coal pits was said to be more than half the city's total industrial output in 1969. CNS, no. 312 (March 19, 1970): A1–A7. Also CNA, no. 784 (December 5, 1969): 1–7. See also Carl Riskin, "Rural Industry: Self-Reliant

cultural machinery has also been decentralized to the commune and district levels, resulting in some disruption of the output of large tractors, but an increase in the production of hand-operated small tractors.[104]

(2) There is little doubt that greater scope was given to market forces in 1960–64 than they received during the Leap. The use of the market is by no means unprecedented in China, but, following the Leap, Party control was reduced and greater play was allowed for the market mechanism than ever before in the exchange of both agricultural and industrial commodities. This policy resulted in rural fairs or village markets for the exchange of small handicraft items produced by domestic side-line industries, commodity exchange exhibitions, the beginnings of market research and commercial advertising.[105] As a necessary precondition to the flexibility required by the market, a degree of entrepreneurial initiative and control over resources almost tantamount to private property was permitted.[106] The program

---

Systems or 'Independent Kingdoms,' " in untitled book (New York, forthcoming), ed. Jim Peck and Victor Nee.

[104] For example, in Kiangsi, the output of hand-operated tractors in 1968 increased six-fold over 1967. Radio Honan, August 8, September 28, 1968, quoted in Chu-yüan Cheng, "The Effects of the Cultural Revolution on China's Machine-Building Industry," *CS* 8, no. 1 (January 1, 1970): 7.

[105] Rural fairs, popularized by extensive press coverage, were encouraged at the end of 1960 and developed not only as a medium of exchange between individual peasant and state stores but also between villages and towns and between communes and other production units. The Ninth Plenum in January 1961 directed that small and medium firms might buy raw materials directly from the market, rather than through wholesale corporations whose allocations were determined by central plan. A planned market existed alongside the open market as a legitimate medium of exchange. Attempts were made to introduce market research (enterprise visiting teams were sent to department stores or consumers; exhibitions and quality contests were held), commercial advertising (hand-painted billboards and magazine and newspaper ads), rural "service departments," whose function was to buy and sell and to "organize" links between producers and merchants. Jan Prybyla, *The Political Economy of Communist China* (Scranton, Pa., 1970), *passim;* Gargi Dutt, "Some Problems of China's Rural Communes," *CQ*, no. 16 (November–December 1963): 112–137; George Ecklund, "Protracted Expropriation of Private Business in Communist China," *Pacific Affairs* 36, no. 3 (fall 1963): 228–249.

[106] By 1965, slightly more than 8 percent of the cultivated land had been distributed to the peasants in private plots, and these plots' average yield was twice that of community-owned land. Shahid Javed Burki, *A Study of Chinese Communes, 1965* (Cambridge, Mass., 1969), pp. 37–40. Collective farms began leasing sideline operations, such as fishponds, to individual farmers; after April 1962, a policy was adopted of allowing city dwellers to obtain licenses to practice service trades and to operate repair shops, after paying a fixed fee, they were entitled to keep all profits. Farmers' stalls and peddlers flourished. The ownership and control of economic resources was officially assigned to various levels of local administration; e.g., teams were to own lands and farming tools and to control the agricultural labor of their populations. "Independent accounting" status meant

combined central supervision through economic accounting with relatively wide freedom of action at the enterprise level in contracting, and quasi-market systems in agriculture and wholesaling. Equalization was stressed less than economic responsibility and enterprise, and "politics" was no longer so undisputably "in command."

"Profit in command," is on the other hand an overstatement. Although a brief debate arose among academic economists (abruptly stifled in 1962), several of whom advocated almost exclusive reliance on profit an an indicator of efficiency as well as the reduction of Party control over farms, factories, and individual producers and a laissez-faire policy regarding the direction of investment, these proposals were never implemented, and the relative importance of profit as an indicator of enterprise efficiency in fact remained fairly constant from 1957 through 1966.[107] Furthermore, the SEM did issue more stringent regulations on sideline occupations and private trade and sought to curtail individualism by bolstering the internal solidarity of the production unit (team, brigade, commune): after 1963, use of the market was overwhelmingly by the collective unit rather than the individual and distribution of unit income remained thoroughly collective. Restrictions on private trade included the classification of retail merchandise at the rural trade fairs into three categories, only one of which might be traded freely.[108]

---

that each unit was required to pay the costs of the facilities it controlled out of its after-tax income. In 1960, special instructions provided that communes and battalions must always pay for any manpower they mobilized for basic construction, and that mobilization should not exceed 3 percent of total manpower. Reiitsu Kokima, "Construction of a 'Self-Sustaining National Economy' in China," *Sekai*, November 1966, in *Survey of Selected Japanese Magazines* (Tokyo), November 14, 1966, pp. 1–15; John C. Pelzel, "Economic Management of a Production Brigade in Post-Leap China," in *Economic Organization in Chinese Society*, ed. W. E. Wilmott (Stanford, Calif., 1972), pp. 387–417.

107 Actually, the Party demoted the "gross output value" target from its "commanding" position and virtually substituted profit in its formulation of the decentralization decisions of November 1957, as Schurmann points out. "China's 'New Economic Policy,'" pp. 68 ff. This regulation of profits appears to have remained in force with little major alteration throughout the 1960s, except that an effort was made to reduce the size of the retained portion. In addition to profit, other success indicators, such as fulfillment of output quotas, were utilized. Barry Richman notes that profit was one of the most important success indicators at most of the enterprises he visited, but the clear-cut top indicator at only a few. *Industrial Society;* also Dwight H. Perkins, "Incentives and Profits in Chinese Industry: The Challenge of Economics to Ideology's Machine," *CS* 4, no. 10 (May 15, 1966): 1–10.

108 The categories: (1) first-category goods (e.g., grain, cotton, and oil-bearing materials), which cannot be sold at rural trade fairs; (2) second-category goods, which can be sold only after farmers meet their quotas for compulsory sale to the states; (3) third-category goods (vegetables, poultry, and handicrafts) which may be traded freely. Buyer and seller agree on prices, but only sales between producer and final consumer are permitted, eliminating transactions by middlemen for exchange value. George N. Ecklund, "Protracted Expropriation."

Liu's penchant for administrative efficiency, as exemplified by the introduction of "socialist trusts," allowed economic considerations to take precedence over political values (such as worker participation or equalization) at the enterprise level. Reference to 1964–65 issues of *Economic Research* (*Ching-chi yen-chiu*), *Ta-kung pao*, and *PD* confirms that coordination was introduced between similar industrial processes, with extensions of planning to allow three- to six-month contracts between factories and their suppliers; for example, by 1964–65, the Agricultural Mechanization Ministry's functions were subordinated by the newly emerging "trusts," and by 1965 nearly half the smaller local plants were shut down. These "trusts" involved "specialization" and sharing operational—but not policy—responsibility with factory managers in a more "perpendicular" reorganization of industries, which increased coordination between plants and subcontractual relationships with suppliers. Criticisms of Liu's emphasis on "big, foreign, comprehensive" (*ta-yang-ch'üan*) industries seem slightly misconceived, for, in the trusts, large, inefficient, "self-contained" plants were to give way to small and medium-sized "specialized" plants: *function*, not size, formed the basis for reorganization.[109] As E. L. Wheelwright and Bruce McFarlane point out, the animus of the program was not exactly populist:

Physical evidence from power, chemical, and coal-mining industries during 1960–62 shows definitely that the concept of small-scale and medium-scale development continued to be applied. But the policy of "walking on two legs" was increasingly associated with emphasis on mechanization and modernization of small and medium enterprises, and with the spread of technological improvements. There was a greater emphasis on quality of output and expansion of a variety of types in the product-mix.[110]

Criticisms of the principle of "managing the economy by economic methods" ("It is undesirable to bring other questions into the matter, Liu is quoted as saying. "What is to be considered is the question of rationalization on the principle of economic management.") are based only in part on Liu's implicit denial of the general applicability of Mao's Thought. Liu also invoked the functionally specialized expertise of the technical and managerial disciplines to justify his injunctions against "administrative," "supra-economic" local Party interference in enterprise affairs; according to his critics, this approach sub-

109 Editor, "Industrial Development in China: A Return to Decentralization," *CS* 6, no. 22 (December 20, 1968); Editor, "The Conflict Between Mao Tse-tung and Liu Shao-ch'i over Agricultural Mechanization," *CS* 6, no. 17 (October 1, 1968). By 1966, two-thirds of the value of agricultural machinery production came from local medium and small plants.

110 E. L. Wheelwright and Bruce McFarlane, *The Chinese Road to Socialism: Economics of the Cultural Revolution* (New York, 1970), pp. 50 ff.

verted proletarian dictatorship by subtracting power from both the masses and the Party bureaucracy and placing it in the hands of a professional intelligentsia.[111] Measured in terms of the economic criteria for which they were chosen, however, Liu's techniques appear to have been successful: one official estimate is that industrial production rose by 15 percent in 1964, and by more than this in 1965.[112] In agriculture, the Liuist developmental strategy of concentrating resources in the most efficient base (viz., the rich farm areas and the old industrial cities) and expanding from there along lines dictated by economic considerations had, by 1964, secured a satisfactory rate of farm output at low cost, which was firmly rooted in the supply of industrial inputs to agriculture: farm output, using the benchmark years of good crop weather, grew by 6 percent annually in 1964–67.[113]

Liu's fall has been followed by good faith attempts to reorient the industrial sector in a direction more consistent with GLF policies, which have nonetheless been implemented with prudence. The relative importance of profit among post-GPCR enterprise success indicators seems to have declined, with the result that "infant industries" have been permitted to operate at a loss under government subsidy.[114] Control of a professional elite over industrialization has been supplanted by a more regulative bureaucracy headed by enterprise RCs,

111 At the Ninth Plenum in 1961, authority at the enterprise level was shifted from the Party committee to the administrators and technicians, so that factory managers would be in a position to exercise the flexibility that the 1957 decentralization decisions had granted to their cadre predecessors. Since 1961, there had been a stress on the "independent managerial authority" inherent in the concept of "economic accounting": factory managers were given broad discretion to set their own commodity mixes; banks, financial officers, and technical accountants in enterprises and state organs acquired authority over financial transactions; engineers gained control over the production process; factory adminstration was recentralized, with major decisions being made at the executive level. "If the Party were suddenly to disappear from the country, and given all the other tendencies we have already described, it is not hard to imagine that China would revert to a kind of state capitalism, politically based on a ruling class of professional intellectuals." Schurmann, "China's 'New Economic Policy,'" p. 86.

112 Harald Munthe-Kaas, "Sweeping Dust Away," FEER 53, no. 13 (September 29, 1966): 606–612.

113 Edwin F. Jones, "Economic Planning: In Search of a Model," CS 10, no. 10 (October 1972): 18–25.

114 "For us production is a matter of quantity; that is, statistics, not bookkeeping," a factory official told Mehnert in 1971, suggesting the high priority given to gross output. "We've filled our quota for the past year, and that's all there is to it." Klaus Mehnert, China Returns (New York, 1972), p. 78. Peking seems to have figured that any new business will lose money for a year or two and so assumes broad responsibility for the survival of initially unprofitable infant industries. One report told of workers who proclaimed, "to benefit agriculture we are determined to run these factories, even if we make a loss for a time." NCNA, May 11, 1969, in Editor, "Peking's Program to Move Human and Material Resources to the Countryside," CS 7, no. 18 (September 15, 1969): 10.

which include workers in leadership positions and provision for the regular rotation of management.[115] Technical expertise has been debunked in a campaign to publicize the ingenuity of untrained proletarian innovators, whose contribution in undercapitalized conditions has often been impressive.[116] Emphasis on "big and modern" industries has been supplanted (there has been little new capital construction in the "big and modern" sector since 1966) [117] by revival of the "walking on two legs" policy, which stresses "small local industry" and creation of labor-intensive intermediate technology, based largely in the countryside (hence exempt from the state minimum wage legislation and able to draw on a cheaper rural labor pool). The emphasis on more primitive industry includes workshops, electric power stations, even a small iron-mill program—reminiscent of, but more sophisticated than, the GLF "backyard steel" project. The commodity markets have been subjected to more stringent political controls in what Peking terms "completion of the socialization of commerce": the state market now dominates, and even supply and marketing cooperatives do business on the basis of a state plan; the peddlers and hawkers have been organized into cooperatives, and the fairs in the countryside are also under state management with controlled prices.[118] Planning has been

[115] In addition to supervisory positions on factory RCs, "workers' investigation groups" have been set up to act as "watchdog" teams on management. At the beginning of 1970, the Hung Hsiang-chiang machinery plant was assigned to trial produce a new product, and it requested sixty sets of new equipment. A "special investigation group" set up by workers found that 14 percent of the equipment in the factory had been lying idle and 17 percent had "hardly been used at all." The group wrote a poster containing "sharp criticism" of certain leaders, and the situation was rectified.

[116] Methods have been devised to convert waste gas with a low content of sulphur dioxide into sulfuric acid; to expand China's chemical industry by making nitrogenous fertilizer, synthesizing benzine, producing methanol at low cost, and developing antibiotics. *China Science News* 1, no. 2 (March 1970): 1 ff. (hereafter *CSN*). With the opening of CPR trade contacts with the West and Japan, the campaign against the "foreign slaves mentality" has, however, abated. "We oppose the traitorous policy of 'imports first,' but at the same time we do not want to deny the necessity of importing technical know-how," a recent statement phrased it. *CSN* 1, no. 3 (June 1970). The current Five-Year Plan (begun in 1971) proposes to draw on foreign technology and increase foreign trade. See J. K. Galbraith, "Galbraith Has Seen China's Future—and It Works," *NYT Magazine*, November 26, 1972, pp. 38 ff.

[117] With regard to large plants subordinate to the ministries in Peking, the policy has been to increase output by "raising the capacity of the existing equipment, instead of by building new factories or installing additional equipment." NCNA, April 20, 1969. The fact that most press reports made no mention of direct control of factories by ministries in 1968–1970 suggests that the industrial expansion during these years was almost entirely locally financed and controlled.

[118] This information is based on Robert Scalapino's interview with an official of the Commerce Department in Peking during a visit to China from December 11, 1972 to January 6, 1973.

reinstituted but operates "from the bottom to the top": the central planning authorities deal only with consolidated plans forwarded by the provinces (the center does set the main priorities, however, and the planning authorities to which a unit must report are also determined by the source of that unit's original capital).[119] Peking's overall industrial production apparently recovered in 1969 to the 1966 pre-GPCR level; industrial production in 1970 was reportedly not only higher than in 1966 but reached the record level attained in 1959. In 1969, Peking's two-way foreign trade volume reached about $3.9 billion, 5 percent higher than 1968, but still some 8 percent below the 1966 level.[120]

(3) The criticisms of Liu's "economistic" labor policies are accurate and essentially valid. In accord with the socialist principle of "pay according to labor and exchange of equal values," Liu attempted to extend the influence of money, to rationalize income payment generally, and to base payments on a clearly differentiated wage scale and an exact accounting of labor input in both industry and agriculture. This approach entailed recognition and acceptance of inequality, rather than leveling those who excelled (as during the Leap): productive workers were regarded as "models" for their less productive colleagues and rewarded in both material and moral terms. As Liu put it in a 1963 conversation with Po I-po:

It appears that promotion . . . of comparing with, learning from, catching up with the advanced and helping the backward is better than the past method of abstractly calling for exertion of efforts and aiming high, for it [the latter] can produce blindness.[121]

In industry, piece-rates, though preferably for teams rather than for individuals, were stressed; by the end of 1961, almost all Chinese industry was run on a time-rate plus bonus basis or on a strict piecework basis.[122] The "double-track labor system," which made possible the exploitation of seasonal farm labor at lower cost on a contractual basis, did not originate with Liu (in fact, during the Great Leap, 26.5

119 Joseph Alsop, "Doing It Yourself," NYT Magazine, March 18, 1973, pp. 16 ff.; see also Robert Dernberger, "Radical Ideology and Economic Development in China," AS 12, no. 12 (December 1972): 1963.

120 NYT, November 19, 1969, p. 10; January 19, 1970, pp. 1, 58; January 18, 1971, p. 46; Tai Sung An, Mao Tse-tung's Cultural Revolution (New York, 1972), p. 118.

121 Conversation of October 21, 1963, in "Selected Edition," SCMM, no. 652 (April 28, 1969): 23

122 Cf. Charles Hoffman, "Work Increases in Communist China," Industrial Relations no. 2 (1964): 96–98; "Work Incentive Policy in Communist China," CQ, no. 17 (January–March 1964): 92–111; and Work Incentive Policies and Practices in the People's Republic of China, 1953–1965 (Albany, N.Y., 1967), p. 106 et passim.

percent of the work force, or 12 million workers, were contract workers), but he apparently opted for its extension. In 1963, the State Council issued a directive that all who were temporary or contract workers should be made permanent workers, but on the basis of his fact-finding trip to Hupei in 1964, Liu objected. On the strength of his report, the Labor Ministry formulated a "Revision of the Draft Regulation on the Use and Management of Contract Workers" (1964) which encouraged their use; subsequently the contract worker system became widely publicized as the "part-worker, part-peasant" system.[123]

In agriculture, the attempt more precisely to correlate rewards with work led, on the one hand, to continual reduction of the unit of production and accounting [124] and, on the other, to elaborate schemes to correlate work points to labor input. Cadres were instructed to "set norms scientifically and record work-points strictly." [125] Because of the accounting acumen and complex organizational requirements of the preferred piece-rate (an chien chi ch'ou) measurement method for individual reimbursement or for the reward of bridgades and teams responsible for implementing their own production norms (the san pao i chiang system),[126] in certain localities (e.g., Anhwei, Fukien) there was a reversion to reward systems that were simpler to administer and corresponded to the previous experience of both cadres and peasants. "Three selfs and one guarantee," which appeared in July–October 1961, put peasants and cadres in a position analogous to the accustomed landlord-tenant relationship: the team controlled the land

123 Lao-tung chan-pao [Workers' battle news], February 3, 1968; also Shou-tu hung-wei-ping [Red Guards of the capital], no. 21 (January 10, 1967), in John W. Lewis, "Commerce, Education, and Political Development in Tangshan, 1956–1969," in Lewis, The City, pp. 163–165.

124 In February 1959 the decision was made by Party leaders under Liu to decentralize the accounting unit from the commune to the production team [sheng-ch'an tui] of 200 to 300 households; in the winter of 1960, the production team of this size was renamed the production brigade [sheng-ch'an ta-tui] while the production sub-team [sheng-ch'an hsiao-tui] of forty peasants was renamed the production team. In the winter of 1961, the accounting unit was further decentralized from the brigade to the team. The size of the team was further reduced during the early 1960s, until it finally comprised only twenty to thirty households. Even so, there were repeated reports of peasants' efforts to "split the production team."

125 Kung Shih-ch'i, "Serious Implementation of the Principle of Exchange of Value," PD, May 20, 1961, in SCMP no. 2508 (June 2, 1961): 5–11.

126 One production team, for example, was lauded for maintaining 1,192 different daily quotas for various tasks, all of which had to be examined at year's end for possible revision. Of this total, 226 were frequently revised according to changing conditions. A sliding scale was devised for many tasks to provide suitable adjustments for bad weather and for "shock effects" when work was accelerated. Only a few jobs remained on a flat day-rate system. "How a Production Team in the Peking Suburbs Enforces Quota Control and Assesses Work and Awards Wage Points," PD, May 22, 1961, in SCMP, no. 2515 (June 13, 1961): 10–18.

and the individual household assumed "responsibility" for it and supplied the labor. The method was popular among local cadres because it supplied a strong incentive for high production (peasants were not rewarded in cash but in work points whose value was determined after the annual harvest) and was easy to administer; peasants liked it because they had a part in negotiating the contracts, and it gave them more freedom than other work measurement methods. The center disliked it because it encouraged individualism (peasants tended to work on their contracted plots and to neglect collective plots) and disrupted state planning. Liu admitted that he was present when these proposals were raised and did not object to them, allowing them to acquire legitimacy.[127]

At the same time, it should be noted that Mao and other surviving elites have also quietly acquiesced to such capitalist measures in the countryside at various times in the history of cooperation.[128] Moreover, these experiments had a short lease on life, both because of Mao's attacks on "three selfs and one guarantee" at the Peitaiho Politburo Conference (August 1962) and at the Tenth Plenum (September 1962), and because reforms of the incentive system did not produce adequate results; after 1962, increased centralization was undertaken to plug gaps in the control system. Polemical hyperbole should not lead one to lose perspective: incentive policy under Liu operated within relatively narrow limits, well below those applied in China's first five-year plan or in the Soviet Union.[129]

Post-Liu reforms of the wage system have largely eliminated differ-

127 "Self-Examination" (October 23, 1966), in *LSWTC*, pp. 621–625.

128 The "three selfs and one guarantee" policy has a long history. Its appearance since 1956 has coincided with agricultural production crises, to which it was regarded as a stopgap solution; e.g., in 1956–1957, when collectivization was getting under way, and during the "three bad years" after the Leap. Reports of the application of this solution in areas close to cities suggest even more flagrant use in deeply rural areas where cadres exercised looser control, because reporters usually investigate conditions near their home base. There seems also to be a correspondence between those areas reporting *san tzu i pao* and rice-producing areas in South China where Buck found the landlord-peasant system most deeply entrenched. John Lossing Buck, *Land Utilization in China* (New York, 1968), 1: 194–196.

After a period of debate, the Party decided to repudiate this method in late summer of 1957; after a negative speech by Teng Tzu-hui in October of that year, all press conferences on the method repudiated its use. The striking absence of commentary from the center on the issue (only three articles in the national media between 1957 and the GPCR) may be a sign of continued disagreement; most references denouncing the method originated in the provincial press. Frederick Crook, "Labor Production Contracts to Households, 1956–1970" (unpub. paper, Washington, D.C., 1971). See also Crook's "Chinese Communist Agricultural Incentive Systems and the Labor Productive Contracts to Households, 1946–1965," *AS* 13, no. 5 (May 1973): 470–482.

129 Hoffman, *Work Incentive*, p. 106.

entials based on *market* exigencies (i.e., the complex bonus system has been abolished, piece-rates have been replaced by time payments, wages are stipulated and not related to enterprise results) while maintaining moderate differentials based on *status* (within a factory, visitors report that the rate tends to vary between 35 and 110 *yüan* per month, variations being based largely on the seniority principle, which serves a welfare as much as an incentive function). This system entails a basic departure from allocation of workers through a "labor market" to reliance on a mixture of moral incentives and administrative fiat to allocate labor.[130] Reforms of the structure of material incentives in the countryside seem to have been more moderate, perhaps because the peasantry was less affected by the revolutionizing impact of the GPCR. In any case, the work-point system and the "three selfs" (private plots, rural free markets, domestic industries) seem to have survived, despite periodic experimentation with (and radical agitation for) more egalitarian alternatives; only the "one guarantee" (fixing of output quotas based on the individual household) has been repealed.[131] Visitors to a "model" commune near Shanghai in 1971 were surprised to find that 25 percent of the peasant families' income still came from private plots.[132]

[130] For an economic analysis of the moral incentive system in the allocation of labor in another socialist economy, cf. Robert M. Bernardo, *The Theory of Moral Incentives in Cuba* (University, Ala., 1971).

[131] Following publication of a favorable article in March 1966 by Ch'en Yung-kuei there was widespread promotion of the Tachai "pace-setter" work-point system, according to which peasants worked collectively at tasks set by the team leaders and then at the end of the year voted rewards for the tasks that were based on both ideological and work merit. *PD* stated on November 24, 1968, that the system was not perfect and was still evolving. In late 1968, there were reports that a reorganization of the communes, including a change in the work-point and supply system, would take place in 1969. Discussions were initiated among peasants on the best method of distributing incomes and supplies, and in some communes new systems were implemented. Discussion continued into the spring farming season of 1969, when the campaign was quietly dropped. Then, on February 23, 1970, *PD* carried an authoritative article prescribing the socialist principle of "from each according to his ability, to each according to his labor." Since then, the earnings system in most places has been adjusted to reward those who worked hard, even apparently at Tachai; articles have appeared blaming "swindlers like Liu Shao-ch'i" (reference to Ch'en Po-ta) for banning "rational rewards" and "work points based on fixed quotas." *NYT*, May 7, 1972, p. 17; Editor, "Pre-Cultural Revolution Economic Policies to the Fore," *CS* 10, no. 8 (August 1972): 21–23. The 1969 Party Constitution formalized the "three-level" ownership system, with the team remaining the "basic accounting unit."

[132] Committee of Concerned Asian Scholars, *China: Inside the People's Republic* (New York, 1972), p. 170.

CULTURAL THEMES

CRITIQUE

The Chinese define "culture" (*wen-hua*) very broadly (as in "Cultural Revolution"); it seems to include the arts, education, journalism, science and technology, and medicine. The criticisms of Liu in all these fields concentrated on two tendencies: functional specialization of knowledge, which fractures ideological unity; and hierarchical institutionalization, which stratifies society and inhibits popularization.

Functional Specialization—Liu seemed to feel that each field had its own immanent laws requiring a functional differentiation of knowledge and the methodology to comprehend them; hence he advocated relaxation of the political controls inherent in the Party's claim to a monopoly on truth. In art, this approach entailed artistic freedom to create and audience freedom to consume. "Banning a book is like shooting a person to death," he rebuked a censor in 1952. "Who had authorized you people to ban publications?" His misinterpretation of Mao's "Hundred Flowers" policy to mean "bourgeois liberalization" ignored the persistence of bourgeois memories in China's largely Western-educated cultural elites, who exploited liberalization to revive the "dead" (the pre-1949 literary heritage, including "writers of the 1930s") and "foreign" (Soviet or Western films, music, and literature).[133]

In education, Liu cultivated "expertise" and downplayed "redness," advocating study "behind closed doors" rather than revolutionary practice. "You have to concentrate on your studies," he admonished students in 1948; "You may inquire about things happening outside the window, but you should not be distracted from your studies thereby." To motivate acquisition of "skills," he appealed to competi-

[133] In 1949 he said, "There is nothing to fear from propagandizing feudal art . . . haven't we triumphed after all?" He declared in 1955 that reprinting old books was permissible "so long as they are wholesome, harmless and salable. Parts of such old books that seem harmful need not be cut out but commentary notes may be added to them in reprinting." Regarding the "foreign," he wrote in a directive to the Cultural Ministry on March 8, 1958: "All cinema films of the world, as long as they are either progressive or harmless, may be imported. These may enable the people to have a glimpse of the social life of other peoples of the world and to gain some worldly knowledge. In short, all good things of the world are wanted by us. . . . The United States meddles with an Iron Curtain, we do not." "Violently Bombard China's Khrushchev," *Chieh-fang chün wen-i* [Liberation army art and literature], no. 12 (August 10, 1967), in *SCMM*, no. 605 (January 8, 1968): 15–26; "Chronology of Events in the Struggle," *Wen-hua ko-ming t'ung-hsün* 11 (May 1967), in *CB*, no. 842 (January 27, 1969): 1–17; "Tempestuous Combat on Literature and Art Front," *Shou-tu hung-wei-ping*, June 7, 1967, in *CB*, no. 842, pp. 17 ff.

tive, egoistic drives rather than altrustic motives, and the school system thus became a ladder for shrewd bourgeois careerists (e.g., the "three-door student," who went from school to college to office and never came into contact with ordinary people), while exams and marks eliminated spirited proletarian children. It is for this reason, not because they "suffered great hardships" and "insults," that Red Guards resented being "sent down" (*hsia fang*) to work in the countryside.[134]

In journalism, Liu advocated an independent editorial policy ("I stand for opening the doors wide," he said in 1948, using one of his favorite metaphors. "Different views should be accommodated. The press should be allowed a bit of liberalism."), and a mixture of "objective, truthful, and impartial" news reporting with feature articles frankly intended to appeal to the tastes of the readers. Liu made "three great accusations" of the media: "formalism and one-sidedness," and "simplification or vulgarization." In the spring of 1961 he said that NCNA's reporting of the Leap was "habitual lying." "You mention only goodness but not defects and mistakes," he complained. "I never read your headlines. Never." "If policies are wrong, you should report the errors and dig out the material proof."

When Premier Chou En-lai reviles the U.S., the news would appear in some U.S. capitalist newspapers. Why can the capitalist papers dare to carry abuse against them, and why don't we have enough courage to publish their invectives against us? [135]

Liu recommended "news for the whole people," urging journalists to "investigate people of various kinds and from various strata" and "report what they dare not say . . . what they are not willing to say,

---

134 The criticisms of *hsia-fang* are internally contradictory, leading one to suspect opposition to *hsia-fang* itself rather than merely to the negative connotation Liu attached to it. On the one hand, Liu is blamed for derogating *hsia-fang* to a channel for downward mobility: "Youths who can neither continue their studies nor find employment in the cities should go to the countryside." *Ko-ming ch'ing-nien* [Revolutionary youth] (Canton), no. 2 (November 10, 1967), in *SCMP*, no. 4093 (January 5, 1968): 1–4. "The first choice is to pursue further study, the second, to enter factories or public organs, and the last, which is worst, to go to the countryside." *Ibid.* On the other hand, Liu is condemned for referring to *hsia-fang*'s favorable career prospects. He promised a bright future to those who "till the soil seriously for three to five years. By then you will have learned all farm work and will be able to do all those things which can be done by the peasants . . . but you have culture, and the peasants have not, and you are better off than the peasants in this respect. On top of this your relations with the masses are good. . . . With these three advantages, the masses will support you and will select you cooperative chairman, *hsiang* chiefs, *hsien* chiefs, and people's deputies." *Nung-ts'un ch'ing-nien* [Rural youth], no. 13 (July 10, 1967): *passim*.

135 "China's Khrushchev Bourgeois Program for Journalism," NCNA, September 2, 1967, in *SCMP*, no. 4015 (September 6, 1967): 22–27.

and what they want but hesitate to say." "We should publish selected news reports put out by the AP, Reuters, and other news agencies," he suggested.[136]

Maoist criticisms of Liu's views on journalism are part of the attack on "bourgeois dictatorship" examined earlier—Liu's proposals illustrate his failure to understand the relationship of ideas to power and the suppressive implications of proletraian dictatorship: "We do not permit the enemy and hostile ideas to have room for expression in our press." Truth, like the authority it sustains, has a necessary class character that "objectivity" ignores; facts that are disheartening to the proletariat are "bourgeois" truths that can "put out the fire of revolution." News for "popular interest" would transform the media into bourgeois "yellow journalism," replete with ads and jejune features: "My Lover's Love Is Thinner Than Paper." [137]

In medicine, as in science and technology in general, Liu's wholehearted advocacy of Western science is counterposed not only to Mao's Thought (which implies a more inductive notion of science and shuns theory) but to Chinese traditional medicine and to a nativist "Chinese science." "In a real technical problem putting politics in command alone will not do," said Liu. "There must be advanced technique." "In the not too distant future, the Western school of medicine will invariably take the place of the Chinese school of traditional medicine," he predicted.[138]

The unresolved status of the scientist or technician in Chinese society seems to be reflected in the criticisms of Liu's science policies. On the one hand, he is attacked for permitting scientists to form "independent kingdoms": "In order to foster experts, intellectuals may be excused from joining the Party and participating in political activities." On the other hand, Liu is also accused of coopting experts into the Party:

Admit a number of engineers into the Party. . . . The barriers should be removed, so that some more experts may join the leading groups. On the one hand this will enable laymen to become experts, and on the other, experts will become Communist Party members.[139]

Institutionalization—Criticisms of Liu's institutionalization of the revolution charge him with promoting the value of "elevation" (*t'i-kao*)

---

[136] *Ibid.*; also "Revolutionary Journalists," NCNA, August 25, 1967, in *SCMP*, no. 4011 (August 29, 1967): 30–33.

[137] *Ibid.*

[138] *PD*, November 3, 1968, in *SCMP*, no. 4302 (December 20, 1968): 8–15; *PD*, September 25, 1969, in *SCMP*, no. 4511 (October 7, 1969): 5–7, 10–11.

[139] "Exposing . . . Liu Shao-ch'i's Doctrine, 'Technique Is the Center,'" *PD*, November 3, 1968, in *SCMP*, no. 4302 (December 20, 1968): 8–16.

instead of "popularization" (*p'u-chi*). The first refers to the need to cultivate and perfect *techniques*, and the latter regards learning as a *service* to be distributed among the masses. As an intellectual, Liu stressed the "elevating" function of learning at the expense of "popularization."

In art, he advocated "professional training for writers" and fostered a cult of the creative personality ("pay close attention to . . . [the] development of the writer's own personality, characteristic traits, and style"). He encouraged intellectual dissent and a literature of social criticism but at the same time tolerated the sequestration of the artist from the masses.[140] Acknowledgment of disciplinary autonomy ("professional training") and a willingness to permit artists to retreat to ivory towers led to an "establishment" that routinized access to artistic values.[141] Liu's consistent promotion of institutionalization brought him into conflict with Chiang Ch'ing's attempts in the early 1960s to "revolutionize" art, to which Liu apparently gave an affirmative but lukewarm response.

In education, Liu scorned the *K'ang-ta*-type revolutionary schools set up in Yenan during the Sino-Japanese War as "unorthodox" and fitting into the "nature of training classes" and praised the universities that were "run according to the experience of Western European countries, Britain, the United States, France, and Japan," claiming these "have done much to elevate the cultural level, scientific level, and knowledge of the Chinese people." Liu allegedly made the European system the model for a post-Liberation form that suffocated revolutionary spirit and cultivated bourgeois careerism. For example, the Peking Union Medical College, founded by John D. Rockefeller, was revived "in its pristine evil" by the Liu "gang" in 1959; its faculty was dominated by bourgeois intellectuals who required heavy curric-

140 In 1964, he said, "You may also write about the weaknesses among the people. . . . You may criticize and promote criticisms, for the sake of amendment, not for the sake of . . . exposing the people in the same way as exposing the enemy." He defended the perquisites of talent, saying that when writers go among the masses, "It is all right for them to stay . . . for only a short period of time," and "they may go there by motorcar so they can eat and sleep in the cars." "Smash the Counterrevolutionary Program of Peaceful Evolution," *PD*, April 23, 1967, in *SCMP*, no. 3935 (May 9, 1967): 17–20.

141 In 1951, he instructed Chou Yang to disband the revolutionary cultural work teams. "All that members of the cultural work teams know is to dance the *yang-ko* and beat the waist drum. They would be ruined for life if things were to go on like this. . . . At present, they are 'tiger balm' cadres without any special skill or high cultural standard. . . . It is necessary to reorganize the cultural work teams, to retrench its staff greatly and to establish regular theatrical troupes." *Hung-se hsüan-ch'uan ping*, no. 4 (May 10, 1967). In 1956, he suggested to the cultural work troupe of the PLA, "Why don't you stage shows for the public? You may also sell tickets and run your troupe as an enterprise." *Chieh-fang chün wen-i*, no. 12 (August 10, 1967), in *SCMM*, no. 605 (December 11, 1967): 15–28.

ulum loads to achieve "high quality" and exploited their graduate students in order to publish in scholarly journals and become famous, while admitting only about 5 percent worker-peasant children (who were later "sifted" out by exams).[142] Liu quietly tabled Mao's 1964 proposal to reform the day schools and pressed forward with his own "double-track" system, which foresaw expansion of a part-work, part-study system while the day schools "should not be augmented and ought to be diminished." [143] Liu held such high expectations for the extension of educational opportunities to the masses promised by this system that he doubted that the job market could keep pace with educational output. Thus, he warned students that "after they graduate, they are still required to work as workers or peasants," predicting that the influx of the educated into unskilled jobs would "gradually eliminate the difference between mental labor and physical labor." Complete conversion of the system to the half-work, half-study schools "can be affected in from fifty to one hundred years"; this length of time was necessary because "the present full-time system is still necessary," and because its supersession was to be voluntary.[144]

Despite Liu's assurance that educational opportunities would be equal and that employers would not discriminate between graduates of the two systems,[145] suspicion centered around the fact that the full-

[142] "Fifty Instances of Liu Shao-ch'i's Opposition to Chairman Mao's Educational Line," *Chiao-yü ko-ming* [Education revolution] (Peking), April 16, 1967.

[143] At an enlarged Politburo meeting in November 1965, Liu said of Mao's proposal: "The question of the reform of the whole-day schools should also be taken up. Chairman Mao put forward this question at the Spring Festival last year. There is yet no solution to it. The Higher Education Ministry . . . has been asked to convene a meeting once more to deliberate on proposed reform measures. It behooves one not to dictate blindly when one has not obtained a clear picture of the thing." *Ibid.* Liu explained his plan for part-work part-study schools in a talk with the Deputy Prime Minister of Cambodia: "We ask them to run work-study or farming-study schools in which the students are required to spend their time to pursue their studies. You should work for your own upkeep with some subsidy from the state. You can attend school half a year in each year, or half a day every day. In this way, you can go to a higher school without interruption. Graduates from a primary school can go to a middle school, and graduates from a middle school can go to the university. . . . Less money is spent by the state, and the burden is also within the means of a family. The money needed to run a full-time school can run four or five work-study schools, and the demand of the students for higher schooling can be met to a fuller extent." "Selected Edition," *SCMM*, no. 653 (May 5, 1969): 21–32.

[144] "If the older group of students fail to see the light, let them cling to the full-day system till their graduation," he said. "This is a quantitative question." The full-day system may persist, but "should not be augmented and ought to be diminished; the part-time system should be expanded." *Ibid.*

[145] "Seventy percent of the work-study students may be allowed to further their studies in a higher school," Liu estimated. He believed graduates from work-study schools were "new men" who "are capable of performing mental labor

time system was left intact, evoking invidious comparisons between the two "tracks." This was a "reprint of the bourgeois 'parallel track system,' which created spiritual aristocrats on the one hand and . . . purely emphasized labor techniques on the other." Moreover, selection was apparently to discriminate on the basis of income as well as talent: "Those who cannot afford the full-time system must make do with the half-day system," Liu said in 1964.[146]

A final example of the hierarchical institutional consequences of Liu's concept of "elevation" comes from medicine. Liu pushed low-risk research in urban hospitals that were well-staffed and equipped rather than high-risk operations to take medical facilities to the peasants. He told his "handful" to "lay stress on protecting the health of the leading cadres of the Party committees at the provincial, municipal, or autonomous regional level, and the provincial people's council," thus spawning elitism. When Mao in June 1965 called the Health Ministry an "urban lord's ministry," which catered only to the 15 percent living in the cities, and ordered that the "majority" of doctors be sent to the countryside (leaving only those "who have graduated for one or two years and are not very experienced"), Liu deferentially proposed to Ch'ien Hsü-chung, a vice-minister, to send half of the medical personnel to the countryside, and if not that, one-third.[147]

ANALYSIS

There is sufficient empirical evidence to establish the following points apropos the critique of Liu's artistic policies, First, broadly speaking, a slightly higher level of artistic freedom seemed to prevail during the pre- than in the post-Liu eras. For a time in the early 1950s, leading cultural institutions like the Academy of Sciences, Peking University, and a number of cultural societies were filled with leading authorities in various fields and their outstanding works were produced in quantity with little revision. A "small hundred flowers" did "bloom" during the presumptive Liu Shao-ch'i stewardship. The intention was to divorce politics from other aspects of the life and activity of the intellectuals, in order to allow more latitude in scholarly

---

as well as physical labor," in distinction to graduates from full-time schools. "And what about the students from the full-time school? The general rule is that those graduated from a junior middle school despise the peasants, those graduating from a middle school despise the workers, and those graduated from a university despise all of them." Because work-study students represent "the future of all of us," they can serve as "engineers, Party committee secretaries, factory superintendants, mayors, or *hsien* magisrates." *Ibid.*

146 *Ibid.*

147 NCNA, January 20, 1969, in *SCMP*, no. 4346 (January 27, 1969): 14–16; *CNA*, no. 738 (January 3, 1969).

pursuits. Following publication of an August 10, 1961, *RF* article, "On Free Discussion of Academic Problems," which stated that the social sciences need not concentrate on subjects directly related to politics, unprecedented discussions occurred, especially in economics. There was a flowering of learned symposia sponsored by the so-called bourgeois democratic parties (including an animated discussion of Confucianism held at the sage's birthplace); anyone taking the minority view was allowed to retain his opinion or offer adverse criticisms. The Propaganda Department issued "Ten Articles on Art and Literature" in July, which stressed literary techniques and professionalism rather than politics, classical Chinese and fine foreign art in addition to contemporary revolutionary works, and let Mao's requirement that artists participate in *hsia-fang* fall into desuetude. Writers used a variety of literary styles and methods of expression in addition to conventional socialist realism and revolutionary romanticism, publishing growing numbers of "miscellaneous essays" (*ts'a-wen*) in the press and journals and writing and producing classical plays, operas, and even several comedy movies.[148]

Due to an already noted hiatus between spontaneous expression and politically orthodox expression, the "Hundred Flowers" spirit was quietly stifled in 1962, but the leadership made no determined attempt to subvert the renewed authority gained by professional intellectuals in 1961. Attempts by Mao and his wife publicly to expose these adulterating influences and restore art to its pristine purity were met by compromising half-measures. For example, to appease increased pressure for more revolutionary content and broader populist appeal, officials in the Propaganda Department in 1963–65 initiated a "culture to the villages" (*wen-hua hsia-hsiang*) campaign. In major cities of China, members of the professional drama, music, dance, art, literary, and science groups were organized into rural cultural work teams to go down to selected villages and entertain peasants; their activities, however, were limited to a combination of entertainment and education, with minor attention to political agitation.[149] The vaunted reform of

148 "Liu Shao-ch'i is not Chiang Kai-shek," as his wife once put it, and revision should be distinguished from reaction. A statistical report in the Red Guard press indicated that of the foreign literary works published by the People's Publishing House from 1959 to 1963, "revolutionary works" accounted for 67.3 percent, while classical works of the eighteenth and nineteenth centuries accounted for 32.4 percent, 70 percent of which had been "decontaminated" by adding a foreword or postscript. "Expose the Big Sinister Schemes," *PD*, June 10, 1967. Among domestic literary works, one would expect the percentage of "revolutionary" works to be higher yet.

149 Wang Chang-ling, "Overt and Covert Struggles Between Mao and Liu over Literature and Art," *IS* 4, no. 3 (December 1967): 1–12; Merle Goldman, "The

Peking opera by P'eng Chen, Chou Yang, et al. consisted of little more than "decontamination" of traditional operas with slight effort to produce "revolutionary" works; according to Chiang Ch'ing, of the 3,000 professional theatrical companies operating in China in 1964, less than one hundred were staging modern dramas, while more than 2,800 were specializing in various kinds of "dead" operas.[150]

Liu's responsibility for the short period of artistic moderation is difficult to demonstrate. His published works are principally concerned with economic and organizational issues; so far as is known, he wrote only one piece about cultural questions, "My View in the Current Polemic in Literature and Art," in 1936. Comparison of this early essay with Mao's roughly contemporaneous "Talks at the Yenan Forum on Literature and Art" (1942) does reveal a different emphasis: "The prime significance of the current polemic . . . lies in overcoming sectarianism and exclusionism," Liu began. He supported writers Lu Hsün and Mao Tun in their sponsorship of a "literature for masses in the national revolutionary war" against Chou Yang's "literature for national defense," pointing out that the latter slogan was not at odds with and could even be subsumed under the former. Liu also said that Kuo Mo-jo was wrong for advocating only *one* literary slogan, which was "nothing but exclusionism." [151] Mao's essay, on the other hand, placed almost exclusive emphasis on populism: "What is the crux of the matter? In my opinion, its consists fundamentally of the problems of working for the masses and how to work for the masses." Mao then concluded that "China's revolutionary writers and artists . . . must go among the masses." He objected to the previous overemphasis on "raising standards" at the expense of popularization —and this popularization does seem to imply "exclusionism." "Some works which are downright reactionary may have a certain artistic quality," Mao concedes. "The more reactionary their content and *the higher their artistic quality, the more poisonous they are* to the people, and the more necessary it is to reject them." [Emphasis added.] [152]

The "two roads" metaphor does not seem to be particularly helpful in construing China's educational development before the GLF.[153]

Unique 'Blooming and Contending' of 1959–1962," *CQ* no. 37 (January–March 1969): 54–84; Goldman, *Literary Dissent in Communist China* (Cambridge, Mass., 1967), pp. 24 ff.

150 Chiang Ch'ing, "On the Revolution in Peking Opera," *Chinese Literature*, no. 8 (August 1967): 118–125.

151 *CW* 1: 23–27.

152 *SW* 3: 257, 263, 275.

153 E.g., the charge that Liu supported Western schools in opposition to revolutionary schools (*PD*, July 18, 1967) is based on deliberate distortion. In 1950 he said, "*The old universities of the past,* on the one hand, *made the Chinese acquire*

Beginning in 1961, there was indeed a shift in emphasis from political to academic (particularly scientific and technical) training and from popularization to quality control. Following Ch'en I's keynote speech in June 1961 and issuance of the "Seventy Article Educational Charter" and the "Sixty Articles on Higher Education" the same year, there was an interdict against undue Party interference in teaching or student affairs, a drastic reduction in time set aside for political studies and physical labor, and increased attention to academic research; available evidence suggests that Liu was in full sympathy with this shift.[154] The quality of education improved perceptibly. By 1964, China was producing 75 percent as many graduate engineers as the U.S.; to one observer, it seemed that "China is being transformed into a technocratic state." [155] At the same time, schools that could not pass "quality controls," many of them set up during the Leap, were ruthlessly chopped down in the budgetary squeeze. The number of institutions of higher learning, for example, decreased from 841 in 1960 to 400 two years later; according to an incomplete statistical report, the number of commune schools sank from 22,715 with 2.3 million pupils during the Leap to 3,715 with 266,000 pupils in 1962.[156]

The formula, "Liu is to elevation as Mao is to popularization" does seem to oversimplify, for Liu did not altogether abandon popularization goals. The post-Leap retrenchment came in the face of a sharp

---

new knowledge, and on the other hand, they committed many mistakes and shortcomings because their basic purpose and policy was erroneous, and their schools . . . were serving the bourgeoisie and oppressing and exploiting the people." Only the italicized portions of the passage were quoted.

154 *PD,* August 12, 25, 31 and September 4, 6, 8, 19, 1961. Liu's higher tolerance of "study" as conventionally understood is already apparent in his earlier writings. In a 1941 essay, "Fan-tui ko-chung pu-liang ti ch'ü-hsiang" [Oppose every unhealthy tendency], the only criterion he laid down for those pursuing intellectual careers was merit: "Even if you do not write a theory like *Capital,* you will be allowed to write any 'theory' as long as you can do it. As long as you can do it well, and make a contribution of benefit to the struggle of the proletariat, the Party will assign you to these tasks with minimum reluctance." In a letter to Sung Liang the same year, he reproached those who "Seem to think you only need practical experience and can lead the revolution to victory without raising the level of theoretical study" (together with those who had an adequate grasp of concrete reality): "those two viewpoints are both wrong." "The study of theory is always indoors," he maintained. "This is the student's important task and it is not right to call him a schoolman [hsüeh-yüan p'ai] . . . any comparison with those who have learned Marxism-Leninism would show that they needed to go through a period of staying inside and reading books." *LSWTC,* pp. 115–127, 114.

155 Immanuel C. Y. Hsü, "The Reorganization of Higher Education in Communist China, 1949–1961," *CQ* no. 19 (July–September 1964): 128–161.

156 Cited in Donald J. Munro, "Egalitarian Ideal and Educational Fact in Communist China," in Lindbeck, *China,* pp. 256–301.

deterioration in educational standards, which was confirmed by others at the time.[157] Liu also may take credit for the vigorous expansion of half-work, half-study schools in 1964–65, which occurred under his program of "double-track" labor and educational systems, an attempt to compromise between popularization and elevation by expanding work-study schools while maintaining educational standards in full-time schools. By the end of 1965, it was revealed that more than 40 million students were attending the nonregular system of schools and this number was on the increase.[158]

Liu's attempt to satisfy the nation's perceived need for a highly trained technocratic sector, at the expense of a more uncompromising egalitarianism, spawned protectionism and elitism and formed the nub of Maoist grievances with his policy. Although Donald Munro's statistics indicate a steadily increasing percentage of peasant and worker students in the student body as a whole from 1950 to 1964, reaching 75 percent in ordinary middle schools in 1964, the percentage of students from worker-peasant families attending Peking University (an elite institution) fell from 67 percent in 1958 to 38 percent in 1962, according to the Red Guard statistics.[159] The "double-track" school system had a close correspondence to the "double-track system" of labor; these tandem systems tended to restrict inter-class and inter-regional mobility, since full-time schools were concentrated in large cities.[160] Mao's repeated criticisms of the education system after 1961 occasioned the convention of five national work conferences (including the Educational, Finance, and Health ministries as well as the CC), but the question of reform of the full-time system was postponed pending further study.

Available evidence confirms the accuracy and validity of the criti-

[157] In 1958, Mao proposed that "education should serve the proletarian dictatorship and should unite with productive labor" and urged an "educational revolution," which Liu endeavored to carry out. The most important innovation was the division of schools into three types: full-time, half-work half-study, and amateur schools. At that time, some of the departments of full-time universities (such as Peking University) switched to the half-work half-study system. In the first few months of 1958, 19,000 ordinary schools were established in 123,000 factories; 1,860 secondary schools were established in 21,000 factories, and 397 schools of higher education were established in 7,240 factories. In January 1959, Liu observed that this development brought a "decline in the quality of learning." K'ang Sheng agreed: "Teaching material cannot be neglected because of labor," CNA, no. 273, quoted in CNA, no. 723 (August 30, 1968).

[158] PD, December 9, 1965.

[159] John Gardner, "Educated Youth and Urban-Rural Inequalities, 1959–1966," in Lewis, The City in Communist China, p. 266.

[160] "Samples of Red Guard Publications," JPRS Special pub., August 1, 1967, pp. 53–54.

cisms of Liu's views on journalism. In a May 1949 speech to a cadre meeting in Tientsin, for instance, Liu complained:

In our newspaper (Tientsin *Daily*) it is only said that workers are good, but whenever capitalists are discussed it is said they are bad, that capitalists have good points is never printed. So capitalists feel that they have no place in our newspaper. There was a period when I'm afraid the Peking *People's Daily* also had this tendency. Capitalists raise this issue, saying: "If workers are bad they are still good, if capitalists are good they are still bad." [Laughter.] [161]

Wu Leng-hsi (former Editor of *PD* and Director of NCNA) reported in his self-criticism that in the summer of 1956, Liu had set forth a "revisionist program in journalism," which envisaged, inter alia, the denationalization of NCNA as an independent "worldwide news agency" on the model of Reuter's or UPI. Liu considered the Soviet Tass "rigid and sterile" but praised Western news agencies as "dynamic," "lively," and "attractive"; he advocated that Chinese news should be "truthful" and "impartial," adopting the "style of objective reporting," and that feature articles should have "universal appeal." [162] Mao's contemporaneous statements on the press indicate a quite different emphasis. "If the newspaper you are publishing will print only bad news, and if you have no heart to work, then it won't take a year [for the nation to collapse], but it will perish in a week's time," he remarked at Lushan. In his "Letter to Journalist Comrades" of January 12, 1958, Mao listed three functions of journalism, each of which is concerned with the hortatory rather than the reportorial function of the press: the first is "to mobilize and organize all people into a powerful force to realize . . . the various great tasks prescribed by the Party." The second is "to integrate the creativeness of the masses with their emotions and energy." The third and "most important" function is the critical one: "to present convincing arguments to attack the various shades of opportunism, conservatism, and destructive capitalism." [163] Despite the clear differences between Mao's and Liu's views of the role of the communications media, the criticisms seem somehow beside the point, since Liu's more liberal policies were not put into effect.[164]

[161] "Tsai kan-pu hui i-shang ti chiang-huo" [Speech at a cadre meeting], in *LSWTC*, p. 208.

[162] "Confessions of Wu Leng-hsi," in *CL&G* 2, no. 4 (winter 1969–1970): 63–87.

[163] Quoted in Frederick T. C. Yu, *Mass Persuasion in Communist China* (New York, 1964), p. 103.

[164] E.g., Wu Leng-hsi recounted that at his own discretion he failed to act on Liu's suggestion that the NCNA be made an independent news agency, because this was in obvious contravention of proletarian dictatorship. One student of the

The rationale of the "small hundred flowers" was to create a favorable atmosphere for scientific research, in which endeavor it was successful: there was a steep increase after 1960 of importations of Western scientific literature, which was reflected in the citation of an increasing range and quantity of foreign scholarly work in Chinese scientific publications and increasingly frequent visits to China by Western scientists.[165] There was greater support for "pure" science during this period: a representative article defended the "relative independence of theory in development"; scientific theories with no tangible connection to production were not criticized as unreal or meaningless and could even guide social practice.[166] By the mid-1960s, almost 800 research institutes were in operation, of which 305 specialized in the life sciences, 205 in the physical sciences, and 271 in engineering.[167] Applied science continued to enjoy high priority, however; beginning as early as 1964, the regime launched a "designing revolution" that encouraged mass participation and attacked specialists for their isolation from the masses.[168]

Notwithstanding "The Sixteen Points'" attempt to exempt the scientific community, the immediate impact of the GPCR was to abrogate the isolation and specialization historically associated with pioneering scientific research and to encourage scientists to mingle with the masses in "communal" research and to work on projects of more immediate relevance.[169] As of 1973, the reopening of the uni-

---

media has, however, expressed the view that in the dissemination of propaganda materials in the early 1960s, materials concerned with "knowledge" outnumbered those on politics. Alan P. L. Liu, *Communications*, p. 56.

165 J. M. H. Lindbeck, "China and the World: The Dilemmas of Communication," in *China Today*, ed. William J. Richardson (New York, 1969), pp. 105–117.

166 Feng Ting, "Concerning Redness and Vocational Proficiency," *KMJP*, June 12–14, 1962, in *SCMP*, no. 2776 (July 12, 1962): 12–13.

167 C. H. G. Oldham, "Science and Education," *Bulletin of the Atomic Scientists* 22, no. 6 (June 1966): 46.

168 "Struggle for Revolutionizing Designing Work," *PD*, April 10, 1965, in *SCMP*, no. 3498 (July 16, 1965): 7; Fa Ting, "Revolutionizing the Designing Work and Developing New Technique," *Ching-chi yen-chiu* [Economic research], no. 11 (November 20, 1965), in *SCMM*, no. 510 (February 7, 1966): 24; in Rennsselaer W. Lee, III, "The Politics of Technology in Communist China," *Comparative Politics* 5, no. 2 (January 1973): 237–261.

169 The Chinese Academy of Sciences was placed under army control beginning in December 1967, and two vice-presidents and about fifteen members had been purged by June 1968. In a 1971 interview, Kuo Mo-jo said that of the 100 resident scientists, sixty were being sent down to the "root levels" (provincial RCs) or shifted to "other organs" (PLA, productive agencies). A further twenty would be placed under the "dual leadership" of Peking and local authorities. The final twenty would remain with the Academy in Peking, to integrate research with practice. Terrill, *800,000,000*, p. 71; also Bruce J. Esposito, "Science in Mainland China," *Bulletin of the Atomic Scientists* 28, no. 1 (January 1972): 36–40.

versities had not yet provided a forum conducive to advanced research, which seems now to be taking place in the institutes, academies,
and ministries. By 1973, five leading officials of the Academy of Sciences had made their reappearance, and scientific links had been
fostered with several countries, with scientific or technical delegations
visiting Albania, Rumania, North Vietnam, Ceylon, North Korea,
the Sudan, France, and the United States.[170]

Very fragmentary evidence also confirms that, although popularization of medical care was not entirely neglected during Liu's stewardship, redistribution goals seemed to take second priority to research
and the construction of modern urban facilities. According to Red
Guard sources, the number of hospital beds in the cities rose from
50,000 in 1954 to 340,000 in 1966, but there was no corresponding
increase in the villages; during post-GLF retrenchment, the number
of health centers in the communes was cut from 290,000 to 70,000,
while the number of urban clinics increased from 43,000 to 84,000.[171]
As for the criticisms of Liu's neglect of traditional Chinese medicine,
the Mao-Liu cleavage seems to have concerned the relative degree of emphasis each should receive, for traditional medicine was not neglected
before the GPCR. Mao, motivated perhaps in part by cultural nationalism, but also by a stronger emphasis on redistribution, advocated
immediate popularization of traditional medical remedies, while Liu
seemed to favor the more cautious strategy of first submitting these
nostrums to scientific test and then standardizing their manufacture.[172]

Nowhere does the sincerity of the Maoist critique seem to be more
clearly demonstrated than in the cultural sphere. In each subfield,
functional specialization is denounced for contributing to the forma-

---

170 *CSN* 2, no. 4 (October 1971); also James A. Berberet, "Science and Technology
in China," *CS* 10, no. 9 (September 1972): 12–19.
171 Peter Kuntze, *Der Osten Ist Rot: Kulturrevolution in China* (Munich, 1970),
pp. 73–79.
172 As early as 1944, the CC urged a fusion of traditional Chinese medicine
[*chung-i*] and Western medicine. Ten years later, concerned lest this fusion result
in the disappearance of the former (and thus of the only medical care available to
most of the populace), a major campaign in support of *chung-i* was launched. In
1955 an Institute for Research on Chinese Medicine was established in Peking, but
1958–1959 seemed to mark the flood tide in public promotion of *chung-i*. In the
1960s, Crozier noted a decline "both in volume and fervor" of publicity, and
surgical achievements seemed to replace herbals and acupuncture as the main
showcase of Chinese medicine. Ideological criticism of modern doctors for their bad
attitude toward traditional medicine also disappeared. "While the relative importance of the separate practice of Chinese medicine seems to have declined, this
process has been matched by the more effective integration of traditional medicine
into modern medical practice," he concludes. Ralph C. Crozier, "Traditional Medicine in Communist China: Science, Communism, and Cultural Naturalism," *CQ*,
no. 23 (July–September 1965): 1–28; see also John Z. Bowers, "Medicine in Mainland China: Red and Rural," *CS* 8, no. 12 (June 15, 1970): 1 ff.

tion of "independent kingdoms" exempt from the values of mass politics; culture is seen as a value to be allocated politically, not "cultivated."

The artistic revolution's most immediate effect was to give the "tool" of literary criticism to the masses; it was first used to excise the poisonous influence of the "three-family village" and in the course of the GPCR included criticism of most works by Shakespeare, Balzac, Stendhal, Pushkin, Tolstoy, Dostoyevski, Gorki, Mayakovsky, Beethoven, and Tchaikovsky for tendencies "antagonistic to the interests of the people." [173] There was a repertory of 200 to 300 traditional operas before 1966, but, according to 1972 visitors, "all have been discontinued." [174] The solution proposed (but not accepted) by the CCRG to the still apparently unresolved question of the future of liberal arts colleges in China was to turn them into "revolutionary mass criticism writing groups." Artistic creation has been transformed via the "mass line" from an individual to a collective endeavor in "three-in-one" teams of Party cadres, professional workers, and masses (with cadres in command); literary and art workers are adjured to maintain intimate and constant contact with manual labor and the masses through such devices as the "open-door rehearsal" [k'ai-men p'ai-hsi].[175] This method has thus far been more successful in revising classic revolutionary texts than in creating new ones, and the staple artistic fare from 1968 to 1973 has comprised the same "ten big" approved productions: one ballet (besides the revised White-Haired Girl), five musical dramas in the Peking Opera Style, and three purely musical numbers.[176] In Sir Herbert Read's view, "the artistic consequences are disastrous from any conceivable standard of aesthetic judgment . . . as dreary as commercial posters in a capitalist country." [177] Implicit in Read's denunciation is an acknowledgment that the vulgarization attending popularization is hardly peculiar to Communist China, however; perhaps some adaptation of the methodology developed in the West for the analysis of "mass culture" might be fruitfully applied.

Two dates of particular significance for the revolution in education

---

173 More than 400 films, among them 300 Chinese films, were censured—including the British film Hamlet, because it "praised personal revenge and served to absolve kings and military leaders," the French film The Three Musketeers, because it "uncritically glorified" the same, the Soviet film Othello, because "love stands over everything," etc. Kuntze, Der Osten Ist Rot, pp. 68–69.

174 NYT, November 8, 1972, p. 56.

175 Hua-yuan Li Mowry, Yang-pan hsi: New Theater in China (Berkeley, Calif., Studies in Chinese Communist Terminology, no. 15, 1973), pp. 17, 25–39, 42–43.

176 Tilman Durdin, NYT, April 24, 1971, confirmed by Gerald Tannebaum (long-term resident of the P.R.C.) in a speech in Berkeley, Calif., in January 1973.

117 The Broadsheet (London) 5, no. 4 (April 1968): 2.

are October 8, 1967, when the CC, State Council, MAC, and CCRG issued an "urgent circular" challenging all governmental institutions to "send all young intellectuals and others down to work in the villages and up to the mountains, with a permanent assignment to remain in the countryside, spread the revolution and grasp production"; and July 27, 1968, when the "worker-peasant Mao Tsetung Thought propaganda teams" were sent to Tsinghua University. The first decision was followed by the displacement of perhaps 30 million "educated youth" to the countryside in the middle of 1970; this *hsia-fang* differs from the pre-GPCR program in that it has included service personnel and elite students and can no longer be considered a mere channel of downward mobility for failures.[178] To the extent that the program is more politically equitable, it may at the same time be less efficient in terms of the rational allocation of skills.[179]

On July 27, 1968, worker-peasant teams invaded Tsinghua and announced that the working class would now cooperate with (reinforce) the PLA fighters in directing the revolution in education and on a permanent basis. In Yao Wen-yüan's words, "Contradictions which have vexed the intellectuals endlessly are quickly solved as soon as the workers participate." Thus, education became intercalated with the economic system, as part of a general effort to resolve the "three differences" between town and country, industry and agriculture, mental and physical work. The work-study model has been generalized to all schools, most of which are attached to factories, laboratories, or experimental farms on which both teachers and students must do manual labor. In the countryside, the primary schools fall under brigade control, the high schools under the commune; in cities, street committees are responsible for primary schools and factories for the high schools; the state assists with financial aid only in emergencies. Workers and peasants participate on school Revolutionary Com-

178 The increased number of young Hong Kong refugees (20,000 in 1972) suggests that it is also less than universally popular. *NYT,* January 14, 1973, p. 10. Visitors from China in the fall of 1971 said downward-transferred youth were being treated as if *hsia-fang* were punishment; none of their skills were used, and they were assigned to the least desirable tasks. John Bryan Starr, *Ideology and Culture: An Introduction to the Dialectic of Contemporary Chinese Politics* (New York, 1973), p. 88, n. 52. The authorities combat resistance by invalidating individual registration and ration certificates in the cities, by making countryside service a prerequisite for urban jobs or university registration, and by exerting pressure on the students' families. Editor, "Educational Reform and Rural Resettlement in Communist China," *CS* 8, no. 17 (November 7, 1970): 1–8.

179 Cf. John Philip Emerson, "Manpower Training and Utilization of Specialized Cadres, 1949–1968," in Lewis, *The City,* pp. 213–214. For a thoughtful dissenting view, see Pi-chao Chen, "Overurbanization, Rustication of Urban-Educated Youths, and Politics of Rural Transformation: The Case of China," *Comparative Politics* 4, no. 3 (April 1972): 361–387.

mittees with students and teachers, help to prepare curricula, and even teach many classes, particularly at agrarian and engineering schools.[180] Teachers no longer have a system of ranks or tenure but are members of the brigade or commune; they work on a "three-thirds" timetable divided between lecturing, attendance at a rural "May 7 school," and field work, for which they receive work points rather than a salary from the workers and peasants. In order to extend the number of schools and make a minimal education accessible to all, the old 6-3-3 system of primary, junior-middle, and senior-middle schooling has been replaced by a seven-year combined primary and junior-middle school, followed by a two-year senior-middle school.[181] The significant extension of the opportunity base into the countryside (by 1972, it was reported that 127 million children, 80 percent of that age group, were attending primary school and 36 million were attending middle schools) [182] has been accompanied by some flattening of the educational pyramid, lowering standards in urban centers and generally derogating higher education.[183]

180 Experienced peasants teach economic affairs; workers teach agricultural machinery maintenance; militia cadres drill the students; and "barefoot doctors" transmit medical knowledge. Due to curriculum reform, academic studies have been almost eliminated in primary and secondary schools; the curriculum is to be prepared to correspond to local economic conditions, but it generally includes five main courses: Mao Tse-tung Thought (every student receives a copy of *SW* as a gift), science, arithmetic, military drill and physical culture, and productive labor. In the rewriting of texts, three aspects of the old must be destroyed: the "history" of math or physics, theories too far "removed from practice," and quotations from so-called experts (particularly foreign and bourgeois experts). Classroom exposure at every educational level is reduced to two or three years, after which the student returns to labor, where his attitudes and abilities must be demonstrated in practice. Ellen K. Ong, "Education in China since the Cultural Revolution," *Studies in Comparative Communism* 3, nos. 3–4 (July–October 1970): 158–177; also Hsia, *The Chinese Cultural Revolution*, pp. 175–185.

181 Radio Canton (December 31, 1970) announced that, in the course of 1970, Kwangtung Province had "basically introduced universal primary education"; in Yünnan Province, 2,560,000 students, 400,000 more than before the GPCR, were reported attending 45,000 primary schools (Radio K'unming, November 13, 1970, quoting incomplete statistics); in areas of Sinkiang and Inner Mongolia, efforts were being made to bring education to children of herdsmen through provisions of mobile primary classes (NCNA, February 3, 1971, and January 7, 1971).

182 Statistics from a key member of the State Council's Scientific and Educational Group, in A. Doak Barnett, "There Are Warts," pp. 36–37, 100.

183 In the summer of 1970, national reopening of technical institutes was announced, but the question of liberal arts colleges remains unresolved. According to travelers' reports the universities have largely converted to vocational training. A large proportion of the original student body was transferred down, and the new entrance requirements omit exams and require a minimum of two years' productive labor to establish eligibility on political as well as intellectual criteria. The student body is far smaller than the old and includes PLA men, workers, and peasants seeking training on a "sabbatical" basis. The training period has been shortened for nearly all professions. Student life has a military pattern and discipline. All

This extremely sweeping reform is more consistent with the ideals of Mao's Thought and at the same time offers the economic advantage of converting the education system into a great pool of cheap labor. Needless to say, there have been problems. Since education's function as a ladder of success has been so thoroughly discredited, students have become more apathetic; they complain that education is pointless (tu-shu wu-yung lun), that they would rather start working as peasants and workers, where they could at least collect work points, than go to school, where they work gratis.[184] Elimination of the notorious test system has resulted in wide differences in standards, classes retarded to the pace of the slowest students, and automatic promotions, and there have recently been reports that tests may be reintroduced in some form.[185] The "method of recommendation and selection," which reportedly resulted in admitting 90 percent Party and CYL members to universities, seems to have been modified by a form of quota system, which includes children of bourgeoisie; entrance requirements still include several years of manual labor, however, and enrollment includes adult workers and peasants.[186]

In medicine, the same principle of maximum redistribution of benefits to the disprivileged, with special emphasis on the peasantry, has swept considerations of professional "standards" or institution building before it. As in all professional fields, the period of training has been reduced and the curriculum simplified (medical colleges no longer teach mathematics, for instance, which is regarded as superfluous for doctors); a one-year training course in Western first aid and Chinese medicine has made available a large task force of "barefoot doctors" for immediate service in the countryside, where they work part-time in the fields to earn work-points. Functional specialization has been reduced, in some cases resulting in the integration of doctoring with nursing, in some cases eliminating such distinctions as that between surgery and medicine.[187]

---

schools are now half-study, half-work. "You wonder at first if you are on a campus at all," writes Terrill. "Here at Communications University in Sian are people . . . threshing wheat (80,000 catties produced on campus this year). In the Middle School attached to Peking Normal University, girls are making chairs. . . . In Canton at Sun Yat-sen University, I found professors tending a vegetable garden." *800,000,000*, p. 120.

184 *RF*, no. 4 (1968); Charles Bohlen, "Studies in Maoism," *FEER* 67, no. 8 (February 19, 1970): 19–22; Réné Goldman, "Chinese Education and the Impact of the Cultural Revolution," in *China: The Peasant Revolution*, ed. Ray Wylie (London, 1972), pp. 33–47.

185 *NYT*, September 25, 1972, p. 3.

186 Terrill, *800,000,000*, p. 120.

187 *CSN* 2, no. 1 (January 1971); *CNA*, no. 138 (January 3, 1969).

CONCLUSION

If Liu Shao-ch'i's life represents the attempt to combine efficiency with equality and order with revolution, the Maoist critique represents application of the Maoist philosophy "one divided into two" (*yi fen wei erh*) to that synthesis, breaking it down to its constituent polarities, and showing how Liu permitted efficiency and order to take precedence and even subvert the achievement of equality and revolution. In Part III, we shall analyze the distortions in the critical characterization of Liu's "line" but here we wish to extract the gist of truth from the critique and try to define the difference Liu's fall makes to China.

Liu's attempt to combine *order* with *revolution* overemphasized organizational constraints to the neglect of ideological or normative incentives. In his concern for the integration and effective operation of the Party, Liu neglected certain frictions in the boundary relationships between the organization and the non-Party masses to which Mao was inordinately sensitive. Liu's attempt to integrate the organization with the masses took the form of cooptation of non-Party elites into a "whole people's" united front, a policy he applied across the board to nationalities and minority religions, technical and managerial personnel, scientists, artists and cultural notables, et al. This resulted in two parallel ladders of upward career mobility: cooptation, based on expertise, and recruitment, based on Party loyalty. Although the former ladder had a low ceiling and coopted personnel were for the most part limited to the cultural establishment and to managerial or staff positions in the heavy industrial sector, Mao apparently saw in this policy the seeds for the growth of a "new class" based on monopoly control of both material and human capital,[188] which would have at best a condescending "tutorial" relationship to the masses, at worst a repressive one. The alienation of this emerging elite from the masses thus forms the basis for the Maoist critique of "bureaucratism," "unconditional obedience," "bourgeois dictatorship," and the like.

[188] There were two patterns of upward mobility in the Chinese bureaucracy, one based on "political" criteria, which was applied to recruit "activists" following campaigns, and one based on criteria of technical and administrative skills, which remained relevant during periods of consolidation. As Ying-mao Kau has demonstrated in an excellent article, technical qualification had shown a slight but steady propensity to increase in importance. "The Urban Bureaucratic Elite in Communist China: A Case Study of Wuhan, 1949–1965," in A. Doak Barnett, *Chinese Communist Politics in Action* (Seattle, Wash., 1969), pp. 216–217. Studies of CC elites suggest, however, that these trends have been confined to lower middle echelons of the apparatus, and that senior elites are consistently recruited on the basis of "revolutionary age."

This critique seems at first to exaggerate the degree of alienation of the elite from the masses. After all, the Liuist system made provision for elite-masses interaction through a Party-mediated "mass line," through cross-cutting mass organizations (to which most of the population belonged), through a network of people's political consultative conferences, through a legal system that accorded each citizen certain minimal rights regardless of class, and through the *hsia-fang* and *tun-tien* (squat on a spot) tactics, both of which seem to have originated with Liu. All of these interactions were organizationally mediated, however; the masses were situated on the bottom tier of the organization and were expected to subordinate themselves to the "higher level" and to conform to various organizational rules, while having minimal share in decision making. The organization was structured in such a way that it systematically ignored cues that did not adhere to prescribed form; although strict adherence to form enhanced the effectiveness of the organization as an administrative apparatus, it also impaired its representative function by stifling the sort of mass spontaneity typical of the "movement." In addition to these inherent structural weaknesses, the organization in the course of time developed other problems: routinized recruitment and promotion policies without a systematic retirement procedure resulted in an overstaffed, top-heavy bureaucracy with self-maintenance and enhancement needs that grew to supplant its primary purposes.[189] Members tended to isolate themselves from sanctions and form "independent kingdoms," identifying with the interests of their working constituency and colleagues and ignoring inconvenient directives from their superiors (the P'eng Chen-Wu Han imbroglio is the best example of this tendency). These tendencies functioned to plug the communications channels between central elites and masses and to facilitate the sort of alienation that permitted the "fifty days" to occur.

Liu's attempt to combine *equality* with *efficiency* and technocratic values assumes the chronological priority of the latter: a constant increase in economic productivity is the dynamic that assures future improvements in popular welfare, and this increase must be purchased with temporary ideological concessions such as wage differentials, func-

---

[189] In the 1949–1966 period, rigid entrance requirements for the Party were followed by bureaucratic step-by-step promotion; at the top level, power was increasingly concentrated among leaders who held multiple posts. Once an individual attained a higher-level position, the probability of purge was rather low; membership in high-level posts depended increasingly on seniority, education, and pre-Liberation record. Paul Wong, "Organizational Leadership in Communist China" (Ph.D. diss., Berkeley, Calif., 1971), pp. 335–342; see also Ying-mao Kau, "Patterns of Recruitment," pp. 262–263.

tional specialization, and market allocation of labor and certain commodities. The principle ordering these concessions is the division of labor: if the "revisionist" principle of combination is the supra-class "united front" based on various criteria of "cultivated" excellence, its principle of division is functional specialization, manifest not only in Liu's complex intra-Party division of powers,[190] but in the functional autonomy ("specific responsibility systems," he called it) he granted economics, culture, science, education, medicine, labor, and mass organizations.

Generally speaking, the principle of functional specialization is ambiguous in its social effects. On the one hand, it makes it possible for the collective knowledge of society to grow much faster than the knowledge of the individual, for the sum total of knowledge is composed of a continually growing mass of systematically interrelated individual knowledge. On the other, it exacerbates divisions between skilled and unskilled labor and between other specialized fields, not merely in terms of differential incomes, but mutual comprehension.

This two-fold effect of the division of labor leads to the understandable, but still surprising, result that in a society whose knowledge is broad enough to steer rockets into outer space, an overabundance of tasks is still . . . being performed that requires less knowledge than the labors of a serf many centuries ago.[191]

Introduction of advanced Western technology into a relatively undeveloped economy tends to widen these divisions, resulting in what one trenchant critic of the process calls "modernization of poverty."

For those who subscribe to the technocratic ethos, whatever is technically possible must be made available at least to a few whether they want it or not. . . . If cobalt treatment is possible, then the city of Tegucigalpa needs one apparatus in each of its two major hospitals, at a cost that would free an important part of the population of Honduras from parasites.[192]

Aside from aggravating maldistribution in some cases (not all—viz., transistor radios, watches, or buses) and deflating Marxist hopes for a "Renaissance man," acknowledgment of the independent validity of various fields of knowledge tends to reduce the explanatory scope of ideology, thus limiting its claim to be morally binding and restricting its mobilizable constituency to those "masses" comprehended by the

190 Ahn calls attention to the post-1962 trend toward greater specialization in the national policy-making organs in his "Adjustments in the GLF," pp. 296–297.

191 Ferenc Janossy, *The End of the Economic Miracle* (White Plains, N.Y., 1971), pp. 201–204.

192 Ivan Illich, "The Alternative to Schooling," *Saturday Review*, June 19, 1971, pp. 44–60.

political subsystem. It also legitimates independent methodological approaches to various fields of knowledge acquired through schooling in a relevant expertise.

The discipline to which Liu seemed to attribute greatest importance was that of science and technology, though he extended "bourgeois liberalization" to other subfields on the basis of the same general principle that legitimated the independent validity of science. Liu's esteem for science and technology is evident in his introduction of agricultural machine stations (to serve the maintenance needs of tractors, not farms), socialist trusts, "scientific" management techniques, and by his general vocabulary of reference (e.g., in recommending "professional training for writers," the first field he mentioned was "natural sciences," including "knowledge of the atomic bomb, because it is the era of atomic energy, chemistry, algebra, geometry, and calculus"). Liu's special interest in this subfield was apparently based on the assumption that science and technology had replaced labor as the most important independent source of surplus value; i.e., that uninterrupted economic progress depends on scientific-technological breakthroughs.[193] The avant garde role of the sciences implies that the school feeding into science replaces "politics" (i.e., mobilization) as the main social mechanism sustaining the growth rate, which is in turn the prerequisite to achieving welfare, equality, and other long-term goals. Those who diligently acquire great "stocks" of expertise in the educational "market" can correspondingly better their life-chances, and an achievement ethic, measured by graded attendance and formal examinations, comes to overshadow altruistic concerns. In this "scientific" cognitive system, the cultural superstructure assumes much less importance, since it comprises habits of thought based on empirical relationships no longer extant, harmless mental heirlooms doomed to natural extinction as the empirical subsystem changes. Implicit in this set of assumptions is a conception of human motivation as a hierarchy of drives, with the "higher" (ideal) motives a dependent function ("ideology") of the "base" (material) drives; the motivation of man hence becomes a technical problem of correlating optimal material reinforcement with desired behavior, and the economic system is steered indirectly by fabricated stimuli rather than guided by norms. The expedient distribution of material rewards suspends class struggle by "buying off" demands and by emphasizing the common interest of all classes in maintaining the efficiency of the system. In sum, the

[193] Cf. "Technology and Science as 'Ideology,'" in Jürgen Habermas, *Toward a Rational Society: Student Protest, Science, and Politics*, trans. Jeremy Shapiro (Boston, 1970), pp. 81–122.

paramountcy of science and technology subordinates distributive justice to the drive for productive efficiency, as informed by the needs of machinery. Society becomes integrated on the basis of a complex division of labor into an "organic" system (*selon* Durkheim) difficult to understand; motives are alienated from action, means from ends, leaders from the led, and there is a dissolution of collective responsibility and consciousness of the meaning of one's actions to the whole: in short, an attenuation of corporate solidarity.

The Maoist critique of revisionism is based on norms derived from indigenous populist utopianism as well as a Marxist vision of the Communist future and is projected well in advance of any norms that have ever been operationalized.[194] The critique of functional specialization seems to imply a dismantling of the assembly line, for instance, and the critique of material incentives and differential pay scales seems to be based on the Communist norm "from each according to his ability, to each according to his need," rather than the Socialist norm, "from each according to his ability, to each according to his work." Criticizing Liu's "mistakes" on the basis of norms yet to be realized obscures the fact that *policy* differences between Liu and Mao were usually quite subtle. These differences concerned degree of change, scope of mobilization, and speed of implementation.[195] By generalizing from the premises on which these minor but fairly consistent differences were based, the critique could project two "roads" leading to entirely different destinations. This projection was based on the assumption that Liu's deviations were not mere tactical concessions but portents of a fundamentally disparate world-view, that "a fraction of an inch at the start can make a world of difference in the long run" (*shih chih hao li, ch'a chih ch'ien li*).

The logic of Mao's "proletarian revolutionary" road does seem to lead in a perceptibly different direction. Alienation between elite and masses, and the "three differences" between town and country, industry and agriculture, and mental and manual work, are resolved by enforcing universal participation in a "sacrament" of manual labor, by prescribing periodic status reversals for elites (*hsia-fang* and rotation of leadership), and by waging a constant campaign against "bureaucratism," including dismissal of a high proportion of staff and secretarial personnel at all levels. Resolution of these "differences" in the con-

194 For a brief review of the traditional populist origins of Mao's Thought, see Jean Chesneaux, "Egalitarian and Utopian Traditions in the East," in *Modern China*, ed. Joseph Levenson (London, 1971), pp. 189–198.

195 Tsou, "Revolution, Reintegration and Crisis in Communist China," in Tsou and Ho, *China in Crisis* 1, bk. 1: 296.

text of a general war against specialization entails derogation of the sciences from their special status as the pace-making productive force and the triumphal reentry of "politics." During the GPCR, "politics" meant the absolute paramountcy of the *volonté générale,* legitimating not only remarkable improvements in the lot of the disprivileged, but the subordination of virtually every realm of thought and endeavor to a uniform set of political bromides. The "united front" principle has been at least temporarily abandoned in a "cleansing of class ranks." "Class" no longer has any determinate relationship to the means of production (which have been socialized) but is defined by relationship to political authority. Moral incentives, in the form of a wide variety of exemplary "models," formal and informal titles arranged in hierarchical order of official and social recognition, have reasserted priority over material incentives: human and capital resources are allocated by a combination of moral incentives and administrative fiat rather than through labor and commodity markets. The general thrust of the collective will is indicated in Mao's Thought, whose meaning Mao is free to expand upon opportunely; the specific meaning is usually worked out on the basis of negotiations among workers, peasants, and local responsible persons. On the assumption that learning is essentially a service rather than an on-going discipline, institutional "standards" have been sacrificed to policies designed to recover the immediate relationship between theory and practice: the rustication of students, teachers, and cadres on a long-term basis, application of the work-study formula to *all* schools, and integration of schools with production units.

The viability of the Maoist road is yet to be demonstrated, and whether or not Liu's road can be abandoned in practice as easily as it could be repudiated in principle remains to be seen. One of the most significant effects of the GPCR has been a general widening and flattening of the pyramids of distribution of power, wealth, and educational and medical services. This development obviously enhances the political values of equality and mass participation, but the priority of equality over efficiency is by no means self-evident in a nation at China's stage of development, particularly if the two goals should turn out to conflict. Thus far, devolution of power to local levels has provided a great stimulus to investment in small rural industry, but conflicts of interest have already arisen between centrally planned and locally sponsored projects, resulting in recentralization tendencies.[196]

196 According to a recent report by the Hofei Party Committee in Anhwei in 1971, projects assigned to the province by central authorities were competing with small, locally planned enterprises for labor, materials, and funds. The problem was

Returning power to the "people" also opens the way for the "independent kingdom" syndrome to be transferred from the middle bureaucracy to grass-roots production units, where local vested interests may stymie central pressures for redistributive reforms and pit the values of grass-roots democracy against the values of the greatest good for the greatest number, as defined by the center. For instance, local units have used their influence to resist relocation of the unit of accounting from the team to the brigade or commune levels, a shift that would result in redistributive benefits for poorer production teams.[197] Finally, the democratization and expansion at the base of the educational pyramid was achieved at the cost of a poorer quality of education, turning the higher education system into little more than vocational training. Unless a necessarily "elitist" higher education system is reconstructed, China will be forced into dependence on other countries for purchase of technical innovations for development of its modern industrial sector.[198] The use of moral rather than material incentives seems feasible, but it necessitates regimentation as well as mobilization and presupposes an ideological uniformity potentially stifling to individual initiative, particularly to intellectual endeavor. The heavy reliance of the morale-building functions of the mass media

solved by a drastic cut-back in the local construction program: in Hofei alone, the reduction of the number of small projects from 245 to 128 released sufficient resources to fulfill the state construction project. Local reports implying that several other areas seem to have encountered similar problems suggest a reduction in the number of new units built and greater efforts to ensure that the projects are well run and in accord with the needs of the state economic plan as well as those of the area concerned. *The Economist* Intelligence Unit, *Quarterly Economic Review Summary*, no. 2 (June 20, 1972): 8; also Riskin, "Rural Industry," pp. 43 ff. (prepublication text).

197 Provinces richly endowed with natural resources also experience a spurt in industrial growth while those less endowed do not, presumably as a result of a "self-reliant" industrialization strategy. Claims for success in agricultural mechanization, for example, come from areas known to have deposits of iron and coal and a previously established industrial base: Shansi, Honan, Hupei and Liaoning have not only manufactured the machine tools necessary for the operation of local machine-building and repair factories but have also provided raw material and equipment and sent technicians to the localities to train personnel in the production, repair, and operation of agricultural technology. Kansu and Ninghsia, on the other hand, have weak industrial foundations, and agricultural mechanization has made little progress there. On resistance from more prosperous teams to attempts to transfer the unit of accounting to the brigade or commune, see Jonathan Unger, " 'Learn from Tachai': China's Agricultural Model," *CS* 9, no. 9 (September 7, 1971): 1 ff.; also *CS* 10, no. 8 (August 1972): 21–23. Peasants have at times resorted to kulak-like tactics to frustrate attempts at redistribution, such as poisoning private fish-ponds and engaging in "go-slow" tactics; though it is impossible to estimate the extent of such incidents, continued failure to socialize domestic industries or private plots hints at their efficacy.

198 *CS* 10, no. 8 (August 1972): 21–23; *CNA*, no. 853 (September 3, 1971).

tends to subvert the accuracy of its reporting and accounting functions, turning "truth" into a matter of prescriptive ("political") rather than empirical relationships.

In a brief preliminary assessment of the recharted Maoist roads, we may distinguish between three sectors of the Chinese political system: organizational, economic, and cultural. Although the GPCR has had an enduring impact on each sector, its impact on the cultural superstructure seems most secure. Its organizational impact was profound but still in contention with the outcome uncertain, and its impact on the economic system seems to have given way to extensive inroads of Liu Shao-ch'i-ism without Liu Shao-ch'i.

In the organizational sector, the GPCR broke the power of Liu's Party apparatus, reduced the perquisites of the bureaucratic "new class," and popularized the idea that political power may be legitimated only by active participation of the masses in government and simultaneous participation of elites in labor. The center's voluntary abdication of power to the localities, however, had the unanticipated consequence of giving free rein to continued factional indiscipline and local corruption, as an immediate result of which there was a militarization of the bureaucracy. To avoid the obvious dangers of this stop-gap solution, the Party was reconstructed in 1970 along the organizational lines of "democratic centralism," with the RCs at each level administratively subordinated to the Party committees. The result is an uneasy compromise between GPCR participatory values (as realized in "open-door rectification," *hsia-fang*, and so on) and a neo-Liuist emphasis on organizational discipline meant to combine the political benefits of the former with the administrative efficiency of the latter. In the economic sector, strong impetus was given to the redistribution of commodities and services to the peasant masses; there has been some reduction in wage differentials but not as much as might have been expected. Ch'en Po-ta's disappearance after the 2nd session of the 9th CC in August–September 1970 was followed the next spring by a campaign against "swindlers like Liu Shao-ch'i" who opposed "rational rewards," "work points based on fixed quotas," and cost accounting.[199] The campaign against functional specialization has been focused on political distinctions, meanwhile allowing quiet reinstate-

---

[199] Indeed, there has been a remarkable increase in purchases of Western and Japanese technology, financed beginning in 1972 by loans with 5-year terms. In the last few months of that year, state trading corporations placed orders for "hundreds of millions" of dollars' worth of high technology from the West, consisting primarily of transport, communications, and power equipment. *NYT*, November 13, 1972, pp. 57–58; January 21, 1973, p. 51; personal communication from Stanley Karnow upon his return from the PRC in the spring of 1973.

ment of "an absolute majority" (95–98 percent) of managerial and technical cadres, usually to their functionally specialized fields.[200] As the still miniscule modern industrial sector grows, it seems likely to require an increasingly minute division of labor that will necessitate training in relevant technical or managerial "expertise" and possibly create pressure for vertical stratification to correspond to the educational investment in various skills—although the depth of nativist opposition to such trends should not be underestimated.

The cultural sector was the one in which the Maoists had clearly articulated an alternative model prior to the GPCR and was also the one most detached from the economic system upon which the populace depends for its immediate sustenance. Maoist innovations in this sector (presently coordinated by Chiang Ch'ing, with a State Council "Cultural Group") seem to have been most sweeping and to have sustained the fewest post-GPCR retrenchments.[201] If Mao's judgment about the causal importance of ideas in history is sound, we may expect the revolution in culture to contribute significantly to the creation of new socialist men.

From an historical perspective, Liu Shao-ch'i and Mao Tse-tung are ephemeral personifications of great ideals and social interests that may be expected to interact long after both men are dead. Perhaps the greatest and most lasting impact of Liu's repudiation will be to give a new impetus and direction to political reform in China, henceforth to be implemented through somewhat more conventional and less disruptive means. Whether it will fall prey to institutional stagnation and spiritual attrition as it becomes integrated with everyday socio-economic reality cannot be predicted with certainty, but, in any case, "Maoism" may rank with ascetic Protestantism and Bolshevism as one of the great this-worldly ethics to have profoundly moved the modern world.

[200] *KMJP*, March 7, 15, 30, 1972; *PD*, January 26, March 29, 1972; quoted in Martin K. Whyte, " 'Red vs. Expert': Peking's Changing Policy," *Problems of Communism* 21, no. 6 (November–December 1972): 18–28.

[201] The opening to Western tourism that accompanied China's attainment of quasi great power status has been followed by a neo-nationalistic display of cultural treasures under the slogan, "Using the past to serve the present." Since 1970, D. W. Fokkema has detected an extremely cautious and limited thaw in the arts, entailing publication of several novels in 1970–1973 (none at all were published from 1966 to 1970). There have been minor concessions to expertise in the education system, including the return of examinations (in a more circumscribed role) and admission of some children of the bourgeoisie to schools on achievement criteria. Personal communications from D. W. Fokkema and from John Jamieson.

PART III
Criticism and Self-Criticism

The weapon of criticism certainly cannot replace the criticism of weapons; material force must be overthrown by material force; but theory, too, becomes a material force once it seizes the masses. Theory is capable of seizing the masses once it demonstrates *ad hominem*, and it demonstrates *ad hominem* once it becomes radical. To be radical is to grasp matters at the root. But for man the root is man himself.

—MARX, *Critique of Hegel's Philosophy of Right*

Marxism can develop only through struggle, and not only is this true of the past and the present, it is necessarily true of the future as well. What is correct invariably develops in the course of struggle with what is wrong. The true, the good and the beautiful always exist by contrast with the false, the evil and the ugly, and grow in struggle with the latter. As soon as a wrong thing is rejected and a particular truth accepted by mankind, new truths begin their struggle with new errors. Such struggles will never end. This is the law of development of truth and, naturally, of Marxism as well.

—MAO, "On the Correct Resolution of Contradictions Among the People"

8

TOWARD A THEORY
OF MASS CRITICISM

Criticism and self-criticism, the collective state's ironic testimony to the importance of the individual, is one of the primary categories of political action in China. During the GPCR, criticism and self-criticism became integrated with a second category of Chinese political action, the "mass line," and the resulting hybrid we term "mass criticism." In this chapter, we shall analyze mass criticism as a system of communication of intended meanings, first setting forth an heuristic model for the comparative study of target-oriented criticism movements, then proceeding to an examination of the Liu Shao-ch'i case in terms of this model.

What may we hope to achieve? We have in the course of this study had frequent occasion to refer to the ambiguous character of the criticism movement: its primary function is that of a *rectification* technique designed to correct political errors; its secondary function is that of a *mobilizational* technique meant to incite the masses to "educate themselves" through participation in the "mass line." A satisfactory theory should show how these two functions, "criticism" and "mass line," relate to each other, and how this relationship has changed over time. In Chapter 7, we encountered a confusing and apparently patternless mélange of true and false criticisms of Liu. Here, a satisfactory theory should do two things: first, it should explain the general process whereby criticisms are generated; second, it should set forth the rules according to which certain criticisms become distorted. A theory that fulfills these objectives would provide a useful methodological tool for the decodification of Chinese criticisms, which might be more generally applicable to other aspects of Chinese studies.

A MODEL OF MASS CRITICISM

According to Remy Kwant's phenomenological analysis of the functions of "critique," criticism presupposes a query as to whether the object in question is as it should be.[1] A negative answer confronts the person criticized (target) with his error (the object of criticism) and calls upon him to fulfill certain demands to rectify his error, while also leaving him free not to fulfill them; i.e., he is placed in a position of moral obligation. This moral obligation implies that both the critic (hereafter abbreviated C) and the target (T) know how the object of criticism (O) ought to be. This "ought to be" is the *norm* (N) of the criticism. T has a relationship of responsibility to O, and a relationship of obligation to N; the relationship between N and O is a logical one of contrariety (e.g., if O is "suppression of class struggle," then N is simply "nonsuppression of class struggle"). "Criticism" is thus "the evaluation of facts in the light of a norm," or C's evaluation of T's responsibility for O in the light of N. Now the Chinese have made a significant innovation in this process by staging it before an engaged mass audience (M): one of the functions of *mass* criticism is to induce the masses, by actively participating in C's criticism of T-O, to embrace N. In this respect, mass criticism may be understood as an important component of the moral incentive system, which is intended to replace material incentives and organizational discipline. It is not a "pure type" of moral incentive, however, for it entails coercive social sanctions against those who fail to embrace N and who thus become assimilated to T: "human targets" may be "dragged out," criticized, and publicly humiliated.

The entire process may be illustrated by a simple topological diagram, in which a solid line indicates the communication of criticism, a broken line a moral relationship (responsibility or obligation), and a dotted line indicates logical entailment (contrariety).

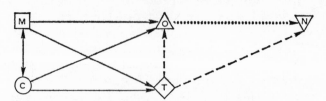

FIG. 2 THE PROCESS OF MASS CRITICISM

The system thus consists of five nodes: three roles (C, T, and M) and two symbols (O and N). C is the initiator of the process and the

[1] Remy Kwant, *Critique: Its Nature and Function* (Pittsburg, Pa., 1967), *passim*.

pivotal role in the system. As the "telescope and microscope" with the charismatic vision first to descry the hiatus between O and N, and as the source of many of the "model" criticism themes, the reputation of C is enhanced even as that of T declines. Who is C? In the GPCR, C was the "center," which was publicly (and usually correctly) understood to mean Mao Tse-tung. One cannot always strictly equate the two, because Mao's personal associates, such as Chou En-lai, Lin Piao, and various "comrades of the CCRG," often authoritatively quoted Mao's *in camera* remarks while adding their own interpretative glosses, or even acted on their own initiative, claiming plenipotentiary status (viz., the CCRG during the "fifty days").

M is the "revolutionary subject" whose most hateful instincts are given critical catharsis in order to awaken his noblest. In the GPCR, M was the "masses"—a deceptively monolithic term subsuming a congeries of violently antagonistic factions. As noted in Chapter 5, "revolutionary masses" were defined normatively (rather than socio-economically) on the basis of "Mao's Thought," which stipulated two criteria for inclusion: relative deprivation and maximal mobilization. The first criterion defined the "underdog" image of the masses, which made their moral and their physical power inversely proportionate. The second criterion bespoke a genuine attempt to square the real constituency of "masses" with its nominal definition. As a *PD* editorial announced on June 8, 1966, "Only when all 700 million engage in criticism can there be a clean-up." Anna Louise Strong's estimate that 200 million Chinese became actively engaged in criticism seems excessive,[2] but it is probable that the GPCR was more inclusive than any previous movement, with the possible exception of the land reform movement of 1946–52.

The most ambiguous role in the system is played by T, who was, of course, Liu Shao-ch'i. The "precritical" system comprised only M and N, with a vector leading from the former to the latter. The criticism process begins when C points to the N-O discrepancy and to T's responsibility for O. T is criticized for being situated at the point O when he "ought" to be at point N; in the criticisms, this situation became alternately formulated: T *appears* to be at point N, but *actually* he is at point O (i.e., he "waves a red flag to oppose the red flag"). The traditional imagistic polarities of ghosts versus men, appearance versus reality, light versus darkness, purity versus filth, and exposed versus concealed are evoked in the polemical literature to dramatize the relationship between O and N, and T's ambiguous relationship to his contradiction. This triangular relationship lends emotional dynamism to the criticism process.

[2] *PD*, June 8, 1966; A. L. Strong, *Letter from China*, no. 51 (September 23, 1967).

We may slightly anticipate Chapter 10 by noting that the system of "mass criticism" described here is an historical outgrowth of the system of "inner-Party struggle" developed at Yenan, which was structurally identical except that M was consigned to a passive role.[3] The primary function of "criticism and self-criticism" or inner-Party struggle was rectification of the O-N hiatus and the redemption of T; the *secondary* function was the education of M.[4] The practice of "criticism and self-criticism" was governed by the formal rules of "principled struggle": first, it must "submit to reason"; second, it must concern "points of issue" rather than be "against the person." Both rules, the second more directly than the first, functioned to maintain a distinction between O and T and to isolate T from the process.

In "mass criticism," M is assigned a much more active role in the process, and the C-M relationship changes from the "educational" one Liu described in 1941 to the more reciprocal (if not yet symmetrical) "mass line." Although the O-N hiatus is *prima facie* considered an opprobrious deviation from the proper relationship between M and N, in terms of the "mass line" relationship between C and M, it may be valued positively as a mobilizing and teaching device ("negative example").[5] Act O challenges the integrity of N and "calls for" N's reaffirmation; if M can be brought to criticize O, this situates M on the straight-line continuum between the negative O-pole and the positive N-pole and reflexively impels M in an N-ward direction. "The sharper and the more thorough our criticism, the less rightist we can be," a Red Guard tabloid cogently argued, resolving a factional identity crisis. "When our criticism is 'leftist' of course we cannot be rightist,

[3] Chou En-lai alludes to the more passive role of the masses in a comparison of the GPCR with the Yenan Cheng-feng Movement: "The rectification campaign was carried out during wartime and could be carried out only among the cadres of higher levels. Moreover, not many of the cadres of higher levels were able to hoist high the great red flag of Mao Tse-tung's thought." "Premier Chou Talks about Why Firepower Must Be Concentrated on Criticizing the Top Party Person Taking the Capitalist Road," *Hung-se chan-pao* [Red battle news] (Canton), no. 15 (November 9, 1967): 1–4, in *JPRS*, no. 44574 (March 4, 1968): 28.

[4] While approving the educative role of struggle, Liu reproved those who led struggles of educative value unrelated to the views of the victims: "They purposely look for 'targets of struggle' (comrades inside the Party) and conduct the struggle against them as representatives of opportunism. They sacrifice this one comrade or these few comrades, 'killing the rooster to frighten the dog,' as the Chinese saying goes, in order to make other comrades work harder and fulfill the task." "On Inner-Party Struggle" (July 1941), *CW* 1:345.

[5] A. L. Strong noticed this reversal of priorities. "The aim of the Cultural Revolution is not to remove from office those 'top Party persons in authority taking the capitalist road,'" she observed. "The real aim is to educate hundreds of millions of people that they may detect and then correct the 'symptoms of revisionism' when these appear." Strong, *Letter*, no. 51.

but we must be opposed to the Right." [6] The most successful "drives" in the history of Chinese Communist mass movements have been based on the definition of a positive objective by means of a negative counterpole.[7] Just as American advertising men have learned to transmute sexual desire into a demand for specific commodities, Chinese publicists have learned to transform diffuse, idiosyncratic grievances into a drive for political change. "What was it that won over most villages to us? The expositions of bitterness," Mao told André Malraux. In 1957, he wrote:

What is correct invariably develops in the course of struggle with what is wrong. The true, the good, and the beautiful always exist in comparison with the false, the evil, and the ugly, and grow in struggle with the latter.[8]

The following story (one of many) illustrates how this "reflexive normative incentive" functioned in the course of the mass criticism of Liu Shao-ch'i:

They welcomed PLA men assigned the task of supporting revolutionary peasants in the area saying, "He has been overthrown and discredited completely and fortunately this place is so far away from him that we haven't been hit by his influence." The PLA men pointed out a lot of revisionist things that had been occurring and compared China's Khrushchev's teachings with Mao's thought. "Communist members now understand that the root of reaction in their own area lay in the line leading to restoration of capitalism which was constantly encouraged by China's Khrushchev. . . . The commune members came to realize still more profoundly the importance of the revolutionization of their own thinking in order to uproot revisionism. . . . The effect of the mass repudiation is now showing itself in the heightened enthusiasm of the commune members, the beautifully cultivated farmland, and the rich crops.[9]

---

[6] "Pursue Remnant Foes with Courage Still Left to Us," *Ping-t'uan chan-pao* [Pingt'uan battle news] (Peking), no. 4 (December 16, 1966); 1, in *JPRS*, no. 40234 (March 13, 1967): 89–90.

[7] Yu notes that "grievance" is "probably the single most important power-producing element, serving to generate the necessary heat and energy for the operation of class struggle." The Communists exploit grievance, he notes, by transforming personal into mass hatred and individual into class hatred. Frederick T. C. Yu, *Mass Persuasion*, pp. 31–34.

[8] Quoted in *PD* editorial, June 8, 1966, also in *RF*, no. 9, 1966. Mao has frequently taken note of the importance of negative examples. "We should award Khrushchev a medal weighing one ton for the valuable lessons his mistakes have taught us," he once remarked. Terrill, *800,000,000*, p. 78.

[9] NCNA, July 28, 1967, in *SCMP*, no. 3992 (August 1, 1967): 10–12. A world-famous example of Chinese skill in linking emotionally salient symbols by analogy to political reform movements was the mass propaganda drive in 1952 against alleged U.S. bacteriological warfare in Korea, which was integrated with domestic health work in the Patriotic Health Drive. The movement proved so successful and so

In the GPCR, the importance attributed to stimulating an effective C-M "mass line" interaction grew to rival and even (as we shall demonstrate in Liu's case) eclipse the importance attached to rectification of the O-N hiatus and redemption (or purge) of T. Due to conflict between the need to close the O-N gap (for rectification purposes) and the need to preserve or even amplify it (for pedagogic purposes), the rising salience of the "mass line" function of criticism naturally introduced certain distortions in its primary redemptive function. These will be examined in greater detail in Chapter 10, but we may list these distortions summarily. First, the iterative C-M relationship ("mass line") exhibited a constant escalatory tendency that transformed the O-N relationship from logical contrariety to political contradiction (A: anti-A): through "exclusion of the middle," all that is not Mao's Thought is seen to negate it. Second, T's "principled" isolation from the process is discontinued, and attacks "against the person" are launched. Third, activation of M in the reciprocal C-M interaction results in a heterodox and sometimes contradictory admixture of criticisms, which do not necessarily "submit to reason."

A chronological dimension is also superimposed on the system in order to suppress traditional "golden age" or cyclical (dynastic cycle) notions of time and reinforce commitment to the highly optimistic Marxist view of history, in terms of which T/O is viewed as an interloper from an onerous past. Thus Liu's purge is linked with the purges of P'eng Te-huai, Kao Kang and Jao Shu-shih, Ch'en Shao-yü, and even with the battle against the Kuomintang. Liu represents an "invasion of the repressed." In an example from the criticisms:

This quiet woman took the floor and hit out hard at the senseless talk of China's Khrushchev that "exploitation has its merits." She gave instances from her own experience, describing how child workers toiled twelve to thirteen hours a day in the old days and led a life of starvation. She contrasted the old life with the earth-shaking changes since Liberation when the working class, as masters of the state, began building socialism and helping the world revolution. "Socialism saved us," she declared. "We must not let China be dragged back onto the capitalist road!" [10]

---

economical to the government that it was established as an annual health drive. *A Regional Handbook on East China* (Human Relations Area Files, New Haven Conn., Subcontract HRAF-29 Stanford-3, 1956) 1:414.

[10] "We Must Not Let China Be Dragged Back onto the Capitalist Road!" NCNA, Shanghai, December 14, 1967, in *JPRS*, no. 44241 (February 9, 1968): 61–63. "The more one hates the old society, the more one will love the Party and the new society." *Ta kung pao* [Daily worker] (Peking), editorial, September 8, 1963, in *SCMP*, no. 3072 (October 3, 1963): 3–6.

THE LIU SHAO-CH'I CASE

In order to analyze the Liu Shao-ch'i case in terms of the model of criticism presented above, it is necessary to abstract our evaluation of the validity of the various criticisms against him in more easily comparable form. The purpose of tabular and graphic presentation most assuredly is not to give the impression that the judgments are either precise or objective, for they are neither, but to make those judgments explicit and thus facilitate further analysis. The various criticism themes are evaluated on the basis of the evidence presented in Chapter 7, and on the same logical criteria: (1) "Confessed": Was the criticism conceded in any of Liu's three available self-criticisms or in Wang Kuang-mei's Tsinghua "trials"? (2) "Accurate": Can it be verified by independent valid documents? (3) "Valid": Is it at odds with Mao's stated views, or with central policy, at the time? (4) "Sincere": Was the policy in question rectified after Liu's removal? To these four criteria we have added in column 5 a summary evaluation of "truth": if the criticism satisfies the first four criteria it is rated "true," but if it clearly fails to satisfy even one, it is considered "false." The only exception to this rule is column 1, "confessed": a negative answer in column 1 does not falsify a criticism if it is contradicted by a positive answer in any other column. Answers are coded Y-yes, N-no, M-indeterminately mixed, and O-no data. Neither Ms nor Os are tabulated.

We may now "translate" Table 1 into the terms of the model presented in Figure 2. Rule 1 ("confessed") corresponds to the relationship between Target, Object, and Norm; it consists of T's acknowledgment of the contradictory relationship between O and N, as noted by C, and of his personal responsibility for that relationship. Liu's confirmation ratio in column 1 under Criteria is quite high (4 Ys, 1 N): he stubbornly denied "subjective opposition" to Mao (criticism IIA.3), and, although he admitted approving dissolution of 200,000 APCs in 1955, he added that he had "made every effort to advocate the socialist transformation of capitalist industry and commerce" (the M in criticism III.A.2).

Rule 2 ("accuracy") has an extremely high confirmation ratio (12:1), which may be skewed somewhat by the imbalance between vast amounts of anti-Liu material made available by his critics and limited amounts of pro-Liu or objective material. This makes it easy to confirm an accurate criticism but difficult to verify an inaccurate one.

Rule 3 ("validity") refers to the relationship between C's current definition of N and his definition of N at the time O was committed;

Table 1

THE CRITICISMS: A LOGICAL EVALUATION

Criticisms	Confessed	Accurate	Valid	Sincere	True
I. Philosophical	Y	M	M	Y	Y
II. Political					
A. The Liberal					
1. Anti-"proletarian dictatorship"	O	M	N	Y	N
2. Anti-"class struggle"	Y	Y	N	M	N
3. Anti-Mao	N	N	N	Y	N
4. Foreign policy	O	Y	N	N	N
5. Party-building policy	O	M	N	Y	N
6. Nationalities and religions policy	O	Y	N	Y	N
B. The Dictator					
1. Oppression of non-Party masses (SEM & GPCR)	Y	Y	Y	Y	Y
III. Economic					
A. Opposition to socialism					
1. "Shielding" bourgeoisie	O	Y	N	M	N
2. Otherwise obstructing socialization	M	M	Y	O	M
B. "Revisionism"					
1. Agricultural mechanization	O	Y	Y	Y	Y
2. Business and commerce	O	Y	Y	Y	Y
3. Labor	Y	Y	Y	Y	Y
IV. Cultural					
A. Art and Literature	O	Y	Y	Y	Y
B. Education	O	Y	M	Y	Y
C. Journalism	O	Y	Y	Y	Y
D. Science and technology	O	I	M	Y	Y
E. Medicine	O	Y	Y	Y	Y
Totals: Ys	4	12	8	14	10
Ns	1	1	7	1	7

Code: Y = yes; N = no; M = indeterminately mixed; O = no data.

more simply put, it may be said to refer to the "true" distance between C and T. The unusually *low* confirmation ratio for rule 3 (8:7, lowest on the chart) indicates that the C-T gap, at any given time prior to criticism, was much narrower than the criticisms suggest. The difference between C and N—representing, respectively, Mao's Thought at the time of O's *commission* and Mao's Thought at the time of *criticism*—is defined by the difference between rules 3 and 4; the magnitude of this difference is a measure of the radicalization of Mao's thought between 1939 and 1966 (whereas only eight of Liu's "crimes" contradicted Mao's Thought at the time of commission, fourteen contradicted Maos' thought at the time of criticism). Liu's guilt was to a considerable degree defined by this radicalization of norms. Dai Hsiao-ai recognized this when he said:

It seemed to me and my friends that Mao had changed his demands and was condemning Liu and a host of lower officials who were doing what they always had done. . . . Mao had, in effect, changed the definition of Communist and these others had failed to keep pace or had opposed him.[11]

The great, "true" distance between T-N (as defined either subjectively, in column 1, or objectively, in column 2), as contrasted with the short distance between T-C (defined by column 3) suggests that, although Liu's purge was certainly "sincere," it was more sincerely "revolutionary" than it was "critical." This observation seems to militate against the frequently heard argument that the GPCR was a power struggle disguised as a revolution; to the contrary, it was a *revolution* disguised as a *power struggle,* at least insofar as Liu Shao-ch'i was concerned. (Of course, insofar as secondary power-holders or "Liuists" were concerned, the GPCR involved a true power struggle.) In Liu's case, the N-O hiatus was artificially polarized for educational purposes.

Is it possible to impute a causal relationship between the truth of the criticisms (column 5) and Liu's fall? Of a total of eighteen discriminable themes, ten were judged true, seven false, one indeterminate. The relationship between this in itself unimpressive truth ratio (55 percent) and subsequent mass criticism or purge can only be judged by comparison with other criticism or purge victims. Although a systematic analysis has not been undertaken, superficial comparison suggests the importance of distinguishing between criticism and purge: the

[11] Bennett and Montaperto, *Red Guard,* p. 146. What Dai failed to recognize was first, that the decision was not solely Mao's but the outcome of a dynamic process of "mass criticism" in which Mao played an initiatory but not always dominant role, and second, that the redefinition of norms was not solely for the purpose of implicating Liu, but to reorient the polity toward higher goals.

relationship between a reasonably high confirmation ratio in column 5 and mass criticism seems to be both necessary and sufficient; the relationship between a high ratio and purge is necessary but not sufficient. This point is clearly indicated (though not systematically demonstrated) by comparison of Liu's score with the scores and fates of more fortunate "revisionists." [12] Also necessary for purge, it seems, are variables not included among the public criticism themes.

What is the relationship between truth and intensity of criticism? An answer to this question presupposes some measure of the intensity of criticism. Given the comprehensive scope of the anti-Liu campaign, a satisfactory sampling technique is difficult to devise; we thus took a complete sample of translated articles (realizing that reliance on the translation services may still bias the sample geographically in favor of South China) and categorized each article by theme. As Table 2 indicates, there seems to be no relationship between truth and criticism intensity: there are, in fact, appreciably more articles dedicated to themes we judged false (viz., 201) than to "true" themes (viz., 150). In other words, whereas 45 percent of the themes were false, 57 percent of the published criticisms were false. This incongruency evidently arises from the desire of central elites to educate the masses about objective problems that may have no discernible connection to the views of the target, a task that is facilitated by the closed public arena and high degree of central control over public information.

Having already dealt with the "true" criticisms in the conclusion to Chapter 7, it may be of interest to analyze more closely the process of polemical distortion accounting for the 57 percent "false" criticisms.

One of the most perceptive attempts to formulate a theory to account for the distortion of political actions into culpable offenses is Nathan Leites' and Elsa Bernaut's analysis of the Moscow purge trials. They detected the operation of a set of "rules of translation" in the

---

[12] For example, Li Hsien-nien repeatedly opposed rapid collectivization in the 1960s (Chang, "Power and Policy," p. 13); he admitted that he first "wavered" at the Lushan Plenum, and in the post-Leap retrenchment period as a Vice-Premier and concurrent Minister of Finance, he played an active role in introducing "revisionist" economic policies. In 1964 he was involved in the formation of "trusts." In 1966 he sent work teams to the Ministry of Finance to suppress the revolutionaries: his policy of "three simultaneous sweepings—simultaneously up and down and back and forth and right and left" allegedly resulted in attacks on 90 percent of the cadres in the Minstry of Finance, yet, as late as February 1972, he continued to defend his "sweeping" policy as an error of scope rather than a basic error of line. Gordon Bennett, "Chou to the Rescue," *FEER* 59, no. 11 (March 1968): 448. Although he was criticized in the winter and spring of 1967, Li was neither purged nor demoted; in fact he is, as of 1973, the third or fourth most powerful figure in the Politburo. Ch'en Yün, author of the notorious "responsibility field system" in the early 1960s, is also a Politburo member. Ch'en I, Li Fu-ch'un, and Chou En-lai were also associated with various Liuist policies, and all were criticized, yet none was purged.

Table 2

A. CRITICISM FREQUENCIES

Criticisms	Frequencies*			Truth[a]
	Official	Red Guard	Total	
I. Philosophical	27	2	29	Y
II. Political				
A. The Liberal				
1. Antiproletarian dictatorship	20	0	20	N
. 2. Anticlass struggle	44	4	48	N
3. Anti-Mao	4	3	7	N
4. Foreign policy	6	0	6	N
5. Party-building policy	29	2	31	N
6. Nationalities	1	2	3	N
B. The Dictator				
1. Oppression	15	8	23	Y
III. Economic				
A. Opposition to socialism	53	4	57	N
B. "Revisionism"	61	6	67	Y
IV. Cultural				
A. Art and literature	23	4	27	Y
B. Education	8	6	14	Y
C. Journalism	6	2	8	Y
D. Science and technology	5	0	5	Y
E. Medicine	6	0	6	Y
Yes =	124	26	150	7
No =	184	17	201	7

* As indicated by number of critical articles appearing in *SCMP, SCMM, CB* and their supplements, 1966–69.
[a] As indicated in Table 1.

extraction of punishable confessions. These rules, to which both prosecutor and defendant tacitly agreed, related the defendant's act to the formal charge in somewhat the same way that wishes are related by an imagined sequence of events to a desired end in the process of daydreaming. In distinction from a day-dream, the fact that translation proceeded according to set rules (however implausible in themselves) indicates that the fabricated charges bore a determinate relationship to reality.[13]

[13] Nathan Leites and Elsa Bernaut, *Ritual of Liquidation* (Glencoe, Ill., 1954), pp. 111 ff. Succinctly formulated, these rules were: (1) The end is in the beginning;

The term "rule of translation" may be used only with reservation in the case of Liu Shao-ch'i, inasmuch as "translation" implies a fidelity to the original "text," whereas in GPCR criticisms such fidelity was often overriden by the critic's faithfulness to a preconceived *model of guilt*. Not only would facts be chosen to fit translation rules, but translation rules would be interchanged to fit the facts, in keeping with the exigencies of the model. The term "translation" is helpful in pointing out the critic's need to find his raw material in the target's language; it must simply be borne in mind that the range of translation was limited by the confines of the model.

This model of Liu's guilt was not fixed but rather was based on an ensemble of objective exigencies that arose in the course of the movement and constantly shifted in relative importance according to the evolving constellation of forces and circumstances. These exigencies projected four broad parameters for the formulation of criticism themes, or "formation rules."

(1) The "true" criticism themes, as defined in column 5 of Table 1, formed *prototypes* for the construction of other criticisms on the basis of analogy. Criticisms of Liu's most *recent* "crimes" also formed a prototype for criticisms by analogy to incidents in his more remote past. In fact, the two categories tended to coincide: the most frequently repeated criticisms referring to errors committed between 1960 and 1966 also tended to be true.[14] These comprised oppression of non-Party masses (IIB.1.), economic "revisionism" (III.B), and the entire category of "cultural" criticisms (IV). False criticisms to the effect that Liu shielded the bourgeoisie and consistently obstructed socialization (III.A) were apparently selected on the basis of their perceived resemblance to Liu's policies during the retrenchment period. False criticisms of Liu's Party-building policies (IIA.5.) seemed to be extensions of true criticisms of his oppression of non-Party masses

---

with time, small beginnings have enormous sequels; (2) exclusion of the middle— intermediate positions are impossible, or at least unstable and inefficient; (3) motives are irrelevant; (4) predicting is preferring; and (5) means are equivalent (since they are chosen purely on the basis of expedience). Superficial comparison suggests that the first, second, fourth, and fifth also apply to the mass criticism of Liu Shao-ch'i; the third rule emphatically does not apply, for malevolent motives were always imputed, even when the deeds were innocuous. This seems to betoken the significant Chinese departures from the Bolshevik "ethic of consequences" (*Verantwortungsethik*) for an "ethic of ultimate ends" (*Gesinnungsethik*); the latter encourages "inner-directed," ultimately "religious" conduct. H. H. Gerth and C. Wright Mills, *From Max Weber: Essays in Sociology* (New York 1958), pp. 120–121.

14 See Figure 4, which indicates that 11.1 percent of the criticisms focus on the 1925–48 period, 39.2 percent on the 1949–59 period, and 49.6 percent on the 1960–66 period.

(IIB.1.) False criticisms of Liu's pre-1960 "revisionist" cultural policies were also based on analogy to his post-1960 cultural policies.

(2) The model reflected the interests of the critics, which were in turn shaped by their respective social backgrounds and political experience. As Table 2 indicates, the disproportionate concern of the official press with Liu's alleged opposition to proletarian dictatorship, class struggle, and Party-building policies reflects an interest of the elites in maintaining a structure of authority. The official press also devoted much more attention than the Red Guard press to the relatively sophisticated issues of economic policy, using its privileged access to information for public educational purposes. The experience of the Red Guards had been for the most part confined to family and school, at most including low-level employment. The relatively high concentration on lèse majesté (which is much less apparent in the gross categorization of articles in Table 2 than in a paragraph-by-paragraph reading of each article) is perhaps related to the fact that Red Guards (whose salient status was that of children in Chinese families) saw Liu's relationship to Mao in essentially filial terms. The Red Guards, as culture consumers who had not yet been fully integrated into the political or economic systems, generally showed less concern for political themes and more for cultural themes, with an understandable emphasis on education (10 percent of all Red Guard criticisms were concerned with Liu's educational policies, as compared to only 2 percent of all official criticisms). Among political categories, Red Guards showed no evident concern with the erosion of proletarian dictatorship but made a stronger protest against oppression of non-Party masses than did the official press (13 percent of all Red Guard criticisms, versus 5 percent of official criticisms). This is, of course, due to their location at the bottom of the Chinese socio-economic pyramid, to their status as long-term victims of domestic, school, and political authorities, as well as to their suppression during the "fifty days" (though protests against work team oppression comprised the bulk of criticisms in IIB.1. in Table 2, no doubt because it was sanctioned).

(3) There was a need to formulate "crimes" serious enough to justify severe organizational sanctions, whose application was probably decided in early 1967, at any rate certainly before the official media campaign started at the beginning of April. This pragmatic imperative [15] is the only factor that seems capable of accounting for the

[15] Mao seems to have yielded to the same imperative in his prosecution of the "Anti-Bolshevik Corps" at Fut'ien in 1930, as in later purges. See Ronald Suleski, "The Fu-t'ien Incident, December 1930," in Early Communist China: Two Studies (Ann Arbor, Michigan, 1969), pp. 1-28.

egregious fabrications that make up the formal charges brought against Liu at the Twelfth Plenum in October 1968.

(4) In an interesting permutation of the first "formation rule," analogies first used to lend rhetorical force to an accusation were transformed from virtual to literal status and a figure of speech would become an earnest, documented criticism. For example, the term "counterrevolutionary coup d'état" was first coined by Lin Piao to dramatize his attack on P'eng Chen in a May 1966 speech; it was subsequently reified and elaborated into an allegation involving extensive troop movements, secret meetings and communications, and convocation of a CC Plenum for the purpose of ousting Mao.[16] Although both Chou En-lai and K'ang Sheng repudiated the "coup" theory in the spring of 1967 for lack of evidence,[17] it became so widely accepted that anyone involved with the "February Outline" (including K'ang Sheng, who was on the original Group of Five) fell under a pall of suspicion.

This "model of formation rules" was used by polemical writers in much the same way a social scientist uses a conceptual model:[18] it was projected against Liu's past life, and every point of tangency between event and model was then "translated" by the appropriate rule into one of the categories of "crimes." "Tangency" was defined according to the following four criteria:

(a) Perceived analogy to frequently repeated or recent criticism themes (*supra*).

(b) Spatio-temporal contiguity. For example, although allegations of treason and espionage were unfounded, it is true that Wang Kuang-mei served as a Communist interpreter for the Americans during CCP-KMT negotiations in 1945, so she *could* have been spying for the Americans. Many of the concrete details surrounding Liu's alleged betrayals were also accurately described. The critic thus moves *a posse ad esse* from a convincing documentation of the possibility of the criminal event to infer its probability.

(c) The importance attached to certain pivotal historical periods was the third criterion of "tangency." The criticisms of Liu tend to accumulate at certain points at which the CCP made watershed decisions, many of which were subsequently felt to be inconsistent with

16 Cf. B. Bogunovic, "The Storm in July," *Politika*, in *SCMP*, no. 3855, (January 9, 1961): 1–5.

17 *Asahi*, May 8, in *DSJP*, May 9, 1967, p. 39.

18 The difference, hopefully, is that social scientists are disinterested and report negative as well as confirming cases. The process also bears a certain resemblance to psychoanalysis, in which the physician attempts to bring to light a relationship between certain consistent syntactic "errors" (parapraxes) and a traumatic prototypical "scene" in the patient's history. Cf. Jürgen Habermas, "On Systematically Distorted Communication," *Inquiry* 13, no. 3 (autumn 1970): 205–219.

the later course of the movement and all of which conceivably involved intense inner-Party disputes. Figure 3 suggests that criticisms
tend to be concentrated at certain "crucial points" when major decisions were made: 1936 (a transition period one year after the disastrous Long March in flight from the KMT reached Yenan and one

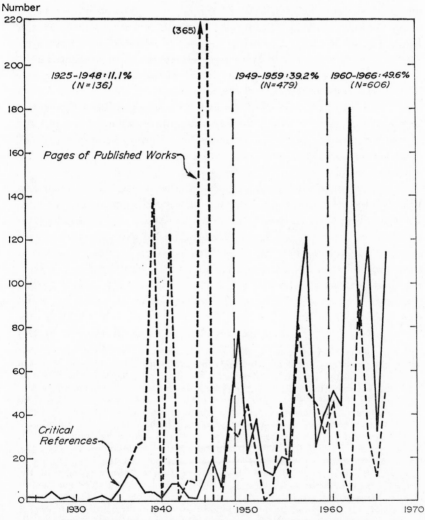

FIG. 3 LIU SHAO-CH'I'S CHRONOLOGY OF CRIMES, 1925–66
Indicates the frequency of references to guilt for particular years, in a selected
sample of itemized critical life histories compiled by Red Guard/official presses,
as compared with the chronology of Liu Shao-ch'i's literary output. Indexed
by pages per year over the same time span in his (unofficial) *Collected Works.*

year before the conclusion of a second united front with the KMT), 1945–46 (a period of uneasy true and negotiation with a once and future enemy), 1950 (transition of governments, land reform), 1955 (the decision to collectivize agriculture and establish joint public-private ownership of industry), 1957 (transition from "thaw" as represented by the "Hundred Flowers" to "freeze" as represented by the anti-rightist campaign and the GLF), 1960–62 (transition from GLF to retrenchment), and 1964 (launching of SEM and would-be transition from retrenchment to ideological revival). The criticisms thus corresponded in their unevenly clustered frequencies to the repeated allegation that "at every crucial point" in the history of the CCP, Liu and his cohorts "came out" to attack the revolution.[19]

(d) The fourth criterion of "tangency" was a possible relationship between availability of sheer quality of documentary evidence and the chronological distribution of criticisms, but Figure 3, comparing Liu's annual literary output with the frequency of criticisms, indicates no apparent correlation.

It will be noted that these criteria for the translation of events in Liu's life into crimes are arranged according to a progressively more indulgent conception of truth. Although a systematic test of this hypothesis has not been attempted, an examination of the diffusion process suggests that the application of progressively less rigorous translation rules proceeded in sequence as each step was exhausted through repetition of that particular set of themes.[20] The timing of this logical regression was unevenly staggered, however, following the lag in the geographical diffusion of themes. The initial parameters for the translation process seemed to be set by considerations of *timeliness:* Liu

19 This however seems to contradict a second tenet of the chronology implicit within the polemic, which is the absolutely immutable quality of Liu's villainy. Liu was born in sin and grew to manhood as a "filial scion of the landlord class"; he "wormed" his way into the Party at the time of its founding to "speculate on revolution," and he "usurped" every office he ever held. This characterization seems to be an expression of the vigorous ideological imperialism that characterized GPCR polemics, a quest for moral absolutes that vaulted both spatial and temporal barriers. Mao's thought (and Liu's opposition to it) became eternal and universal; history became an undifferentiated extension of the revolutionary present. The Communists attempt to reconcile the contradiction between the immutability of guilt and the periodicity of crime by reference to the "people/enemies of the people" distinction: contradictions among the people are mutable and contradictions between the people and the enemy are immutable. In Liu's case, superposition of this conceptual framework on Liu's career resulted in a deep cleavage between Liu's appearance and his essence—Liu's essential guilt was immutable, its appearance opportunistic; his intention to do mischief was constant, his ability dependent on circumstances.

20 For a study of the diffusion of criticism at an earlier point in the GPCR, see Clifford Edmunds, "Historicism, Ideology and Political Authority in Communist China: The Case of Chien Po-tsan" (Master's essay, University of Chicago, 1968), pp. 135 ff.

functioned as a "negative example" to stimulate the masses reflexively to achieve certain normative goals, which shifted with the "flux and flow" of the movement. In the fall and winter of 1966–67, for instance, Liu was blamed for cadre suppression of Red Guards. In the spring of 1967, however, Liu was attacked for hitting at "a large number of good or comparatively good cadres" in order to protect "a handful": the reflexive normative message was that "Revolutionary Cadres Must Be Treated Correctly." The unfounded accusation that Liu fostered a "mountain-stronghold mentality" or "theory of many centers" first appeared in the fall of 1967, when the Maoists took a hard line against Red Guard factionalism.[21] The attack on Liu's "economism" coincided with a wave of strikes and demonstrations by contract laborers; the criticism of his Party-building policies coincided with the effort to rebuild the Party in the fall of 1968. In the initial stages of the GPCR, Liu was denounced for demanding "absolute obedience"; this essentially accurate criticism did not disappear in later stages when order was being restored but was coupled with an increasingly stressed injunction to restore "revolutionary discipline." Thus, each period in the movement, depending on the balance of forces and moral prestige, called for a limited assortment of criticism themes; with these themes in mind, the critics would scrutinize the evidence at their disposal and formulate criticisms, following the sequence of rules shown in Table 3.

Table 3

PROJECTED DECISION SEQUENCE FOR FORMULATION
OF CRITICISMS

Rule	Time			
	1	*2*	*3*	*4*
1. Is the criticism true?	Yes	No	No	No
2. Is it analogous to a true criticism?		Yes	No	No
3. Is is objectively possible?			Yes	No
4. Did it occur at a crucial point in history?				Yes

21 A more adequate explanation of the inability of factions to unite would take into account the competition of polyarchal groups in a political culture that defined polyarchy as illegitimate (and "class struggle" as legitimate), with the result that each group struggled to achieve hegemony by overpowering its competitors. Cf. Robert Dahl, *Polyarchy: Competition and Opposition* (New Haven, Conn. 1971), pp. 105–123; also Robert Dahl, ed., *Regimes and Oppositions* (New Haven and London, 1973), pp. 1–27.

CONCLUSION

The purpose of this chapter has been to construct a general semiotic model of the "mass criticism" process and to apply this model to the Liu Shao-ch'i case. The model makes clear that mass criticism is *ambiguous* in its action implications, with an inherent contradiction between its primary purpose, which is to rectify the gap between norm and object of criticism and redeem (or purge) the target, and its secondary purpose, which is to create an effective pedagogic relationship between critic and mass audience by using the N-O relationship as an heuristic device. Application of the model to the Liu Shao-ch'i case indicates that the hiatus between norm and object was not altogether fabricated but that it was artificially polarized into an antagonistic contradiction in order to sustain the is-ought tension from which the process derives its moral impetus and reflexively to stimulate the masses to attain given political objectives. To the extent that its primary purpose was thus superseded by its secondary purpose, the mass criticism of Liu Shao-ch'i was "a revolution disguised as a power struggle"; Liu's self-criticisms might have been publicly accepted only if Mao had decided to terminate the process.

The introduction of the masses to an active role in the criticism process dictated the sacrifice of earlier tenets of "principled" criticism (i.e., impersonality and rationality) in order to maximize popular participation in the "mass line" relationship between critic and mass audience. It also entailed the distortion or fabrication of criticisms and the dramatization of contradictions with indigenous religious or folk imagery in order to teach lessons not always related to the views of the target. Our model implies that political evil in China is generally perceived as an empirical manifestation of an abstract system of ideas, which are linked by analogy. The "translation" of biographical events in the life of the target into punishable "crimes" seemed to follow rules of progressively less rigorous character, applied within the periodically shifting parameters projected by the evolving balance of forces and moral prestige in the movement.

9

MASS CRITICISM AND MASS LINE

The significance of the criticism of Liu Shao-ch'i in China's process of development, we suggested in the introduction to Chapter 8, lay in the attempt to unite mass line and criticism and self-criticism into what we have termed mass criticism. This attempt, however, took place in a social context altogether different from the one in which the norms governing these processes were first set forth and had quite different social ramifications. In this chapter, we analyze the "mass line" component of mass criticism; in the final chapter, we shall summarize the structural evolution of "criticism and self-criticism."

ORIGIN AND DEVELOPMENT OF THE MASS LINE

Both the mass line and criticism and self-criticism (also called "inner-Party struggle") seem to have assumed definitive theoretical form during the Yenan Party rectification movement of 1942–44. Whereas criticism–self-criticism was intended primarily to function as a mode of decision making and conflict management among cadres at the same hierarchical level (often members of the same work team or Party committee), the mass line was meant to facilitate communication and create policy consensus *between* hierarchical levels. "We must teach the masses clearly what we received from them confusedly," Mao explained to André Malraux; politically relevant information was to travel "from the masses, to the masses." [1] The "masses" in question included both rank-and-file members of the CCP and "non-Party masses," as Mao made clear in "Some Questions Concerning Methods of Leadership" (June 1, 1943); "Get Organized!" (November 29, 1943); and "On Strengthening the Party Committee System" (September 28,

[1] André Malraux, *Anti-Memoirs*, pp. 369–370.

1948). Cadres first observed the masses' "scattered and unsystematic views" in order to identify problems; they then summed up these scattered views in reports, which were forwarded to the highest committee responsible for that region. That committee then issued authoritative directions or instructions, which were sent back through the apparatus to be explained and popularized among the masses. To emphasize the fluidity and interconnectedness between discrete steps in the process, John Lewis condenses his description into a single monstrous neologism: "Problem identification–investigation–preliminary decision–testing-revision–report–authoritative decision–implementation–supervision–new problem comprises the life cycle of the action affecting a particular policy decision." [2]

The mass line was developed in the primitive conditions of the Yenan base area. Due to the peasant backgrounds and low literacy rate of its participants, communication was predominantly oral and face-to-face and usually took place within small meetings. The content of these discussions was both "educational" and "critical": the educational element consisted of group "study" (hsüeh-hsi) of selected CCP documents; the critical element consisted of reflexively apprehending the norms implied in criticisms of earlier purge victims, such as Ch'en Tu-hsiu or Ch'en Shao-yü, or of members of the group found to have committed analogous errors.

When the CCP acquired national sovereignty in 1949, both criticism-self-criticism and the mass line became integrated into the structure of authority. The fairly loose relationship between the two became functionally and chronologically distinct: as we shall see in the following chapter, criticism and self-criticism became a mechanism of decision, conflict resolution, and discipline at the highest levels of leadership and an educational or disciplinary device at lower echelons; the "mass line" governed the relationship between elites and lower-level masses and cadres. The distinction between the two became clearly visible

---

[2] John W. Lewis, *Leadership in Communist China* (Ithaca, N.Y., 1963), pp. 72–73. The CCP exposition of the mass line may be found in Boyd Compton, ed., *Mao's China: Party Reform Documents, 1942–1944* (Seattle, Wash., 1952), pp. 1–9, 69–74, 176–184; John W. Lewis, ed., *Major Doctrines of Communist China* (New York, 1964), pp. 182–186; Liu Shao-ch'i, "On the Party's Mass Line" (1945), in *The Chinese Communist Regime: A Documentary Study*, ed. Theodore H. E. Chen (San Diego, Calif., 1965); Mao Tse-tung, "The Mass Line," Chapter 11 in *Quotations from Chairman Mao Tse-tung*, ed. Stuart R. Schram, pp. 118–134. Western commentaries and analyses may be found in Chapter 3, "The Mass Line as a Concept of Leadership," in Lewis, *Leadership*; Franz Schurmann, "Organizational Principles of the Chinese Communists," in *China Under Mao*, ed. MacFarquhar; and Mark Selden, "The Yenan Legacy: The Mass Line," in *Chinese Communist Politics*, ed. Barnett, pp. 99–155.

during the two high-level purges that took place between 1949 and 1966: Kao Kang and Jao Shu-shih in 1954–55, and P'eng Te-huai in 1958. In both cases, organizational sanctions were first decided through inner-Party criticism and self-criticism, and the mass line was used later to invoke mass criticism as a way of generating reflexive moral enthusiasm for some unrelated project—in the former case, the First Five-Year Plan, in the latter, adjustment to the failure of the Leap.[3]

As the regime's concern with rapid economic growth and efficient administration became more pronounced, and its communicative capacity increased, whatever representative or grievance-redress function the mass line had formerly served tended to diminish. The regime acquired a monopoly over political communication which, in the words of Frederick Yu, "encompasses almost all feasible vehicles of human expression and means of influencing attitudes and behavior."[4] Moreover, as Franklin Houn has noted, efforts to increase the flow of communication between elites and masses were consistently combined with increases in political control; although the regime received feedback from the masses, it seemed to be insensitive to it,[5] for Party leaders had their own ideological vision of the future and were wary of "tailism." In consequence, growing apathy on the part of the masses toward attempts by elites to mobilize them became apparent.

As noted in Chapter 3, Mao's concern with the general problem of bureaucratic alienation between elites and masses has been visible since Khrushchev's denunciation of Stalin and the Hungarian uprising in 1956 and became fully articulate during the Sino-Soviet dispute. In his first attempt to give the masses a voice in political affairs, the masses said altogether too much, but the "Hundred Flowers" did leave one legacy to the rather top-heavy Chinese communication system: the "big-character poster" (ta-tzu pao), which had made its appearance before but never on so large scale. A poster could easily be written by anyone with high local efficacy, though communication between cities or campuses was interdicted by the Party.[6]

---

3 Simmonds, *China*, p. 101.

4 Yu, *Mass Persuasion*, p. 4.

5 Franklin W. Houn, *To Change a Nation* (New York, 1961), pp. 230–237.

6 Cf. Yu Ming-sheng, "The Power of *Ta-tzu pao*," *PD*, March 28, 1958, quoted in Vincent V. S. King, "Propaganda Campaigns in Communist China" (Cambridge, Mass., the M.I.T. press, Jaunary 1966), p. 80. Cf. also Réné Goldman, "The Rectification Campaign at Peking University," *CQ*, no. 12 (October–December 1962): 138–154. Posters were again used in the "anti-waste" campaign in February 1958 and the "double-anti" campaign in 1958, but poster-writing was kept under organizational control. Every government department and bureau was ordered to establish a poster-publishing unit and put up posters regularly. *PD*, March 27, 1958, in King, p. 82.

The big-character poster turned out to be the opening wedge for a number of communicative innovations that were completely to destroy the Party's institutional monopoly over elite-mass communication during the GPCR. Posters, of course, "covered every available wall and mat," and they were augmented by Red Guard tabloids (*hsiao-pao*), some of which appeared daily, others every third or fourth day; some printed, others hectographed; some original, others plagiarized; some with national circulation (e.g., for several months in 1967, Tsinghua's *Chingkangshan* had a circulation second only to that of *PD*).[7] The interdict on inter-city communications was placed in abeyance to maximize mobilization, and Red Guards set up a network of liaison stations, which functioned like diplomatic missions and were connected by envoys, commercial telegraph facilities, and tabloid newspapers. The stations were extremely effective in disseminating information (e.g., in July 1967, Chiang Ch'ing's instruction to "attack with reason and defend with force" was followed within a few hours by arms seizures—it was not until a few days later that the instruction was published in the official press). The new, alternative communication system was characterized by frankness, spontaneity, and lack of uniformity and seemed to reach a younger and more urban audience.[8] Yet, it was impossible to limit this form of communication to any particular class or group; indeed, its "public" character systematically

[7] The first issue of *Hung-wei-ping* [Red Guard], the first Red Guard tabloid, appeared on September 1, 1966, apparently as a replacement for *Chung-kuo ch'ing-nien pao* [China youth news], which ceased publication on August 20, 1966. In addition to *Chingkangshan*, Red Guard tabloids that attained national circulations were *Hsin Pei-ta* (Peking University), *Red Flag* (Peking Aeronautical Institute), and *Tung-fang-hung* (Peking Geological Institute), all representative of the more radical elements in the movement. T. K. Tong, "Red Guard Newspapers," *Columbia Forum* 12, no. 1 (spring 1969): 38–41. The position taken by elites, including Maoist elites, toward these unofficial publications was rather consistently hostile but ineffectual until late in the movement. On March 3, 1967, the Peking Municipal RC ordered that only ten main Red Guard organizations be permitted to publish newspapers (according to a Peking poster of June 12, 1967), but these instructions were ignored. On July 18, 1968, the Peking RC again issued a notice, which stipulated that (1) Red Guard media might publish only directives of the CC and CCRG and directives published in *PD, RF,* and *LAD;* (2) there should be no spreading of "counterrevolutionary rumors"—the Red Guards were forbidden to "collect, print, or distribute 'alley-way news' and 'street information'"; (3) the circulation of internal articles, conference materials, and speeches by responsible cadres should be carried out strictly in accord with regulations and not printed without permission. This notice was reprinted in provincial papers in Kirin, Anhwei, Liaoning, Heilungkiang, Chekiang, Hunan, Kwangtung, and Shantung. The following month, "Mao's Thought propaganda teams" moved into the newspaper offices and the Red Guard press was finally shut down.

[8] Editor, "Mass Factionalism in Communist China," *CS* 6, no. 8 (May 15, 1968): 1 ff.; also Starr, "Mao Tse-tung's Theory," pp. 417 ff.; Oskar Weggel, *Massenkommunikation in der Volksrepublik China* (Hamburg, 1970), p. 88.

thwarted attempts to enforce ascriptive criteria for participation in the movement. The *raison d'être* of this alternative press was the availability of extraordinary information, specifically polemical information that had never before appeared in the official press in such rich and specific detail; the Red Guard press became dedicated exclusively to polemics and showed an inherent tendency to sensationalize.

The advent of a nationwide extra-Party press (compounded by rebel power seizures of key journals of the official press) [9] was only one of the unique features of "mass criticism" as practiced in the GPCR. A second feature, already alluded to in the introduction, was the dissolution of the distinction between "criticism–self-criticism" and "mass line": Mao opted to proceed with his purge even before receiving "slight majority" approval for his plans at the Eleventh Plenum, and the "mass line" was thus initiated *prior to elite agreement on criticism targets*. This uncertainty as to the identity of targets tended to result in an indiscriminate attack on all "authorities," since the masses lacked the political information to distinguish between capitalist-roaders and proletarian revolutionaries when both "waved a red flag." Third, having grown suspicious of the Party organization, which he believed harbored many of his opponents, Mao tried to *divorce ideology from organization* and to dispense with the latter altogether. The new communication network changed from well-structured channels along a hierarchical line of organization to direct communication between elites and masses; this pattern was characterized by multiplicity of channels (Red Guard rallies, "special instructions," speeches delivered by leaders in person, leaked black materials, and the like) and the absence of any "gatekeeper" to regulate the flow of information. The main channel was the editorials and keynote polemical articles of the major news media, such as *RF, PD,* and *LAD;* an unprecedented number of speeches by Maoist leaders at big rallies and small group interviews supplemented editorials with authoritative interpretations suited to local conditions. Although this new communication network had

9 By the end of 1966, five papers and three magazines had been closed, three papers and two periodicals had been renamed, and at least twenty-six magazines had been temporarily suspended. National papers that managed to maintain normal publication without succumbing to the rebels simply introduced directives and editorials on Party policies as printed in *PD* or published articles generally lauding Mao and Lin Piao. Professional publications lost their specialized character and devoted their pages to polemics. Most provincial papers were reported taken over by rebels, becoming vehicles for the faction that controlled them. Shanghai's *Wen-hui pao* and *LD* were taken over on January 4–5, and by May 1967 NCNA had come under direct control of the CCRG and Ch'en Po-ta warned Peking students it was no longer to be interfered with. *CTK* (the Czech news agency), May 29, 1967.

the desired effect of dissolving "bureaucratic" barriers to elite-mass relations, it had the dysfunctional effect of exposing elites to direct mass pressure, exacerbating factionalism at both elite and mass levels by permitting alliances to form between members of the elite and ideologically sympathetic rebel constituencies.

All three of these problems—the (limited) polemical autonomy of an alternative communication system, the indiscriminate attack on all authorities, and factionalism among both Red Guards and elites— reached critical proportions during the January 1967 "movement to seize power." One solution to the crises brought about by Mao's radical attempt to eliminate alienation between elite and mass would have been for him to request the PLA and chastened Party cadres to restore order, but such action would have militated against the enhanced mass activism the GPCR was meant to achieve, and Mao resorted to this solution only sporadically and with obvious reluctance. It was in order to resolve these problems *without* repudiating or suppressing the mass criticism he had unleashed that Mao decided in early 1967 to turn the force of the movement against Liu Shao-ch'i.

LIU SHAO-CH'I AS SYMBOL AND SCAPEGOAT

If Liu Shao-ch'i was politically impotent after the August 1966 Eleventh Plenum, the *meaning* of Liu Shao-ch'i lived on in the minds of all involved in the GPCR. Because the organizational apparatus that had previously been used to lead mass movements was discredited quite early, and because any use of the PLA to suppress the masses was so sharply at variance with the values the GPCR was meant to promote, the Maoists attempted to manipulate the meaning of Liu Shao-ch'i through the mass media in order to guide and control the movement reflexively.

An inspection of the relationship between criticisms of Liu and criticisms of all "Party persons in authority taking the capitalist road" indicates that at different times and for different reasons Liu was (1) a *symbol* for all "capitalist-roaders" that was used as a rallying call for rebellion against an entire category of elites; (2) a *scapegoat* for other capitalist-roaders, a villain against whom both friend *and* erstwhile foe could unite in common vilification.[10] It seems clear that within both the Red Guard and official presses, Liu functioned to some extent as a

[10] The "scapegoat/symbol" conceptualization refers to Liu's substitutability for other targets and does not exhaust his polemical "meaning." As we noted in the preceding chapter, Liu came to stand for a comprehensive system of evil, in part properly imputed to him, in part not.

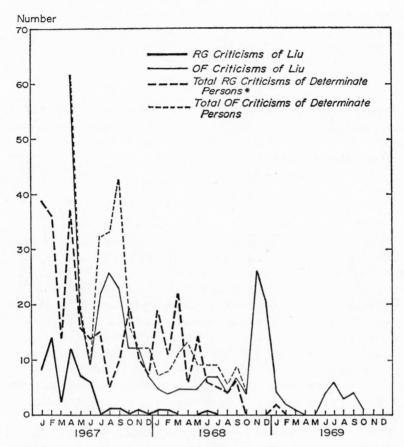

FIG. 4 CHRONOLOGY OF CRITICISM
* As distinguished from criticisms of ideas or groups.

symbol. This is indicated by the positive correlation both between Red Guard criticisms of Liu and Red Guard criticisms of other targets (i.e., between the solid thick line and the dashed thick line in Figure 4) and between official criticisms of Liu and official criticisms of others (between the solid thin and dashed thin lines).[11]

However, a comparison of the two presses indicates considerable variation in the symbolization achieved: the centrally controlled official press was able to achieve a much higher concentration of criticisms against Liu Shao-ch'i than was the Red Guard press throughout the

[11] The correlation coefficients within Red Guard and official presses are .55 and .138, respectively; only the correlation between Red Guard criticisms of Liu and Red Guard criticisms of others is statistically significant (p < .01).

period under study. The clear and highly significant (p < .00001) relationship between *source* of criticism and relative concentration on criticism *targets* is shown in Table 4.

Table 4

RELATIONSHIP BETWEEN TARGET AND SOURCE OF CRITICISM

Target	Source	
	Official Press	Red Guard Press
Liu	243	31
Other	78	197

Furthermore, inspection of Figure 4 indicates that, whereas the proportion of criticisms of Liu among total official criticisms remained relatively constant and even increased after August 1968, the proportion of criticisms of Liu among total Red Guard criticisms tended to decrease over time. The renewed outburst of criticism of "capitalist-roaders" in both official and Red Guard presses in the spring of 1968 was not matched by an increase in Red Guard criticisms of Liu, and by August of that year Red Guard criticisms had ceased entirely. Thus, Red Guard enthusiasm with the criticism of Liu was relatively short-lived—by the summer of 1967 most Red Guards had concluded that Liu was a "dead tiger" and unneedful of further polemical attention.

Whereas within the two presses Liu functioned to some extent as symbol, in the relationship *between* the two presses (i.e., between both thin lines and both thick lines) he clearly functioned as a *scapegoat*. To be more specific, the official press invoked Liu to prevent Red Guard criticism from proliferating to other targets, including factional rivals, PLA authorities, and "liberated" Party cadres. The use of Liu as a scapegoat to deflect attacks on lesser targets is evident in the inverse relationship between official attacks on Liu and Red Guard criticisms. Over the seventeen-month period when both presses were operating (from April 1967 through August 1968), there was a statistically significant negative correlation (Pearson $r = -.47$, $p < .01$) between official criticisms of Liu Shao-ch'i and total Red Guard criticisms; there is also a negative correlation ($r = -.66$, $p < .01$) between official criticisms of Liu and Red Guard criticisms of *other* targets.

To summarize our findings concerning the alternate functions of Liu in the Red Guard and official media, the data suggest that the

Red Guards were inclined to use Liu as a "symbol" for attacks on diverse local targets, whereas the official press tried to use him as a "scapegoat" to *deflect* attacks from these same targets. In the course of the movement there was a cyclical, contrapuntal interplay between "democracy" and "centralism," and Liu's function alternated accordingly. The operation of the factors responsible for the alternation of function between symbol and scapegoat can be elucidated by a time-series analysis of the dynamics of the movement.

One can discern, with varying degrees of clarity, several trends. The long-term trend, as noted in Chapter 5, was for criticism to mount in a series of *steps* beginning in the fall of 1966 and culminating in an all-time high with the launching of the official press campaign in April 1967, then generally diminishing from that high point to the Twelfth Plenum in October 1968, which precipitated another surge, this one entirely dominated by the official press.

The seasonal trend was for criticisms to escalate sharply after New Year's and during the spring months of March, April, and May; in the ensuing summer months criticisms tended to proliferate and become extreme, even violent; in the late summer and autumn the authorities interceded and imposed settlements between conflicting Red Guard factions, and there was a season of consolidation. The first year (1966) did not altogether fit this pattern: after the spring offensive (directed not against Liu Shao-ch'i but the "three-family village" and the P'eng-Lo-Lu-Yang "black gang" who shielded them), criticisms subsided during the June–July "fifty days" under the suppressive impact of the work teams. Criticism briefly revived in August without being directed at any distinct target group, subsided somewhat in September, then resumed steady escalation (without official sanction) through November and December, to climax in the "January storm." This seasonal pattern seems to reflect the plant-and-harvest exigencies of China's agricultural economy. As J. D. Simmonds has noted in an analysis of policy making from 1959 to 1966, the late summer and early autumn months tend to be a time for major policy discussion, for crops are entering the late stage of the growing period and the national agricultural exchequer can be assessed (see p. 100). The two seasonal "revolutionary high tides" thus followed completion of autumn harvest in December and completion of spring planting at the end of March.

The monthly trend was for criticisms to escalate at the first of each month and to diminish in the second half of each month. The variables that determined the intramonthly dynamics of criticism are presented in Table 5.

Table 5

INTRAMONTHLY CRITICISM DIFFUSION AND DEPLETION VARIABLES

Targets	Month	
	First half	Last half
Liu	A	B
Others	C	D

Actually, two intramonthly propensities were exhibited in the course of the criticism movement: first, a greater total number of criticisms tended to be published in the first half of the month than in the second half, which we call the intramonthly *depletion* propensity. This was measured simply in terms of AC's percentage of ACBD and is charted in Figure 5. We propose the hypothesis that this propensity arose from the need to coordinate amorphous groups without regular internal communication channels to participate in the demonstration through the use of convenient monthly publication schedules. If this hypothesis is correct, one would expect the depletion propensity to vary directly with the extent and intensity of organized mass demonstrations. If one considers the pattern of demonstrations during the period, this expectation seems to be sustained by Figure 5, though the evidence is far from conclusive. The intramonthly depletion propensity was high for the Red Guard press (a more irregular "movement" epiphenomenon) and almost nonexistent for the official press. In the twenty-one-month period from January 1967 to September 1968, the ratio of depletion to accumulation in the Red Guard press was sixteen months to five; in the corresponding eighteen-month period in the official press (which did not initiate criticism until three months later), eight months showed depletion, seven accumulation, and three an even distribution. The average *percentage* of criticisms to appear in the first half of the month during this period was 63.7 percent for the Red Guard press ($t = 2.37$, $p < .025$) and 53.7 percent for the official press (statistically insignificant). The extinction of the Red Guard press after August 1968 immediately follows the nationwide dispatch of "worker-peasant Mao Tsetung Thought propaganda teams" to the campuses and newspaper offices in July to impose compulsory arbitration on factional disputes and terminate "spontaneous" demonstrational activities.

The second propensity is that of intramonthly *diffusion:* the month

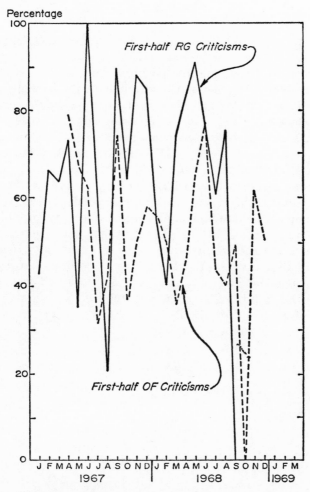

FIG. 5 INTRAMONTHLY CRITICISM DEPLETION PROPENSITY FOR LIU SHAO-CH'I
Indicates the percentage of total monthly criticisms to appear in the first
half of each month, from January, 1967, to June, 1969.

would begin with a high percentage of Red Guard attacks against
Liu Shao-ch'i and a low percentage of attacks against other targets
and end with a high percentage of attacks against others and a low
percentage of attacks against Liu, reflecting the inability of the
leadership to sustain its control in the face of "democratic" impulses
to spread the attack to more immediately threatening local targets; in
other words, elite attempts to use Liu as a scapegoat were usurped by

mass attempts to use him as a symbol. The diffusion propensity may

be formulated A:C::D:B, or more simply, $\frac{A}{C} : \frac{D}{B}$. Because this propen-

sity was associated with the interplay between centralism and democracy in the movement, it was not apparent in the centrally directed
official press. In the Red Guard press, it was most striking during the
months when concerted drives were launched: in January 1967 (a
month that showed accumulation rather than depletion of total criticisms), 41 percent of the first-half criticisms attacked Liu but only
4 percent of the last-half criticisms did so; in February, 48 percent of
the first-half criticisms attacked Liu and 23 percent of the last-half
criticisms; in March, 22 percent of the first-half criticisms attacked
Liu and none of the last-half. April showed concentration rather than
diffusion (12 percent as against 70 percent), probably because the Red
Guard press was successfully diverted from its tendency to multiply
targets by the massive official press drive against Liu beginning
March 31, but May and June also showed diffusion. The statistically
significant relationship ($X^2 = 2.8$, $p < .10$) between choice of target
and half of the month in the Red Guard press during this six-month
period (when criticism was most intense) is shown in Table 6.

Table 6

INTRAMONTHLY CRITICISM DIFFUSION, JANUARY–JUNE, 1967

Targets	Month	
	First half	Last half
Liu	36% (32)	22% (12)
Others	64% (65)	78% (47)
	100% (97)	100% (59)

Thereafter no diffusion propensity was apparent; this was perhaps
partly because the official press (whose leading organs were controlled
by the radicals from January 1967 until September 1967, when the
"May 16 Group" was repudiated) succeeded to some extent in usurping the demonstration-guiding role of the Red Guard press, partly
because the Red Guards seemed to lose all interest in "dead tiger"
Liu Shao-ch'i. After August 1967, no more than one polemical attack
on Liu per month appeared in the Red Guard press.

INNOVATION AND DIFFUSION OF CRITICISMS

In the mass criticism campaign against Liu Shao-ch'i, there were roughly three patterns for the innovation and diffusion of criticism. The first was innovation at the (Red Guard and Revolutionary Rebel) grass roots, which attracted the favorable notice of a member of the elite and was followed by diffusion through the national media. According to the accounts of most eyewitnesses, the charge that Liu exercised "bourgeois dictatorship" and "white terror" by sending CCP work teams to manage the GPCR at various schools during the "fifty days" in June–July 1966 originated in this manner. Mao did not oppose the dispatch of work teams at first; although it was later recalled that Mao had expressed reservations, Chiang Ch'ing said that "we have also gone through a process of development (kuo-ch'eng) in our understanding of work teams." The work-team criticism can be traced in its progress "from the bottom to the top": in early September 1966, those students who had been harshly treated by the work teams during the "fifty days" captured control of the "Third Headquarters" (and with it a highly effective communications apparatus). From that vantage point, they pursued those responsible for their dispatch—first Li Hsüeh-feng, Mayor of Peking, and then in mid-October Liu Shao-ch'i as "Li Hsüeh-feng's wirepuller."

A second criticism that seemed to originate at the grass roots was the personal exposé, which disclosed lurid details about the target's private life. These Red Guard "scoops" were based on highly enterprising investigative reporting: Ken Ling noticed during a "link-up" trip to Peking in the fall of 1966 that the Tsinghua rebels had visited practically every place Liu or his wife had ever worked to collect information; in T'aoyüan especially, nearly every commune cadre had been questioned "dozens of times." "We went to the NCNA and the Nationalities Commission, the Overseas Chinese Affairs Commission, and the Ministry of Education—all distributors of Red Guard investigation team reports—to ask for more materials," a Tsinghua rebel told him. "We took everything they gave us . . . ending up with quite an assortment." [12] The most widely lampooned victim of this criticism technique was, of course, Wang Kuang-mei, whose pearl necklace and silk ch'i-p'ao (worn during a 1963 trip to Indonesia) became symbols of bourgeois decadence. Although central authorities discouraged this type of criticism after January 1967, it continued to appear.

It should be noted in qualification that the success of grass-roots in-

12 Ling, Revenge, pp. 198–199.

novation was dependent upon attracting a favorable response from the center (or at least not provoking a critical response). "This was a calculated risk and we won by sheer luck," recalled Ken Ling. "If we aimed at the wrong target . . . we should have been put down as 'counterrevolutionaries.' Many times, we Red Guards had this kind of worry." [13] It seems clear, for example, that protests against the work teams would have been "strangled in the cradle" by the end of June had not the Maoists decided to champion the cause of the rebels. Most decisive in this regard was Mao himself: he wrote encouraging letters to rebels at Peking University and the middle school attached to Tsinghua University, ordered Nieh Yüan-tzu's big-character poster nationally publicized on June 1, and, in his own big-character poster of August 5, first called attention to the existence of an "opposite road" at the center and called on radical (i.e., anti-work team) students to "bombard the headquarters" of the "bourgeois reactionary line." It was only after the August Plenum, and after Mao, wearing a *hung-wei-ping* brassard, had received Red Guards atop the T'ienanmen reviewing stand and declared that the Red Guards were "a legal organization under the dictatorship of the proletariat," that the Red Guards became a nationwide movement.[14]

The Maoist reaction to the escalation of criticism in the fall of 1966 seemed to be less activist than earlier, but not until after the "January storm" did the Maoists begin explicitly to repudiate such devices for mass innovation of criticism as mass struggle rallies, personal exposés, and pursuit of responsibility for work teams up the organizational hierarchy. The persistence of mass initiative in the selection of targets beyond this point is due partly to the fact that the movement had acquired a self-sustaining dynamic that did not respond predictably to elite appeals, partly to an apparent split within the leadership between the "center" and the incipient "May 16 Group."

The second pattern for the innovation and diffusion of criticism was for Maoist elites to pronounce a general criticism, which was diffused through the media and used by lower-level polemicists, who supplied details, marshaled supporting evidence, and added variations adapted to local conditions and grievances. Most of the polemical imagery and slogans of the campaign (e.g., "Rebellion is justified!")

13 *Ibid.*
14 In the words of one Red Guard, "The big change was when Chairman Mao had the big August 18 rally in T'ienanmen Square and said he was joining the Red Guards and let us put the armband on him. . . . Then the Red Guards burst their dykes and spread all over the country. People of all ages wanted to join, even children and old people." Hans Granquist, *The Red Guards*, trans. E. G. Fries (New York, 1967), p. 108.

derived directly from the "little red book," *Quotations from Chairman Mao Tse-tung*. Mao also originated the standard epithets, "revisionist," "Party persons in authority taking the capitalist road," and "bourgeois reactionary line," thus establishing broad parameters for subsequent criticisms. Yet, because Mao was a universally acknowledged symbol of ideological legitimacy, his name and his "Thought" were sometimes invoked to justify causes for which he may have felt little sympathy, but he found it difficult to repudiate them without seeming to contradict his own quoted words.

The third pattern operated surreptitiously: initially, the center "leaked" highly detailed, confidential "black materials," which were then published in the Red Guard and sometimes the official press. Liu's October 1966 self-criticism could not have become available without elite collusion, and nearly all criticisms of Liu's errors during the 1962 retrenchment from the Leap and during the SEM are based on quotations from previously unpublished data, including private conversations with friends, *in camera* speeches and *obiter dicta,* and personal letters. It seems that these leaks were facilitated by members of the CCRG. The CC-State Council issued directives prohibiting Red Guard raids on confidential files on September 8, 1966, February 17, 1967, and August 31, 1967—only the last directive was co-signed by the CCRG, signaling a break between the "May 16 Group" and Chiang Ch'ing.[15] "Actually, it has collected black material on every one of us, and it may throw it out in public at any time," Chiang said of her erstwhile colleagues on September 5. In his speech to the Ninth Congress, Mao also attributed the leaks to "Wang [Li], Kuan [Feng], Ch'i [Pen-yü]." [16]

Though the appearance of these three patterns for the innovation and diffusion of criticism was not entirely dependent on the wishes of Maoist elites, their respective influence over the process of escalation seemed ultimately subject to Mao's veto power. The escalation of criticisms against Liu seemed to follow a step-like progression, and the impact of each pattern varied from step to step. In Chapter 5, we identified four phases in Liu's implication, in only the last three of which was mass criticism involved. (1) The first phase extends from Liu's demotion at the Eleventh Plenum in August 1966 to the publication of his October self-criticism in the Red Guard press on December 26. The first pattern (innovation from below, diffusion from above) seems to be mainly responsible for this step, although the second and

15 *CCP Documents*, pp. 72, 309, 503.

16 "Mao's Speech to the 1st Plenary Session of the CCP's 9th CC." (April 28, 1969), in *IS* 6, no. 6 (March, 1970): 94–99.

third patterns were also in evidence.[17] (2) The second phase followed the January "movement to seize power," which precipitated the "February adverse current": this "current" implied a temporary decrease in the amount of criticism of Liu, but, at the same time, the exemption of other "power-holders" from criticism implied a step forward in the *concentration* of criticism. Liu's meaning thus began to shift from symbol to scapegoat. (3) The third step (initiation of the official press campaign at the end of March) was decided between March 14 and 18 at a joint meeting of the Politburo Standing Committee and MAC and announced at a central work conference of March 27–28. The decision was made and implemented by a coalition of CCRG, PLA, and mainstream elites and was intended to facilitate revival of the movement with Liu as pure scapegoat. As a scapegoat, Liu was meant to function as a reflexive moral incentive to channel the criticism movement toward constructive—or at least nondestructive—goals. Liu's role as a scapegoat was only effective for as long as his credibility as a threat could be sustained, however, whereupon attacks proliferated upon the "authorities" and rival factions whom he was intended to represent, and Liu's meaning reverted from scapegoat to symbol.

The use (and limitations) of the "scapegoat" to control factional tendencies in Chinese rectification movements is intelligible as an attempt to combat the implications of what William H. Riker has termed the "size principle": "In social situations similar to the N-person, zero-sum game with side-payments ["antagonistic contradictions," in Maoist terms], participants create coalitions just as large as they believe will ensure winning and no larger." True to this principle, constituents of the Maoist coalition tended to fragment into internecine conflict groups just as soon as they believed the Liuists had been defeated. To avoid this tendency, the polemicists sought to create an artificially incomplete information system that grossly overestimated the power of Liu Shao-ch'i, intuitively realizing that "the greater the degree of imperfection or incompleteness of information, the larger will be the coalition that coalition-makers seek to form and the more frequently will winning coalitions actually formed be greater than minimum size." This attempt to manipulate the information system foundered repeatedly on the Maoist loss of monopoly control of the media; the Red Guards conveyed the true ratio of forces between Mao and Liu in their own media system, and the formation of

---

[17] Examples of the second pattern are Mao's August 5 big-character poster, "The Sixteen Points" of the Eleventh Plenum, and public speeches of Ch'en Po-ta, Lin Piao, and Chiang Ch'ing at rallies. The best instance of the third pattern is publication of Liu's October self-criticism in *Chingkangshan* on December 26.

a grand coalition against a fictively potent opponent became possible only after the Red Guard media had been shut down and Maoist monopoly control over the communication system restored.[18]

CONCLUSION

To what extent were the promises of mass-line theory fulfilled by its revival under altered circumstances? The original mass line had three analytically distinct purposes: (1) to *facilitate vertical communication* between elites and masses; (2) to *achieve consensus* between elites and masses; and (3) to *enhance the masses' sense of political efficacy* by apparently deferring to their will in making and implementing decisions. Our inquiry is concerned not only with the success of mass criticism in realizing these purposes but with the likely durability of that success.

(1) Vertical communication between elites and masses was enhanced by each of three patterns of innovation and diffusion described above. Although mass innovation was really only permitted in the first pattern, each pattern encouraged mass involvement in repeating and elaborating upon given polemical themes, thus relating abstract criticisms to personal experience. The first pattern (innovation at the grass roots, followed by national dissemination through the media) played an influential role in the first step of the escalation process; in the second step (the "February adverse current"), excesses in struggle tactics and goals had the counterproductive effect of stemming mass initiative in selecting targets and deflecting concentration onto authoritatively designated targets. Thereafter mass initiative was manifest only in attacks on local power-holders or struggles between factions; the incapacity of the anti-Liu campaign fully to coopt this initiative finally led to the forcible suppression of revolutionary initiative in the autumn of 1968. The third pattern ("leaks" from the center) lasted from August 1966 to around September 1967, when Mao sealed off the leaks by shutting down *RF* and starting a purge of the radical "May 16 Group."

In sum, the GPCR unquestionably increased vertical communication between elites and masses. In assessing the likely durability of this reform, it seems useful to distinquish between mass-local elite relations and mass-center relations. Through such devices as the regular rotation of leadership, diminution of functional specialization wherever feasible (to prevent meritocracies from forming), reduction of organizational structures and cadre strengths by 40 to 70 percent

18 William H. Riker, *The Theory of Political Coalitions* (New Haven and London, 1962), pp. 32–33, 66, 88–89.

under the slogan "better army and simpler administration" (*chin-ping chien-cheng*) to reduce institutional barriers to the mass line, and provision of seats for representatives of the "revolutionary masses" on RCs at every production unit and at every political level, the Maoists have tried to facilitate mass-elite communications, and these efforts appear to be quite successful at the local level. The shut-down of the Red Guard press has resulted in a net decline in the content and quantity of *mass* media since the GPCR, but this should be weighed against a general revival of local *popular* media. Big character posters are regularly used to discuss elections and local issues; correspondence teams (composed of workers, peasants, and soldiers) are sent "to every basic unit of factories and workshops, rural production brigades, PLA companies, and militia organizations" to write articles for local broadcasting stations and the local press; new publications produced by workers' organizations to provide material for study sessions have appeared; the use of radio diffusion stations (which permit translation into local dialects) has been resumed; local nonprofessionals have begun producing short commentaries, short dramas, poetry, and revolutionary stories for local consumption; there are reports of amateur film teams, amateur itinerant film groups, story-tellers, and even children's drama groups.[19]

With respect to communication between mass and *center,* only the second pattern has survived the GPCR, which is no more (or less) than existed previously. This pattern tends to move "from the elites, to the elites": general themes originate at the center, iteration and elaboration of these themes in the local media is permitted, and the "feedback" that returns to the center is little more than an amplified echo of the original themes.

(2) The mass-criticism campaign failed conspicuously to generate reasoned consensus between elites and masses: consensus was eventually achieved only by purging fractious elites and using the army (or worker-peasant propaganda teams) to impose compulsory arbitration on rebellious "masses." Instead of leading to consensus, the process of mass criticism led to sharpened antagonisms between groups, which threatened at times to culminate in civil war. We submit that the reasons for this change lie in three crucial differences between mass line and mass criticism.

First, there was a change in *function.* The GPCR was a criticism movement; as such, it deliberately undermined inhibitions on the expression of grievances and sensitized people to "contradictions," which

19 *CNA*, no. 828 (January 15, 1971); and Donald McInness, "Communications Media and the Grass Roots," in *China Notes* 9, no. 2 (spring 1971): 18–21.

could be properly resolved only through "struggle." Praise of the martial virtues and a taboo on "unprincipled" compromise encouraged parties to a contradiction to escalate their attacks on each other without limit. In contrast, the original mass line was intended to function as part of a policy-making process. By divorcing the mass line from any connection to policy, the process was deprived of any chance for reality-testing, and the only limit to the unfolding logic of Mao's Thought was often physical conflict with another faction holding a variant interpretation.

Second, there was a change in *organization*. Early capture of the pace-making sector of the official press and the construction of a comprehensive alternative media network made it possible for the first time to carry on a mass movement outside, even against, the Party organization. The advantage of conducting a media campaign outside the organizational hierarchy was the possibility of evoking instant, spontaneous mass response. Oskar Weggel puts it well:

From this magic center directives emerge which in their abstract form and terseness say almost nothing. The directives from Mao are like a signal, which flashes on at times and triggers a Pavlov-effect on the entire political system. What comes from above is no longer a practical direction, which is filtered through routinized machinery, but abstract commands, which have only the purpose of arousing the spontaneity of the masses.[20]

If Mao's complaint with bureaucratic mediation was that it alienated the leaders and deadened mass spontaneity, he soon learned that the problem with immediate dissemination of ideological guidelines through the media was the opposite difficulty of controlling the mass response. The only type of message that could be distributed simultaneously to everyone over the mass media was so abstract that it lent itself to diverse interpretations. As Chang Ch'un-ch'iao observed of the "little red book" in 1968:

The reading of quotations has become nothing but a war of words. I will only read passages from the quotations which are favorable to me, but will not read anything which is unfavorable to me.[21]

As noted above, the attempt to use Liu as a condensation symbol around whom heterodox grievances could coalesce was successful only so long as the credibility of threat could be sustained. Eventually the Red Guards in most cities merged along functional or occupational

20 Weggel, *Die Chinesischen Revolutionskomitees*, p. 88.
21 "Comrade Chang Ch'un-ch'iao's Speech at Chiao-t'ung University of Shanghai" (January 18, 1968), *Tzu-liao chuan-chi* [Special collection of information material] (Canton), February 10, 1968, in *SCMP*, no. 4146 (March 26, 1968): 3.

lines into "two opposing factional organizations" with links to adult elites: the radical faction aligned with the CCRG, the conservative faction aligned initially with the Party apparatus, later with the PLA.[22]

Third, there was a change in *communication*. The second innovation and diffusion pattern was supplemented by the third and first. The third pattern, involving "leaks" from the center, proved capable of blowing up elite disputes into factional struggles by leaking word of internal differences, which might otherwise have been resolved internally, to the respective constituencies of the disputants. The first pattern involved rapid growth of a quasi-autonomous communications network at the grass-roots level, which was identified as the voice of the "masses." This alternative media system also functioned as a channel for upward mobility based on skills in symbol manipulation, as the meteoric careers of K'uai Ta-fu, Nieh Yüan-tzu, et al. demonstrated. Thus, there were strong tendencies to sensationalize the critique and push the "cult of personality" to extravagant extremes.

(3) The elites expressly deferred to the will of the masses during the GPCR, paying repeated tribute to their political efficacy. As Mao said in January 1967, "Neither I nor you have solved the question of T'ao Chu, but the rise of the Red Guards has solved it." Not only T'ao Chu, but virtually all criticism or purge victims were accused of failing to defer to the will of the masses. There are reports that this emphasis on elite deference has enhanced the masses' sense of political competence and led to greater popular participation in local politics. Ross Terrill reports:

There is a greater sense of involvement. The lady from whose roadside stall I buy tea in Nanking knows which four provinces still have not established new Party committees. Shopkeepers in Shanghai venture comment on world affairs. . . . Drivers and Luxingshe aides showed no timidity or subservience —in 1964 there had been some.[23]

The durability of the enhanced mass *sense* of political efficacy is ultimately dependent upon an enhancement of their actual political efficacy. We may measure political efficacy with two indicators: participation in political decisions, and the size of the "cut" obtained in the authoritative allocation of values. By the first criterion, the creation of seats for mass representation at all levels of the hierarchy at least legitimates the principle of mass representation in government, and although these mass representatives tend to be excluded from important decisions and to have less power the higher one ascends the

22 *CS* 6, no. 8 (May 15, 1968): 1 ff.

23 Ross Terrill, "The 800,000,000: Report from China," *The Atlantic* 228, no. 5 (November 1971): 90–121.

hierarchy, their very existence is an improvement over the prior arrangement. If their political power is often nominal, mass representatives also function to aggregate public opinion and serve as ombudsmen for the redress of grievances. Since the GPCR, the RCs, and particularly their mass representatives, have become the main correspondents for letters: the Kiangsu RC, for example, received about 12,500 letters from November 1967 to the middle of March 1968, of which 95 percent had been answered by the beginning of March.[24]

By all accounts, the share of disprivileged groups (particularly peasants) in the authoritative allocation of both goods and services has appreciated considerably: this is evident in improved rural medical services, more egalitarian educational facilities, and in an immediate consumers' windfall (which has, however, been somewhat exaggerated in recent visitors' reports): since 1969, more than 2,000 types of Chinese traditional and Western medicines have been reduced in price by an average of 30 percent, according to various reports, and such goods as bicycles, motor bicycles, sewing machines, wrist watches, and radios have been made available for mass sale.[25] By both criteria, then, the political eficacy of the masses seems to have been enhanced. At the same time, we must take note of a subtle postrevolutionary devaluation of semantic coinage, whereby "masses" has been defined to exclude the original agents of revolution and refer primarily to the most quietistic elements in the GPCR: the peasants. For the Red Guards, the GPCR's effect has been counterproductive, leaving them to draw what comfort they may from their improved chances to implement the ideals of public service they had helped to prevail.[26]

24 Weggel, *Massenkommunikation*, pp. 34–35. Weggel also notes that prior to the GPCR, political communication was controlled through a net leading to the CC Propaganda Department; control has since been decentralized to the provincial level, where each RC (now, presumably, each Party committee) has its own "political department" in charge of "public opinion" (pp. 37–38).

25 *CSN* 2, no. 1 (January 1971): 1 ff. *L'Unita* reported that the sale of goods to the population increased by 15.7 percent in 1970 over the previous year. *FBIS*, October 30, 1970, p. B1. During his 1972–1973 visit, Robert Scalapino obtained a list of prices for common consumer commodities that presents a somewhat more sobering picture of the consumer bonanza, however.

26 Thus one cadre taunted reluctant students with their own words: "Some of these students, when rebelling, shouted about 'daring to climb a mountain of knives and plunge into an ocean of flame.' Now, when Chairman Mao tells them to go to the mountains and to the countryside, they don't even dare to speak!" These words "hit the young generals on a sore spot," and "all of them quickly applied to go to the countryside." On September 3, 1968, *LD* published a "Comment on 'If I Had Only Known This Day I Would Not Have Done It,'" which acknowledged the commonness of such rueful feelings.

10

THE STRUCTURAL EVOLUTION OF
CRITICISM AND SELF-CRITICISM

Criticism and self-criticism, or inner-Party struggle as it is sometimes called, has always been a major mechanism of inner-Party decision making and discipline among Chinese Communist elites, but during the GPCR it emerged as a form of mass mobilization and rectification as well. This chapter interprets this climactic development as the consequence of a series of contingent political decisions and cumulative structural changes in the Chinese communications system.

One of the bases of the apparent elite solidarity, which persisted with rare interruption prior to 1966, was the operation of a particular process of mediated and regulated conflict among members of that elite. As Richard Solomon has correctly pointed out, the introduction of regulated and mediated conflict marks a significant departure from prevailing cultural patterns of emotional expression and conflict management, according to which annoyance would be repressed until it reached a certain threshhold, whereupon it would explode chaotically.[1] In the new pattern, as long as conflict took place within a stipulated organizational context according to certain rules, it was deemed salubrious for both the Party and the individual. According to Liu Shao-ch'i:

Experience proves that whenever a comrade in a responsible position seriously practices sincere and necessary self-criticism before the Party membership and the masses, . . . their internal solidarity will develop, their work will improve and their defects will be overcome, while the prestige of the responsible comrade will increase instead of being undermined. There is a great deal of evidence, both in the Party and among the masses, to prove this. On the other hand, where a responsible comrade lacks the spirit of

[1] Richard H. Solomon, "Mao's Effort to Reintegrate the Chinese Polity: Problems of Authority and Conflict in the Chinese Social Processes," in *Chinese Communist Politics*, ed. Barnett, pp. 271–365.

self-criticism, refuses or fears to reveal his own defects or mistakes, or tries to cover them up; when he expresses no gratitude for criticism and instead of being pleased to be told of his faults blushes to the ears and makes acrimonious retorts or looks for a chance to revenge himself on his critics, the result is just the opposite.[2]

The process of criticism and self-criticism was meant to facilitate the open airing of differences between Party members and to encourage the discussion of alternative policies. It was meant not only to maximize the policy options considered but to provide a forum for the expression of grievances and a small-group disciplinary technique. A refugee with experience in both the KMT and the CCP contrasted the sense of catharsis achieved in the CCP through criticism and self-criticism with the KMT's tendency to stifle potentially distressing communication:

The Communists always encourage people to talk, and to express their opinions. . . . If you talk about problems you prevent misunderstandings and maintain unity in work. During the Nationalist era things were not this way; you would hold back your opinions and eventually you would become enemies.[3]

Franz Schurmann describes the process of criticism and self-criticism as a small-group disciplinary technique:

Essentially, the technique consists in the usually temporary alienation of a single member from the group through the application of collective criticism. One member is singled out for criticism, either because of faulty ideological understanding, poor work performance, or some other deviance. He is not only subjected to a barrage of criticism from the members, but also joins in and begins to criticize himself. . . . The avowed purpose is to "correct" (kai-tsao) the individual. Under normal circumstances, the individual is "reintegrated" into the group after the "temporary alienation." The experience of temporary alienation of the one criticized and collective criticism by the group members is, in theory, supposed to have the general effect of maintaining the group's cohesion and effectiveness. Great fear exists on the part of those potentially criticized that they may become victims of a more permanent alienation. Fear of such permanent alienation serves to strengthen the bonds within the group.[4]

But for the person criticized, criticism and self-criticism could be an exceedingly trying experience. During the 1959 Lushan Plenum, P'eng Te-huai used obscene language to characterize his forced self-

---

[2] *CW* 2: 65.
[3] Quoted in Solomon, "Mao's Effort," pp. 328–329.
[4] Franz Schurmann, "Organization and Response in Communist China," *Annals of the American Academy of Political and Social Science* 321 (January 1950): 57.

criticism after forty days of "struggle" at a 1945 North China conference and complained that the Lushan Plenum, which had criticized
Mao's policies, did not last long enough.[5] P'eng's wife divorced him
after his purge in 1959, compounding his misfortunes.[6] During the
GPCR, Chu Te was forced to make a self-criticism; in disclosing
the incident, Lin Piao said, "It was the Party Center which made him
take off his pants." [7]

Criticism and self-criticism, as it is practiced in China, seems to be
a unique disciplinary and decision-making institution among ruling
Communist parties; it differs appreciably from the pattern of external
control networks and occasional "show trials" based on extraction of
false confessions that has prevailed in the Soviet Union and Eastern
European Communist states. To what does China owe this unique
development? Partly to its cultural legacy from "traditional" China, we
surmise, which has influenced the development of criticism and self-
criticism in at least two ways. First, China at the time of the birth of
the CCP was aptly characterized as a "sheet of loose sand," consisting
of a congeries of small, exclusive, self-regulating units (including
guilds, secret societies, and *Landsmannschaften,* as well as political
parties) modeled more or less after the clan. The CCP resemblance to
these groups in drawing a clear distinction between in-group and
out-group is reflected in two categories of "struggle": principled, redemptive struggle against deviant insiders, and expedient struggles
against outsiders. Second, the perceived beneficent impact of "self-
criticism" upon the group and the target derives in part from the
integral position of confession in traditional moral and legal codes,
which in turn derives from a Confucian emphasis on educating and
transforming the wrong-doer rather than simply punishing him. According to the Ch'ing code, if confession is voluntary (i.e., an antece-
dent to demonstration of guilt), punishment must be waived or mit-
igated. But if the accused refuses to confess in the face of evidence
proving his guilt, application of torture to extract confession is sanctioned.[8] Confession is a prerequisite to sentencing in either case, but

5 "The Wicked History of Big Conspirator, Big Ambitionist, Big Warlord P'eng
Te-huai—Collected Materials Against P'eng Ten-huai," comp. Tsinghua Chingkangshan, November 1967, in *CB,* no. 851 (April 26, 1968): 14.

6 "Shen-hsü P'u An-hsiu" [Investigate P'u An-hsiu], ed. Ting Wang, *Chung-kung,*
pp. 17–18, cited in *Tsu-kuo,* no. 89 (August 1, 1971): 2.

7 *Ko-ming kung-jen pao,* no. 5 (February 19, 1967): 4; quoted in Tang Tsou,
"The Cultural Revolution and the Chinese Political System," *CQ,* no. 38 (April–
June 1969): 63–91.

8 Derk Bodde and Clarence Morris, *Law in Imperial China: Exemplified by
190 Ch'ing Dynasty Cases* (Cambridge, Mass., 1967), pp. 42, 97–98; also George

its relationship to the verdict depends upon the particulars of the case. According to the tacit "rules" of criticism and self-criticism that seemed to operate prior to the GPCR, public self-criticism also signaled the resolution of criticism and was followed by a disposition of the case that granted forgiveness or imposed sanctions of various kinds.[9]

The development of inner-Party struggle was also favored by the particular sociopolitical circumstances surrounding the CCP accession to power. The CPSU, prior to the October Revolution, was split into two distinctive environments staffed by different types of activists who rarely interacted, especially during the 1914–17 period. On the one hand, there were cosmopolitan ideologue-intellectuals who had spent years abroad writing, proselytizing, and thinking about ultimate ends, such as Lenin, Trotsky, Zinoviev, Kamenev, Bukharin, and Rykov. On the other hand, there were the organization men who had never left Russia and spent most of their time hiding or in prison (viz., Stalin, Kuganovich, Molotov, Ordzohnikidze, and Kirov); due to the security threat posed by the Tsarist Okhrana and its network of informers, these men abrogated democratic principles to create a secret and highly centralized "organizational weapon." The CPSU seized power through a quick urban coup d'état, followed by a short and conventional civil war to consolidate its urban power base. The Party then assumed control of the apparatus of state, therewith coming into possession of an apparatus of control and manipulation that it had previously lacked: the government bureaucracy. The ideologues, after the premature death of Lenin, for the most part lacked any appreciation of the importance or workings of the bureaucracy (for example, Trotsky declared on his appointment as the People's Commissar for Foreign Affairs, "I will issue a few revolutionary proclamations to the people of the world and shut up shop"). Also, lacking any alternative means

---

Alexander Kennedy, *Die Rolle des Gestaendnisses in chinesischen Gesetz* (Berlin, 1939), pp. 5–12, 37.

[9] For instance, in June 1957, two deputy chairmen of the Democratic League were accused of leading a nationwide clique to overthrow the Party; neither admitted it, and so "the campaign against them was pushed relentlessly forward until January 1958 when Shih Liang claimed that they had confessed their crimes and their clique had been destroyed." MacFarquhar, *The Hundred Flowers*, p. 26. Similarly, Ch'en I sought to exempt Liu from criticism by maintaining that "Liu and Teng have been thoroughly defeated and have confessed their crimes." In the first case, confession resulted in punishment, whereas in the second it was intended to result in acquittal. In general, once confession or self-criticism is accepted as satisfactory, the process of criticism and self-criticism comes to an end and a decision is reached on the individual case. But the process of criticism and self-criticism continues on policy issues raised by that individual's mistakes.

of creating a mass power base, they soon succumbed to the organization men, who proceeded to use the same methods they had learned to survive in enemy-occupied territory to organize and operate the state apparatus.[10]

During the CCP's initial period of legality in the 1920s, when it was centered in the cities and dominated by ideologue-intellectuals like Li Ta-chao and Ch'en Tu-hsiu, its elite structure bore a strong resemblance to that of the CPSU. The repressive measures undertaken by Chiang Kai-shek in the April 12, 1927, coup and afterward nearly wiped out the Party's urban base and forced its survivors into the countryside, where the Party underwent a basic change of tactics that coincided with the rise of a new leadership under Mao Tse-tung and the eclipse of the Soviet-educated urban intellectuals. For the next twenty years the Party engaged in continuous warfare, during which it controlled extensive regions, but was unable to seize the state in Bolshevik fashion because the balance of coercive power was initially overwhelmingly on the side of the KMT and could be reversed only through a "protracted struggle." But due to the lack of political unity and extensive social dislocation, the Kuomintang regime could not effectively control many areas in China. This condition enabled the CCP to create its own base of support through nationalist appeals and social reforms, wooing a constituency by skillfully intermixing ideology with the manipulation of popular interests and discontents. In these years when the CCP was trying to capture national power, it could not rely on exclusively bureaucratic methods of control, which require a reasonably settled political order to function effectively. Because centralized control from the top was impossible, the Party granted wide autonomy to local units, which were to maintain dicipline, commitment, and enthusiasm through small-group activities such as "criticism and self-criticism." Cadre policy had to be managed with exemplary rectitude in order to avoid alienating the "wavering" petty- and national bourgeoisie, whose support or at least neutrality was deemed essential for victory.[11] In sum, the fact that the CCP was a Party out of

[10] The Trotsky citation is from E. H. Carr, *The Bolshevik Revolution, 1913–1923* (New York, 1953) 3: 16. The developmental parallels are examined in David Luck, "Soviet and Chinese Political Development," *Survey*, nos. 74–75 (winter-spring 1970): 29–49; Bodo Zeuner, "Innerparteiliche Demokratie," *Zur Politik und Zeitgeschichte* (Berlin), nos. 33–34 (1969): 26–28; Franz Schurmann, "Organizational Contrasts Between Communist China and the Soviet Union" (Hong Kong, 1961), pp. 29–30; and Schurmann, "The Organizational Functions of the Communist Party in China" (Berkeley, 1959), pp. 15–16. The last two sources are unpublished papers.

[11] "The leaning of the middle-of-the-road forces and the middle elements possesses a decisive significance in relation to the revolution we are making. Because

power during its formative years established a predisposition to tolerate a sphere of legitimate inner-Party freedom of expression and to develop a mobilizational rather than an administrative approach to the masses.

Despite this tendency toward freedom of expression within the Party, there was an important cleavage within the CCP regarding inner-Party struggle, a cleavage whose existence and significance were first clearly revealed during the GPCR. The CCP also had a split elite environment, consisting of "red area" forces comprised of peasant armies and guerrilla generals under Mao Tse-tung on the one hand, and "white area" forces consisting of urban students, workers, and peasants operating under Liu Shao-ch'i on the other; during the war years, contact between these two elite groups was minimal. Both "red" and "white area" elites relied extensively on mass mobilization and inner-Party criticism and self-criticism, but whereas the "red area" forces operated from secure base areas, the "white area" forces were "fish" in a non-Party "human sea" and were exposed to much more serious problems. The reduced security problem in the "red areas" is one reason for Mao's fairly uncomplicated approach to inner-Party struggle (the other having to do with his distinctive political style). Mao would simply call for inner-Party struggle whenever he noted tendencies within the Party that he wished to see corrected, as he did in his 1929 resolution, "On the Rectification of Incorrect Ideas in the Party," which called for a rectification of "absolute equalitarianism, absolute democratization, adventurism," and so on.[12]

Liu Shao-ch'i, as the ranking Communist leader in "enemy-occupied areas" during most of the war—from 1935 to 1942, he was Secretary of the North China Bureau (1936), Secretary of the Central Plains Bureau (1939) and its successor, the Central China Bureau (1941)—elaborated a rather complex casuistry laying down detailed conditions and qualifications for the *institutionalization of* inner-Party struggle, thus making the process invulnerable to the loss of any particular leader. He stressed the need to "organize well, prepare well, and have good leadership." Liu alluded to the reason for his more centralist approach in his 1944 discussion of the feasibility of the Cheng-feng technique behind the lines:

Some of it can be used, but much of it cannot be used. . . . If you use Yenan's method and hold a discussion meeting in which you say all you want

---

this is a society of 'small at both ends and large in the middle,' . . . it may just mean victory, whomever the middle-of-the-road forces will side with. Otherwise, there is no victory." Liu, "Fan-tui tang-nei ke-chung," in *LSWTC*, pp. 115–127.

12 *SW* 1: 105–114.

to say, of course sometimes you talk one day, two days . . . you're not finished in a month! But before the talking is finished the enemies will break
in. . . . So if you want to convene a discussion meeting it is just as well . . .
not to talk so much, to keep it under your belt. . . . When you come back
here [Yenan], you can relax a bit, it doesn't matter if the meeting breaks
up in confusion.[13]

Liu said that it was of little value to "say generally, 'Our work
shows errors of bureaucracy or liberalism,' you want to say that affair
is such-and-such, that person is such-and-such . . . you should speak
of concrete matters." [14] Yet these "concrete matters" should concern
"points of issue" and not be a "struggle against a certain Li or a certain
Chang." In an attempt to strike a balance between "excessive and mechanical" struggles and "liberalism," he drew a basic distinction between "principled" and "unprincipled" struggles, which had the general effect of repressing personal and idiosyncratic grievances and
rationalizing political conflict. "Principled" struggle involved "the
methods of observing and treating problems according to general rules
of development. . . . If errors arise in principle, not only specific
errors arise, but also systematic consistent errors." Questions of principle must be settled through struggle: "No compromise or 'middle
road' will bring about a solution," wrote Liu. "We must resolve these
through debate and reach unanimity." But "unprincipled" conflicts
over more practical or idiosyncratic problems can ("and must") be
resolved through informal compromise. Liu noted that "it is impossible to judge who is right and who is wrong in such unprincipled disputes" and concluded that:

Issues such as that a certain comrade does not fully trust another or still
suspects another, etc., should in general not be brought up for discussion, because discussion on such issues will be of no avail. Such issues can be settled,
and a particular comrade can be proved trustworthy and can be cleared of
suspicion only in the course of his work, his struggle, and his practice.[15]

In possible connection with the need for security in the "white
areas," Liu also insisted on a sharp distinction between "inner" and
"outer." He imputed a *theoretical* relationship between inner- and
extra-Party (class) struggle, saying that the former is coeval with and
"reflects" the latter, but he precluded any *practical* relationship between
the two. The prescribed social context for struggle is "inside the Party"
(*tang-nei*), and Liu condemned those comrades ("although they cannot

13 "On the Expansion of Democracy" (1944), in *LSWTC*, pp. 134–142.
14 *Ibid.*, p. 138.   15 *CW* 1: 330–367.

still be called comrades") who avail themselves of extra-Party resources, such as "newspapers, magazines, and various conferences outside the Party and even those of the bourgeoisie and the enemy," to
influence the outcome of intra-Party disputes. Once a decision is
reached, the minority is obligated to follow the majority, but, "on condition that they absolutely abide by the decision of the majority in
respect to organizational matters and in their activities," those who
disagree with the decision should reserve their opinions against the
possibility that they might eventually prove correct. "One must in
principle hold on to one's opinions," wrote Liu.[16]

Retrospective comparison of Mao's writings with regard to inner-
Party criticism and self-criticism reveals four underlying differences.
First, Liu's criteria for successful "struggles" stressed adherence to
certain prescribed *forms,* while leaving the substantive content of the
argument open; Mao's corresponding criteria were careless of form and
emphasized "correct" *substance.* For instance, Mao's famous distinction between "antagonistic" and "nonantagonistic" struggles purports
to be formal but is in fact substantive, based on whether or not the
criticism strengthens the "leadership of the Communist Party" and
"socialist solidarity"—if it does not, it is "antagonistic" and should be
"resolved by the practice of dictatorship." Second, Liu's "principled/
unprincipled" distinction is based on characteristics of the *object;*
Mao's corresponding distinction purports to be objective but, by
resting partly on the way contradictions are "handled," turns out to
be a *subjective* distinction ultimately dependent on the definition of
an authority standing above the conflict.[17] Third, whereas Liu put
strong emphasis on impersonality and the rationalization of conflict
(e.g., disputes should be "appropriate and well-regulated," conducted
"within proper limits," and so forth), an emphasis quite consistent
with his conception of "cultivation" as the repression of incalculable
emotions, Mao placed greater emphasis on the maximum possible involvement of the "uncultivated" masses, which entailed higher tolerance for dramatic display of emotions and demonstrative attacks
"against the person." For example, Mao "listened attentively to their
reports and collected a great deal of material" when peasants told him
how they had paraded humiliated landlords in tall hats and placards
during the 1927 Hunan peasant uprising. "This is what some people
call 'going too far' or 'overreaching the proper limits in righting a

16 *Ibid.,* p. 363.
17 Robert Fahrle and Peter Schoettler, *Chinas Weg: Marxismus oder Maoismus?*
(Frankfurt/M., 1969), pp. 85–115.

wrong.' . . . Such talk may seem plausible, but it is wrong," Mao wrote. "Revolution is not a dinner party." [18] Finally, whereas Liu's inner/outer distinction was consistently applied to the CCP and conceded a theoretical but never a practical relationship between class conflict and inner-Party struggle, Mao had been groping for some time for a formula that would include the masses within the in-group. His first attempt to do so, in 1956–57, was his introduction of a "people/enemies of the people" distinction that cross-cut class categories. "Within the ranks of the people, the contradictions among the working people are nonantagonistic while those between the exploited and the exploiting classes have a nonantagonistic aspect in addition to an antagonistic aspect." [19] Following setbacks in the "Hundred Flower" Campaign and the Lushan Plenum, he returned to class categories and introduced the idea that there were "bourgeois elements" within the Party, a warning that was made more specific in the 1965 "Twenty-three Points," which referred menacingly to "Party persons in authority taking the capitalist road," some of whom might be in the CC.[20] During the GPCR ,the theoretical connection between the inner-Party opposition and class struggle was for the first time to become actual—but this gets ahead of the story.

Between publication of Liu's paradigmatic essay on inner-Party struggle in 1941 and the launching of the GPCR in 1965, six structural changes occurred in the institutional and technological parameters of criticism and self-criticism. The first three occurred in 1949, when the CCP seized the state apparatus, acquiring monopoly control over the instruments of violence, state patronage, and mass communications.

(1) The first change meant that leaving the Party or defection to the KMT was no longer an available alternative to those who were criticized or who disagreed with the Party line.[21] In other words,

---

[18] "Report on an Investigation of the Peasant Movement in Hunan" (March 1927), in SRWM, pp. 23–40.

[19] "On the Correct Resolution of Contradictions Among the People," in SRWM, pp. 432–479.

[20] Baum and Teiwes, Ssu-ch'ing, pp. 118–126.

[21] According to Chang Kuo-t'ao's later account, this is the way the 1937 dispute between Chang and Mao was resolved. When a stalemate developed with Mao in control of the Politburo and Chang in control of the Second Provisional Central Authority, Chang simply stopped attending Politburo meetings for three months. When Mao sent Tung Pi-wu to ask him to stop "sulking," Chang told Tung, "I don't want to attend Politburo meetings, or to receive comrades to discuss Party affairs. Furthermore, I wish to withdraw from the central leadership of the Party. I'm now teaching economics with you at the North Shensi Public School; isn't this just fine?" "Introduction," in Liu, CW, p. vii. For a more detailed account, see "Wo-ti hui-i" [My memoirs], Ming pao yüeh-k'an 6, no. 2 (February 1971): 85–90. In January 1925, Mao Tse-tung resigned under pressure from both the KMT

there was now no escape from the coercive sanctions that the post-Liberation leadership could always adopt as a final resort in case ideological or organizational sanctions failed. The post-Liberation leadership was no longer inhibited by the possibility that dissidents could always opt out or defect. It continued to feel the need to demonstrate exemplary organizational behavior to the Party masses but was less restrained by this need than before, since the Party's survival was assured by its monopoly over legitimate violence.

(2) Control over governmental patronage enormously increased the disciplinary powers of organizational elites over middle- and lower-level cadres by placing criticism and self-criticism within a bureaucratic context, in effect eliminating the possibility of nonmanipulated struggle at any but the highest ranks, where power was more equally distributed. Seizure of the state apparatus gave the Party dispensation over an increased quantity and variety of resources (e.g., power, wealth, and deference) and created expediential pressures on cadres to exempt their superiors or colleagues from avoidable criticism.

(3) Through their control over the instruments of mass communication—the press and radio, television, motion pictures, and the popular and fine arts—CCP elites could take advantage of a technology whose rapid expansion across the country introduced a qualitatively different communication system to China.[22] The face-to-face oral communications network became augmented by a multiplicative network, so that any written or spoken message issued from the center could in theory reach every participant simultaneously in identical form.[23] This innovation had important structural implications for the "mass

---

Central Executive Committee and the CCP CC Organization Department on the pretext of ill health and returned to Hunan to "recuperate" shortly before the Fourth Congress of the CCP. "In fact," Rue infers, "he was expelled from the CC." Again in November 1927, Mao was purged from all Party positions but allowed to remain a Party member in Chingkangshan. John E. Rue, *Mao Tse-tung in Opposition, 1927–1935* (Stanford, Calif., 1966), pp. 38, 49 ff.

[22] Newspaper circulation increased from 3.4 million in 1951 to 15 million in 1958; magazine circulation jumped from 900,000 to 17 million during the same period. Yu, *Mass Persuasion*, p. 90. The Chinese claimed in 1960 that radio transmitting power was about five times greater than the sum of twenty years of transmitting power under the KMT from 1928 to 1947. The GLF in 1958 produced more than a million radios; ten years earlier, there were scarcely more than a million sets throughout the whole of China. Hugh Howse, "The Use of Radio in China," *CQ*, no. 2 (April–June 1960): 59–69. Western observers have been amazed by the speed and penetration of this communications revolution; according to Houn, "This is perhaps the most extensive propaganda effort of all time, and one likely to be of the greatest consequence in the course of world affairs." *To Change a Nation*, p. 1.

[23] Paul Kecskemeti, "Review of *Nationalism and Social Communication*," *Public Opinion Quarterly* 28, no. 1 (spring 1954): 102–105.

line," which was predicated on the possibility of two-way communications "from the masses, to the masses." The primarily oral communications system established under more primitive conditions for the Cheng-feng Movement made two-way communication technically feasible, but the new media greatly increased elite capabilities to transmit messages without correspondingly increasing the capability of the masses to do likewise, and thus time subtly altered the nature of mass contact through human transmitters. Instead of oral agitators roving the countryside (the oral agitation system atrophied quickly after 1953, as the CCP shifted emphasis to mass media), human transmitters were attached to each medium, and newspaper-reading groups, radio-listening groups, book-reading groups, and film-discussion groups were organized.[24] The integration of human transmitters and multiplicative media tended to enhance the authority of the former (the cadre could now point to the passage in the newspaper), while decreasing his flexibility in tailoring the message to the audience, and perhaps reducing his susceptibility to feedback.[25]

As the multiplicative network grew, it tended to supplant the limited-copy, limited-access organizational network.[26] This had little immediate import, since the two networks normally operated in tandem and were coordinated by the same Propaganda Department bureaucracy, but the multiplicative network's growth and demonstrable independent mobilizing efficacy created the possibility for high-level elites to "short-circuit" the bureaucracy and gain immediate contact with the masses through multiplicative media. The structural conditions existed for "Caesarism" by elites prepared to use skills in symbol manipulation to create a mass following, a possibility first fully realized in the GPCR.

In sum, CCP acquisition in 1949 of monopoly control over the instruments of governmental patronage, legitimate violence, and multiplicative media resulted in the differentiation of inner-Party struggle into two distinct arenas: First, a relatively clandestine and orderly purge mechanism emerged *within* the Party, which relied upon con-

---

24 Alan P. L. Liu, *Communications*, p. 115.

25 I owe these points to a personal communication from Alan Liu. James R. Townsend has noted a corresponding transition from a more nearly symmetrical mass-line relationship to a manipulative, apparently alienating one. *Political Participation in China* (Berkeley, Calif., 1969), concluding chapter.

26 For example, in 1954–1955 the "propaganda outlines" [*hsüan-ch'uan ta-kang*] and "propaganda handbooks" [*hsüan-ch'uan shou-ts'e*] periodically diffused through organizational channels by the CC Propaganda Department during mass movements were superseded by Party newspapers such as *Chung-kuo ch'ing-nien, Hsüeh-hsi* [Study], and later *Hung-ch'i* [Red flag]. Yu, *Mass Persuasion*, pp. 88–89. After the GLF's failure, the internal organizational network became completely esoteric.

trol over patronage enforced by implicit threat of coercion. This development resulted in an apparent elite monolithicity, which masked a constant shifting of positions; when conflict was irreconcilable, organizational sanctions were applied with rather little ex post facto publicity, following the Soviet mode. Second, a series of well-prepared, highly organized mass criticism campaigns were directed by the elite against carefully "labeled" targets through a nationally coordinated network of oral meetings and multiplicative media.[27]

(4) The fourth structural change took place as a natural extension of the Party's "united front" policy of accommodation with traditional elites. During the 1950s and early 1960s, although periodic campaigns were launched against dissident literati, between campaigns there was a quiet but steady cooptation of cultural notables. Also, certain sectors of the bureaucracy began to appropriate their offices (i.e., form "independent kingdoms") in order to protect themselves from the purges that sometimes swept the Party; thus, they tended to identify their interest with those of their constituency whose cooperation was deemed essential for successful implementation of central policy. The campaign against Wu Han, which initiated the GPCR, may have been originally intended as a normal continuation of the series of criticism campaigns against cultural notables that had taken place periodically since 1949, but it ignored the extent to which the cultural establishment had become interlocked with the political elite. "I did not realize until I was told by the Premier that once a person like Wu Han was exposed there would be many more like him," Chiang Ch'ing related in 1967. "That was where the real difficulty lay." [28] When this establishment was threatened from the outside, it locked in a united front so tight that "you couldn't stick a pin in," as Mao put it. This made it impossible for him to isolate and pick off the "handful" of his enemies, even asuming he knew who they were, and, as each falling victim exposed the patronage of others ("black backers"), entire chains of officials linked by formal or informal ties of organization or prior association were purged. The exposure of these hidden links seems to have fed Mao's suspicions of an oppositionist conspiracy and finally won his approval for an almost indiscriminate attack upon the establishment.

27 For studies of these earlier campaigns, see Yang I-fan, *The Case of Hu Feng* (Hong Kong, December 1956); Chalmers Johnson, *Freedom of Thought and Expression in China: Communist Policies Toward the Intellectual Class* (Hong Kong, 1959); Theodore H. E. Ch'en, *Thought Reform of the Chinese Intellectuals* (Hong Kong, 1960); Guy Alitto, "Thought Reform in Communist China: The Case of Chou Ku-ch'eng" (M.A. Thesis, Chicago, 1966).

28 Chiang Ch'ing's April 12, 1967 speech to the MAC.

(5) The fifth structural change became visible in the early 1960s. A perceptible and enduring gulf gradually developed between two factions in the top-echelon leadership because the original "rules of the game" granted the dissenting minority the right to "reserve opinions." This right was compatible with the continued efficacy of inner-Party struggle only insofar as the identity of the adversary shifted from issue to issue; if "opinion groups" hardened into permanent factions, the result was a loss of the sense of solidarity and mutual trust necessary for criticism and self-criticism.[29] Available evidence about policy making in the 1950s indicates that there was a constant turnover of opinion-group membership within the inner core of the leadership,[30] but during the 1960s the Maoists began to "reserve opinions," [31] and the inner-Party debate and exchange of opinions became less open and frank and tended not to follow organizational channels so closely as before.

There seem to have been two reasons for the Maoist disaffection. First, Mao noticed a systematic distortion of his directives when they were transmitted through the Party apparatus, resulting in a policy output subtly different from the Maoist input; when he left the bureaucracy to its own routine, its policies also differed from those he might have wished, and he periodically intervened. Second, Parris Chang has shown that the key locus of decision in the Party shifted in the 1960s from the ad hoc meetings which Mao had frequently used in the 1950s and could easily dominate to the large and formal "central work conferences," where those in charge of the Secretariat were able to exercise control over the agenda and the preparation of policy proposals. Because the policy process was relatively open, not monopolized by a few leaders but accessible to a significant number of Party officials below the Politburo, the importance of the Politburo (and its Standing Committee) in the policy process tended to decline.[32] This growth of formal inner-Party democracy did not completely deprive Mao of his influence over policy—his national stature permitted him to inter-

[29] For a perceptive analysis of the theory and practice of "opinion groups," see Schurmann, *Ideology*, pp. 48 ff.

[30] Roderick MacFarquhar, "Communist China's Intra-Party Dispute," *Pacific Affairs* 31, no. 4 (December 1958): 323–336; Parris Chang, "Struggle Between the Two Roads;" and "Power and Policy," p. 46.

[31] That Mao reserved his opinions is revealed by a passage in Liu's first self-criticism: "As Mao was not in Peking then [1962], I went to him and delivered a report. *Afterwards* I learned that Chairman Mao was not at all in agreement with my appraisal of the situation." *CW* 3: 361 [emphasis added]. Mao also permitted his wife secretly to prepare the original attack on Wu Han, as previously indicated.

[32] Chang, "Research Notes on the Changing Loci of Decision in the CCP," *CQ*, no. 44 (October–December 1970): 169–195.

vene in the process and achieve his ends throughout the 1960s—but Mao may have frequently been in the minority, and at the Eleventh Plenum he obtained a bare majority only with extraordinary effort and strenuous maneuvers. The sheer frequency and size of these central work meetings reduced the impact of a Supreme Leader with only a small personal staff whose style was to rule by occasional fiat.[33]

(6) The sixth structural change followed from the fifth, the formation of durable conflict groups at the center. Members of inner-Party struggle sessions have always had access to extra-Party power bases, such as field armies (in the 1940s and early 1950s), local constituencies, government bureaus, and so on. A cardinal rule for the successful operation of the criticism and self-criticism process was each leader's forfeiture of access to these extra-Party resources, so that his fate was at the mercy of a closed circle of intimates.[34] The growth of organization (with its attendant maintenance and enhancement needs) outside that circle and the erosion of trust within it led its members to consolidate their hold over extra-Party power bases, resulting in "parallel and competing bureaucracies." It was at this time that the alliance between Mao and Lin Piao was formed.

As the log-jam of repressed hostilities slowly broke into open conflict in the winter and spring of 1965–66, members of incipient conflict groups in the struggle process openly appealed to constituencies in extra-Party power bases in order to break the deadlock. This indicated that:

Political conflicts which cannot be resolved by elite groups or politically relevant groups within the existing pattern of participation-mobilization will give rise to attempts by one or both sides to enlist active support of other groups to break the deadlock, thus changing the scope and form of . . . participation-mobilization.[35]

The case of Liu Shao-ch'i, however, suggests two qualifications to this conclusion. First, the temptation to break the deadlock by introducing outside forces only arises when one party has a decisive pre-

---

[33] According to Chang, there were nineteen central work conferences in 1960–1966: one in 1960, three in 1961, four in 1962, three in 1963, four in 1964–1965, and four in 1966. In addition to work conferences, there was a congeries of other meetings, some with institutional labels, such as "enlarged Politburo meetings," others known only by the place and time they were held. *Ibid.*

[34] For example, the public charges against both Kao Kang in 1954–1955 and P'eng Te-huai in 1959 included the accusation that they went outside the Politburo to cultivate support among CC members.

[35] Tang Tsou, "The People's Liberation Army and the Cultural Revolution: A Study of Civil-Military Relationships in China" (unpub. paper, University of Chicago, 1970).

ponderance of inside or outside resources. If all participants were equal in both intra- and extra-Party resources, the deadlock would conceivably continue indefinitely, for anyone who mobilized outside forces to break it would be met by equal force. Mao's special temptation (and justification) to appeal to non-Party forces derived from the disproportion between his diminishing power inside the Party and his decisively preponderant power outside it. The second reservation seems more decisive. Breaking a deadlock could not have been Mao's *sole* intention, for this end was achieved at the Eleventh Plenum with the criticism and demotion of his enemies within the CC and passage of "The Sixteen Points"; yet the August Plenum marked the *beginning*, not the end, of the GPCR. Because Mao's victory over his inner-Party opposition was already assured at the outset, we may safely assume that his motives for "pushing the GPCR through to the end" went beyond a desire to break a deadlock and depose his enemies. For this he could presumably have used the PLA (as he later used the PLA to subdue extremist rebel groups),[36] but he refrained for two reasons: first, because his enemies had earned considerable mass support by their remarkable resuscitation of the economy after the Leap, Mao felt it necessary to legitimate his purge through a mass educational campaign; second, he wished to prolong the criticism campaign to gain popular backing for a domestic reform program of unprecedented sweep and depth.

The GPCR mass criticism campaign employed rhetoric originated a quarter-century previously (e.g., "unity–struggle–unity," and "struggle–criticism–transformation") to characterize a struggle that took place under drastically altered structural circumstances: a struggle that was thrown open to the masses through an unprecedented proliferation and decentralization of informal communications media, including big-character posters, hectographed leaflets, and tabloid newspapers (of which there were more than one hundred). Any nationally coordinated defense by the Party apparatus was rendered ineffective by the early demotion and subsequent purge of its leaders, Liu and Teng. The Maoist strategy was to destroy the Party's legitimacy by systematically circumventing its gatekeeping monopoly over center-mass communications and to recruit ad hoc paramilitary bands from disaffected sectors of the populace to "bombard the bourgeois headquarters" with the tacit (and later explicit) backing of the PLA. In

36 As the Chinese have apparently also noted. A July 1, 1971 *PD* editorial observed that some people have asked, "Since Liu Shao-chi . . . usurped part of the power . . . it needs only an order from Chairman Mao to dismiss him from office, why should the present method [the GPCR] be adopted?" Quoted in Chang, *Radicals and Radical Ideology*, p. 55.

this altered context, an institution originally designed to achieve political redemption and renewed unity within a closed circle of elites resulted in nonredemptive purges and rampant factionalism in society; unity and order were restored only by reassertion of dictatorship.

The original institution was premised upon a solidarity ("unity") among all participants (Liu's "family" metaphor for the Party is not accidental), which had been temporarily disturbed by an offense by one of them. To induce remorse, the offender is isolated from the others and criticized; he then confesses and solicits forgiveness from the others to obviate the distance between them. In so doing he affirms that he has indeed committed the acts of which he stands accused, but denies that he is *in* those acts; his appeal for forgiveness is a demonstration that he transcends his acts and his past and is not identical with them. In accepting his self-criticism and granting forgiveness, the others in turn acknowledge that their earlier critical characterization of the offender was partly incorrect or incomplete. The process is resolved in the externalization of the offense and the reintegration of the offender into a group newly purified and united by this emotional opening and surrender on the part of both the person criticized and his critics.[37]

Both the structural evolution of criticism and self-criticism in the years since its inception and the special circumstances characterizing the GPCR made this process unworkable, for the following reasons:

(1) The process of criticism and self-criticism was ultimately premised on the distinction between inner and outer, which Mao opted to destroy, along with most other conventional distinctions, in order to facilitate maximal mobilization of the masses. "To say that 'there is a difference between inside and outside' is to be afraid of the revolution," Mao said in July 1966. "It will not do to fix frames for the masses." [38] This distinction was destroyed by counterphobic rhetoric, by elites writing anonymous articles in the press denouncing other elites, by "leaks" to Red Guard media, and by open manipulation of outside pressure groups through speeches and "instructions" in order to influence inner-Party verdicts. The closed circle could be penetrated almost at will, with the result that ties to outside pressure groups preempted commitment to the group's decisions, and the underlying assumption of ultimate "unity" no longer stood.

(2) Enfranchisement of the "uncultivated" masses resulted in a

37 Joseph Beatty, "Forgiveness," *American Philosophical Quarterly* 7, no. 3 (July 1970): 246–255.
38 "Speech to Responsible Persons of the CC" (1966), *CNS*, no. 284 (August 21, 1969): A4.

breakdown of Liu's "principled/unprincipled" distinction to permit the expression of nonrational grievances. Opening the doors to the masses augmented the original circle of "comrades" with great numbers of newcomers to the political process—particularly middle-school and university students and young workers not yet sufficiently socialized into the rules of criticism and self-criticism. So they translated the issues into a more familiar framework to which they could emotionally relate: Mao was perceived as a father, Liu as an ambitious and unfilial son; Liu's personal foibles assumed high salience. The circumscription of faults was progressively widened by the increase in participants, each of whom wished to translate Liu's crimes into his own terms and make a critical contribution, with the result that so many aspects of Liu's thought and life were drawn in and attacked from various perspectives that he could not hope to atone for his "crimes" without becoming all things to all men. Certain groups also acquired vested interests in the criticism movement, which they exploited to storm the power structure and expropriate offices; they needed to discover more and ever more serious "crimes" in order to sustain the indignation of the masses that propelled the campaign, adding to the pressure for polemical escalation. As a result, Liu tended to "resist" in the sense that his definition of his crimes (in his self-criticism) failed to keep pace with the expanding popular indictment.

(3) Previously, the process of criticism and self-criticism was conducted according to what Max Weber called the "principle of collegiality" within a forum of formal equals, all of whom could use the same theoretical calculus in a fairly objective way to determine guilt or innocence.[39] With the opening of the conflict to the public, and because the popular perception of its leadership was monocratic rather than collegial and Mao's personal popularity far surpassed that of any of his colleagues, the principle of autocracy temporarily superseded the principle of collegiality. This "autocracy" was effective only ideologically, however, for the organization was reputed to be riddled with "capitalist-roaders" and was deliberately short-circuited. In the GPCR, the Maoists therefore utilized the mass media to promote Mao's Thought as a new calculus for determining innocent or guilt. This ideological calculus eclipsed the elaborate and time-consuming procedures that were normally enforced by the Party organization prior to "labeling" criticism targets,[40] just as the rise of the Red

[39] Max Weber, *Economy and Society*, ed. G. Roth and C. Wittich (New York, 1968), 1: 271–282.

[40] For a discussion of "labeling" in the GPCR, see Gordon Bennett, "Political Labels and Popular Tension," *CS* 7, no. 4 (February 26, 1969): 1 ff.

Guards eclipsed the Party organization itself, but Mao's Thought proved impossibly vague as a criterion for selecting targets. Mao's Thought provided a *structural* critique, which said no more than that the oppressed were "justified" in rebelling against "authorities" who were "taking the capitalist road"; this left rebel factions considerable latitude in choosing targets, particularly at provincial and local levels. But the indeterminancy of Mao's Thought as a calculus of guilt meant that criticism had no intrinsic limits. Once a person came under attack, there was an immanent dynamic to the criticism process that propelled it toward his destruction: as soon as the target acquired a public "hat," he was isolated, because those who maintained any contact with him risked implication; his self-criticisms were indignantly rejected for the same reason. This escalatory dynamic vitiated the intended function of criticism as a sort of ordeal by fire for aberrant cadres, simply because *no* target could "pass the test" unless he managed to secure the outside intercession of Mao, Chou En-lai, or Lin Piao; even if one faction forgave him, a competing faction was sure to assail the verdict and demand a reversal.

Due to the indeterminacy of Mao's Thought as a calculus, and to the rejection of organizational criteria, there was a tendency for rebels to act on cues from elite leaders or to revert to ascriptive criteria. Targets were labeled on the basis of various "contagion patterns" linking them with "dead" targets, such as prior association or place of origin; these criteria tended to operate on a "domino" principle, making it possible to implicate entire chains of officials (by May 28, 1967, no less than 2,500 members of Liu Shao-ch'i's "faction" had thus been discovered by Red Guards).[41] Similarly, "comradeship" as a basis for political loyalty gave way to "friendship"[42] or even kinship, which began to assume an importance unprecedented in CCP history as a criterion for recruitment and coalition formation among elites.[43]

As Edgar Snow has noted, the emergent pattern of conflict resolu-

---

[41] *Yomiuri*, April 4, 1967, quoted in Rice, *Mao's Way*, p. 345.

[42] Cf. Ezra Vogel, "From Friendship to Comradeship: The Change in Personal Relations in Communist China," *CQ*, no. 21 (January–March 1965): 46–61.

[43] Chiang Ch'ing named her first daughter Hsiao Li "person in charge" (chief editor) of *LAD* after the reorganization of the editorial board on August 23, 1967, and placed her second daughter Li Ming in one of the subordinate units of the Science and Technology Commission for National Defense, a department in charge of the nuclear weapons testing program. Lin Piao named his wife Yeh Ch'ün one of the nine members of the reorganized PLA Cultural Revolution Group in 1967, placing her sixth in rank, and assigned his daughter Tou-tou to the editorial staff of *K'ung chün pao*, the air force paper. Chien Yu-shen, *China's Fading Revolution: Army Dissent and Military Divisions, 1967–1968* (Hong Kong, 1969), p. 125.

tion bears a certain resemblance to the Western "critical election" in that deadlocked elites seek a decisive popular constituency to win backing for a political platform and to defeat an opposition by employing all available communications media for mass mobilization.[44] However, the Chinese Communist pattern differs in at least two respects. First, there was no precisely measurable calculus of consent. Opinion was to be expressed exclusively through criticism, and not everyone had equal access to the media. Anyone could write a wall poster, but the multiplicative media, including the pace-making sector of the official press as well as the Red Guard tabloids, were seized by radical publicists, who had reached their positions by dint of demonstrated polemical skills. The criticisms they wrote were not meant to persuade an inert majority to vote one way or another (as in the West) but were "performative utterances," which themselves constituted "votes," for it was thought that the appearance of a sufficient number of telling criticisms could in itself destroy an authority's legitimacy and make it impossible for him to rule. Under this arrangement, Mao's opponents had no chance to defend the alternative platform they were said to uphold, nor did the "silent majority" have any real avenue of expression, but the Party's monopoly over authoritative opinion was temporarily broken, and this control was distributed among a network of symbol specialists, who gave the movement its radical thrust.

Second, the Maoists had no viable alternative "slate" of candidates, as Mao came to realize in the course of the "January 1967 storm." Mao concluded that the rebels were "politically immature," that if they seized power one day they might be "swept away" the next, and he found it necessary to persuade the same cadres who had been disgraced and purged to "liberate" themselves from bourgeois thinking and reassume leadership positions on the RCs.

The GPCR was clearly no election, and yet its most significant departure from previous decision-making procedures was in penetrating the inner/outer distinction and establishing a liaison with constituencies of extra-Party masses and polemicists. Michel Oksenberg has suggested that this innovation in making important decisions might become institutionalized in a form of "interest-group politics." Modernization and industrialization will result in increasing functional differentiation, he argues, and as these new professional and functional groups acquire greater resources and the society grows more complex, their backing will become indispensable to maintain economic effi-

44 Snow, *The Long Revolution*, p. 67.

ciency, and elite factions will increasingly seek backing from the interest group concerned in order to promote a given policy proposal.[45]

Oksenberg's projection seems based on the assumption that "revisionism" will return to post-GPCR China. The tendency for elites to become identified with particular interest groups was apparent under Liu Shao-ch'i, most notably in the case of P'eng Chen, Lu Ting-yi, and the cultural-educational establishment. Yet Okensberg overstates his case by overlooking the passivity of Chinese interest groups.[46] This passivity may be attributed to the absence of any ideological legitimation for the concept of *pluralism* in China, a concept that possibly evokes memories of the short-lived experiment with constitutional government and a multi-Party system in 1911, which was followed by an extended period of national disunity and weakness. Even during the "revisionist" heyday, "interest-group politics" consisted of paternalistic solicitude by certain members of the elite rather than any active pressure for favors by the interest groups. Furthermore, "revisionism" was thoroughly repudiated during the GPCR, and with it the prospect of interest-group representation within the leadership; this is not to say that it will not reappear, but that ideological sanctions would militate against its reappearance.

But what of the prospect of a continued liaison between the *masses* and certain high-level elites? The mandate that was issued to Red Guards to participate in the political process by writing polemics or demonstrating has been revoked; the rival factions have been disbanded, their printing presses confiscated, and their nationwide liaison networks broken up. Nonetheless, the big-character posters remain a feature of the political scene at the lower levels, introducing contestation into local elections that were previously rubber-stamp affairs.[47] A place has been made for "mass representatives" on RCs at all levels; as noted in Chapter 9. Even if their power is only nominal, this is an important concession to the principle that non-Party masses should have permanent representation on leadership councils that make decisions immediately affecting their lives. While it is possible that the drastic cut-back in secretarial and staff personnel may impair the technical and planning functions of the leadership, it may also

[45] Oksenberg, "Occupational Groups in Chinese Society and the Cultural Revolution," *The Cultural Revolution: 1967 in Review* (Ann Arbor, Mich., 1968), pp. 1–45.
[46] Tang Tsou, "Interest Groups and the Political System in Maoist China" (unpub. paper, Chicago, 1969).
[47] Maria Antonietta Macciocchi, *Daily Life in Revolutionary China* (New York, 1972), pp. 316–320.

contribute to decentralization, making the government more responsive to its constituency.[48] Finally, and of far-reaching historical importance, the GPCR emancipated ideology from organization, breaking down the impermeable "line of demarcation" between elites and masses through such organizational innovations as "open-door rectification" and routinized *hsia-fang* of various categories of cadres. In the winter of 1970–71, for instance, "radicals" in various provinces availed themselves of their improved access to elites to attack local Party committees for failing to implement the more egalitarian norms implicit in GPCR polemics; agitation continued until *PD* published an edict from the Chairman on February 18, 1971, proscribing further alteration of the commune system.[49] This suggests the way disadvantaged groups may continue to use Mao's Thought to legitimate the expression of grievances without going through formal channels, and at the same time illustrates how the integral link between ideology and Supreme Leader provides a court of last resort to arbitrate conflicts arising from ambiguities within the ideology.

At the highest level of leadership, however, Mao has moved to reestablish the old distinction between "inner" and "outer." As he said at the First Plenum of the Ninth CC:

We adopted the method of issuing a communiqué so that foreign newsmen could no longer get our news. [Laughter.] They said we had a secret meeting; we were both open and secret. . . . We may have eliminated all the traitors and spies they planted in our ranks. In the past, news about every meeting immediately leaked out and then appeared in the tabloid newspapers of the Red Guards. Since the overthrow of Wang [Li], Kuan [Feng], Ch'i [Pen-yü], Yang [Ch'eng-wu], Yü [Li-chin], and Fu [Ch'ung-pi], they have been shut out from any news about the central leadership.[50]

Whereas pre-GPCR plenums were given considerable publicity, usually including publication of important speeches and reports (for example, at the Eighth Congress, every address was immediately released to the public), beginning with the Twelfth Plenum of the Eighth CC in October 1968, central meetings have been held under quasi-secret conditions, publicized only by release of a communiqué, if by that. Since the Ninth Party Congress in April 1969, Mao has discontinued his practice of issuing "latest instructions" directly to the masses through the media and is seldom seen in public.

In short, the emerging distribution of authority just reverses the

[48] Tsou, "Maoist Revolutionary Values."
[49] See Chapter 7 of this book.
[50] "Mao's Speech to the First Plenary Session of the CCP's Ninth CC" (April 28, 1969), in *IS* 6, no. 6 (March 1970): 94–99.

pre-GPCR pattern: whereas at lower levels of the bureaucracy there has undoubtedly been an increase in "democracy," at the center there has been an increase in "centralism." [51] Under the Liu-Teng collective leadership, policy was made through a process of consultation among three organs, the CC, the Politburo and its Standing Committee, and the Secretariat, each of which convened frequent enlarged sessions. In the post-GPCR leadership, the Secretariat appears to have been eliminated, the CC meets rather infrequently, and the Politburo has been halved in size (reduced from twenty-one to ten) as a consequence of continuing purges.

At the highest level, there appear to be two modalities of conflict resolution in the new authority structure. First, the normal mode of redemptive inner-Party criticism and self-criticism seems to have been reinstituted in much the same form as it functioned in the 1949–66 period. For example, a recent *Red Flag* article reassured apprehensive cadres:

Of course, in the course of bearing responsibilities, weaknesses or mistakes may also appear. But this is not serious; in our Party we have always had an old rule, which is to undergo criticism and self-criticism, to publicly expose one's weaknesses and errors and promptly and fundamentally to reform, and then it's all right.[52]

Second, during extraordinary circumstances, a precedent exists for opening the process of mediated and regulated collegial conflict to the public in harness with the dialect of class struggle, forfeiting the redemptive character of the process in order to maximize mass mobilization (see Chapter 8). The circumstances under which such a metamorphosis may take place are undefined, but they seem to include the existence of an enduring stalemate at the highest policy levels, elite access to alternative avenues of mass mobilization, and the presence of a mobilizable mass (i.e., sectors of the populace who may be mobilized without seriously disrupting economic production, such as students or the underemployed).

The introduction of this second form of conflict resolution, and the fluid relationship between the two modes has an ambiguous impact on the continuing structural evolution of criticism and self-criticism. With regard to *elite-mass* relations, the second method entails the

---

51 In Liu's formulation of the pre-GPCR pattern, "Leaders in the Party and higher-level organizations should pay more attention to democracy, and subordinates should pay more attention to obedience." *CW* 1: 397. The post-GPCR pattern is modeled after Mao's directive, "Concentrate the great authority, diffuse the small authority." Quoted in Schurmann, "Organizational Contrasts," pp. 29–30.

52 *RF*, no. 11 (October 30, 1972): 19–22.

legitimation of public opinion to decide major issues of state. It remains to be seen whether the network of RCs will become institutional foci for the aggregation of public opinion, acting as "ombudsmen" to mediate communication between Party committee and masses, but in any case a precedent has been set for an occasional "jubilee" in which disadvantaged and normally inarticulate sectors of the populace are encouraged to express their grievances and achieve redress.

With regard to *intra-elite* relations, it seems that the prospect of a transformation of the normal mode into the extraordinary entails a significant escalation in the disciplinary sanctions available to those members of the elite who can command a mass constituency. On the one hand, memories of the GPCR and the spectre of its repetition seem likely to make the normal mode a somewhat less candid and more provisional "game," since each player is aware of the option of "turning the tables" and suddenly raising the "stakes" from defeat on the issue at hand to political survival. In the absence of any tradition of legitimate political opposition, this creates regime instability. With the monopolization of the means of production, legitimate violence, mass publicity, and patronage, there is also the potential for "nationalization" of guilt.[53] The prospect of becoming a national guilt symbol is so unnerving that its likely targets might prefer suicide (e.g., Lo Jui-ch'ing, Teng T'o) or a preemptive bid for total power or flight (as the bizarre Lin Piao episode suggests). While this situation has surely made life at the top much more hazardous, it has also given the regime a means to generate a mandate for change and to avoid the loss of impulsion said to characterize the Soviet collective leadership.[54]

[53] Georges Henein, "Autocritique," *Petite Encyclopédie Politique* (Paris, 1969), pp. 16–19.

[54] Michel Tatu, "Possibilities of Evolution in the Soviet Union," in *The Atlantic Community and Eastern Europe: Perspectives and Policy* (Paris, Atlantic Institute, 1967), pp. 19–25.

SELECTED BIBLIOGRAPHY

FREQUENTLY CITED PERIODICALS

China News Analysis. Hong Kong.
China Notes. New York: Far Eastern Office, Division of Foreign Missions, National Council of Churches.
China Science Notes. New York: Committee on Scholarly Communication with Mainland China, National Academy of Sciences, American Council of Learned Societies, Social Science Research Council.
Current Background. Hong Kong: U.S. Consulate General.
Current Scene: Developments in Mainland China. Hong Kong.
Daily Summary of the Japanese Press. Tokyo: U.S. Embassy.
Far Eastern Economic Review. Hong Kong.
New York Times. New York, N.Y.
Selections from China Mainland Magazines. Hong Kong: U.S. Consulate General.
Summaries of Selected Japanese Magazines. Tokyo: U.S. Embassy.
Survey of the China Mainland Press. Hong Kong: U.S. Consulate General.
U.S. Joint Publications Research Service. Arlington, Va.

BOOKS AND MONOGRAPHS

Althusser, Louis. *Reading Capital.* Translated by B. Brewster. London: New Left Press, 1970.
An, Tai Sung. *Mao Tse-tung's Cultural Revolution.* New York: Pegasus, 1972.
Arendt, Hannah. *The Human Condition.* Chicago: University of Chicago Press, 1958.
Asian Research Center. *The Great Cultural Revolution in China.* Hong Kong: Green Pagoda Press, 1967.
Barnett, A. Doak, ed., *Chinese Communist Politics in Action.* Seattle, Wash.: University of Washington Press, 1969.
Baum, Richard and Teiwes, Frederick C. *Ssu-ch'ing: The Socialist Education Movement of 1962–1966.* Berkeley, Calif.: University of California, Center for Chinese Studies, 1968.

359

Baum, Richard, ed., *China in Ferment: Perspectives on the Cultural Revolution.* Englewood Cliffs, N.J.: Prentice-Hall, 1971.

Bennett, Gordon C., and Montaperto, Ronald N. *Red Guard: The Political Biography of Dai Hsiao-ai.* Garden City, N.Y.: Doubleday and Co., 1971.

Bernardo, Robert M. *The Theory of Moral Incentives in Cuba.* University: University of Alabama Press, 1971.

Blumer, Giovanni. *Die Chinesische Kulturrevolution, 1965–1967.* Frankfurt am Main: Europaeische Verlaganstalt, 1968.

Bodde, Derk and Morris, Clarence. *Law in Imperial China: Exemplified by 190 Ch'ing Dynasty Cases.* Cambridge, Mass.: Harvard University Press, 1967.

Bowie, Robert R., and Fairbank, John K., eds., *Communist China, 1955–1959: Policy Documents with Analysis.* Cambridge, Mass.: Harvard University Press, 1967.

Brzezinsky Zbigniew K. *The Soviet Bloc: Unity and Conflict.* 2d ed. Cambridge, Mass.: Harvard University Press, 1967.

Buck, John Lossing.. *Land Utilization in China.* 3 vols. 3d ed. New York, N.Y.: Paragon, 1968.

Burki, Shahid Javed. *A Study of Chinese Communes: 1965.* Cambridge, Mass.: Harvard University Press, 1969.

Chang Man, *The People's Daily and the Red Flag Magazine During the Cultural Revolution.* Hong Kong: Union Research Institute, 1969.

Chang, Parris H. *Radicals and Radical Ideology in the Cultural Revolution.* New York: Columbia University, Research Institute on Communist Affairs, 1972.

Chen, C. S., ed., *Rural People's Communes in Lien-chiang.* Translated by Charles Price Ridley. Stanford, Calif.: Hoover Institution Press, 1969.

———, ed. *Mao Papers.* London: Oxford University Press, 1970.

Ch'en, Jerome, ed. *Mao.* Englewood Cliffs, N.J.: Prentice-Hall, 1969.

Chen, Nai-ruenn, and Galenson, Walter. *The Chinese Economy Under Communism.* Chicago: Aldine Publishing Co., 1969.

Chen, Theodore H. E. *Thought Reform of the Chinese Intellectuals.* Hong Kong: Hong Kong University Press, 1960.

———, ed. *The Chinese Communist Regime: Documents and Commentary.* New York: Praeger Publishers, 1967.

Chen, Yung Ping. *Chinese Political Thought: Mao Tse-tung and Liu Shao-ch'i.* The Hague: Martinus Nijhoff, 1966.

Ch'eng, Tien-mu. *Maos Dialektik des Widerspruchs.* Hamburg: Holsten Verlag, 1971.

Chesneaux, Jean. *The Chinese Labor Movement, 1919–1927.* Stanford, Calif.: Stanford University Press, 1968.

Chien Yu-shen. *China's Fading Revolution: Army Dissent and Military Divisions, 1967–1968.* Hong Kong: Centre of Contemporary China Studies, 1969.

Chuang, H. C. *The Great Proletarian Cultural Revolution: A Terminologi-*

cal Study. Berkeley: University of California, Center for Chinese Studies, 1967.

Chung Hua-nin and Miller, Arthur C. *Madame Mao: A Profile of Chiang Ch'ing.* Hong Kong: Union Research Institute, 1968.

Committee of Concerned Asian Scholars. *China: Inside the People's Republic.* New York: Bantam Books, 1972.

Compton, Boyd, ed. *Mao's China: Party Reform Documents, 1942–1944.* Seattle: University of Washington Press, 1952.

Daim, Wilfried. *Die Kastenlose Gesellschaft.* Munich: Manz Verlag, 1960.

Daubier, Jean. *Histoire de la Révolution Culturelle Prolétarienne en Chine.* Two vols. Paris: François Maspero, 1971.

Devillers, Philippe. *Mao.* Translated by Tony White. New York: Schocken Books, 1969.

Domes, Jürgen. *Die Ära Mao Tse-tung.* Stuttgart: Kohlhammer Verlag, 1971.
———. *Von der Volkskommune zur Krise in China.* Duisdorf b. Bonn: Selbstverlag der Studiengesellschaft zur Zeitprobleme, 1964.

Doolin, Dennis. *Communist China: The Politics of Student Opposition.* Stanford, Calif.: Stanford University Press, 1964.

Dutt, Gargi and Dutt, V. P. *China's Cultural Revolution.* New York: Asia Publishing House, 1970.

Eberhard, Wolfram. *Guilt and Sin in Traditional China.* Berkeley and Los Angeles: University of California Press, 1967.

Ebon, Martin. *Lin Piao: The Life and Writings of China's New Ruler.* New York: Stein and Day, 1970.

Esmein, Jean. *La Révolution Culturelle Chinoise.* Paris: Éditions du Seuil, 1970.

Fahrle, Robert and Schoettler, Peter. *Chinas Weg: Marxismus oder Maoismus?* Frankfurt a. Main: Verlag der Marxistischen Blaetter, 1969.

Fan, K., ed. *Mao Tse-tung and Lin Piao: Post-Revolutionary Writings.* Garden City, N.Y.: Doubleday and Co., 1972.

FitzGerald, C. P., ed. *Quotations from President Liu Shao-ch'i.* New York and Tokyo: Walker/Weatherhill, 1968.

Fokkema, D. W. *Report from Peking: Observations of a Western Diplomat on the Cultural Revolution.* London: C. Hurst, 1971.

Garaudy, Roger. *Le Problème Chinois.* Paris: Union Générale D'Éditions, 1967.

Gigon, Fernand. *Vie et Mort de la Révolution Culturelle.* Paris: Flammarion Éditeur, 1969.

Glaubitz, Joachim, ed. *Opposition Gegen Mao.* Olten, Switzerland: Walter Verlag, 1969.

Goldman, Merle. *Literary Dissent in Communist China.* Cambridge, Mass.: Harvard University Press, 1967.

Goodstadt, Leo. *Mao Tse-tung: The Search for Plenty.* London: Longman Group, 1972.

Granquist, Hans. *The Red Guards.* Translated by E. G. Fries. New York: Praeger Publishers, 1967.

Gray, Jack and Cavendish, Patrick. *Chinese Communism in Crisis: Maoism and the Cultural Revolution*. New York: Praeger Publishers, 1968.

Habermas, Jürgen. *Toward a Rational Society: Student Protest. Science and Politics*. Translated by Jeremy Shapiro. Boston: Beacon Press, 1970.

Harrison, James Pinckney. *The Long March to Power: A History of the Chinese Communist Party, 1921–71*. New York: Praeger Publishers, 1972.

Heinzig, Dieter. *Die Krise der Kommunistischen Partei Chinas in der Kulturrevolution*. Hamburg: Mitteilungen des Instituts für Asienkunde, No. 27, 1969.

Helwig, Paul. *Dramaturgie des Menschlichen Lebens*. Stuttgart: Ernst Klett Verlag, 1958.

Hindels, Joseph. *Lebt Stalin in Peking? Die Ideologische Auseinandersetzung im Kommunismus*. Vienna: Europa Verlag, 1964.

Hoffman, Charles. *Work Incentive Policies and Practices in the People's Republic of China, 1953–1965*. Albany: State University of New York Press, 1967.

Houn, Franklin W. *To Change a Nation*. New York: The Free Press, 1961.

———. *A Short History of Chinese Communism*. Englewood Cliffs, N.J.: Prentice-Hall, 1967.

Hsia, Adrian. *The Chinese Cultural Revolution*. Translated by Gerald Onn. New York: McGraw-Hill, 1972.

Hsiung, James Chieh. *Ideology and Practice: The Evolution of Chinese Communism*. New York: Praeger Publishers, 1970.

Hung-ch'i p'iao-p'iao [The red flag waves]. 16 vols. Peking: Chung-kuo ch'ing-nien ch'u-pan she, 1957.

Hunter, Neale. *Shanghai Journal: An Eyewitness Account of the Cultural Revolution*. New York: Praeger Publishers, 1969.

Johnson, Chalmers. *Freedom of Thought and Expression in China: Communist Policies Toward the Intellectual Class*. Communist China Research Series, vol. 21. Hong Kong: Union Research Institute, May 1959.

———. *Peasant Nationalism and Communist Power*. Stanford, Calif.: Stanford University Press, 1962.

Keesing's Publications. *The Cultural Revolution in China: Its Origins and Course up to August, 1967*. Keynsham, Bristol: Keesing's Publications, 1967.

Kent, A. E. *Indictment without Trial: The Case of Liu Shao-ch'i*. Canberra: Australian National University, Department of International Relations, Working Paper No. 11, 1968.

Klein, Donald W., and Clark, Anne B. *Biographic Dictionary of Chinese Communism, 1921–1965*. Cambridge, Mass.: Harvard University Press, 1971.

Kuo, Heng-yü. *Mao's Kulturrevolution: Analyse einer Karikatur*. Pfullingen, Germany: Verlag Guenther Neske, 1968.

Kwant, Remy. *Critique: Its Nature and Function*. Pittsburgh, Pa.: Duquesne University Press, 1967.

Labedz, Leopold, ed. *Revisionism: Essays on the History of Marxist Ideas*. New York: Praeger Publishers, 1962.

Lasswell, Harold D. *Power and Personality*. New York: W. W. Norton and Co., 1948.

Leites, Nathan and Bernaut, Elsa. *Ritual of Liquidation*. Glencoe, Ill.: The Free Press, 1954.

Lewis, John Wilson. *Leadership in Communist China*. Ithaca, N.Y.: Cornell University Press, 1963.

———, ed. *Major Doctrines of Communist China*. New York: W. W. Norton and Co., 1964.

———, ed. *The City in Communist China*. Stanford, Calif.: Stanford University Press, 1971.

Lifton, Robert J. *Revolutionary Immortality: Mao Tse-tung and the Chinese Cultural Revolution*. New York: Random House, Vintage Books, 1968.

Lindbeck, John M. H., ed. *China: Management of a Revolutionary Society*. Seattle: University of Washington Press, 1971.

Lindqvist, Sven. *China in Crisis*. Translated by Sylvia Clayton. New York: Thomas Y. Crowell, 1963.

Liu, Alan P. L. *Communications and National Integration in Communist China*. Berkeley and Los Angeles: University of Calif. Press, 1971.

Liu Shao-ch'i. *Collected Works*. 3 vols. Hong Kong: Union Research Institute, 1969.

———. *Liu Shao-ch'i wen-t'i tzu-liao chuan-chi* [A special collection of materials on Liu Shao-ch'i]. Taipei: Chung-kung wen-t'i yen-chiu so, 1970.

Ling, Ken. *The Revenge of Heaven: Journal of a Young Chinese*. Translated by Miriam London and Ta-ling Lee. New York: G. P. Putnam's Sons, 1972.

Macciocchi, Maria Antonietta. *Daily Life in Revolutionary China*. New York: Monthly Review Press, 1972.

MacFarqhar, Roderick, ed. *China Under Mao: Politics Takes Command*. Cambridge, Mass.: The M.I.T. Press, 1966.

———, ed. *The Hundred Flowers Campaign and the Chinese Intellectuals*. Epilogue by G. F. Hudson. New York: Praeger Publishers, 1960; London: Stevens and Sons, 1960.

Malraux, André. *Anti-Memoirs*. Translated by Terence Kilmartin. New York: Holt, Rinehart and Winston, 1968.

Mao Tse-tung. *Selected Works*. 4 vols. Peking: Foreign Languages Press, 1965.

———. *Mao Tse-tung chi* [Collected works]. 12 vols. Tokyo: Pei Wang, 1971.

———. *Selected Readings from the Works of Mao Tse-tung*. Peking: Foreign Languages Press, 1971.

Marcuse, Herbert. *Soviet Marxism*. New York: Random House, 1961.

Mehnert, Klaus. *Peking and the New Left: At Home and Abroad*. Berkeley: University of California, Center for Chinese Studies, 1969.

———. *China Returns*. New York: E. P. Dutton and Co., 1972.

Merleau-Ponty, Maurice. *Humanism and Terror: An Essay on the Communist Problem*. Translated by John O'Neill. Boston: Beacon Press, 1969.

Mills, C. Wright. *The Sociological Imagination*. New York: Grove Press, 1961.

Mu Fu-sheng. *The Wilting of the Hundred Flowers.* New York: Praeger Publishers, 1962.

Munro, Donald J. *The Concept of Man in Early China.* Stanford, Calif.: Stanford University Press, 1969.

Myrdal, Jan and Kessle, Gun. *China: The Revolution Continued.* New York: Random House, Pantheon Books, 1970.

Nee, Victor. *The Cultural Revolution at Peking University.* New York: Monthly Review Press, 1969.

Oksenberg, Michel C. *China: The Convulsive Society.* New York: Foreign Policy Association, Headline Series, no. 203, December 1970.

———, ed. *China's Developmental Experience.* New York: Praeger Publishers, 1973.

Payne, Robert. *Portrait of a Revolutionary: Mao Tse-tung.* New York: Abelard-Schuman, 1961.

Peng Shu-tse, *et al. Behind China's "Great Cultural Revolution."* New York: Merit Publishers, 1967.

Peterson, Joseph. *The Great Leap: China.* Bombay: B. I. Publishers, 1966.

Prybyla, Jan. *The Political Economy of Communist China.* Scranton, Pa.: International Textbook Co., 1970.

Pusey, James R. *Wu Han: Attacking the Present through the Past.* Cambridge, Mass.: Harvard University, East Asian Research Center, 1969.

Pye, Lucian W. *The Spirit of Chinese Politics: A Psychocultural Study of the Authority Crisis in Political Development.* Cambridge, Mass.: The M.I.T. Press, 1968.

Rice, Edward E. *Mao's Way.* Berkeley and Los Angeles: University of California Press, 1972.

Richman, Barry. *Industrial Society in China.* New York: Random House, 1969.

Robinson, Joan. *The Cultural Revolution in China.* Baltimore, Md.: Penguin, 1969.

Robinson, Thomas W., ed. *The Cultural Revolution in China.* Berkeley and Los Angeles: University of California Press, 1971.

Rue, John E. *Mao Tse-tung in Opposition, 1927–1935.* Stanford, Calif.: Stanford University Press, 1966.

Scalapino, Robert A., ed. *Elites in the People's Republic of China.* Seattle; University of Washington Press, 1972.

Schram, Stuart R., ed., *Quotations from Chairman Mao Tse-tung.* New York: Praeger Publishers, 1967.

Schurmann, Franz. *Ideology and Organization in Communist China.* 2d ed. Berkeley and Los Angeles: University of California Press, 1968.

Schwarz, Henry G. *Liu Shao-ch'i and "People's War": A Report on the Creation of Base Areas in 1938.* Lawrence, Kans.: Center for East Asian Studies, University of Kansas, 1969.

Service, John Stewart. *The Amerasia Papers: Some Problems in the History of U.S.–China Relations.* Berkeley: University of California, Center for Chinese Studies, 1971.

Shapiro, David G. *Neurotic Styles.* New York: Basic Books, 1965.

Siao, Emi. *Mao Tse-tung: His Childhood and Youth.* Bombay: People's Publishing House, 1953.

Siao Yü. *Mao Tse-tung and I Were Beggars.* Syracuse, N.Y.: Syracuse University Press, 1959.

Simmonds, J. D. *China: Evolution of a Revolution, 1959–1966.* Canberra: Australian National University, Department of International Relations, Working Paper no. 9, 1968.

Smedley, Agnes. *Battle Hymn of China.* New York: Alfred A. Knopf, 1943.

Smelser, Neil J. *Theory of Collective Behavior.* New York: The Free Press, 1963.

Snow, Edgar. *Random Notes on Red China, 1936–1945.* Cambridge, Mass.: Harvard University Press, Chinese Economic and Political Studies, 1968.

————. *Red China Today: The Other Side of the River.* Rev. ed., New York: Random House, 1970.

————. *Red Star Over China.* 5th printing. New York: Grove Press, 1961.

————. *The Long Revolution.* New York: Random House, 1971.

Snow, Helen Foster [Nym Wales]. *The Chinese Labor Movement.* New York: The John Day Co., 1945.

————. *Notes on the Chinese Student Movement, 1935–1936.* Stanford, Calif.: Hoover Institution, 1959.

Starr, John Bryan. *Ideology and Culture: An Introduction to the Dialectic of Contemporary Chinese Politics.* New York: Harper and Row, 1973.

Tang, Peter S. H., and Maloney, Joan. *Communist China: The Domestic Scene, 1949–1967.* South Orange, N.J.: Seton Hall University Press, 1967.

Taylor, Charles. *Reporter in Red China.* New York: Random House, 1966.

Terrill, Ross. *800,000,000: The Real China.* Boston: Little, Brown and Co., 1972.

Ting Wang, ed. *Chung-kung wen-hua ko-ming tzu-liao hui-pien* [Collected materials on the Chinese Communist Cultural Revolution]. 3 vols. Hong Kong: Ming Pao Yüeh-k'an she, 1967.

Townsend, James R. *Political Participation in China.* 3d impression. Berkeley and Los Angeles: University of California Press, 1969.

Trumbull, Robert, ed. *This Is Communist China.* By the staffs of Yomiuri Shimbun, Tokyo. New York: David McKay, 1968.

Tsou, Tang and Ho, Ping-ti, eds. *China in Crisis.* 2 vols., 3 bks. Chicago: University of Chicago Press, 1968.

Union Research Institute. *Communist China, 1967.* Hong Kong: Union Research Institute, 1969.

————. *Communist China, 1968.* Hong Kong: Union Research Institute, 1969.

————. *The Case of P'eng Te-huai, 1959–1968.* Hong Kong: Union Research Institute, 1968.

————. *CCP Documents of the Great Proletarian Cultural Revolution, 1966–1967.* Hong Kong: Union Research Institute, 1968.

U.S. Department of State. *The China White Paper*. Stanford, Calif.: Stanford University Press, 1967.

Van Ness, Peter. *Revolution and Chinese Foreign Policy: Peking's Support for Wars of National Liberation*. Berkeley and Los Angeles: University of California Press, 1970.

Van Slyke, Lyman P. *Enemies and Friends: The United Front in Chinese Communist History*. Stanford, Calif.: Stanford University Press, 1967.

Vogel, Ezra F. *Canton Under Communism: Programs and Politics in a Provincial Capital, 1949–1968*. Cambridge, Mass.: Harvard University Press, 1969.

Wakeman, Frederic, Jr. *History and Will: Philosophical Perspectives of Mao Tse-tung's Thought*. Berkeley and Los Angeles: University of California Press, 1973.

Wang Ch'ao-t'ien. *Wo shih i-ko hung-wei-ping* [I am a Red Guard]. Taipei: Chung-kuo ta-lu wen-t'i yen-chiu so, 1967.

Weber, Max. *Economy and Society*. Guenther Roth and Claus Wittich, eds. 3 vols. New York: Bedminster Press, 1968.

Weggel, Oskar. *Die Chinesischen Revolutionskomitees, oder der Versuch, die Grosse Kulturrevolution durch Parzellierung zu Retten*. Hamburg: Mitteilungen des Instituts für Asienkunde, no. 25, 1968.

———. *Die Partei als Widersacher des Revolutionskomitees*. Hamburg: Mitteilungen des Instituts für Asienkunde, no. 34, 1970.

———. *Massenkomunikation in der Volksrepublik China*. Hamburg: Mitteilungen des Instituts für Asienkunde, no. 38, 1970.

Wheelwright, E. L., and McFarlane, Bruce. *The Chinese Road to Socialism: Economics of the Cultural Revolution*. New York: Monthly Review Press, 1970.

Whitson, William W. *The Chinese High Command: A History of Communist Military Politics, 1927–1971*. New York: Praeger Publishers, 1973.

Wilmott, W. E., ed. *Economic Organization in Chinese Society*. Stanford, Calif.: Stanford University Press, 1972.

Wilson, Dick. *Anatomy of China*. New York: Weybright and Talley, 1968.

Yu, Frederick T. C. *Mass Persuasion in Communist China*. New York: Praeger Publishers, 1964.

ARTICLES

Ahn, Byung-joon. "Adjustments in the Great Leap Forward and their Ideological Legacy, 1959–1962." In *Ideology and Politics in Contemporary China*, edited by Chalmers Johnson, Seattle: University of Washington Press, 1973, pp. 270–282.

Bastid, Marianne. "Origines et Développement de la Révolution Culturelle." *Politique Étrangère* 32, no. 1 (Summer 1967): 68–87.

Baum, Richard. "China, Year of the Mangoes." *Asian Survey* 9, no. 1 (January 1969): 1–18.

Bennett, Gordon. "Political Labels and Popular Tension." *Current Scene* 7, no. 4 (February 26, 1969): 1 ff.

Birrell, Ralph J. "The Centralized Control of the Collectives in the Post-Great Leap Period." In *Chinese Communist Politics in Action,* edited by A. Doak Barnett, pp. 400–447.

Boorman, Howard L. "Liu Shao-ch'i." *Biographic Dictionary of Republican China.* Vol. 2: 405–410. New York: Columbia University Press, 1968.

———. "Liu Shao-ch'i: A Political Profile." *The China Quarterly,* no. 10 (April–June 1962): 1–23.

Bowers, John Z. "Medicine in Mainland China: Red and Rural." *Current Scene* 8, no. 12 (June 15, 1970): 1 ff.

Bridgham, Philip. "Factionalism in the Chinese Communist Party." *Party Leadership and Revolutionary Power in China,* edited by John W. Lewis, pp. 203–239. London: Cambridge University Press, 1970.

———. "Mao's Cultural Revolution in 1967: The Struggle to Seize Power." *The China Quarterly,* no. 34 (April–June 1968): 6–38.

Buchanan, James. "Equality as Fact and Norm." *Ethics* 81, no. 3 (April 1971): 228–241.

Chang, Parris H. "Mao's Great Purge: A Political Balance Sheet." *Problems of Communism* 18, no. 2 (March–April 1969): 1–11.

———. "Research Notes on the Changing Loci of Decision in the CCP." *The China Quarterly,* no. 44 (October–December 1970): 169–195.

———. "Struggle Between the Two Roads in China's Countryside." *Current Scene* 6, no. 3 (February 15, 1968): 1 ff.

Chao Ts'ung. "Wen-ko yün-tung li-ch'eng shu-lüeh" [An account of the Cultural Revolution]. *Tsu-kuo* [China Monthly], appears seriatim, 1966–1972.

Charles, David A. "The Dismissal of Marshal P'eng Te-huai." In *China Under Mao: Politics Takes Command,* edited by Roderick MacFarquhar, pp. 2–34.

Cheng, Chu-yuan. "Power Struggle in Red China." *Asian Survey* 6, no. 9 (September 1966): 469–484.

Chesneaux, Jean. "Egalitarian and Utopian Traditions in the East." In *Modern China,* edited by Joseph Levenson, pp. 189–198. London: The Macmillan Co. 1971.

Crozier, Ralph C. "Traditional Medicine in Communist China: Science, Communism, and Cultural Nationalism." *The China Quarterly,* no. 23 (April–June 1966): 1–44.

Domes, Jürgen. "Chinas Spaetmaoistische Führungsgruppe: Die Soziopolitische Struktur des IX. Zentralkomitees der Kommunistischen Partei Chinas." *Politische Vierteljahresschrift* 2, no. 3 (September 1969): 191–219.

———. "The Cultural Revolution and the Army." *Asian Survey* 8, no. 5 (May 1968): 349–364.

Draskic, Milan. "Happenings in China." *Socialist Thought and Practice,* no. 26 (April–June 1967): 98–109.

Dreyer, June. "Traditional Minorities Elites and the CPR Elite Engaged in Minority Nationalities Work." *Elites in the People's Republic of China,* edited by R. A. Scalapino, pp. 416–451.

Dutt, Gargi. "Some Problems of China's Rural Communes." *The China Quarterly,* no. 16 (November–December 1963): 112–137.

Ecklund, George N. "Protracted Expropriation of Private Business in Communist China." *Pacific Affairs* 36, no. 3 (Fall 1963): 228–249.

Fan Shu-cheng. "Liu Shao-ch'i ti tzu-wo chien-ch'a pao-kao" [Report on Liu Shao-ch'i's self-examination], *Ming Pao Yüeh-k'an,* no. 14 (February 1967): 30 ff.

Feng Wen. "Assumptions and Proofs of Mao-Liu Power-Struggle." *Chinese Communist Affairs* 3, no. 4 (August 1966): 47–56.

Fitzgerald, Stephen. "China Visited: A View of the Cultural Revolution." In *China and Ourselves,* edited by Bruce Douglass and Ross Terrill, pp. 1–30. Boston: Beacon Press, 1969.

Gelman, Harry. "Mao and the Permanent Purge." *Problems of Communism* 15, no. 6 (November–December 1966): 2–14.

Gittings, John. "Inside China: In the Wake of the Cultural Revolution." *Ramparts* 10, no. 2 (August 1971): 10–20.

————. "The Party Is Always Right." *Far Eastern Economic Review* 64, no. 23 (June 5, 1969): 574–575.

Habermas, Jürgen. "On Systematically Distorted Communication." *Inquiry* 13, no. 3, (Autumn 1970): 205–219.

Harding, Harry, Jr. "Maoist Theories of Policy-Making and Organization." In *The Cultural Revolution in China,* edited by Thomas W. Robinson, pp. 113–165.

Harding, Harry, Jr., "China: Toward Revolutionary Pragmatism." *Asian Survey* 11, no. 1 (January 1971): 51–68.

Henein, Georges. "Autocritique." *Petite Encyclopédie Politique,* pp. 16–19. Paris: Éditions du Seuil, 1969.

Hinton, William. "Hundred Day War: The Cultural Revolution at Tsinghua University." *Monthly Review* 24, n. 2 (July–August 1972).

Howse, Hugh. "The Use of Radio in China." *The China Quarterly,* no. 2 (April–June 1960): 59–69.

Hsiao, Gene T. "The Background and Development of the 'Proletarian Cultural Revolution.' " *Asian Survey* 7, n. 6 (June 1967): 389–405.

Hsü, Immanual C. Y. "The Reorganization of Higher Education in Communist China, 1949–1961." *The China Quarterly,* no. 19 (July–September 1964): 128–161.

Hsü Kuan-san. "Ko-jen li-i i-ting yao chao-ku" [Be sure to eliminate self-interest]. *Jen-wu yü ssu-hsiang* [Men and Ideas], no. 22 (January 15, 1969): 9–16.

————. "T'u-p'o Yenan ch'uan-t'ung, fa-chan ch'uan-min wen-i" [Broadcast the Yenan tradition, develop the art and literature of the whole people]. *Jen-wu yü ssu-hsiang* [Men and Ideas], no. 22 (January 15, 1969): 9–16.

————. "Mao, Liu chih-chien ti ken-pen fen-ch'i tsai na-li?" [Where is the real difference between Mao and Liu?]. *Jen-wu yü ssu-hsiang,* no. 33 (December 15, 1969): 9 ff.

————. "Yenan shih-tai ti Liu Shao-ch'i" [Liu Shao-ch'i in the Yenan period]. *Jen-wu yü ssu-hsiang*, no. 38 (May 15, 1970): 9–16.

————. "Tang-ti ta chien kung-shih" [The great work of the Party]. *Jen-wu yü ssu-hsiang*, no. 40 (July 15, 1970): 8–15.

————. "Ts'ung pei-fang ch'ü ch'i-fei" [Beginning in the northern area]. *Jen-wu yü ssu-hsiang*, no. 41 (August 15, 1970): 7–13.

Illich, Ivan. "The Alternative to Schooling." *Saturday Review*, June 19, 1971, pp. 44–60.

Israel, John, "The Red Guards in Historical Perspective: Continuity and Change in the Chinese Youth Movement." *The China Quarterly*, no. 30 (April–June 1967): 1–33.

Jahuda, Michael. "Kremlinology and the Chinese Strategic Debate." *The China Quarterly*, no. 49 (January–March 1972): 45–48.

Joffe, Ellis. "China in Mid-1966: 'Cultural Revolution' or Struggle for Power?" *The China Quarterly*, no. 27 (July–September 1966): 123–132.

Johnson, Chalmers. "The Cultural Revolution in Structural Perspective." *Asian Survey* 8, no. 1 (January 1968): 1–16.

Kau, Ying-mao. "Patterns of Recruitment and Mobility of Urban Cadres." In *The City in Communist China*, edited by John W. Lewis, pp. 97–123.

————. "The Urban Bureaucratic Elite in Communist China: A Case Study of Wuhan, 1949–1965." In *Chinese Communist Politics in Action*, edited by A. Doak Barnett, pp. 216–277.

Klein, Donald W. "The Party and the Leaders." In *The China Giant*, edited by C. P. FitzGerald, pp. 47–56. Glenview, Ill.: Scott, Foresman and Co., 1967.

————, and Clark, Anne B. "Liu Shao-ch'i." In *Biographic Dictionary of Chinese Communism*, 1921–1965. Vol. 1: 616–626.

————, and Hager, Lois B. "The Ninth Central Committee." *The China Quarterly*, no. 45 (January–March 1971): 37–57.

LaBarre, Weston. "Some Observations on Character Structure in the Orient. II. The Chinese, Part 1." *Psychiatry* 9, no. 3 (August 1946): 215–239.

Lewis, John W. "Leader, Commissar and Bureaucrat: The Chinese Political System and the Last Days of the Revolution." *Journal of International Affairs* 24, no. 1 (1970): 48–74.

Li Ming-hua. "A Study of the CCP Two-Road Struggle in the Countryside." *Issues and Studies* 4, no. 8 (August 1968): 7–19.

Lieberthal, Kenneth. " 'Mao versus Liu?' Policy Towards Industry and Commerce: 1946–1949." *The China Quarterly*, no. 47 (July–September 1971): 494–521.

Lindbeck, John M. H. "China and the World: The Dilemmas of Communication." In *China Today*, edited by William J. Richardson, pp. 105–117. New York: Friendship Press, 1969.

Liu, Alan P. L. "Mass Media in the Cultural Revolution." *Current Scene* 7, no. 8 (April 20, 1969): 1 ff.

Lowenthal, Richard. "Development vs. Utopia in Communist Policy." In *Change in Communist Systems*, edited by Chalmers Johnson, pp. 33–107. Stanford, Calif.: Stanford University Press, 1970.

Luck, David. "Soviet and Chinese Political Development." *Survey*, nos. 74–75 (Winter–Spring 1970): 29–49.

MacFarquhar, Roderick. "Communist China's Intra-Party Dispute." *Pacific Affairs* 31, no. 4 (December 1958): 323–336.

"Mao Tse-tung tsai ch'i-ch'ien jen ta hui shang-ti tzu-wo chien-ch'a" [Mao Tse-tung's self-examination at the meeting of 7,000]. *Jen-wu yü ssu-hsiang*, no. 40 (July 15, 1970): 27–33.

Montaperto, Ronald N. "From Revolutionary Successors to Revolutionaries: The Transformation of an Elite." In *Elites in the People's Republic of China*, edited by Robert A. Scalapino, pp. 575–609.

Munro, Donald J. "Dissent in Communist China: The Current Anti-Intellectual Campaign in Perspective." *Current Scene* 4, no. 11 (June 1, 1966): 1–19.

———. "Egalitarian Ideal and Educational Fact in Communist China." In *China: Management of a Revolutionary Society*, edited by John M. H. Lindbeck, pp. 256–301.

Nathan, Andrew J. "A Factional Model for CCP Politics." *The China Quarterly*, no. 53 (January–March 1973): 34–67.

Neuhauser, Charles. "The Chinese Communist Party in the 1960s: Prelude to the Cultural Revolution." *The China Quarterly*, no. 32 (October-December 1969): 3–37.

———. "The Impact of the Cultural Revolution on the CCP Machine." *Asian Survey* 8, no. 6 (June 1968): 465–489.

Nivison, David S. "Communist Ethics and Chinese Tradition." *Journal of Asian Studies* 16, no. 1 (November 1956): 51–75.

Oksenberg, Michel C. "Policy Making Under Mao, 1949–1968: An Overview." In *China: Management of a Revolutionary Society*, edited by John M. H. Lindbeck, pp. 79–115.

———. "Occupational Groups in Chinese Society and the Cultural Revolution." In *The Cultural Revolution: 1967 in Review*, edited by Chang Chun-shu, James Crump, and Rhoads Murphy, pp. 1–45. Ann Arbor: University of Michigan, Center for Chinese Studies, 1968.

Ong, Ellen K. "Education in China since the Cultural Revolution." *Studies in Comparative Communism* 3, nos. 3–4 (July–October 1970): 158–177.

Pelzel, John C. "Economic Organization of a Production Brigade in Post-Leap China." In *Economic Organization in Chinese Society*, edited by W. E. Wilmott, pp. 387–417.

Perkins, Dwight H. "Agriculture." In *The China Giant*, edited by C. P. FitzGerald, pp. 80–87.

———. "Incentives and Profits in Chinese Industry: The Challenge of Economics to Ideology's Machine." *Current Scene* 4, no. 10 (May 15, 1966): 1–10.

———. "Mao Tse-tung's Goals and China's Economic Performance." *Current Scene* 9, no. 1 (January 7, 1971): 1 ff.

Powell, Ralph L. "The Increasing Power of Lin Piao and the Party Soldiers, 1959–1966." *The China Quarterly*, no. 34 (April–June 1968): 38–66.

Pye, Lucian. "Hostility and Authority in Chinese Politics." *Problems of Communism* 57, no. 3 (May–June 1968): 10–23.

Riskin, Carl. "The Chinese Economy in 1967." In *The Cultural Revolution: 1967 in Review,* edited by Chang Chun-shu, *et al.,* pp. 45–72.

————. "Rural Industry: Self-reliant Systems or 'Independent Kingdoms'?" In untitled book, edited by Jim Peck and Victor Nee. New York: Pantheon, forthcoming.

Robinson, Thomas W. "Chou En-lai and the Cultural Revolution in China." *The Cultural Revolution in China,* edited by Thomas W. Robinson, pp. 165–313.

Schram, Stuart R. "Mao Tse-tung and Liu Shao-ch'i, 1939–1969." *Asian Survey* 12, no. 4 (April 1972): 275–294.

Schurmann, Franz. "China's 'New Economic Policy'—Transition or Beginning?" *The China Quarterly,* no. 17 (January–March 1964): 65–92.

————. "Economic Policy and Political Power in Communist China." *Annals of the American Academy of Political and Social Science,* Vol. 349 (September 1963): 49–70.

————. "Organization and Response in Communist China." *Annals of the American Academy of Political and Social Science,* vol. 321 (January 1959): 57 ff.

————. "Peking's Recognition of Crisis." In *Modern China,* edited by Albert Feuerwerker, pp. 89–105. Englewood Cliffs, N.J.: Prentice-Hall, 1964.

Schwarz, Henry G. "The Nature of Leadership: The Chinese Communists, 1930–1945." *World Politics* 32, no. 4 (July 1970): 496–518.

Selden, Mark. "The Yenan Legacy: The Mass Line." In *Chinese Communist Politics in Action,* edited by A. Diak Barnett, pp. 99–155.

Solomon, Richard H. "Communication Patterns and the Chinese Revolution." *The China Quarterly,* no. 32 (October-December 1969): 88–110.

————. "Mao's Effort to Reintegrate the Chinese Polity: Problems of Authority and Conflict in the Chinese Social Process." In *Chinese Communist Politics in Action,* edited by A. Doak Barnett, pp. 271–365.

————. "One Party and 'One Hundred Schools.'" *Current Scene* 7, nos. 19–20 (October 1, 1969): 1 ff.

Spitz, Alan. "Mao's Permanent Revolution." *The Review of Politics* 30, no. 9 (October 1968): 440–445.

Strong, Anna Louise. *Letters from China,* nos. 41–62 (1966–1967).

Suleski, Ronald. "The Fu-t'ien Incident, December, 1930." In *Early Communist China: Two Studies,* edited by Chang Chun-shu, et al., pp. 1–28. Ann Arbor: University of Michigan, Papers in Chinese Studies, 1969.

Teiwes, Frederick C. "The Purge of Provincial Leaders, 1957–1958." *The China Quarterly,* no. 27 (July–September 1966): 14–33.

Tong, T. K. "Liu Shao-ch'i, the Liu Shao-ch'i Faction and Liu Shao-ch'i-ism." In *Collected Documents in the First Sino-American Conference on Mainland China,* edited by Wu Chen-tsai, pp. 235–259. Taiwan: Institute of International Relations, 1971.

————. "Red Guard Newspapers." *Columbia Forum* 12, no. 1 (Spring 1969): 38–41.

Tretiak, Daniel. "The Chinese Cultural Revolution and Foreign Policy." *Current Scene* 8, no. 7 (April 1, 1970): 1 ff.

Tsou, Tang. "The Values of the Chinese Revolution." In *China's Developmental Experience*, edited by Michel C. Oksenberg, pp. 27–41.

————. "The Cultural Revolution and the Chinese Political System." *The China Quarterly*, no. 38 (April–June 1969): 63–91.

————. "Revolution, Reintegration, and Crisis in Communist China: A Framework for Analysis. In *China in Crisis*, edited by Tang Tsou and Ping-ti Ho, vol. 1, bk. 1: 277–348.

Vogel, Ezra F. "From Friendship to Comradeship: The Change in Personal Relations in Communist China." *The China Quarterly*, no. 21 (January–March 1965): 1–28.

————. "The Structure of Conflict: China in 1967." *The Cultural Revolution: 1967 in Review*, edited by Chang Chun-shu, et al., pp. 97–125.

Walker, Kenneth R. "Collectivization in Retrospect: The 'Socialist High Tide' of Autumn 1955–Spring 1956." *The China Quarterly*, no. 26 (April–June 1966): 1–44.

Wang Chang-lin. "A comparison of the Ideologies of Mao Tse-tung and Liu Shao-ch'i." *Issues and Studies* 4, no. 12 (September 1968): 22–31.

Wang Hsüeh-wen. "The Nature and Development of the 'Great Cultural Revolution.' " *Issues and Studies* 4, no. 12 (September 1968): 11–22.

Wang Ta-hung. "The Mao-Lin Group's Anti-Liu Offensive." *Chinese Communist Affairs* 3, no. 4 (August 1967): 47–56.

Weidenbaum, Rhode Sussman. "The Career and Writings of Liu Shao-ch'i." In *Researches in the Social Sciences in China*, edited by John E. Lane, pp. 53–78. New York: Columbia University, East Asian Institute, 1957.

"Wen-chien chieh-hsiao" [Document introduction]. *Chung-kung yen-chiu* [Studies of Chinese Communism] 3, no. 1 (January 1969): 149–155.

Wen Shih. "Political Parties in Communist China." *Asian Survey* 3, no. 3 (March 1963): 157–165.

Wu, Yuan-li. "Communist China's Economic Prospects and the Cultural Revolution." In *Communist China*, edited by Alan A. Spitz, pp. 33–43. Seattle: Washington State University Press, 1967.

Zeuner, Bodo. "Innerparteiliche Demokratie." In *Zur Politik und Zeitgeschichte*, nos. 33–43. Berlin: Colloquium Verlag, 1969.

UNPUBLISHED OR LIMITED CIRCULATION DOCUMENTS

Alitto, Guy. "Thought Reform in Communist China: The Case of Chou Ku-ch'eng." M.A. Thesis, University of Chicago, 1966.

Blecher, Marc J. "Liu Shao'ch'i: The Formative Years." Seminar paper, University of Chicago, autumn 1970.

Chang, Parris H. "Power and Policy in China." Manuscript, University of Pennsylvania, 1972.

Crook, Frederick. "Labor Production Contracts and Households, 1956–1970." Paper prepared for the U.S. Census Bureau, Washington, D.C., summer 1971.

Edmunds, Clifford G. "Historicism, Ideology and Political Authority in Communist China: The Case of Chien Po-tsan." Master's essay, University of Chicago, 1968.

Farrell, Martin F. "Mao, Stalin and Economism: A Comparative Study." M.A. Thesis, University of Chicago, 1969.

Flanders, Steven. "Remunerative Rewards and Rationality in Movement-Regimes: The Chinese Case." Paper delivered at the annual meeting of the American Political Science Association, Chicago, September 1971.

Hiniker, Paul. "Chinese Attitudinal Reactions to Forced Compliance: A Cross-Cultural Experiment in the Theory of Cognitive Dissonance." Center for International Studies, M.I.T., May 1965.

Han, Susan. "The Concept of the Proletariat in Chinese Communism." Ph.D. dissertation, University of Chicago, 1955.

Lee, Hong Yung. "The Nature of Radicalism in the Cultural Revolution." Seminar paper, University of Chicago, December 1972.

Lee, Peter Nan-shong. "A Comparative Study of Managerial Personnel: Soviet Russia, Communist China and Yugoslavia." Departmental paper, University of Chicago, Summer 1971.

Meisner, Mitchell R. "Modernization and Revolution: The 'Three Great Revolutionary Movements' in China, 1963–1967." Master's essay, University of Chicago, 1968.

Schurmann, Franz. "Organizational Contrasts Between Communist China and the Soviet Union." Paper presented at Hong Kong, March 13, 1961.

———. "The Organizational Functions of the Communist Party in China." University of California, Berkeley, Center for Chinese Studies Colloquium Paper, February 26, 1959.

Starr, John Bryan. "Mao Tse-tung's Theory of Continuing the Revolution Under the Dictatorship of the Proletariat: Its Origins, Development and Practical Implications." Ph.D. dissertation, University of California, Berkeley, 1971.

Tsou, Tang. "Interest Groups and the Political System in Maoist China." Paper presented at the University of Chicago, 1970.

———. "The People's Liberation Army and the Cultural Revolution: A Study of Civil-Military Relationships in China." Paper delivered at University of Chicago, 1971.

Womack, Brantly. "Theory and Practice in the Thought of Mao." Seminar paper, University of Chicago, 1971.

Wong, Paul. "Organizational Leadership in Communist China." Ph.D. dissertation, University of California, Berkeley, 1971.

INDEX

Academy of Sciences, 273, 280
Afghanistan, 236
Agrarian Reform Law:
Liu Shao-ch'i's 1950 report on, 26
Agricultural Producers' Cooperatives (APCs), 42, 255
Agriculture:
Liu Shao-ch'i's policies toward, 246–48, 257–59
production of private farm plots, as percentage of total production, 267
Albania, 280
All-China General Union, 14
Althusser, Louis, 88
Anhui, 18
Anhwei Province, 265
An Tzu-wen, 16
Anyüan, 20
Anyüan Coal Mine, 12–13
Anyüan Labor Organization, 13
Anyüan Miners' Labor Union, 12–13
Arendt, Hannah, 117
Asian and Australian Trade Union Conference (1949), 25
August 1st Regiment, 84, 106
Austria, 237

Bangladesh, 237
Belgium, 237
Bennett, Gordon, 124
Bernaut, Elsa:
analysis of Moscow purge trials by, 306–7
Big-character posters:
origin of, 78, 328
role of, in communication of the cultural revolution, 317–19
See also Nieh Yüan-tzu

Boorman, Howard, 6
Bridgham, Philip, 32
Bukharin, 339
Bureaucratism:
Liu Shao-ch'i's attitude toward, 182–83
Mao Tse-tung's attitude toward, 181–82
Bureaucrats:
criticized by Mao Tse-tung, 47
purge of as goal of "Hundred Flowers," 35–37
Burma, 226, 236
Business and commerce, Liu Shao-ch'i's attitude toward, 248–50, 259–64

Canada, 237
Canton, 14, 42, 50, 125, 133, 149
"Capitalist road," 214–93. See also Mao Tse-tung, criticism of Liu Shao-ch'i
Central Cultural Revolution Group (CCRG), 76, 77, 83, 89, 105, 106, 122–37 passim, 147, 148, 150, 154, 158, 159, 166, 167, 169–70, 281, 282, 334
designates Liu Shao-ch'i as scapegoat, 330
formation of, by Chiang Ch'ing (May 1966), 60
a leak source for mass criticism, 329
"Paris Commune" formed by, 151–52
political power of, explained, 148
radicalization of, 150–51
role in cultural revolution, 138–44
role in mass criticism model, 299
Ceylon. See Sri Lanka
Chang, Parris, 348–49
Chang Ch'eng-hsien, 80